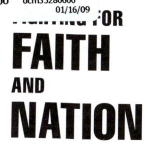

FIGHTING FOR
FAITH
AND
NATION

D0074515

University of Pennsylvania Press
SERIES IN CONTEMPORARY ETHNOGRAPHY
Dan Rose and Paul Stoller, Series Editors

A complete list of books in the series
is available from the publisher.

FIGHTING FOR
FAITH
AND
NATION
DIALOGUES
WITH SIKH MILITANTS

CYNTHIA KEPPLEY MAHMOOD

PENN

University of Pennsylvania Press
Philadelphia

Published by
University of Pennsylvania Press
Philadelphia, Pennsylvania 19104-6097

Library of Congress Cataloging-in-Publication Data

Mahmood, Cynthia Keppley.
  Fighting for faith and nation : dialogues with Sikh militants /
Cynthia Keppley Mahmood.
     p. cm. — (Series in contemporary ethnography)
  Includes bibliographical references and index.
  ISBN 0-8122-3361-1 (alk. paper). — ISBN 0-8122-1592-3 (alk.
paper)
  1. Sikhs—Politics and government.   2. Punjab (India)—Politics
and government.   3. Human rights—India—Punjab.   4. Sikhism.
I. Title.   II. Series.
  DS485.P88M25   1997
  954.91'4'00882946—dc20   96-34959
                                                                      CIP

CONTENTS

ILLUSTRATIONS

PREFACE

This book is the result of a difficult project that could not have been undertaken without the guidance, generosity, tolerance, and trust of a great many people. First to be mentioned must be the Khalistani Sikh community, whose members put themselves at risk by welcoming an inquisitive stranger. The hospitality of countless Sikh households and *gurudwaras* made the interviews on which this research is based possible, and many individuals spent hours and days away from their homes and their work to answer my endless questions. In particular, I appreciate the grace with which militant Sikhs have greeted my disagreements with them and encouraged me to put these divergent opinions in speeches and writings. This generosity of spirit and sense of respect for difference will be, I hope, the enduring cornerstone of the Sikh community.

With regard to the Sikhs, I want to make a few things perfectly clear at the outset, though they will be made clear throughout the book as well. First, the Khalistani militants form a very small subset of the Sikh community as a whole. This book is not about "the Sikhs." It is about the militants. Any attempt to treat what is written here as a generalization about Sikhs in general would be highly misguided, and I would condemn it wholeheartedly. The book is not even about all of those Sikhs who support the idea of an independent homeland; it focuses specifically on those who have taken up arms in order to achieve it and on the communities that support them.

Three years of intermittent fieldwork with expatriate Sikhs in ten North American cities forms the basis for this book, which is both an oral history of the militant movement and a dialogical ethnography of a cultural community. Some of the people with whom I worked are permanent residents or citizens of the United States or Canada, others are here as recent refugees, and still others live outside of North America but met me in various locations for the purpose of recording their narratives. The tapes on which they were recorded have been destroyed, and for the protection of my interlocutors no record of names, places, or other identifying information has been preserved.

The photographs in this book require special comment. Some of them I took myself, and publish here with the full consent of the people portrayed. Others, however, are part of a collection of photos that circulate around the human rights and Khalistani communities. A few were taken out of Punjab under difficult conditions and have been reprinted many times, which accounts for their poor quality. The inherent drama of their subject matter, I believe, more than compensates for their technical deficiencies. I chose not to enhance them in any way.

Though I cross-checked most of what was told to me with other sources, I cannot vouch for the veracity or accuracy of every episode reported to me by Sikh militants. There will obviously be divergent accounts of many of these, particularly from their enemies. The portrait of militancy in this book is therefore *not* an "objective" or "balanced" description of the Punjab conflict. It is a glimpse into the world of Sikh militants as I have experienced it. I will welcome the broader contextualization of this work by other scholars.

Finally, let me be entirely forthright about my own political stance here, about which readers may be rightfully curious. I am not a supporter of Khalistan. I think the Sikh militants have some serious grievances with the state of India. I abhor many of the methods militants have chosen to address them. Since I am not a Sikh, nor a Punjabi, nor an Indian, I don't have a "position" on the question of Khalistan, and I feel that the idea of what Khalistan would be is unclear enough at this point to make taking such a position inadvisable in any case. I don't think the militants are crazy or evil, however; I don't think India has seen the last of Sikh separatism; and I think that the best way to understand why militants fight is to talk with them about it. I think that the only way to prevent outbreaks of violence such as Punjab has witnessed over the past fifteen years or so is to ensure human rights and freedoms, including attention to the principle of self-determination. These are my political views, in short.

Not all scholars are comfortable with highly sensitive topics such as this one, and some of them are my close colleagues. I therefore thank members of the Department of Anthropology at the University of Maine for their tolerance of this work, and I particularly value the guidance and support of Henry Munson throughout the project. Steve Bicknell worked on the illustrations, and Kris Sobolik was a constant source of encouragement.

A wide circle of anthropologists who are pioneering the ethnographic study of conflict provided necessary intellectual and moral support. Jeff Sluka, Carolyn Nordstrom, Tony Robben, and Kevin Avruch have been particularly helpful. The courage and insight of Joyce Pettigrew continues to be a major source of inspiration, and her comments and criticisms of my work have been indispensable. Mark Juergensmeyer, Peter van der Veer, Al Wolfe, and Paul Wallace also read the manuscript of this book and offered excellent suggestions for revision. Bertrand Masquelier was a source of encouragement and support not only during this project but over the past fifteen years.

Finally, I must comment on Patricia Smith of the University of Pennsylvania Press, who supported this book from the start and persisted through various ups and downs to ensure its realization. I consider her a colleague—an "intellectual comrade"—as well as an editor. Others at the Press contributed substantially to this project, and I thank them for their energy and effort.

None of these individuals, however, bears any responsibility for the final form taken by this book. Mistakes and indiscretions, and certainly all opinions, are entirely my own.

As for my husband Khalid, no one else could have been as steadfast in support of a highly problematic research project, as reliable in keeping confidences, and as acute in political judgment.

My daughter Naintara cheered me up when too much thought of conflict got me down, and with her sunny presence reminded me daily of why we have to figure out a way to live without violence.

1

OF NIGHTMARES AND CONTACTS

LAST NIGHT I was awakened by a nightmare, the same recurring dream I have been suffering for the past year or so. I was in Cambodia, a Cambodia I know only through TV images of Vietnam War vintage. It was hot, humid; the air was heavy with tropical smells but vibrating with danger. I was climbing a long stone stairway in a kind of tower, looking down through crumbling windows at a busy marketplace below. People carrying baskets of fruit on their heads; bald-headed monks begging for alms. Suddenly, I heard shots, the rat-tat-tat of automatic weapons fire, and men in camouflage suits started running here and there in the crowd. I stood on the steps, frozen in fear and horror. People in the marketplace were screaming and falling down, but I was too far away to see blood. Gathering my wits about me, I ran, breathless, out of the tower and away from the market square. After running for some time, I looked back to see the entire area blow up in a sudden inferno of flame. I fell to the ground and woke up, bolt upright, in a cold sweat.

The story of my research on Sikh militancy is also a story about my personal confrontation with violence. To mask it here as more neutral, more distanced than it is would be to deny the nights of terror, displaced to another, safer, venue, that I experienced off and on since I began this project. And to write about Sikh militants as if I had not become personally, existentially entangled with them and their quest would be an inexcusable hypocrisy. As a scholar, I know what it means to look for all sides of a question, to be critical of sources, to be "objective." As an anthropologist, I am familiar with the peculiar inside-outside stance of the ethnographer, which allows glimpses into other realities while retaining a quintessentially Western academic outlook. In trying to understand what militant Sikhs are doing, however, I find that the anthropology of another era is also useful, not the anthropology claiming to be science but the one that sees the confrontation of "man with man" in all his naked mystery as the heart of the anthropological enterprise. Like many anthropologists of my generation, I find myself questioning some of the basic axioms of my field, which, however stimulating intellectually, seem somehow inadequate to the task of understanding real human beings.

Immanuel Kant, a forgotten ancestor of contemporary anthropology, took the traditional "What is man?" question to be the heart of what an academic discipline of anthropology should be. But for Kant this question subsumed three subsidiary issues that have been largely ignored: "What can I know?" "What ought I to do?" and "What may I hope?" It is this last query in particular that is rather jarringly out of place in the modern academic climate, though Edward Burnett Tylor, too, author of our classic 1871 definition of culture, emphasized not only the "habits" of human beings but their "capabilities" as well.[1] Is it not part of the anthropologist's enterprise to ask what heights humans are capable of reaching? Our discipline's insistence on the value of the everyday, so important in countering neglect of the ordinary in other areas of scholarship, also has the effect of somewhat eclipsing the reality of the out-of-the-ordinary, the truly heroic, in human endeavor. Taken as a whole, the picture painted of humankind by the collections of ethnographic literature many of us have on our bookshelves is sadly inadequate. True, most human beings live quotidian, habituated, ordinary lives most of the time. But what about when they don't? What are people capable of when the everyday is disrupted by famine, by war or pestilence, when they are called upon to do more than fetch water and grow crops and make love and rear children, to be more than "just human?" Our literature doesn't contain many portraits of people in extraordinary, rather than ordinary, circumstances.

Sikh militants in the northwestern state of Punjab in India have been engaged in an armed insurgency for the past decade and a half. Their ultimate aim is the formation of a sovereign nation of Khalistan, "land of the pure." It is not clear what percentage these militants and their supporters form of the total Sikh population; there are many others who would like to see an independent nation emerge but reject violence as a means of achieving it, and still others who are firmly loyal to India and reject the Khalistani ideology outright. Conditions in Punjab have been so disrupted by violence on the part of both the militants and the government forces arrayed against them, and the exchange of ideas has been so severely curtailed by various forms of censorship, that assessing accurately what the people there really want is probably impossible. What is clear is that tens of thousands of people—militants, government troops, and bystanders—have been killed in the past fifteen years or so of the conflict.[2] This level of violence is equivalent to that of many of the so-called "low-intensity conflicts" that dot the global landscape today (compare, for example, the 3,000-odd casualties of the Northern Ireland conflict) and places most members of the Sikh community in what we might well call "extraordinary" circumstances. Certainly the Khalistani militants, now scattered in exile across several continents, live their lives at an emotional pitch far from the everyday reality of most of the people we know and study.

Anybody who has thought about whether the Nicaraguan *contras* were "freedom fighters" or "counter-revolutionaries" or whether the PLO is a "terrorist" or "nationalist" organization will recognize the element of relativism that comes into any serious discussion of political conflicts like the one in Punjab. Unfortunately, the rather obvious fact that things look different from the inside of one of these groups than from the outside has been lost on many people involved in policymaking and negotiation, who tend to underestimate the radical differences in world view that obtain between the U.S. State Department, for example, and militant Islamists intent on blowing up the World Trade Center. The fact is, we don't know enough about how the latter think to effectively talk with them. We can't easily imagine what the world looks like from extraordinary viewpoints. And ethnographies of village life in Egypt, however important in themselves, don't enlighten us much about World Trade Center bombers.

There is a growing feeling among younger anthropologists that our discipline has suffered a not entirely unwarranted marginalization over the past few decades. Even as the methods and language of ethnography are being taken up by colleagues in fields as diverse as political science and English literature, and even as "cultural studies" usurps anthropology's primary concept of culture, the discipline itself cannot be said to be a central voice on the current intellectual scene. It is particularly worrisome that anthropologists are called on as infrequently as they are in the policy arena, which depends on accurate information about and assessment of actors whose worldviews may be wildly different from our own. In a culturally plural world, those whose calling is translation across cultural divides have a critical role to play.

Anthropologists, professionally oriented to recognize the kind of radical otherness represented by Sheikh Omar Abdel Rahman and his band, are in an especially good position to explore the nature of the extraordinary cultures that emerge in conditions of conflict. We are habituated to the situation of listening to people with judgment suspended, whether they be Philippine headhunters (Renato Rosaldo, *Ilongot Headhunting*) or impoverished mothers in Brazil (Nancy Scheper-Hughes, *Death Without Weeping*). That anthropological "translation" occasionally comes across as exoneration is a particular problem when we are dealing with political violence, a subject far nearer to most readers than the traditionally exotic subject matter of classic ethnography. A scholar who chooses to study the culture of a street gang or a guerilla army will certainly find herself in a more difficult ethical and methodological predicament than a scholar who studies kinship patterns in highland New Guinea. But, convinced that street gangs and guerilla armies are at least in some sense "cultures" amenable to the same kind of ethnographic exploration anthropologists have pursued in the jungles of Africa or the outback of Australia, more and more scholars have turned to the study of cultures of violence as one important way in which anthropology can make a contribution to the public discourse of our times.

MEETING SIKHS

My interaction with Khalistani Sikhs began at a South Asian restaurant in Berkeley in November 1992. A friend somewhat involved in the Kashmir issue knew that I had written about the problems that various communities in India faced and asked whether I would like to meet some Khalistani activists from the Bay Area. I agreed, albeit hesitantly, and mulled over and over again in my mind whether I really wanted to meet people associated with a major guerilla insurgency in a foreign country. I had just returned from India the previous spring, where I had become embroiled in a debate about the fate of tribal peoples in Bihar, entangled in that state's notoriously contorted politics (which includes academic politics), and at the end, physically assaulted by a street gang in Patna. As it was, I wondered whether I had any future research career in India. To study Khalistani Sikhs, known to be among the most violent of the many groups today challenging Indian state authority, would mean perhaps relinquishing further hopes of extended visits to India. Scholars I worked with in Patna virtually forbade me to pursue "the Punjab problem" further. The topic is extremely volatile, and despite a strong commitment to academic freedom in India, a fair amount of self-censorship goes on all the time, particularly in peripheral locations.

Nevertheless, I went to the Berkeley dinner, inspired in part by Carolyn Nordstrom's session on "Dangerous Anthropologies" at the American Anthropological Association meetings then being held in San Francisco. I was not the only anthropologist to find that the study of culture leads, in today's world, to the study of politics, and, in many cases, to the study of violent conflict. With both trepidation and overwhelming curiosity, I met three Sikhs at the office of our common friend and we went on to a local South Asian restaurant.

Over vegetarian curries we talked about India, Sikhism, and conflict. They were noncommittal; I was curious. Of the three Sikhs present, one had short hair and a trimmed beard, and the other two sported classic flowing beards and saffron turbans. One of the turbaned Sikhs was obviously the spokesperson, while the other was silent. The silent one had dark, clear eyes that never left my face. I was very conscious of his gaze as I talked with the others.

Rightly suspicious, these three Sikhs, whose position in "the movement" I didn't know at the time, asked more questions than they answered. But what they did say struck me as remarkably open; they were not a bit furtive or evasive in talking about Khalistan and seemed to speak from heartfelt feelings rather than from ideology. They asked me about my family background; I told them about my father, who was a labor activist and a pacifist. They asked about my research on Buddhism; I told them about the ancient Buddhists and how I believed their movement to have been social and political as well as religious, putting them in a dangerous position vis-à-vis the powerholders at the time. I told them about my recent trip to India in which I became convinced that the rights of tribal peoples, now involved in their own insurgencies, were being severely abused—sometimes with the complicity of academics. The Sikhs listened intently. When we were through with our meal, they all shook my hand warmly, and the solemn one grasped my hand in both of his.

My second contact with Khalistani Sikhs took place about eight months after that Berkeley dinner. Letter and phone conversations with Dr. Amarjit Singh, the vocal one at the restaurant, resulted in my flying out to the West Coast again. Amarjit and another gentleman took me to the San Pedro detention facility in Los Angeles harbor, where several dozen Sikhs were imprisoned for immigration offenses. That was the first of a series of encounters with Sikhs, varying in content and form but always quite intense, that forms the basis of this book. Over the course of the next three years, I interviewed dozens of militants at length, stayed in the homes of militant families, spoke in Sikh *gurudwaras* (temples) and attended Sikh conventions. That first trip to San Pedro nonetheless remains crystal clear in my mind, for it was then that I really committed to the idea of writing a book about Sikh militancy.

As the gates of the jail clanged behind us, I realized that I had never actually been in a prison before, although I had seen so many in movies that the scene felt not at all strange. After the two Sikhs with me deposited their daggers at the entryway (all orthodox Sikhs carry swords of some form with them at all times), we proceeded upstairs to a large room that had been set aside for Sikh religious services. Amarjit and the other gentleman with us had agreed to conduct prayers for the inmates, providing a neat excuse for our access to the prison. Slowly the Sikh prisoners filed into the room, their regulation orange uniforms incongruously matching the scraps of saffron cloth, sacred to Sikhism, pinned or tied in their hair. They were barefooted, and left tracks on the dusty linoleum. As each passed us, he gave the traditional gesture of respect and greeting, palms together in front of the chest, or bowed down quickly to try to touch the feet of Amarjit. He seemed embarrased by this gesture, and discouraged it. I later learned why the men were showing him this honor, however: Amarjit, among the first Sikhs I met, was spokesperson for a committee that plays a leading role in the Khalistani insurgency. Though his own role is purely political, it quickly became clear to me that he was respected by many Sikhs involved in both militant and non-militant sides of the struggle.[3]

The men, some quite young, boys, really, gathered in one corner of the room and sat cross-legged on the floor. Before I knew what was happening, I was in front of them, standing by as the other Sikh led them in the recitation of verses from the Sikh scriptures. When they stopped, Amarjit started explaining who I was.

"Why don't you say a few words?" he suggested.

Totally unprepared for this, I was, not surprisingly, hesitant. The men with dark hair, dark beards, dark eyes, and all those orange uniforms, sat expectantly—respectful but wary. One or two looked quite dazed. I glanced out the window and saw an exercise yard and barbed-wire fencing beyond. Again, the ridiculous memory of TV movies crossed my mind. Television encourages a kind of game-playing mentality, I believe, especially in the realm of violence that many of us suburbanites have never really experienced in any other form. But this was not a game. I remembered my own minimal experience with violence—the assault in Bihar, a rape in New Orleans—and this brought me back to the grim reality of the people before me. There was nothing exciting about their situation. There was no music, as one Vietnam vet commented about buildings blowing up in the non-cinematic real world.

I caught the eye of one young fellow at the back, and his mouth crinkled very faintly at the corners in a wisp of a smile. Taking that as encouragement, I thought of what I could say. I knew that many Sikhs have suffered in the counterinsurgency that has swept Punjab in the past twelve years, and I decided to try to establish a link with these prisoners through the natural sympathy one feels for victims of repression. Some of them might well have also been on the trigger end of acts of terrible violence, but I knew that if I highlighted that possibility in my mind a wall between me and them would rise up quickly to block out our human bond. I knew that I couldn't be afraid of them, or I would never manage to understand what they were doing. So I decided to insinuate myself into their world gently, getting to know them first as sufferers, only later as fighters. I now find that though I disagree with and condemn many of their actions, I am never paralyzed by the amorphous sense of fear that enters most of our discussions about "terrorism." If only militant Sikhs were monsters, psychopaths, criminals, or "evil men" (Khushwant Singh's term[4]), it would be easy. But they're not, and my hope is that bringing out the world of Sikh militancy in human terms here will make clear the real problem of conflict resolution: that both sides are populated by human beings, in most cases behaving as decently as they know how in immensely difficult circumstances.

"I know that many of you have been through great ordeals," I started, slowly. I didn't know what to say, and the enormous chasm between signing Amnesty International letters and facing the victims of human rights abuses eye to eye suddenly yawned before me. I knew I was inadequate to the task of saying anything meaningful to people who had probably been tortured, maybe raped, certainly humiliated and harassed before they fled India.

"Nobody knows what is happening to the people of Punjab," I continued. "I know just a little bit about it, enough to know that your stories are worth hearing and worth retelling. I want to hear them from you, if you will allow me to. I want to write a book about Punjab and tell them to other people as well."

I went on in this vein. I no longer remember just what it was that I was saying, but I do remember with acute clarity the expressions on the faces of my audience. As a teacher, I am used to paying attention to how my audience is reacting, but I think I never scanned the faces of the crowd more earnestly than during those initial moments at San Pedro. Many of them remained totally blank throughout my talk. When I was through some of the men stayed where they were but others came up to greet me.

"I didn't know what to say," I confided apologetically to Amarjit.

"It's all right," he said. "They were listening not to your words but to your heart. They can hear that you are sincere."

Sincere. This was a word I was to hear many times over the next few years, for sincerity, authenticity, being who one says one is, is a trait especially valued by Sikhs. Conversely, insincerity, duplicity, or failure to live up to what one should be is the greatest sin. "He's not sincere," can be a scathing insult; "He is sincere," a compliment applied even to enemies.

Amarjit and I sat down at a long table and one of the prisoners, an older man with gray in his beard, sat down across from us. He was thin; bones stood out everywhere.

"I used to be a farmer," he said. "My family was farming for many generations. We are simple people without much education, but we work hard." He glanced at me to see, I imagined, whether not being educated might affect my estimation of him.

"My family was simple, too," I said. "They left Germany when they couldn't practice their religion the way they wanted to, and came to Pennsylvania to farm. I was the first member of my family to go to college."

At this gesture of empathy, he seemed to relax. He then told a story that I came to see as typical: the Indian army's attack on the holiest shrine of the Sikhs in 1984 prompting a renewed identification with the faith; a relative who got involved in the militant resistance; repeated harassments and finally arrest at the hands of Punjab police. I didn't know how to ask about torture but I had read enough human rights reports to be aware of how frequent it was in that part of the world.

"Would it be all right if I ask him about torture?" I asked Amarjit.

He nodded. But I hesitated, looking for words, and Amarjit finally jumped in for me.

"Were you abused while in police custody?" he asked. "The Doctor [an honorary reference to me] would like to hear about those experiences so she can put them in her book."

I got ready to write down what he said in my notebook, but at the same time recognized an certain inhumanity in the mere gesture of picking up my pen. I put it down again and shoved my notebook to one side.

"First I was stripped naked," the man recounted. "The police officers started shouting questions at me, in very insulting ways," he said. "They were quite drunk."

"Were they Hindu or Sikh?" I inquired.

"Sikh," he responded, bringing out one of the features of the Punjab problem too easily skimmed over by media centered on "communal" (interreligious) conflict.

"One of them started hitting me, and he hit me again and again. He started beating me with a *lathi* [night stick]. After a while when I didn't say anything they hung me up by the arms, like this." He demonstrated a position I would later know as "the airplane," arms pulled up behind to put the strain on the shoulder girdle. In some cases the feet were weighted to pull on the joints even further.

"I got electric shocks on my head and on my private parts. I told them I didn't have any information, I didn't know anything, but they kept on shocking me and abusing me with that stick."

Amarjit said quietly by my side, "Sometimes they are abused anally too, but they won't talk about it." Amarjit had a medical background, and found it easier than other Sikhs to talk about anatomy. I nodded in response to his comment, banishing the image conjured up by it, and listened as our interlocutor continued.

"After that they took me down from there and threw me in a cell. There were two other guys there, but no toilet or anything. Just a bucket in the corner, and it was overflowing. One of the guys was badly bruised and he was moaning and groaning, lying on the wet floor. We kept trying to rub his legs. He was in a lot of pain.

"That night we three prayed for hours. We didn't sleep. We just prayed and prayed."

"Did you think that you might not survive?" I asked.

"No one knows whether they will live or die when they are picked up by police. I put my trust in Waheguru [God]."

He cleared his throat. "Next day, I was taken out again and more of the same was done. More the next day. Then they made me sit on the floor and put the roller on me."

I later learned what "the roller" was. A heavy wooden cylinder is rolled across the thighs of a prisoner, weighted by people standing on both ends, to crush and tear the muscles of the upper leg. Months after this interview, I was able to see the results of "the roller" on the legs of one Sikh unembarrassed enough to show me. That one also had burns from a hot iron staggered up and down his back and chest.

"What were you thinking as you were being tortured? Can you tell me what was going through your mind?" I asked, indelicately.

"Nothing. My mind was empty. When I thought of something I only thought to say the name of my God, Waheguru."

Again, I later learned how common it was for people under torture to lose all sense of their surroundings, and literally, their wits. Elaine Scarry, who wrote an intriguing book about torture and war called *The Body in Pain,* pointed out that this fact of radical narrowing of one's world while in extreme pain calls into question the alleged aim of torture, namely, to get information. Even when people do have information to give, they typically lose track of it utterly in the torture situation. The goal of torture therefore must be understood in terms other than the mere acquisition of knowledge, despite the common claim of torturers the world over that that is why they torture.[5]

"After several days of this treatment some people of my village managed to gather up some money and they demanded my release. I got out and then decided to leave India. But I came to the United States without proper papers and now I am in jail."

"How long have you been here?" I asked.

"Four months."

"Are you being treated all right?" I queried.

"Yes, but . . ." Suddenly this gaunt survivor was looking away from me, his face contorted with emotion. I hardly dared to ask, but I did.

"What is it?"

"My wife . . . I was . . . since I have been here I got a letter, she . . . was taken into custody . . ."

He couldn't go on. I saw water filling his eyes, and he turned away.

"Your wife was dishonored?" asked Amarjit. It's a euphemism for rape.

He nodded, and I watched a tear drop onto his beard. I didn't know whether it was appropriate or not, but I reached across the table and put my hand on his arm. He didn't move it away.

Later I would sit through many sessions like this, see many eyes full of tears. Amarjit, however hardened to the realities of what he sees as a guerilla war, became watery quite often. He has a peculiar gesture of swiping at the corners of his eyes with one finger, which he does surreptitiously, as if no one notices. But I do, and seeing that raw emotionalism in a man at the forefront of a major separatist movement always prompts me to recognize anew the complexity of trying to write effectively about people involved in conflict.

I heard tale after tale of atrocities suffered by Sikhs during the course of my research, some of which I share in these pages. Reports of Amnesty International and Human Rights Watch are also replete with them.[6] The texts alone, however, in their understated neutrality, do not show one very critical aspect of the Sikh experience of abuse: that is that physical insults, no matter how horrific, are not as agonizing as attacks on one's dignity. The really hurtful things involve the humiliation of women, the indignity of anal and genital torture, the slurs on the Sikh faith represented by tearing off turbans and cutting hair (kept long by Sikhs as a crucial religious symbol). At one point I was sitting with some Sikhs looking through an album of photos that had been smuggled out of Punjab at great cost. One page was worse than the next for sheer blood and gore. The picture that really caught my attention, however, showed a Sikh man with turban removed, hair flying, crouching in abject fear as an Indian police officer, with an expression of supreme disdain, prepared to slap him. I kept returning to this photo. Sikhs around me who noticed my response said that I must have been a Sikh in a previous life to recognize this particular scene as a particularly and uniquely horrifying one.

Eventually, I did make contact with people who had not only suffered but fought back. Although some individuals declined to talk with me or talked only in highly guarded terms, others were, after a time, willing to tell me their stories. I was actually surprised at the cooperation I received from people involved in the guerilla struggle. Why should they take the risk? Why trust me? What did they have to go on, other than my "sincerity?"

Sincerity, however, may be enough, or at least as good as any other criterion one might apply in a situation like this one. Jeff Sluka, who studies the IRA and other paramilitaries in Northern Ireland, says

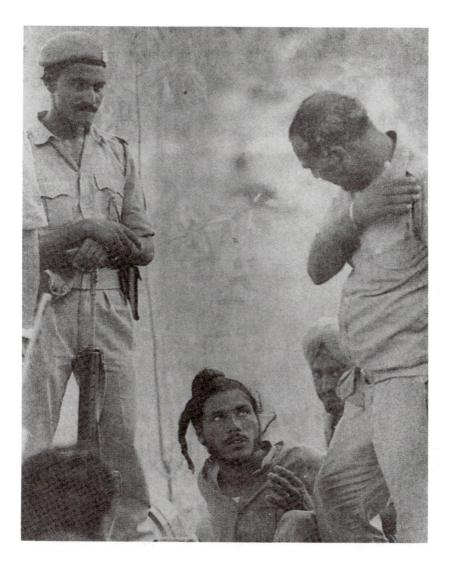

1. Sikh prisoner, turbanless, being abused by Central Reserve Police. This is one of the photos used in the international documentation of human rights violations in India.

frankly that friendships are among the most important factors in conducting research in arenas of conflict. (Sluka's articles on "Participant Observation in Violent Social Contexts" and "Reflections on Managing Danger in Fieldwork" are the clearest guidance available for those interested in this kind of study.[7]) Sluka also suggests that one start at the top of any organization of interest, since access guaranteed by leaders will typically be respected all the way down. Though I had not consciously chosen this strategy, serendipity put Amarjit, a very highly placed individual, in my path. Now my circle of acquaintances among Sikhs has widened, but it is clear that the reason people talked to me at first was solely Amarjit's presumed approval. After the initial entree, however, I was on my own. There was a snowball effect: one militant would introduce me to another, that one to a third, and so on.

Once I realized that I would indeed be talking with people involved on both receiving and initiating ends of acts of violence, I thought carefully about how best to protect both them and me from legal repercussions. (Anthropological fieldnotes can be subpoenaed, a fact some have learned to the detriment of their "informants.") I first developed an informed consent statement, which I read or told to people at the outset of interviews, which stated that I had no legal privilege and that information told to me could be requested by a court of law. Because of this, I asked Sikhs with whom I talked to change names, places, and details as necessary to disguise their stories. I knew I needed to remain in ignorance of certain things despite the problems it might cause my research, because otherwise I might become inescapably compromised (for example, finding out who committed an unsolved crime).

Most of the conversations I had with militants were conducted in English, spoken fluently by many Sikhs. Some of the narratives, however, were recorded in Punjabi and translated with the help of other Khalistanis present, usually highly placed ones. The situations in which a translator was required were occasionally particularly interesting, as a telling phrase or two would be purposely left out or modified, apparently not by mistake but in the interests of security. I never pressed at these points; I didn't *want* to know whatever it was that highly placed Khalistanis felt I shouldn't know. The translation process served as a kind of screening for the most sensitive subjects, and I believe I had to allow that screening to take place if I hoped to retain access to the militants.

I learned that one of the really important skills in talking with people involved in conflict is having a strong sense of this information threshold, of knowing when to stop probing, when to simply let a topic drop and pursue something else. Paradoxical though it may seem, I believe that a certain gentleness of style here is critical in interviewing people who are involved in armed conflict. Being accustomed to responding to violence with violence, they open up best in a nonconfrontational setting. Observing the way that journalists tend to interview people on television and radio, often "putting them on the spot," I find it unsurprising that what they are able to elicit from people engaged in violence is sometimes less than useful. In my experience, putting people on the spot is probably the last thing an effective interviewer in an arena of conflict would want to do.

Having made a plea for gentility, however, I would hasten to add that honesty in expressing one's differences with interlocutors and firmness in standing by them are also crucial to winning the respect of people in conflict. Perhaps particularly for Sikhs, any hint of fearfulness on the part of an interviewer would be disastrous. Thoughout this research, I had the sense that if I started being afraid around Khalistani Sikhs I might as well drop the project entirely. Sometimes, after an absence from the community for a month or two, reading other accounts of their activities that made them seem frightening indeed, I would start to grow uneasy, feel my heart beat more rapidly at the thought of what I was getting into. But a dose of real Khalistanis would always restore my sense of balance. When I got scared, I knew it was time to touch base with reality—that is, touch base with human beings, not their near-monstrous images—again.

I also told Sikh militants individually and in groups what my book would be like and made sure they understood that they could refuse to participate or end the conversation at any time. When I could, I showed them parts of the finished manuscript to solicit their comments and suggestions. Sometimes I revised the text based on what they said, other times I did not.

This kind of research arrangement is obviously highly problematic. Usually guarantees of confidentiality and anomymity are given, but the researcher herself knows the masked information. Purposely keeping oneself in the dark means most critically that one is unable to verify a lot of information. I don't see any way around this dilemma. If you don't want to become a partisan (i.e., are not ready to perjure yourself on behalf of the group or suffer the consequences of sharing sensitive information), you have to keep yourself innocent of many concrete details.

I believe, however, that for the purposes of anthropology (as opposed to, for example, the purposes of intelligence gathering), it is in some sense not the concrete details in which we are interested. Was it in Gurdaspur or Ludhiana that the bomb went off? Was it in this jail or that that the "roller" was used? These are not the kind of things I wanted to learn from militant Sikhs. What I did want to learn about was how it felt to be somebody whose legs have been permanently crippled by torture, or alternatively, somebody who set off a bomb. (Often, not surprisingly, the two are related.) And the trust the Sikhs extended to me was reciprocated by an important trust I had to extend to them: to protect me from becoming compromised by unwanted information. I did not want to become a Khalistani; I wanted to remain an anthropologist, and I had to have help from my interlocutors to retain this fragile inside-outside position.

The wrist bands worn by Sikhs (*kara*) represent many things. I got one at a *gurudwara* near Chicago at one point, and I sometimes wear it and other times take it off. I find myself taking it off when I am feeling too much in danger of "going native" through my close association with the people I study—too much the participant, too little the observer. But I always wear it when I write, and for me that clink of steel around my wrist serves as a constant reminder of two values. First is the commitment to write the truth as I, in my best effort, understand it; "Truth is pure steel," says the founder of Sikhism, Guru Nanak. But in another way the *kara* reminds me of my indissoluble link to real people in the real world; more generally, the impact of what I do as a scholar on the world outside the academy. We are too easily oblivious to the practical consequences of our work, claiming arrogantly that truth is truth, we will write it as we see it and let the chips fall where they may. I am too much of a pragmatist to ever be that kind of scholar. I know that what I do affects real people, and I have to try to think through the possible repercussions. Another aphorism of the Sikhs comes to mind: "Truth is the highest good," they say, "but higher still is truthful living."

How to reconcile adherence to truth with commitment to human beings is, of course, one of the big challenges facing concerned scholars today. It is also one with which Sikhism as a philosophical tradition has grappled extensively. Maybe we can learn something from them, and they from us.

CONFRONTING VIOLENCE

In this spirit, I began interviewing men and women involved in the armed side of the Khalistan conflict, renegotiating my stance as independent-scholar-yet-constrained-by-politics at every step. There were missteps, too. But in bumbling my way into the lives of people in conflict, I found myself personally engaged in a way that I had not foreseen, not on a political level but on a deeply philosophical one—what Nordstrom and Robben call existential, rather than cultural, shock.[8] I had never really sat down and talked with people who openly accepted the necessity of dying, and killing, for a cause—and who were ready to do either at the drop of a hat. Being around people like this makes you think, and not only about the viability of the state of India. For what am I willing to die? To kill? And aside from this nearly automatic reflexive impulse, what does it mean to live in a community circumscribed by violence, to witness lives in which violence, and the threat of violence, and the memory of violence weave a sinuous path through daily activities and define a world in which survival alone seems a substantial accomplishment?

At the tail end of a generation whose attitudes were largely shaped by the Vietnam War, looming over our consciousness even decades later, I was always generally opposed to military action. Gulf War, no, Somalia or Bosnia, better give it deep thought, and so on. Unlike my father, I was never a pacifist—couldn't be a pacifist in a world in which the strong so clearly dominated the weak and so clearly would not give up that power by moral pressure alone. One thing was clear, however—violence was a last resort, at best an unfortunate strategic necessity in a world in which power was distributed unequally. One might have to grit one's teeth, go against one's better instincts, and make short-term sacrifices in the interests of long-term justice. The idea that violent actions could be meaningful in themselves was a troubling one all too glibly avoided in mainstream Western circles.

At the same time (the sixties and seventies) there was a new academic literature that tried to define aggression as an inherent part of human nature. Books like Konrad Lorenz's *On Aggression,* Robert Ardrey's *Territorial Imperative,* and Lionel Tiger's *Men in Groups* had great popular appeal because they seemed to live up to widespread *ideals* of peace, while also neatly justifying capitalism, patriarchy, and other aspects of modern Western society. Most anthropologists hated this kind of literature and devoted much teaching time to demonstrating that humans were not genetically wired for violence; there were various "harmless peoples" to be found around the globe—look at those Semai, for example, who had such an abhorrence of violence they would not tolerate even a parent reprimanding a child. Yet oddly enough Robert Dentan, one of the key ethnographers of the Semai, noted that when Semai were recruited into the Malaysian army they became fantastic soldiers, experiencing a "blood drunkenness" in battle that horrified onlookers. The Kalahari San turned out to occasionally murder each other, fought with valor in the South African Defense Force, and later joined the guerilla organization SWAPO in some numbers when they realized where their interests lay. Conversely, initial reports of "fierce people" like the Yanamamo were supplemented by more balanced portrayals that showed that even they were also capable of gentle and loving actions and sustained peace for substantial periods between their famous bouts of warfare.[9] The picture turned out to be complex: every society seemed to exhibit both peaceful and violent behavior, however various the interpretations placed upon them. "We are all capable of violence" is one of those truisms that seems to be, in fact, true, at least as far as societies as wholes are concerned.

Outside the halls of academia, the most important forums where matters of human violence are discussed are the military headquarters of the world. Pragmatists all, military writers are rarely inclined to speculate about whether we are "instinctually" aggressive or simply culturally inclined or disinclined to violence. They are interested in one question only: given war, how can we (whoever the "we" is) win it? Yet despite their pragmatic stance much of the work by military theorists is oddly abstract, talking in coldly rationalistic terms that seem eerily to exclude breathing human beings. Classical military theory is therefore as inadequate to the task of understanding actual violence as the sociobiological literature that reduces it to genetics and the "cultural" literature that makes it epiphenomenal to social circumstance.

Working with Sikh militants has made clear to me that abstract explanations of group violence that neglect the highly individualized quality of participation in violent activities, whether on the part of victims or perpetrators, are insufficient. Wars are fought between groups, but pain, death, and risk are deeply personal. Treating people's actual experiences of violence as central gives a wholly different perspective from that of military theory, and it brings to life Corbin's insight that human violence is mostly *conceptual*, not instinctual, emotional, customary, or blind.[10] Sikhs, drawing on an elaborate theology of violence, are particularly articulate about the conceptual order behind their armed resistance, an order fully ensconced in individual, conscious, decision-making human beings. Anyone who attempted to understand Sikh militancy or predict militant actions based on the hyper-rationalized military theory of ROTC textbooks would find themselves wholly out of their element, as in another arena the U.S. military establishment also discovered with regard to the Viet Cong.

Though many academics would like to see ROTC programs out of the universities and have little respect for military writers, it is important to look carefully at military theories about violence because they are spawned by and in turn shape general attitudes toward political violence in our culture. In particular, the legitimation of murder carried out by states and the criminalization of murder carried out by non-state groups or by individuals is a legacy of the Western military tradition that haunts us today, distorting, for example, analyses of the World Trade Center bombing. "How can you sit around talking with people who are responsible for murder?" I was asked by one student with regard to interviews with Sikh militants. I presume that "sitting around talking" to war veterans would not provoke the same sense of outrage. To be sure, there are important differences between state and nonstate political violence, and glossing over these differences can be both intellectually irresponsible and pragmatically dangerous. Nevertheless, the very strong sense of disjunction between the two spawned by traditional military theory continues to inhibit the effective resolution of conflict.

Modern military theory in the West derives largely from the work of Carl von Clausewitz, whose classic essay *On War*[11] still frames the thinking of people involved in the war industry over a century after its publication. The Clausewitzian worldview, sometimes called the "trinitarian" model, places people, army, and state in a triangular relationship, each aspect independent but interrelated. Being tied to the notion of the state as a political order, the model is therefore limited to a particular moment in Western history, usually defined as the period dating from the Treaty of Westphalia in 1648 to the present, in which the state is under attack from both substate identities and superstate allegiances. The model also prompts rejection of any violence carried out by non-state (that is, powerless) groups as acts of "terrorism" or outright criminality. When leftists like Noam Chomsky, then, turn the terrorist label around to apply it to states, they pose a direct challenge to the presumptions of the Clausewitzian mental map.[12] If generals and colonels can be "terrorists," can Khalistani Sikhs then be legitimately thought of as "soldiers?" We can go only so far with this reasoning, as we shall see. But the axiom that states alone are authorized to commit murder complicates the picture of intergroup violence considerably. At the most extreme, it even prompts nonstate groups to claim statehood as a way of legitimizing the violence in which they engage.

Clausewitz's famous dictum, "War is a continuation of politics by other means," points to a second critical feature of the modern military universe: its emphasis on strategy. (Many radical leftists have taken over this notion as well, accepting the strategic necessity of violence without much further consideration of what that violence means to the individuals who engage in it.) People in Clausewitz's universe commit acts of violence rationally, because they are part of trained armies that obey orders. It follows from this way of thinking that the most powerful states with the best-trained troops and the best military strategies will win wars.

That this conclusion is in fact patently untrue is illustrated by the Vietnam case, among others. Martin van Creveld uses the U.S. failure in Vietnam as one of the centerpieces of his sustained critique of Clausewitzian theory, *The Transformation of War*. In this important book van Creveld proposes that the "low-intensity conflicts" now prominent in the world are not a minor variant or modification of state-based warfare but are, in fact, wars, and that ideas about what warfare is have to shift to accommodate this new reality. In guerilla conflicts, unlike wars that follow the

Clausewitzian model, the state is not the sole legitimator of violence, and people and army (the other two arms of the trinitarian triangle) are intertwined, even, at times, identical. Van Creveld also points out that countering guerilla insurgencies with Clausewitzian strategy nearly always fails. Moreover, the experience of combat itself is quite different for the guerilla; indeed it recaptures some aspects of the kinds of warfare that preceded the establishment of nation states. Personal commitment makes the crucial difference.[13]

It is one of the great tabooed facts of our age that men and women who have experienced the heat of battle sometimes feel nostalgia for it. War is hell, we're not supposed to like it, and any hint that there is something attractive about killing and risking death might, we feel rather superstitiously, make us all cross the threshold into World War III and Armageddon. Any realistic perusal of war literature, however, reveals that for all the horror of the battlefield, it creates a special pathos that is for many people not replicable in any other human endeavor. Many veterans, for all their nightmares, view their moments in battle as the high points of their lives. What are we to make of this? To talk about aggressive biological instincts is too reductive; to talk of psychopathology, too trivializing. Most of us would rather not face the fact that coming to grips with death, which is largely what the war experience is, is one of the existential tasks facing every human being. It is not an entirely unnatural idea to suggest that this confrontation with human mortality is worthy of some kind of celebration, whatever the circumstances under which it occurs. Figuring out how to approach this difficult topic without contributing to a "pornography of violence," without glorifying murder, is one of the challenges that face anthropologists trying to write realistically about the human experience of conflict.

The question of why violence occurs in the broad sense raises with it, then, the insistent question of how individuals engaged in violence experience that engagement. To say either that they are, in their thousands, "just following orders" in the rational sense is absurd; so is accusing them all of insanity. Why people fight, why they willingly face death and cause it, is explored historically in John Keegan's excellent soldier's-eye view of war, *The Face of Battle,* which compares what battle was like for combatants at Agincourt, Waterloo, and the Somme.[14] The brave new world not of armies but of peoples, of low-intensity, non-state guerilla struggles defined less in terms of massed battles than of individual encounters, however, invites more of this kind of ethnography of violence that draws on real people's experiences of what it feels like to face that fusillade or pull that trigger. Unless we understand why it makes some kind of sense for somebody to put a bomb in the World Trade Center, we will not be able to prevent this kind of atrocity from happening again.

Heightened security measures are more an admission of defeat than a meaningful remedy.

Anthropologists have in fact established a considerable literature on the lived realities of human violence, and the ethnographic study of terror and resistance has become something of a subfield of its own. Only a small number of anthropologists are, however, engaged in this important work, and there is still a fair amount of skepticism on the part of colleagues about the validity of our involvement in arenas of violent conflict. Philippe Bourgois, who has studied political violence in Central America as well as urban drug wars in the United States, commented that colleagues seem to take his interest in conflict as personal adventurism rather than a serious academic pursuit (personal communication). Happily, the recent publication of several collections of essays on the ethnography of violence,[15] and the increasing involvement of anthropologists in the field of conflict resolution,[16] bode well for the future of the field. Anthropologists have now studied violence in Central America, Northern Ireland, the Balkans, southern Africa, and elsewhere, and they continue to produce deeply challenging ethnography centering on the human experience of conflict.

Militant Sikhs, suffering and causing pain, loss, and death every day, are living in extraordinary, not ordinary, circumstances. Their actions can't give us a window on everyday human life; they are not "typical" even for Sikhs generally. But to return to Kant's forgotten question for anthropology, "What may I hope?" I think we can well look to communities under fire like this one to see just what we human beings are capable of. Dignity in the face of unutterable insults, physical and mental, is part of that equation. Unflinching courage in the face of nearly certain death in combat is another. Love for one's comrades, generosity toward one's community, devotion to one's God; these are other qualities of Sikh militants that inspire and instruct. "These people are *magnificent*," one of my students commented after hearing some of my stories, and indeed, in an important sense, they are. Obviously, their victims would not agree with this assessment. But this is, in fact, the point: they are magnificent, and the havoc they wreak is devastating. We won't understand them better by denying either part of that formula.

Seen as a resistance movement, certainly the most heroic light in which to see it, Sikh militancy can be placed along an axis with other respectable resistances like those of the Tibetans, the Kurds, and even the French in World War II. It is also, however, a movement for the consolidation of the Sikh religion. From the viewpoint of loyalist Sikhs who have no interest in Khalistan, the militants are not only dangerous terrorists but also fundamentalists who appoint themselves bastions of orthodoxy from which no deviation is tolerated. There is, then, an axis of religious revivalism along which militant Sikhism must also be placed, less flatteringly (for most of us), beside Ayatollah Khomeini and Jerry Falwell. Mark Juergensmeyer has attempted to reconcile these divergent but intersecting axes by calling such politicized fundamentalists "religious nationalists," a term probably acceptable to people both within and outside of these movements.[17]

The fact is that though scholars may debate whether the Sikh militant movement is "primarily" one of resistance or one of fundamentalism (a debate largely revolving around the extent of personal sympathy for the movement), it is clearly both. Militant Sikhism has flourished during the 1980s and 1990s as an obvious reaction to state persecution, but its origins in the 1970s cannot be understood without recourse to the notion of religious consolidation. The two have worked in tandem to create that volatile mix characteristic of religious nationalist movements. In the Sikh case, too, the militancy is marked by a certain unpredictability that drives those interested in containing it wild and brings pause to every thoughtful observer. There are too many diverse pressures and too much of a "hothouse atmosphere"[18] within the militant community to make clear predictions about what a future state led by current militant leaders would be like.

This observation brings me, still reflecting on Kant, to a fourth question I would add to his composite query "What is man?" In knowing Sikh militants, I have a better sense of what I may hope for "man," but I also find myself asking "What must I fear?" I don't fear religious nationalism per se, at least not the Sikh kind, but I would not want to write the element of tragedy-in-the-making out of my meditations here. As the ancient Greeks taught us, the noblest human beings can finish tragically. A movement full of verve and moral right, populated by "magnificent" human beings, can end up creating a political situation that is an abomination. (From the French revolution on, we've seen this tragedy too many times to be over-optimistic about revolutions.) The same "saints" who uphold with valor and grace every ideal of the Sikh way of life look the other way when less saintly companions slaughter women and children on buses. These are the contradictions of being human, and they apply equally to the police torturer who nightly tucks his daughter into bed with consummate gentleness and to the Sikh guerilla who bows his head in prayer before gunning down a local official. Each does the best he can to serve what he sees as a just cause, and a hell on earth (as one Amnesty International worker called Punjab, off the record) is created. What must we fear? That good intentions, nobility of effort, will not be enough, neither for police officers nor for guerilla fighters, nor for scholars.

Most of the Sikh militants with whom I speak are sadly (or perhaps

happily) unaware of the problematic tendency of revolutionary movements to turn sour. Like revolutionaries everywhere, they are convinced
of the uniqueness of their cause and are in any case too busy fighting to
worry much about outcomes. The struggle for Khalistan is, perhaps, best
envisioned as a quest; the process of striving itself provides an important
source of meaning. The evocative quality of the Khalistan theme in Sikh
rhetoric far exceeds political issues like borders and national flags, and
it makes nobility of effort virtually an end in itself. (The pervasiveness of
this theme also explains why Clausewitzian containment efforts have not
in fact dampened Khalistani ardor; it is only partially explicable in terms
of rational strategy.) Today, when counterinsurgency efforts have in large
part succeeded in driving the militant movement underground or overseas, the persistence of a deep commitment to the idea of Khalistan on
the part of Sikh "freedom fighters" can only be understood in terms of
philosophy, which persists through the ups and down of politics and
battles. To ignore this side of things is to suppose that once the militants
have been sufficiently repressed the struggle for Khalistan will be over.
My experience with Sikh militants strongly indicates that this will not be
the case.

My task here, then, is to convey the sense of meaningful striving, the
sense of being at the peak of one's humanity in spite of the hellish conditions around one, that animates Sikh militants as they fight and die for
a sovereign Sikh nation. The same sense of participation in a holy quest
sustains them in exile overseas as they read reports of the "pacification"
of Punjab that seem so at odds with their own experience. Despite the
probable accusation from some quarters that I am providing a platform
for "terrorists," I use the militants' own words where possible to bring to
the reader a sense of the immediacy of the Sikh militant world. It is less
distant and more accessible than most people think. The militants are
more like *us* than most people think, and I hope this book will make that
clear while problematizing what they (and we) are doing.

My relationship with Amarjit continued to grow after that first set of
encounters in California. We traveled to many cities of the United States
and Canada together, sometimes speaking in tandem at *gurudwaras*,
other times interviewing militants for hours at a stretch, still other times
sitting up nights talking about religion, politics, or both. I also started
attending meetings of organizations and groups different from or even
antagonistic to Amarjit's, and talked with people bluntly hostile to him.
I learned about the controversies and ambiguities of his own position
and eventually came to rely more on my own assessments and intui-
tions regarding the militants. I started meeting non-militant Khalistanis,
who want sovereignty but seek peaceful means to get it, as well as loyalist Sikhs, not supportive of Khalistan at all. Eventually, I wrote a few

academic papers and started testifying on Sikh refugee matters in the United States and Canada.

It is critically important to make an effort to contact people in various wings of a political movement, otherwise one will be branded as a spokesperson of a particular faction. This became of particular concern to me as I gradually learned about the factional disputes with which the Khalistani community is riven. Amarjit himself was aware of this danger, and encouraged me to make contacts of my own with various groups, even with people who regarded him as an enemy or rival. Eventually I developed my own network of Khalistanis, some connected in one way or another with Amarjit but others not. Sometimes I found myself awkwardly listening to accusations and counter-accusations across factions, or hearing wildly different versions of the same event. But I *never* carried tales from one person or group to another. This kind of discretion is as important in developing trust as keeping confidences with the community generally. I took no positions on internecine rivalries and tried to steer clear of local politics.

What did the Khalistani separatists want from me? Although it became clear that the dialogue between me and some of the militants acquired a personal dimension as we grew to know each other better, it would be naive to supose that the individuals leading the insurgency didn't have an agenda into which they saw me fitting. Clearly, they are hoping for good PR. "If you just tell the truth, that *will* be good PR," says Amarjit confidently. "We know that our movement can stand any amount of scrutiny."

So I do scrutinize it, I criticize it regularly and publicly, and I write this book telling the truth as I see it with some confidence that Khalistani Sikhs will respect and even appreciate what I have done. Of course, there are zealots; a speaker in a *gurudwara* once introduced me as "a supporter of Khalistan," whereupon Amarjit picked up the microphone and corrected, "She is just a scholar concerned to find out the truth about the situation in Punjab and the Khalistan movement." Since from their viewpoint almost nobody else is concerned to get behind the massive propaganda on the subject put out by the Indian government, my interest alone makes a huge impression. One elderly woman ran up to me after I had recited the litany of human rights abuses in India that somehow never do get the publicity of those in Latin America or China; she gripped me by the shoulders and said in heavily accented English, "The mothers of Punjab thank you." I didn't know what to say, feeling wholly inadequate to the task of living up to that kind of approbation. I can't do much for the mothers of Punjab, except my usual academic thing: tell the truth as I see it.

I am often asked whether it is depressing to engage in this kind of research. In being around militant Sikhs I was in fact reminded of a medical project I once worked on that focused on melanoma, an often fatal form of skin cancer. My job involved keeping track of survival statistics of a large array of patients, and though I found the science part of the work fascinating it was very depressing to produce those incessant downward-sloping curves that illustrated the poor chances of survival beyond a few years past diagnosis. When I got the chance to actually talk with melanoma patients on a W.H.O. project in Australia, I worried about whether I would be able to cope with being around dying people day after day. But the funny thing was that actually being with the people who had melanoma was far *less* depressing than dealing with all those tragic numbers. In the abstract, all it looked like was a lot of death. But in the flesh, on the ground with real human beings, there was also courage and humor, creativity and spirituality, love. I was inspired, not depressed, by being with them.

I experienced the same phenomenon as I researched violence in Punjab. The very first prescription for somebody trying to understand what violent conflict is all about, I therefore suggest, is to talk to, be with, learn from the people involved in it. Without this face-to-face encounter, all one sees is downward-sloping lines.

At one point a meeting was held in which a roomful of militant Sikhs asked me questions about what I was up to and what the product of my research with them might be like. It was, needless to say, a particularly intense example of the kind of thing anthropologists now go through in the attempt to engage in dialogue with the people they study. After our public exchange, one fellow came up to me and hinted that I might like to avoid writing about the episodes in which militants killed innocent noncombatants. Drawing myself up, I commented that as a Sikh, as someone for whom "truth is pure steel," this individual could hardly be asking me to refrain from telling the truth about the Khalistan struggle (part of which is that innocent people get killed). After a momentary silence, in which everybody around us seemed to be waiting to hear his response, the militant gave a slight bow and said, "Madam, it seems you are a better Sikh than I." He shook my hand and left.

Oddly enough, the risks of engaging in research on ongoing conflicts are usually either blown utterly out of proportion or totally ignored by colleagues involved in more traditional subject areas. For every colleague who feared that Sikh militants, or the Indian government, or both, might set off a bomb in our building, there was another who dismissed any hint of danger as sheer melodrama. ("You're in the United States, after all.") When I started coming into contact with other scholars studying similar insurgencies, I realized that my experience was fairly common. It makes for a certain kind of loneliness and a strong sense of being on one's own resources in terms of making decisions about the advisability of a particular course of action. I follow my gut instincts, thus far successfully. As Sluka points out, there's a lot of luck in it, too.[19] Not every confrontation will turn out as well as the one described above.

I still have nightmares about violence. Violence *is* my worst nightmare, which makes this research project the most difficult I have undertaken. Though the differences between me and militant Sikhs are vast—aside from myriad cultural differences, they are devoutly religious and I am not—the thing that puts them and me on different sides of an immense divide is the fact that they are involved in a war and I am not. Yet I am haunted by the realization that had I been born in different life circumstances, I might well be the one dodging, or throwing, that grenade. Like most anthropologists, I am intrigued by lives not lived, attracted to windows into other possibilities. I rejoice in the richness added to my life by my encounter with Sikh militants, while recognizing the disagreements, many extreme, between us.

Rupinder Singh Sodhi, the Indian Supreme Court attorney who defended two Sikhs involved in the assassination of Indira Gandhi, said that his aim was not to "get them off" in legal terms but to create a space in which their voices could be heard with dignity.[20] I sometimes see my mission here in similar terms and, like Sodhi, believe that militant Sikhs respect it. I am "in the system," I am committed to following the rules, I can't be a partisan who helps insurgents ("criminals") evade the law. Assassins get hanged; they and we know that and accept it. But we still can benefit from hearing what they have to say. What makes it worthwhile for somebody to face the gallows? A Sikh later hanged for the murder of an Indian army general said that he imagined the rope around his neck as a lover's embrace. What sort of worldview does a comment like that spring from?

A strong sense of the incommensurability of different cultural realities pervades American anthropology alongside an equally strong sense of common human ground. Only recently has greater attention been paid to the actual experiences of ethnographers doing fieldwork, which, more than a set of methods, means reaching out to other human beings across a sometimes immense cultural gulf. That fieldwork is such a momentous personal experience for most anthropologists has traditionally been belied by our rhetorical style, which conformed to the misguided notion that a pretended distance from one's "subjects" was prerequisite to "science." Now, thankfully, there is more latitude for a range of ways in which ethnographers can viably relate to the people they study and learn from. Exploration of relationships developed through fieldwork (as in Vincent Crapanzano's *Tuhami* or Marjorie Shostak's *Nisa*) has itself become a subgenre of contemporary anthropology. In fact, ethnography is now best understood as dialogical rather than "objective" (if it ever was), and it is in this spirit that I write about my relationships with Sikhs as well as about Sikhs themselves.

Amarjit attended a few sessions of the American Anthropological Association meetings in 1993, his presence epitomizing the challenging moment at which we are now trying to do ethnography. The people we study have started scrutinizing *us*, penetrating even to the heart of our professional meetings. Sitting there in his saffron turban, dagger tucked tactfully under a suit jacket, he raised his hand to ask a question after one provocative paper. I got nervous, wondering what he was going to say, whether it would be appropriate, how it would make me look. After he made his comment (a perfectly reasonable one), I told him about my trepidation and my subsequent relief that in fact he knew how to behave in my world. "Now you know how I feel every time you walk into a *gurudwara*," he replied, turning the anthropological tables.

Jewish theologian Martin Buber talks about the *I-Thou* relationship as crucial to human nature: the recognition, in the very otherness of the other and in the wholehearted acceptance of that otherness, of kinship.[21] Those I-Thou relationships, impossibly intimate, are at the heart of the anthropological enterprise, whether it concerns Sikh militants or New Guinea tribespeople. This is when "informant" or even the now-chic "interlocutor" are pitifully inadequate terms, "friendship" too maudlin to capture the ontological embrace of the alien as, like oneself, wholly human. The moments of epiphany in fieldwork are those in which one confronts the "anguish and expectation" (Buber's phrase) of being human in another, the "what must I fear" and "what may I hope" we all confront in such very different forms. It is in this space between one self and another, fraught with meaning, that the ultimate question, "What is man?" might be answered. When that space is wide, as in the confrontation across cultures, this question can be explored in its fullest exuberant richness.

Anthropology as a discipline has lost something of this philosophical wealth. But individual anthropologists find it regularly, and it may help some of us figure out the answer to that other segment of Kant's query, "What ought I to do?"

2

THE FRAGRANCE OF JASMINE

N THIS CHAPTER I look at the basic history and doctrines of the Sikh faith, as seen through the eyes of the orthodox. Their vision of Sikhism and their understanding of what it means to be a Sikh is somewhat at odds with the perspective of Western academia, which is at the moment a source of considerable controversy. This controversy, and what it can tell us about the value of "inside" and "outside" scholarship, is considered further in Chapter 10. Here, the aim is to get a feel for what the pious Sikh understands of his or her faith that serves as motivation, justification, or explanation for current political actions.

FOUNDATIONS OF FAITH

Guru Nanak, the founder of the Sikh faith, was born in C.E. 1469 in what is now Pakistani Punjab. His birthplace, called Nankana Sahib, attracts thousands of pilgrims every year from all over the world (though the closed border between India, where most Sikhs live, and Pakistan, its sometime enemy, makes this pilgrimage problematic for many). Guru Nanak was probably influenced by both of the major faiths of his time and place, Hinduism and Islam, though Sikhs are upset when scholars emphasize these historical influences over the revealed quality of Guru Nanak's pronouncements.[1] It is certainly clear that the first Guru rejected much of both Hinduism and Islam, at least in terms of how they were practiced. One of the verses in the Guru Granth Sahib, the holy book of the Sikhs, narrates Guru Nanak's rejection of the Brahmin habit of wearing a sacred thread over the shoulder. In this verse Guru Nanak heaps scorn on those who believe that one can use a thread to reach spiritual truth:

Though people commit countless thefts, countless adulteries, utter countless
*   falsehoods and countless words of abuse,*
Though they commit countless robberies and villainies night and day against
*   their fellow creatures;*
Yet the cotton thread is spun, and the Brahmin comes to twist it.

Guru Nanak then proposes, characteristically, a thread not of cotton, but of truth:

Out of the cotton of compassion
Spin the thread of contentment
Tie knots of continence,
Give it the twist of truth.
That would make a garland for the soul . . .
Such a thread once worn will never break
Nor get soiled, burnt or lost,
The person who wears a thread like this is blessed.

Not only did Guru Nanak reject what he saw as the empty ritualism of the Hindu tradition, but he also famously renounced its most characteristic social organization, the caste system. People from all castes became his *sikhs* or disciples, and they ate together in the community kitchen or *langar* which today remains characteristic of Sikh life. All the *gurudwaras* contain these kitchens, which are not only important symbols of egalitarianism but serve a charitable function as well. (After the Rodney King riots in Los Angeles, local Sikhs went out into the streets with pots of food to help those displaced from their homes.) The most famous *gurudwara*, the Harmandir Sahib at Amritsar (popularly, "the Golden Temple"), also has four doors facing the four directions, to signify welcome to anybody who chooses to enter. Although caste continues to play a role in Sikh society (expressed, for example, in marriage patterns) despite the clear ideology against it, the egalitarian strain in Sikh culture has been noted by observers from British times to the present.[2]

Islam, the faith of the rulers of the region at the time of Guru Nanak, also rejected caste hierarchy, including its ban on interdining. But Guru Nanak felt that many Muslims, like many Hindus, were going about their worship devoid of the true spirit behind the prayers. He says in the Guru Granth Sahib:

Five prayers you say five times a day,
With five different names;
But if truth is your first prayer,

The second to honestly earn your living,
The third to give generously in God's name,
If purity of mind is your fourth prayer,
And praise of God your fifth;
If you practice these five virtues . . .
Then you can call yourself a Muslim.

Sikhs today typically express a close solidarity with Muslims, primarily because both minorities in India claim to suffer the same discrimination at the hands of the Indian government, but also because they both share a monotheistic tradition. (The fact that the greatest persecution of the Sikhs occurred at the hands of Mughal rulers, who were Muslim, is a historical fact that does not seem to hamper the current Sikh-Muslim alliance.) Because of the egalitarian thrust of both Sikhism and Islam, many of the converts to both faiths historically have come from the Hindu lower castes, a process still going on today. Nevertheless, despite the general affinity of the two faiths, Guru Nanak saw the need for a different kind of spirituality from that practiced by the Muslims. Although it is not clear just how socially separate Guru Nanak's followers were from adherents to the Hindu and Muslim faiths, it is a matter of great importance to contemporary Sikhs that the originality of his teachings be recognized. It is also obviously important to presumed nation builders that the separate identity of the "people" be recognized from the outset.[3]

There were, of course, other traditions in Indian history that also focused on getting behind the ritualization of popular religion. Buddhism and Jainism were two movements whose rhetoric against the empty adherence to tradition sounds very similar to that of Guru Nanak. Both were ancient rebellions against Brahminism, at least partly protesting the materialism that turns people away from recognition of truth. The following verse from the Guru Granth Sahib is quite reminiscent of the Buddhist *sutras*:

Religion doesn't consist of a patched coat, or a yogi's staff, or in ashes smeared over the body;
Religion doesn't consist of earrings worn, or a shaven head, or in the blowing of horns.
Stay pure amid the impurities of the world; that is the way to find religion . . .
Religion doesn't consist in mere words;
One who looks upon everybody as equal is religious.
Religion doesn't consist in wandering to tombs or places of cremation, or in sitting in attitudes of contemplation;

*Religion doesn't consist in traveling to foreign countries, or in bathing at
    places of pilgrimage.
Stay pure amid the impurities of the world, that is the way to find religion.*

Whereas both Buddhism and Jainism developed traditions of renunciation based on this kind of philosophy, mainstream Sikhism remained firmly committed to pragmatism, to living in the real world. Though a few sects developed that did focus on meditative withdrawal (the Udasis, for example, a sect founded by the son of Guru Nanak), the point in mainstream Sikhism was to maintain a state of spiritual bliss while doing the usual things that humans do: marrying, having children, working, fighting wars. Sikhs are proud to claim that their tradition is one in which *practice*, the way one lives, is the true test of faith. One is sincere, one is charitable, one is devoted to truth, one is courageous—these are things that make one a Sikh. (T. N. Madan notes that it is a tradition that is *orthoprax* rather than *orthodox*.[4]) But it is very hard to live this way without the strength that comes from prayer, and that is why even the most worldly Sikhs ideally spend hours each day in the recitation of the Guru Granth Sahib or in listening to *gurubani* ("the Guru's songs"). Guru Nanak instructed as much when he advised,

*As the lotus floats in water, but remains unaffected by its waves;
As the swan swims in it and is not drenched by water;
So by meditating on the Word and repeating God's Name,
You will be able to safely cross the ocean of the world.*

Virtually all Sikhs involved in the militant struggle for Khalistan report the central role of prayer in their lives. In my wanderings among North American Sikhs I stayed in their own homes, and I was able to see for myself just what this kind of devotion means. Mornings, long before I was awake, household members would be up, bathed, and dressed, sitting in poses of silent meditation or quietly chanting verses from the Guru Granth Sahib. The time just before dawn, called "the ambrosial hours" in Sikh tradition, is thought to be especially conducive to communion with the divine. When I would get up, usually long after dawn, Sikh members of the household would already be refreshed and calmed by their prayer session. They would pray again at night, or at any spare moments during the day. (One time I was sitting in the car with one Sikh while waiting for another to make some copies of a document at a commercial Xerox machine; I fumed at the delay while the Sikh assumed the lotus posture in the back seat and chanted. He emerged from the delay energized; I, irritated.)

One militant told me that even while he was hiding underground in Punjab, living in fields, and roaming from place to place, he used to go once a week to the Harmandir Sahib at Amritsar, entering in the evening after most of the pilgrims had departed and staying there through the night until the worshipers started straggling in again at dawn. A sacred pool of water surrounds the Harmandir Sahib, and he used to sit there and listen to the sound of *gurubani* being recited within. Now, in the rush of his political activities among expatriate European Sikhs, he has to find those moments of quiet within.

"It sounds crazy, but I have to say that the time I spent in jail [eighteen months] was the best time of my life," another Sikh told me.

"Why?" I asked.

"Because we were able to pray there sixteen, eighteen, sometimes twenty hours a day. I will never forget that place where I recited so much *gurubani*. I felt so happy there."

I came to recognize the phrase "he prayed twenty hours a day" as a recognition of devotion, often applied to fighters who in realistic terms could not have been literally sitting there reciting *gurubani* for twenty hours. Jarnail Singh Bhindranwale, the leader of the Sikhs who defended the Harmandir Sahib against the 1984 army assault, called "Sant" (saint) by his followers, "prayed twenty hours a day." Granted the hyperbole in this phrase, to which Punjabis are generally prone in any case, I witnessed personally the long hours of meditation of which Sikhs are in fact capable, when the opportunity presents itself. Some explain the phrase "praying twenty hours a day" as meaning that even while one is engaged in everyday activities, somewhere in the back of one's mind one is continuously in prayer.

The Sikh conception of the divine, translated very inadequately as "God," is one that recognizes with awe the incapability of puny humankind to effectively apprehend it. ("At the taste of sweetness, the mute person can only smile.") This sentiment is described in a beautiful verse of the Guru Granth Sahib:

> Were I to live for millions of years and drink the air for my nourishment;
> Were I to dwell in a cave where I beheld not sun or moon, and could not even dream of sleeping,
> I should still not be able to express Thy worth; how great shall I call Thy Name?
> Were I to be felled and cut in pieces, were I to be ground in a mill;
> Were I to be burned in a fire, and blended with its ashes, I still should not be able to express Thy worth; how great shall I call Thy Name?
> Were I to become a bird and fly to a hundred heavens;
> Were I to vanish from human gaze and neither eat nor drink,

I should still not be able to express Thy worth; how great shall I call Thy
   Name?
Had I hundreds of thousands of tons of paper and a desire to write on it after
   all the deepest research,
Were ink never to fail me, and could I move my pen like the wind,
I should still not be able to express Thy worth; how great shall I call Thy
   Name?

The mystical impulse in Sikhism is surely part of what leads some observers to class it with Hinduism, while the explicit monotheism of the tradition resembles that of Islam. But the community of disciples gathered around Guru Nanak quickly established an independent identity, over the centuries elaborated into an entire culture quite different in tone from any other group on the subcontinent. Guru Nanak is believed to have traveled far and wide as he shared his religious insights, expeditions recorded in the *janamsakhis* (biographies) Sikhs rely on for knowledge of the life of the first Guru. They are full of instructive stories illustrating the Guru's wisdom that complement the abstractions, however beautiful, of the Guru Granth Sahib.

One day while visiting the Muslim holy city of Mecca, for example, Guru Nanak happened to be sleeping with his feet facing in the direction of the Kaaba, a sacrilege in Islam. "Who is the infidel sleeping with feet toward the House of God?" a cleric challenged. Guru Nanak replied, "Turn my feet in the direction in which God is not," cleverly showing both the omnipresence of God and the limitations of Muslim understanding.

There are equal numbers of anecdotes putting the Hindus in their place. One day Guru Nanak was at Hardwar, the important Hindu pilgrimage center on the Ganges, during a major festival. At dawn the Hindu pilgrims started splashing water toward the sun. "What are you doing?" asked Guru Nanak. "We are offering water to our ancestors to quench their thirst," someone replied. Whereupon Guru Nanak started throwing water toward the west. "What are you doing?" the pilgrims inquired. "I am watering the fields in my village in Punjab," he replied. The pilgrims laughed, saying "How can the water reach such a distance?" Guru Nanak retorted, "If the water cannot reach my fields which are about four hundred miles from here, how can it reach your ancestors who are not even in this world?"

In most of the places where these episodes are believed to have occurred, *gurudwaras* (literally, "gateways to the Guru") were constructed in honor of Guru Nanak. They form a chain across the dusty plains of north India and beyond (as far as Baghdad and Kathmandu) but cluster most closely in Punjab, "the land of five rivers," now split between enemy states. On the Indian side today there are some fourteen million Sikhs, complemented by two or three million in other parts of India and possibly another three million flung out in diaspora around the world. There are now elegant *gurudwaras* in London, Nairobi, Chicago. The *gurudwaras* dotting the Punjab landscape, however, have a special historical significance that makes them high points in the spiritual geography of Sikhism. This historicity, obviously, plays into the rhetoric of the Khalistan movement, allying it vaguely with Zionism and other religious-cum-nationalist identities. Zionism, having been successful in creating its own state, is drawn on more frequently than others, but it differs from Sikh nationalism in that it involved a *return* to the religious homeland. The Sikhs are already there; as Robin Jeffrey notes, "Unlike most Christians, Muslims or Buddhists, most Sikhs practice their religion in its own holy land."[5]

Guru Nanak was under no illusions as to the real difficulty of following the path of religious truth. As the community of Sikhs, the *panth*, grew, he tested his disciples to show how firm one's resolve must be "to stay pure amid the impurities of the world." In a significant episode toward the end of his life, Guru Nanak set off on a road leading into a forest, enjoining his disciples to accompany him. As the group proceeded they found copper coins scattered across the path. Some of the Sikhs greedily picked them up and left for home. As the remaining disciples advanced, they found the road littered with silver coins. At this point more in the group departed. Finally, gold coins were piled on the path. After this only a few loyal followers pushed on with Guru Nanak.

When they entered the forest the party found a funeral pyre lighted by four lamps, emitting a ghastly smell. The Guru asked, "Is there anyone who will eat this corpse?" The Sikhs turned away in disgust, but one, Bhai Lehna (*bhai* means "brother" and commonly precedes male Sikh names), stood firm. "Where shall I begin, with the head or the feet?" he asked. At this gesture of loyalty and love, Guru Nanak embraced Bhai Lehna and gave him the name Angad, "touch of the Guru."

Guru Nanak composed the most important prayer in Sikhism, the *Japji* or morning prayer:

> *There is but One God,*
> *Eternal Truth,*
> *Almighty Creator,*
> *Unfearful, Without Hate and Enmity,*
> *Immortal Entity,*
> *Unborn, Self-Existent;*
> *By His Grace, you shall worship*

The One Who was True before creation,
The One Who was True in the beginning,
The One Who is True now,
The One Who shall be True forever.

The first phrase of this prayer is especially significant. Guru Nanak put the integer one (*ek*) in front of the sign indicating formlessness (*oankar*) to indicate the oneness and amorphousness of the divine spirit. The phrase "One God" (*ek oankar*) is found in Sikh homes cast in metal, sculpted in wood, and embroidered in cloth. It is considered to be the single most important expression of Sikh belief. That the one god is also expressed through the ten historical Gurus (of which Guru Nanak was the first) is no more problematic to Sikhs than is the humanity-divinity of Jesus Christ for Christians. They use the term "Guru" to refer to any of the ten historical Gurus as well as to *Waheguru* ("Great Guru"), or God.

The element of sacrifice in Sikh theology is best expressed in the lives of the Gurus, who understood that one had to totally relinquish one's own egoistic desires to apprehend truth. Although some were also heralded as great military leaders, they are conceived as self-effacing, gentle, and humble. "If you want to play this game of love," said Guru Nanak, "Come to my street with your head in your palms." The portrait of Guru Nanak that adorns most Sikh homes is evocative of this spirit. Interestingly, the classic portrait of the last Guru, Guru Gobind Singh, unabashedly militaristic, is understood as equally representative of the selflessness that characterizes the spiritually enlightened. Though scholars write about the "evolution" of Sikh consciousness from Guru Nanak to Guru Gobind Singh, orthodox Sikhs, at least, view one as only the historical fulfillment of the other.

When Guru Nanak died in 1539, he passed the guruship on to the loyal Bhai Lehna, who knew that being a Sikh meant making any sacrifice, in preference to his own sons. Saying "The Divine Light is the same, the Way is the same; the Master has merely changed the body," he recognized Bhai Lehna as Guru (Angad), and started the tradition of passing the guruship along from one person to another. This tradition ended when the tenth and last Guru finally turned the spiritual authority of the guruship over to the holy book, the Adi Granth (Guru Granth Sahib) itself.

The biographies emphasize the catholicity of the Sikh community, relating that Guru Nanak was so universally esteemed that Hindus wanted the honor of cremating his body, while Muslims wanted to claim it for burial. (This general high regard is also demonstrated in the eulogy, "Guru Nanak, for Hindus a Sage, for Muslims a Saint.") Sikhs believe, however, that Guru Nanak's body turned to pure light and merged with the Divine Light. The shroud was then cut in two, the Hindus burning one half and the Muslims burying the other half. The apocryphal quality of this narrative should not detract from its clear meaning for Sikhs; Nanak was neither Hindu nor Muslim, but the new spirituality he represented was respected (respectable) by both.

MARTYRDOM AND MILITANCY

As the line of Gurus continued and the Sikh *panth* expanded, persecution and the need to defend the faith against it took an increasingly central role. The Mughals, of course, persecuted not only Sikhs but also Sufis, who were linked to their own Islamic tradition, and the majority Hindu community. (The hatred of Hindus for Aurangzeb extends to this day, when the name itself evokes a response similar to that generated by mentioning Sherman in Georgia.) But the Sikh religious tradition, still young and evolving, incorporated the fact of persecution and resistance to it in a special way.

In a political situation in which Sikhs were being killed by the thousands, the self-sacrifice insisted on by Guru Nanak as prerequisite to spiritual enlightenment came to be interpreted as including physical martyrdom—not just "losing one's head" in the symbolic sense but literally dying for the faith. Sikhs use the Muslim term *shaheed* to describe their martyrs (also used as a title, as in "Shaheed Amrik Singh," the martyred Amrik Singh), but martyrdom in Islam is actually somewhat different from martyrdom in Sikhism. Centrally, Sikhs do not conceive of martyrdom as a ticket to paradise, but focus instead on the *willingness* to give one's head, the readiness at any moment to sacrifice, as key to the "grace" of the Guru-oriented Sikh. (It is not the outcome, but the process, as in the difference in Buddhism between *nibbana* as a kind of place and the *nibutta*-person, walking around in this world in a state of nonattachment.) A theological appreciation for martyrdom has led both Muslims and Sikhs to astounding battlefield bravado (witness all those Iranian boys rushing off joyously to meet their deaths in the Iran-Iraq war), but too hasty a gloss over differences here would be unwarranted.

The first of the Sikh Gurus who was martyred for the faith was Guru Arjun, the fifth in the line, who is also remembered as the compiler of and major contributor to the holy scriptures. Guru Arjun's verses in the Guru Granth Sahib make very clear the idea that Sikhism is a third faith entirely separate from Hinduism and Islam and are hence critical to current debates about the separateness, or lack of it, of the Sikh community. In one verse he writes:

I do not keep the Hindu fast, nor the Muslim Ramadan;
I serve Him alone who is my refuge.
I serve the One Master, who is also Allah.
I have broken with the Hindu and the Muslim,
I will not worship with the Hindu, nor like the Muslim go to Mecca;
I shall serve Him and no other.
I will not pray to idols nor say the Muslim prayer.
I shall put my heart at the feet of the One Supreme Being,
For we are neither Hindus nor Muslims.

Guru Arjun also composed some of the most eloquent and touching prayers in the Sikh collection. Surely the following would move the spiritually inclined of any tradition:

O Lord of Mighty Arms,
Creator of all things,
O Ocean of Peace!
Take me by the hand and raise me
Who am fallen in a pit.

My ears hear not;
My eyes have lost their light;
I am crippled, afflicted,
Like a leper I come stumbling to your door
And cry for help.

You are the Lord of the fallen;
Above you there is no Lord.
O Compassionate One!
You are my Companion, Friend, Father and Mother;
Let Nanak bear the imprint of your feet in his heart.

Guru Arjun was born in 1563 and was martyred in 1606 at the hands of the Mughal emperor Jehangir, who seems to have used the accusation that the holy book of the Sikhs was antithetical to Islam as part of a broader attempt to consolidate his power. The tortures borne by Guru Arjun have become legendary: he was forced to sit on a red-hot pan and have burning sand poured over him; he was boiled in a cauldron of water. Guru Arjun is celebrated in Sikh tradition as bearing all these tortures in silence, refusing to bow before tyranny or to renounce the holy scriptures.

There is another interesting part to this story. Guru Arjun had a Sufi saint named Mian Mir as a close companion, who also laid the foundation stone for the Harmandir Sahib (again, pointed to by Sikhs as evidence of the inherent ecumenicism of the tradition). This Mian Mir had been questioning Guru Arjun about the true meaning of enlightenment and what impact it could have on practical matters. When he witnessed Guru Arjun's composure and serenity under torture, he then, it is thought, understood just what impact spirituality could have. Guru Arjun told Mian Mir not to worry, not to fear, because what he was suffering was the sweet will of the Lord.

Bhai Gurdas, one of the major contributors to Sikh scripture, wrote the following lines with regard to Guru Arjun's torture:

> *The Guru bore all this torture proudly and never uttered a sigh or a groan.*
> *The Guru was unruffled!*
> *The Guru stayed calm and unperturbed like the sea!*
> *The Guru was in absolute bliss!*
> *This was the wonder of the Lord.*

Guru Arjun said, in a famous line, "The true test of faith is the hour of misery." He was eventually thrown into the river Ravi, and Sikhs believe that as everyone watched he turned to light and blended with the Divine Light. The concept of sacrifice for God took on a highly concrete form, then, in the martyrdom of Guru Arjun, pictured wading into the river (that is, fearlessly and calmly embracing death) on wall calendars in many Sikh homes.

Guru Arjun was able to put into effect Guru Nanak's earlier injunction to live "as the lotus floats in water but remains unaffected by waves." Even in extreme pain he retained his state of ecstasy, serving as a model for Sikhs up to the present faced with similar tortures. Another common piece of religious art features Bhai Mani Singh, another victim of Mughal torture, who was supposed to be cut limb from limb but whose torturer, in an attempt to spare him, starting slicing at his wrist. "You were told to cut me limb from limb," Bhai Mani Singh said, "so start with the joint of my little finger and work your way up." Not stoic but calm, unattached to his body in his pure communion with Guru, he is pictured with his fingers dripping blood and his eyes shining with religious bliss. Such a martyrdom is itself a weapon; "I will break this potsherd [my body] on the heads of the rulers in Delhi," another martyr declared.

One Khalistani militant drew directly on this history, which minimizes individual bodily pain in favor of what the victory over that pain can accomplish, as he suffered excruciating tortures at the hands of Punjab police. In the hot, still back room of a *gurudwara* he showed me the scars of this torture permanently inscribed on the flesh of his torso (the scars of the mind exhibited only by a certain hardness around the mouth):

In our daily prayers we remember all our Sikh martyrs during the Mughal period, those who went through terrible hardships. They were cut to pieces, made to survive on a small loaf of bread, and they withstood all those tortures. I used to think, "What type of people were they?" and while I was in the movement there was sometimes a little thought in the back of my mind that if the time came, would I be able to behave as those brave Sikhs, my ancestors, did? But finally when I went through it, it was not me but those other Sikhs who were sustaining that. It seemed they were taking the pain with me. I felt then the satisfaction of knowing that with Guru's grace I was able to pass the test of being a Sikh.

This is required of a Sikh, that a Sikh should withstand everything. What is of the body is anyway just elements and with death everything goes back. But the spirit is something immortal and if this spirit is filled with the love of Guru then that gives all the courage and strength. Me and my friends, we used to sit together and laugh a lot at how the Guru has made us mortals to be in the spirit of those immortal saints and martyrs, at how we lived up to this and passed the test of our generation courageously.

The interpretation of Sikhs like this one of the torture experience subverts the overriding aim of torture, which is the total degradation of the victim. The Sikh understanding of physical suffering, almost welcomed as a test of their spiritual commitment, turns every act of torture into a kind of victory.

A younger interlocutor described his awakening to the power of Guru through the model of a fellow Sikh sufferer. I record his story in some detail here, as it instructively points to the role of state persecution in the nurturing of militancy as well as in itself prompting a religious awakening:

"When the attack on the Golden Temple occurred in 1984, I was just a student in school, only fifteen years old. But we got together at school, about five hundred of us, and started protesting.

"There was at that time a Sikh Students Federation, and one member of that Federation, Kuldip Singh Telham, got arrested. (He was later killed by the government.) We protested against that arrest. Police came to our protest and started shooting at everybody, and a few people got wounded. Later the Federation members who were in hiding came to our school and convened a meeting. We started a school branch of the Sikh Students Federation and we decided to hold a program called 'In Memory of the Martyrs of Khalistan.'

"It was actually very dangerous, but I wasn't afraid. I didn't know then how they tortured, how they killed people. But let me tell you the truth. I actually wanted to go to jail to see if it was really as bad as people said.

"Anyway, I eventually got arrested along with other Federation members. I was arrested many times in the next four years. Finally in 1988 they arrested me once again and said, 'We'll kill you if you don't stop your activities.' I said, 'I'm not doing anything wrong, not killing anybody. I don't have anything to do with violence.' But they said, 'We will kill you anyway.'

"Then I went into hiding at my cousin's house. I knew that if they caught me they would torture me and kill me. My friend got arrested at his college, Khalsa College in Jallandhar, and they tortured and killed him. Another friend was in custody at an interrogation center and I knew he was being tortured. I wondered whether he would tell about me under interrogation.

"My whole family got arrested, my sister, sister's husband, my father, my mother, and my brother. They arrested all of them because I wasn't at home. 'Where is he?' they asked my mom. 'We don't know,' she said. 'He went off to college and he didn't come back.' She was afraid that if they found me they would kill me. She said, 'You can do with us whatever you want, but we don't know where he is.' The officer told her, 'We will kill all of you because your son is a terrorist.' They searched the house for weapons, but we never kept anything like that. All they found were Federation receipts.

"Then they went to my mother's sister's house. They held the whole family at gunpoint. They prodded my brother with the gun and then he said, 'Yes, I know where he is.' He told my mother, 'They will kill us all. Just tell them where he is.'

"So they caught me, where I was sleeping with my cousins. My mom, my sister, and my dad were released. But they kept me, my brother, my sister's husband, my brother-in-law, and my two cousins. They kept all of us because we were young. They want to finish off the 14 to 35 age group. But they took me to one side of the police station and said to the others, 'He's a killer. We'll deal with him separately.'

"Then they took my clothes off and I was without anything. 'Where are your senior party members, where is your president?' they asked. At that time it was Gurjit Singh. There were two other members in hiding, Nirmaljit Singh Nimma and Kanwaljit Singh Sultanwind, who were later killed in a fake encounter. The police were asking me about them. They also asked about a police officer who was killed in our area. 'Who did that? You did that, didn't you?' they said. But I said, 'No, I didn't.'

"They bound my arms behind my back, handcuffed, and hung me

upside down from the ceiling. It's called the 'airplane.' Then they were hitting me and hitting me. It was very hard for me. I was just crying and crying. They were saying, 'Just tell us, we will release you.' But I couldn't do that. If I didn't know about that how could I say anything?

"Then they put me down on the floor. They have a big heavy roller and they put it on my thighs. One police officer stood on one side and the other on the other side and they rolled it across my thighs over and over. It was very painful. I was afraid. I thought they would kill me. But I thought if I say other Federation members' names they would kill me anyway. If they wanted to kill me, they would. That was all there was to it.

"Then the senior superintendent of police came over and asked how come the police were doing so much violence to me. They said 'We arrested him, but he's not saying anything.' 'Bring him to the main interrogation center, then,' the superintendent said.

"On the way over the police kept saying to me, 'We will kill you over here. We will say that somebody tried to help you escape, and that we had to shoot and kill you.' They were trying to make me afraid, but I was no longer afraid. I thought, well, if they want to kill me there is nothing I can do. I knew I was not a criminal.

"As I was getting out of the van at the Criminal Investigation Agency center, they beat me up. Many of them were drunk. Then the superintendent of that center came out and when I saw who it was I thought I would surely be killed. That guy has killed so many people. We called him 'The Butcher.'

"When I got inside they caught me by my arms and legs and put me down on the floor. I was feeling really bad at that time. They were joking around. 'Just tell us. How do you want to be tortured?' They thought they were having fun.

"Then they caught me on my right leg and my left leg and spread them wide, wide like this. And they were hitting me at the same time. 'We killed your friends and they told us about you,' they were saying. Then they got electric shocks and gave me shocks on the private parts of my body. They shocked me and shocked me. They said, 'We will finish you. Now you can't be married, you can't produce any more terrorists.'

"A few of them seemed to be getting tired, so they said, 'Well, he doesn't want to say anything so let's just kill him.' But the inspector said, 'No, we'll do it tomorrow. I still have something to ask him.'

"There was another guy who had gotten killed at that interrogation center and he had had his flesh torn out with a long spear. They showed me that spear and I got really afraid. But then I thought again, 'There is nothing I can do. If they want to kill me they will.' So I forgot everything and everybody. I just got ready to die.

"Beating me and beating me, this continued on and on. I couldn't feel anything on most of my body anymore. But they tried to find out where I still felt pain and then they would hit me there.

"Then the president of our whole Federation was dragged out. He was at the same interrogation center! They started to beat him up and said, 'Here is your partner in this, we will beat him up too.' He was a doctor.

"They were beating him up very badly, just like you beat paddy in the fields. They were saying things to him but I didn't listen. I was just preparing myself to die. Then they told me that he would be killed that night.

"He heard that, too, but as I watched him I saw that he wasn't saying anything to them. He was just saying 'Waheguru' again and again. 'Waheguru,' he would say, 'you take care of me. Waheguru, Waheguru.'

"When I saw this I thought, if he doesn't say anything how can I say anything? I got strength from him. He knew he was going to die and he just turned to Guru. I said, 'Waheguru, Waheguru,' and I got calm.

"They were taking him out and he turned and said, 'God will take care of you. There's a place in heaven for us because we are dying for truth. Don't be afraid.'

"By God's grace I got released. From then on I relied on the Guru."

The concretization of the ideal of selflessness in the self-sacrifice of martyrdom was most effectively demonstrated by a historical hero named Baba Deep Singh, whose head was severed from his body in battle with the Afghans. Sikhs believe that he carried his head in his left palm, following Guru Nanak's injunction quite literally, and advanced toward Amritsar with a raised sword in his right. Not only is Baba Deep Singh's martyrdom a common theme of Sikh religious art, but it was brought to life once again in the 1984 attack on the Golden Temple. Jarnail Singh Bhindranwale, urged to escape by a back route as the Indian army bore down, is believed to have remarked, "Baba Deep Singh came so far to give his head at this place, and I am privileged to be able to give mine right here." Thus another accretion to the powerful generative myth of Sikh martyrdom—Shaheed Bhindranwale now stares down from his own portrait on the walls of Sikh homes, next to those of Gurus and historical martyrs. "Physical death I do not fear," said Bhindranwale. "Death of conscience is the real death." This aphorism has become a favorite in the militant community.

Bhindranwale was, of course, not only a martyr but a fighter as well (at least, an inspirer of fighters; it is unknown whether he ever actually killed anyone himself). It was the sixth Guru, Guru Hargobind (1595–1644), who first took up arms in defense of the faith, calling on the Divine Spirit not only to endure suffering but to vanquish enemies as well. Following the martyrdom of Guru Arjun, his father, Guru Hargobind took up two swords and said they would be called *miri* and *piri,* representing both temporal and spiritual authority (in Indian terms, the combination of *shakti* and *bhakti*). These two swords became emblematic of the Sikh community, and flutter on the saffron or blue banners that hang outside every *gurudwara.* The emblem of the double swords is now a particularly prominent symbol of nationhood for Khalistani Sikhs.

Guru Hargobind enrolled loyal followers as his bodyguards and eventually developed an entire army, enjoining Sikhs to be "saint-soldiers" (*sant-sipahi*) who combine spirituality with valor. As noted previously, militant Sikhs today firmly reject the idea that the Sikh community was somehow transformed from a pacifist sect to a military force during the period from Guru Nanak to Guru Hargobind, believing that what Guru Hargobind did was bring to fruition an idea inherent in Sikhism from the beginning. This conception of the inherent militancy of the tradition is tied, interestingly, to the habit some Sikhs have of wearing a steel emblem of the double swords on their turbans. At one *gurudwara* where these were being sold I heard someone snort, "They don't need to add that frippery; the fact of wearing the turban [i.e., of being a Sikh] implies militancy in itself. Adding that thing can be taken to mean that Sikhism alone doesn't make you a militant." Militants today believe that being a Sikh *means* being a "saint-soldier," and that those who condemn the current militancy are not "true Sikhs." A great deal of venom is expended in these debates, which are not only about Khalistan and the most viable strategy for obtaining it but for the nature of Sikhism itself. Those who tie Sikhism to militancy in a more primordial than strategic sense might agree with the card who, commenting that Indians generally wear their religions on their sleeves, said of Sikhs, "We wear ours on our hips" (a reference to the carrying of swords).

It was Guru Hargobind who was responsible for the construction of the Akal Takht, the "eternal throne" of the Sikhs, to complement the spiritual center of the faith at the Harmandir Sahib. Eventually, other buildings were constructed around these two critical edifices—one representing temporal power, the other spiritual strength—to form what is colloquially called "the Golden Temple Complex." It was this sacred complex that was attacked in 1984, sparking what became the militant movement for Khalistan.

Guru Hargobind is honored by Sikhs as a particularly valiant fighter. He severed enemy heads with a single blow of the sword, never showed his back to a foe, and so on. An important point in all this battle glory, however, is that the four major battles fought by Guru Hargobind are perceived by Sikhs as solely defensive in nature: "not an inch of territory was gained." The sword that became the symbol of Sikhism was intended to defend the weak and smite the oppressor, not to be used for personal gain. The fact that this sword is complemented by the symbol of the kettle, to feed the hungry, is less known outside the Sikh community but forms part of their own consciousness of themselves as protectors of the weak. Militant Sikhs today, however aggressive their behavior seems from outside, see themselves as soldiers for justice in this tradition. One of their central mottos, *"Deg Tegh Fateh"* (Kettle Sword Victory), expresses this sense that it is through defense of the oppressed that victory will be achieved.

One militant affiliated with the Khalistan Liberation Force took a typically universalist view of the Sikh struggle for justice when he pointed to a portrait of Guru Tegh Bahadur, the ninth Guru, who was said to have been martyred for the right of *Hindus* to worship freely:

> That's Guru Tegh Bahadur. His story is so beautiful, because he sacrificed his life for the sake of another religion, for Hindus. At that time they were being persecuted by the Mughals. That's really an inspiration to me. That's why I think Sikhs are in the world, not just for Sikhs alone but for anybody who needs a Sikh.
>
> Honestly, deep in my heart I feel like our work in this world has to be much bigger than just for ourselves. Some of my friends say that when Khalistan is established then we'll be able to kick back and relax! But I say no, the work is just getting started. You have your country but then you need to work on achieving justice in it and then in the rest of the world.
>
> All these wars that are going on today, people are demanding justice at all costs. Bosnia is a clear-cut case. We have to not only be more peaceful in spirit, but we have to be willing to sacrifice our lives. The United Nations doesn't really have any power because there aren't enough parents willing to sacrifice their sons. It's all just a big hoopla. If there is injustice and somebody in Somalia isn't getting food, the United Nations should be able to take care of it.
>
> When Khalistan is established if I have any say I will send 500, 1,000, 5,000 Sikhs right away. You don't get peace and justice without sacrifice and our Gurus taught us all about that.

It was the tenth and last Guru, Guru Gobind Singh, who took the final step of establishing the military brotherhood of Sikhs, the Khalsa, or "pure." Gobind Singh lived from 1666 to 1708, during a period of great tyranny under the reign of Mughal emperor Aurangzeb. He stated from the first that he was born to save the Sikh faith:

The Divine Guru has sent me for the religion's sake.
For this reason I have come into the world;
Extend the faith everywhere,
Seize and destroy the evil and sinful.
Understand this, holy people, in your minds—
I assumed birth for the purpose of spreading the faith, saving the saints and
    extirpating all tyrants.

The most important event in the militarization of the faith conducted by Guru Gobind Singh was the foundation of the Khalsa in 1699. Sending *hukmnamas* (letters of authority) to followers throughout the region, Guru Gobind Singh requested all Sikhs to congregate at Anandpur during the annual harvest festival of Vaisakhi. (The city of Anandpur was to become famous in twentieth-century history as the site of the Anandpur Sahib Resolution, which demanded greater autonomy for the Sikhs.) A small tent was pitched, and Guru Gobind Singh addressed the congregation from its entryway. He drew his sword and demanded, "I need one head. Is there anyone who will volunteer to give his head?" No one answered on this first call, nor on the second, but on the third invitation one Sikh rose and said, "My head is at your service." Guru Gobind Singh took this volunteer inside the tent and emerged shortly with his sword dripping blood. "Now I require another head," he said. "Who can oblige me?" Again one Sikh volunteered, entered the tent, and Guru Gobind Singh emerged with bloodied sword. This happened five times. Then the five heroic volunteers came out of the tent, unharmed. These five, who were willing to sacrifce their lives for their Guru, were called *panj piaras* or "five beloved ones." Guru Gobind Singh took an iron bowl and poured some water in it, then his wife, Mata Sahib Kaur, came and added sugar crystals. Guru Gobind Singh stirred this mixture with a double-edged sword while reciting *gurubani*. This procedure created a sacred nectar called *amrit*, a word that forms the etymological root of the name of Amritsar, the holy city of the Sikhs. Baptism by the sword's nectar, an image both martial and spiritual, replaced the more traditional picture of the devoted Sikh lovingly drinking the water in which a Guru's foot had rested.

Each of the five beloved ones of Guru Gobind Singh drank five palmfuls of the *amrit* and had *amrit* sprinkled in their eyes five times. Each time they repeated the phrase, "*Waheguru ji ka Khalsa, Waheguru ji ki Fateh*" (Khalsa belongs to God, Victory belongs to God). Then they received five sprinkles in their hair and sipped from the bowl of *amrit*. Guru Gobind Singh gave them all the name Singh, meaning "lion," and designated them collectively as the Khalsa. For members of the Khalsa, Guru Gobind Singh would be their father, and his wife would be their mother. They would claim Anandpur, the city where the Khalsa was created, as their home, and would celebrate Vaisakhi as the birthday of the Khalsa.

Women were also initiated into the Khalsa, and initiates were then called *kaur* or "princess." The admission of both men and women, and the veneration of both Guru Gobind Singh and Mata Sahib Kaur as founding parents, are points of pride for members today, freshly aware of gender issues. In the current militancy, the claim of Anandpur as a birthplace and the naming of Guru Gobind Singh and Mata Sahib Kaur as parents has also on occasion been useful for militants refusing to give information about themselves to police interrogators.

Every member of the Khalsa was enjoined by Guru Gobind Singh to wear five symbols of the Sikh faith, called "the five K's." These were *kesh*, unshorn hair; *kanga*, comb; *kachera*, breeches; *kara*, steel bangle; and *kirpan*, sword. The point of the five K's was to ensure that Sikhs would not

2. Portraits painted by Sobha Singh of Guru Nanak (left) and Guru Gobind Singh, as commonly seen in Sikh households and *gurudwaras*.

be able to shirk their duty to defend their faith by blending unnoticed into a crowd. The characteristic turban, used to bind up the uncut hair of the Khalsa Sikh, was and is a conspicuous and undeniable marker of religious identity. Today, the turbans are often saffron, the color of martyrdom.

Khalsa Sikhs today, who sometimes refer to themselves as "baptized" or "confirmed" but are more appropriately described as simply *amrit-dhari*, those who have taken *amrit*, also carry the surname Singh, or, if female, Kaur, though sometimes these designations may be followed by another family or regional name. They continue to wear the five K's scrupulously and have fought major legal battles over the right to wear them in various settings in India and abroad. Two Sikhs who were elected to the Indian Parliament in 1989 (Simranjit Singh Mann and Dhyan Singh Mand) refused to take up their offices since they were not allowed to enter the parliamentary chamber wearing their swords. Recently, Sikhs in Canada won the right to wear the turban while serving in the Royal Canadian Mounted Police. The Sikh prisoners I spoke with at San Pedro, who were not allowed turbans for fear they might use them to hang themselves, won the right to wear scraps of saffron-colored cloth on their heads for purposes of prayer.

Just how important it is to keep the five articles of faith is illustrated by the famous story about Kartar Singh, the former head of a key Sikh seminary, who is believed to have died because he refused to allow surgeons to shave his hair for a necessary operation. Another example is provided by the following brief narrative, told by a guerilla fighter from the Babbar Khalsa force:

One time on a hot summer day I was sleeping in only my underwear, and as it is mandatory for a Sikh that he should always keep five articles of faith on him all the time, I had my sword and swordband on the left arm. As I slept, I was in such a deep slumber that somehow the sword slipped and fell on the floor and I was without it. Then some freedom fighter friends came to my house and they asked my mother, "Where is he?" My mother said I was sleeping in the back room. They came and saw that I was in deep sleep and my sword was on the floor. They went back and told my mother. "Come on," they said, "let us show you something. Look at this boy, he has been baptized and he has taken a vow to keep the five articles of faith and now he has parted himself from his sword." My mother said, "OK, I'll bring a stick. You beat him with this and teach him that he should be loyal to his faith." For this unconscious misconduct I was then produced before five Sikhs, a sort of court in our tradition, and I was given religious punishment for that.

The use of *panj piaras*, five beloved ones, as a kind of court, was begun by Guru Gobind Singh. After initiating the original five volunteers into the Khalsa, he requested that they in turn initiate him. This is taken as a significant indicator of the democratic nature of the Khalsa; authority is vested in any group of five Sikhs who come together to take a decision. The Panthic Committee, which declared the independence of Khalistan in 1986, was likewise a five-member body.

Guru Gobind Singh carried a falcon as a symbol of martial and spiritual strength, and he is often pictured with a falcon on his wrist in Sikh religious art. The falcon remains a powerful mystic symbol, and claims were made that falcons had appeared in various locations around Punjab following the Indian Army assault on the Golden Temple Complex in June 1984. A falcon was said to have appeared at Prime Minister Indira Gandhi's home just before her assassination by two Sikh bodyguards in October of that year.[6] Jarnail Singh Bhindranwale carried a silver arrow, also reminiscent of the quiver of arrows on Guru Gobind Singh's back, at all times.

Though the Khalsa siblinghood is respected by the entire Sikh community (as reflected in the motto *Raj Karega Khalsa*, "The Khalsa Shall Rule"), not all Sikhs took *amrit* in Gobind Singh's time, and today, despite a push for more and more "baptisms" by Bhindranwale and other leaders, it is not known what percentage the *amritdhari* Sikhs form of the total Sikh population. Because of their explicit link to militancy as a philosophical stance, *amritdhari* Sikhs have been particular targets of surveillance and harassment in the current conflict. Many are in fact involved in the Khalistan movement, but others are not, for various reasons. Certainly not all have taken up arms (other than the mandatory *kirpan*), though Bhindranwale advised, "To kill is bad, but to have weapons and not to fight for justice is worse." The taking of *amrit* is said to turn sparrows into hawks; they may not fight, but the talons are there.

The sacred taking of *amrit* as initiation into the Khalsa was mocked in recent years by a notorious Indian police officer called Gobind Ram. Among other atrocities, he became famous for urinating into a pot and saying to a Sikh woman prisoner, "You have drunk the *amrit* of Gobind Singh, now drink the *amrit* of Gobind Ram." Several attempts were made by various militant groups to "deliver justice" to this Gobind Ram, and he was finally blown to smithereens by a bomb hidden under his chair. "They had to sweep him off the floor with a broom," said one informant grimly.

Guru Gobind Singh was also responsible for the code of discipline that still regulates Khalsa Sikh life. The saint-soldier of the Khalsa is to rise before dawn to bathe and to pray. The use of tobacco is strictly forbidden along with other intoxicants, chastity is mandated, and Sikhs are enjoined to be always ready to help the defenseless. Furthermore, and importantly, a Sikh should never show his back to a foe in battle.

Fearlessness under fire has become something of a trademark of the Sikhs. The British colonizers of India recognized the Sikhs as "a martial race," and Sikhs served in the Indian army out of all proportion to their numbers until the recent disaffection. "He who is fearful is not a Sikh and he who is fearless is a Sikh," said Bhindranwale at the Golden Temple entrenchment. One of the venerated martyrs of the Khalistan movement, Bhai Avtar Singh Brahma of the Khalistan Liberation Force, was known and admired for his habit of firing at his targets from a full frontal standing position. He used to use village loudspeakers to challenge the police to come out and get him. This kind of utter disregard for personal risk is what makes the Sikhs great fighters, fearsome enemies, and often, of course, martyrs. Guerilla fighters today all have portraits made of themselves in full regalia, bandolier across the shoulder, to be released to the public after their martyrdoms.

Just what being a saint-soldier means is expressed in the following two comments about Khalistanis:

> I can tell you this not only about myself and my companions, but about all the militants I know. We are very devout people. We wake up at three or four in the morning, bathe, and pray for hours and hours. We pray before we go on a mission, that the mission should be successful. When we come back and it has been accomplished we thank the Guru for that. Our only mission in life is to uphold the value of *dharm*, righteousness. People who are fighting for that, upholding the loftiest ideals, how can they do wrong?

> When they go off to a mission they are not excited or nervous at all. They are totally at peace. They say their prayers, standing before Guru Granth Sahib and asking strength for what they want to do. The way they take out their weapons and ready their weapons, it is close to worship. Then when they come back the first thing they do is lie prostrate before Guru Granth Sahib. They thank Guru if the action was successful. If not, then they pray and say, "Guru, thank you for keeping us alive today, and please give us the strength so that next time our mission will be successful." They are very devout, full of noble spirit.

A major prayer of Guru Gobind Singh, now part of the "National Anthem of Khalistan," expresses the militant ethos clearly:

Lord, these boons of Thee I ask,
Let me never shun a righteous task,

Let me be fearless when I go to battle,
Give me faith that victory will be mine,
And when comes the time to end my life,
Let me fall in mighty strife.

Guru Gobind Singh suffered the martyrdom of his four sons, the elder two when he sent them into battle, and the younger two when they were bricked up alive inside a wall by a Mughal functionary. Despite this terrible loss, Guru Gobind Singh wrote a *zaffarnama* or "letter of victory" to Aurangzeb. "These are just a few candles that you have snuffed out," he wrote. "But the whole blazing furnace of the Khalsa is all around me, and it will make Punjab so hot that your horses won't be able to gallop across the burning plains."

Since Guru Gobind Singh, to make sense of suffering in terms of the larger community, whose momentum is exhilarating and whose ultimate victory is sure, has become commonplace. It accounts for the strange sense of optimism, even joy, that pervades the militant Sikh community. Though I was ready to try to be open-minded about why people decide to take up arms when I started my study of Sikh militancy, I found myself taken aback by the mood of exaltation in Sikh homes and *gurudwaras*. It seemed that the worse things got, the happier they were.[7] I later realized that the cause for celebration was simply knowing a truth worth dying for, having a cause worth living for, perceived by Sikhs as existentially meaningful utterly independent of rational strategies. One young Sikh girl in Canada had to design a T-shirt as part of a school project; the teacher found her subject matter (a bloody martyrdom) too morbid and she suggested, "Why don't you make Tina Turner?" Her father, a militant, said of this, "How sad, unhealthy really, that the only thing Canadian kids have to worry about is rock-and-roll."

On Guru Gobind Singh's death the spiritual authority of the guruship passed on to the holy scriptures and the temporal authority passed to the entire Sikh *panth*. *Granth* (Guru Granth Sahib) and *Panth* are therefore the twin repositories of Guru, making veneration of the Word and defense of the Nation dual modes of worship for the orthodox Sikh. The Sikh militant who listens to *gurubani* on his Walkman while going on missions, so that he faces death not to the sound of bullets but to the sound of prayer, is the embodiment of this philosophy. While the niceties of philosophy may not matter to potential victims of militant violence, for whom the image of an armed Sikh with hymns on his headset is particularly horrifying, there is certainly more behind this figure than simple glosses like "fanaticism" would indicate. Getting behind this superficial fear is crucial to figuring out what to do about religious violence, which differs from other kinds of violence and also differs from one context to another. In this search, the particularism of ethnography can be most helpful, bringing us beyond labels like "terrorism" and "fundamentalism" that often seem to hide more than they illuminate.

When Guru Nanak approached the city of Multan during his travels around the subcontinent, he was met at the gates by a holy man with a cup of milk, who told him that there were already enough holy men in the city, that there was no room for one more. Guru Nanak took the milk and floated a jasmine petal on its fragile surface. "Just as the delicate fragrance of jasmine will add flavor to this milk," he said, "so my teachings will impart beauty and truth to the people of your city."

The landscape of Punjab, saturated with so much blood, is also in Sikh minds fragrant with the scent of jasmine. To understand the blood and the jasmine both is the challenge facing the intruding anthropologist.

3
A SAINT-SOLDIER

MARK JUERGENSMEYER suggests the term "religious nationalism" as a descriptor of the many politicized religious revival movements across the globe. Militant Islam is prominent, in its myriad forms from North Africa to the Middle East to Central Asia to the Pacific, but other movements include the Hindu revitalization now being expressed in India, the Sinhalese Buddhist nationalism in Sri Lanka, the right-wing Jewish militancy in Israel and the West, and more. Though not all the movements that entangle religion and politics aim at the creation of a state (e.g., the U.S. Christian variety), enough of them seek to either establish or transform one that the term "religious nationalism" is a fortunate one. It has the crucial advantage of being more affectively neutral than "fundamentalism," with its connotations of backwardness, intolerance, and zealotry.

Juergensmeyer notes in *The New Cold War: Religious Nationalism Confronts the Secular State* that the religious activists with whom he speaks in various parts of the world are "politically astute and deeply concerned about the society in which they live." [1] Devout they may be, but they are not necessarily anti-modern, intolerant of others, or bent on converting everybody else to their particular brand of belief. "The West is scared to death of religion," one Sikh commented at a recent seminar. This refrain echoes throughout Juergensmeyer's work, in which the West's determination to keep church and state separate is silhouetted against a global backdrop of buoyant movements of religious nationalism. Though he may carry this theme too far in calling the global confrontation between religious nationalism and the secular state "the new cold war," it is clear that there is a deep rift between the world views of most Westerners and that of religious nationalists like Khomeini or Kahane. This rift is exacerbated by the fact that very few people in the West have occasion to sit down and talk with the likes of Khomeini or Kahane and are dependent on the media coverage that naturally emphasizes dramatic acts of violence over conciliatory dialogue. There is in fact a large common ground between secular and religious kinds of nationalism, though differences cannot be swept aside.

I found in my long talks with Sikhs that some of the most interesting and enlightened of them were also the most religious. One *granthi* (scripture-reader) in particular, was an archetypical "fundamentalist" in that his education was primarily religious in nature, he was a strict puritan in terms of day-to-day ethics, and he brooked no challenges to orthodox readings of the Sikh scriptures. But he also had quite a universalist and pragmatic understanding of what Sikhism was and what a Sikh state could be. His story is interesting not only because of his intelligence and eloquence (which he expressed in fluent English) but because he had grown up with Sant Jarnail Singh Bhindranwale, essentially the founder of the Khalistani militancy. I met him early in my research, and I remember the conversation that took place between us vividly. It shows both the potential for real interaction with "religious nationalists" as well as some of the problematic differences between this way of thinking and our own.

THE MOVING UNIVERSITY

"My name is Iqbal Singh," he began our interview session, "from Amritsar. I was born in December 1962. My family background was not very religious. My father and mother were Sikhs but they would go to the *gurudwara* only about once a month. But my elder brother decided to go and learn more about Sikhism. We have a school of Sikh theology called Damdami Taksal, which is in Bhatinda district. He went and studied there."

"How did you feel when he made the decision to go?" I asked.

"I was too young to feel anything. I was only six years old when he went there. But we were very comfortable financially so I couldn't understand why he decided to go on that path. Anyway, after spending six or seven years there, he moved to Bombay to start his career as a *granthi* in a *gurudwara*. I was then in seventh grade. He called up my parents and said that I should learn *gurmat* [Sikh religious teachings]. He was not making any money, but he said he felt mentally satisfied, and he wanted me to feel the same.

"I still have the letter that he wrote to me at that time. 'Iqbal,' he said, 'I meet so many doctors, engineers, and other rich people, but I don't see any peace of mind anywhere. I see myself with my four hundred rupees a month, and I feel very comfortable because at least I have peace of mind. I don't want you to become a doctor or an engineer. If you really want a happy life then go into this profession.'

"Well, my parents resisted. They were not happy. But they eventually listened to my brother and they sent me to Damdami Taksal. I was only eleven years old."

"Just listening to your parents, really," I commented.

"Right. When you are living in a village and your parents are deciding to send you to a city, you are excited no matter what that is. I was excited to go. Especially to avoid housework!" The young *granthi* laughed when he said this.

"Tell me what it was like there," I requested. "What were your first few days like?"

"It was not really that good. After spending one month I called my parents up and I said, 'I don't want to stay.' "

"Why not?" I asked.

"Because it was a totally different atmosphere. At my home we used to get up around eight or nine, according to our school time. But at the Damdami Taksal there is a discipline that you have to get up early in the morning for meditation, *nam simran* [the repetition of the Divine Name]. That discipline was painful. I was not used to it. I called my parents up and my brother came and got me."

"What about the other boys there with you? What were they like?"

"They were OK. But I was only eleven years old and I had no friends there. I had never been away from my parents, my five brothers, and two sisters. So after that first month I gave up and went home. But after two weeks I decided to go back again."

"After you were waking up at eight instead of four, you decided it wasn't really so bad?" The *granthi* was smiling as he recounted his story, so I warmed up to him naturally. He laughed easily and beautifully.

Amarjit, sitting off to one side, told me that at that time, 1974, the leader of the Damdami Taksal was Sant Kartar Singh Bhindranwale. Sant Jarnail Singh Bhindranwale, who was later to die in the attack on the Golden Temple Complex, was a student there then.

"Yes, Sant Kartar Singh ji Khalsa was the head of Damdami Taksal," my interlocutor continued. ("Ji" is used in the name as an indicator of respect.) "Sant Jarnail Singh ji was a student. He was studying there, like me."

"At that time, did you know Sant Jarnail Singh?"

"We were just friends. We did not then have any picture in our minds that he was going to be the next head of Damdami Taksal and a great leader. It was very enjoyable, our friendship. We lived like brothers."

"Did you all sleep in a dormitory?"

"Actually there are two sections of Damdami Taksal. One is in the headquarters in Mehta, district Amritsar. Those people who specifically learn harmonium, baja, and tabla [musical instruments used in *kirtan*, hymn singing], they would stay in that headquarters. Those who wanted to learn speech and interpretation of Guru Granth Sahib ji, they would travel with Santji [at this point he is referring to Sant Kartar Singh] wherever he would go. I was with that group. The whole year long we would stay two weeks here, two weeks there, two weeks in the next town, and so on. We were always on the road."

Amarjit interrupted. "That's why they call it the 'moving university' of the Sikhs."

"Yes, the moving university," the *granthi* assented. "We had two buses and one truck and we always went around in those."

"Were they all boys?" I queried, always on the look out for gender issues.

"All boys. I was the youngest, at the time, of all those in the moving university."

"Did you study other subjects, too? Or just religion?"

"Just religion. Well, we also covered things like Sanskrit, some history like the rule of Chanakya, and so on. But strictly speaking it all had to do with religion."

He continued his narrative. "I spent seven years there at Damdami Taksal. In 1977, Sant Kartar Singh ji, the head of the institution, unfortunately died in a car accident. So after that Sant Jarnail Singh ji was chosen as head of Damdami Taksal."

"How old was he then?"

"Sant Jarnail Singh ji was then 31 years old."

"When you say he was chosen, what do you mean? What is the process of being chosen?"

"Actually that was during the Emergency in India—you know about the history of that, imposed by Indira Gandhi. Well, Sant Kartar Singh ji opposed that. He was so against it. So he knew that he could be arrested at any time and that the Indian government might kill him. One time he was in front of the congregation at Gurudwara Birh Baba Budha Ji, district Amritsar—I know because I was on the stage with him at the time— he announced that if somehow he died, Baba Thakur Singh should be the next head of the Taksal. But after the car accident he did not have time to say anything more. Baba Thakur Singh had the right though to choose to appoint somebody else who could lead."

Amarjit added, "That Baba Thakur Singh is the acting head of Damdami Taksal now."

"That was because Sant Kartar Singh had given him the authority," the *granthi* contributed.

I was curious. "Are they still functioning in the same way, roving around Punjab?"

The *granthi* and Amarjit both nodded. I decided to try to pursue more theoretical concerns.

"Let me just back up a minute. In that time, before Sant Jarnail Singh became head, was there talk about politics among the students at Damdami Taksal?"

The *granthi* thought carefully, then spoke slowly. "I don't differentiate what politics is and what religion is. It is a way of life for us. When someone disrupts your way of life and you try to stop him, for that person it becomes politics. For me it is not politics, it is just a way of life. When someone disturbs the way I want to live, and the Indian government wants me to do it another way, then it becomes politics for them. But not for me. I just have my way of life. I may have to fight for the right to live it that way, but I don't call it politics."

"Anyway, already during the Emergency years, Damdami Taksal was like a thorn in the side of the Indian government, because its head protested Emergency measures?"

"Yes, they were really after us all because of that."

"And everybody agreed, not just the head of Damdami Taksal but all the people within, they all felt the same about it?"

"Exactly. There were many protests conducted by Damdami Taksal during the Emergency."

Amarjit added that there were in fact dozens of protest demonstrations led by Sant Kartar Singh. When I asked whether these were all peaceful demonstrations, both asserted that they were.

"Was anybody talking about Khalistan at that time?" I asked.

"No, there was no talk of anything called Khalistan back then. The question was why the civil liberties of the people were being taken away. But of course that is the real foundation for Khalistan—when it becomes clear that you are not being allowed to live the way you want in India."

"And Sant Kartar Singh was a very charismatic person," Amarjit chimed in.

"Yes, he was," agreed Iqbal Singh. "He was a great man. I feel proud of those three years I spent with him. He used to wash our hair like we were his sons. I can still remember the feeling of his hands in my hair, though I was only eleven years old."

I reaffirmed, "He was like a father to you." In this kind of reaffirmation of what somebody said, which I found myself doing often, I felt like a psychotherapist.

"What did you call him?" I asked.

"I called him Babaji [father] and he used to call me Betaji [child] or various other terms of endearment."

"Was he married, did he have a family?"

"Yes. In fact his son, Bhai Amrik Singh, was a prominent figure in the movement."

I felt the little internal click that comes when you realize you have made an important connection. Bhai Amrik Singh was the head of the Sikh Students Federation and Bhindranwale's right-hand man during the occupation of the Golden Temple Complex. He was martyred in the 1984 assault.

"Oh, that was his son?" was in the event all I thought to ask.

"Yes, and I knew his wife and younger son, too."

"How old were you then, when Sant Jarnail Singh became head?"

"I was eighteen years old."

"When he became head, did things change?"

"Not in political terms. It was just the same way. The Indian government thought that maybe although they could not stop Sant Kartar Singh ji, maybe Sant Jarnail Singh ji would be weaker. That was not the case."

Amarjit then interrupted with a significant point. "Cynthia," he said, "Let me tell you that Sant Kartar Singh's death in an accident was not a natural one. There was something behind it."

"Do you believe that?" I asked the *granthi*.

He thought a moment, then said quietly, "Yes, it is a known fact that there was a conspiracy."

"It was never officially investigated?" I tried to prompt.

"It's unfortunate, but no one took care of that," he said.

Amarjit took over this line of thought. "Sant Kartar Singh had been giving indications that he thought something was going wrong. He kept telling Sant Jarnail Singh that . . ."

Iqbal Singh interrupted to continue the story himself. "As a mystic person Sant Kartar Singh ji was really a saint. I think he knew. One time we were sitting in a village, Mulsehan, in district Jallandhar, and Jarnail Singh ji was not a regular student at that time like we were. He had responsibilities by that time, two sons and a wife, and he had to take care of them. He would come, stay a month, go back, and so on like that. That day when we were ready to leave for our next destination, Sant Jarnail Singh ji came to Sant Kartar Singh ji and said, 'Allow me to go now. I have to go.' Sant Kartar Singh ji said, 'Why are you going? You will be coming back.' No one understood what he meant. But Sant Jarnail Singh ji must have thought something. He did so much *nam simran* [prayer], so much meditation, twenty hours out of twenty-four he was in meditation. He really worked hard, and he had great spiritual powers. Anyway, he went back to his village and the rest of us went on to Solan in the hills. When Sant Jarnail Singh ji heard then what happened to Sant Kartar

Singh ji in his absence, he felt so bad. He spent all his time then in the hospital [with the injured Kartar Singh].

"For thirteen days Santji [Kartar Singh] was in the hospital. When the accident happened, I mean. He kept asking for a pen and a paper, but no one gave him any."

"He couldn't speak?" I inquired.

"No, he couldn't speak because he had severe damage to his chest and his ear was cut off totally. The first question he asked was about the five articles of faith. I was in that bus, that same bus in which Santji [Kartar Singh] was taken to the hospital, so I was standing by when this happened. He made sure about his *kachera, kirpan,* and all. Then he touched his head and discovered his comb was missing. Somebody realized that Santji had no comb and gave him one, and he was reassured by that."

He continued. "After some minutes Sant Kartar Singh ji wanted to write something down, but he couldn't speak. He kept making a movement with his hand, like this." Iqbal Singh demonstrated a pantomime of writing. "If I could understand that he was asking for a pen and paper, why not the others standing by?"

"No one gave him a pen and paper?"

"No one gave him any. After a while he asked again in the same way, but again no one gave him a pen or paper."

"And you think that people didn't give him pen and paper on purpose?"

"I think so. It was a big topic of discussion after his death. He wanted to tell something, but was not provided the means to do so."

"Then later on he was cremated?" I asked.

"Yes. He was cremated at Mehta Sahib [headquarters of Damdami Taksal]. He had died in Ludhiana but was brought to Mehta Sahib for the *saskar* [cremation ceremony of the Sikhs]. At that time the doctor who had treated Sant Kartar Singh ji said something really interesting. That doctor was a Christian, and told how he had explained to Santji that he had to remove the hair of his head and chest for surgery. Santji said, 'You can cut my head off, but don't touch my hair.' That's how devout he was. And he never complained that he had any pain. The doctor said, 'What kind of person is this?' And he said, 'If I can make Santji survive I will see that Jesus has survived.' He thought Santji was so spiritually strong, he was like Jesus.

"After his death the body was cremated and Sant Jarnail Singh ji started as master of Damdami Taksal. We started our journeying again, going around to villages in Punjab, to Bombay, to Calcutta, and so on. We continued with the moving university."

JARNAIL SINGH BHINDRANWALE

"Was it odd for you that you used to have Sant Jarnail Singh as just your friend, and then he was suddenly in a high position like that?"

"No. We understood that he was now the head. And friendship is . . . well, the friendship was of course still there. But we now showed greater respect to him because of his position."

He went on. "Sant Jarnail Singh ji was not really very different as head of Damdami Taksal. He was just like he always was. He had a great peace of mind before he attained this position and after. He used to come to our rooms in the dormitory and we would laugh and laugh. He would ask about our troubles and problems and help us with them. He was so strict, too. If we would do anything wrong, he would not spare us!"

The *granthi* laughed as he remembered, fondly, being disciplined by Bhindranwale.

"Did he call you by your first names?" I asked.

"Yes. But we called him Santji, or Babaji. Not by his first name, to show respect."

"Would you say he was growing in his spiritual power during that time?"

"He had always made a strong impression on people, even before he was Santji. He was the only person that virtually everybody respected. Even Sant Kartar Singh ji, he would not treat Sant Jarnail Singh ji as a student or a disciple, but as an equal, a real *gursikh* [true or orthodox Sikh]. He felt his power.

"Sant Jarnail Singh ji had so much respect for *gurubani* and Guru. Once I know we were sleeping in the same room, and we used to just lie on the floor rather than using beds. There were some prayer books up in the rafters and one time one somehow got loose and fell down at Sant Jarnail Singh ji's feet. He was sleeping and didn't realize what had happened. When he got up and saw the book lying by his feet he cried, 'This is an insult to *gurubani*, how could I do that?' He was very disturbed about this and wouldn't eat or sleep. Sant Kartar Singh ji went to him and said, 'Jarnail Singh, this is not your mistake. You didn't do anything wrong.' But Sant Jarnail Singh ji was in such pain that he read the whole of the Guru Granth Sahib as an apology.

"You only love *gurubani* like that when you know it has provided you so much. There are some people who respect it for nothing, it's just a gesture. Just because of tradition they bow before it. Sant Jarnail Singh ji was not tradition. He was the living image of *gurubani*. If you wanted to see some Sikh out of the Guru Granth Sahib, Sant Jarnail Singh ji was the one."

Amarjit added, in a mood of nostaligia, "Sant Jarnail Singh was such a gentle man, a very loving and spiritual person. Everybody felt this from him. You would have really liked to know him."

Iqbal Singh continued. "On April 13, 1978, I was part of the *jatha* [brigade] who went to stop the Nirankaris. [The Sant Nirankaris are a sect who believe in a living Guru and are rejected by Khalsa Sikhs as blasphemous.] That was really the beginning of the movement, so I'll tell you about this incident. I was there, I was an eyewitness.

"We were staying in Gurudwara Gurdashan Prakash, which had become Santji's headquarters in Amritsar. A group of Sikhs came and told Santji that there was a Nirankari, Gurbachan Singh, who was going to lead a procession in Amritsar and who was saying that on this day, April 13, Guru Gobind Singh created the *panj piaras* [five beloved ones] and that he would now create the *sat sitaras* [seven stars]. Santji got really upset listening to that, it being Vaisakhi day and in the city which is the heart of Sikhism and all.

"Let me say this very clearly: if anybody wants to have his own religion, I don't think Sikhs have any problem with that. But when he is challenging the basic philosophy of the Sikhs, when he is actually naming Guru Gobind Singh and suggesting that he is the equivalent of that Guru, that is a direct challenge to our deepest beliefs. If he were saying something else, anything else, that was not directly against the Sikh religion, Santji would be pleased that he should do whatever he wants. Santji used to tell a Hindu to be a better Hindu, a Muslim to be a better Muslim, and so on. But this person challenged the very basis of Sikhism, and Santji got really upset.

"I know about this because I followed Santji when he went over to Manji Sahib Diwan Hall, a huge auditorium that can fit several thousand people. He spoke to the Sikhs for fifteen minutes and very clearly laid out the situation."

I interrupted. "How many followers did they have, the Nirankaris?"

"There were thousands of them, all over India."

"How can you account for the attraction? Why did so many people join the Nirankaris?"

"Since the Sikh religion came into existence, the Hindu, the Brahmin that is [the highest caste of the Hindu system], always tried to divide us into sections. Divide and destroy. Let me tell you one incident which related to me personally. One of my brothers came to me at one point and said that he wanted to cut his hair. I asked why. He said that there were some actors coming to do a play in our village and they wanted to give him a role. I told him that he could cut it if he wanted to but that he could not come back in the house afterward. See, it was the policy of those people that they wanted to convert those boys who were *amritdhari* Sikhs. They would attract them to quit living like an *amritdhari* by giving them roles in plays which would require them to cut their hair and that sort of thing. They had other attractions, too, like giving small businesses to their followers."

"You think these were purposeful manipulations?"

"It was clearly a matter of purposeful manipulation. There was free sex and liquor involved, too. They tried to lure people away from . . ."

Amarjit cut in. "You have to look at the make-up of the people who joined the Nirankaris, too. Either they were class one gazetted officers, deputy commissioners could allot land plots and all, or they were the poorest of the poor. The rich went there like they would go to a country club. They they used their power to attract greater numbers from among the poor, luring them with money and other things. And the central government, which was the Janata government of Morarji Desai, started manipulating them as a way to undercut the power of Sikhism in Punjab. The sad part was that some members of this government were brought to power by Sant Kartar Singh himself, in leading all those demonstrations and so on. It was very painful to see this happening in a state where Damdami Taksal had itself made such a direct contribution."

"Your brother finally didn't go with them?" I asked Iqbal Singh.

"No. In fact I went myself and I told them that if they tried to come into our village there would be a fight. They did try to come and in fact there was a fight. But then they did not dare come to our village for the next four or five years.

"Anyway, when Santji was told about the Nirankari procession on Vaisakhi day he tried to get a minister in the government to intervene. But he said there was nothing he could do about it. So we vowed to go there and protest openly. There was no intention of fighting. If there had been fighting on our minds we would have prepared ourselves better."

"You didn't have any weapons?" I asked. I later learned that this question doesn't make sense to an *amritdhari* Sikh, because he or she always has the *kirpan* (dagger or sword).

"We were praying to God the whole time as we marched. It was not because of some kind of fear but to show that we were intent on peacefully protesting. When we reached the Nirankaris, they started throwing cola bottles at us. Then some of them started throwing bricks and stones. Some from our group threw them back. Then the Nirankaris started firing. The police came and they also started firing at our group. Even though we were intent on having a peaceful march, thirteen Sikhs got killed in that confrontation."[2]

"How did you feel when you heard the shots, when you realized they were firing?"

"We were all pushing each other back, because we had nothing [no firearms]. It is not good to die without a fight. If you are in the battlefield it is all right, but not to die without standing up for yourself. We all pushed each other to go back, and some of us hid under a truck for about half an hour. Then we went back to Darbar Sahib [Golden Temple Complex]."

"Were some of your friends killed?"

"Bhai Ranbir Singh ji, he was my first teacher at Damdami Taksal, he was killed there. Baba Darshan Singh ji was killed, too, and there were others. I knew them personally."

Amarjit added, "Those who went to protest the Nirankaris were not only from Damdami Taksal but some members of the Akhand Kirtni Jatha went as well [a group devoted to hymn singing]. Bhai Fauja Singh was leading that group. Among those who got killed, some were from Damdami Taksal and some were from Akhand Kirtni Jatha."

Iqbal Singh continued. "Santji wanted to join us to march against the Nirankaris on that day. But five Sikhs got together, including Bhai Fauja Singh, and they said, 'No, we are ordering you to stay here.' He had to obey that [because of the *panj piaras* tradition]."

"They were concerned for his safety?" I asked.

"Yes, they were worried about his safety. They ordered him not to go."

Amarjit continued, "The whole of the Indian press came out in support of the Nirankaris after that episode. Prime Minister Morarji Desai put the entire blame on the Sikhs. Not only that, but the Nirankari head was escorted safely out of Punjab. When the First Information Report was lodged he was the first accused of violence, but he never got arrested. In fact the court was moved out of Amritsar because most of the judges would be Sikhs. Instead the case was brought to Haryana where the judge was a Hindu. The whole thing was heard in camera, so who knows what went on? Finally, the court acquitted all the Nirankaris, and it even passed strictures against the Punjab government for registering the case. As for the Sikhs, they waited patiently while the Nirankari case was being heard. But when the verdict came in and they were all declared innocent, Santji said, 'OK, their justice system has failed, so now our justice system will prevail.' That was why he felt we had to take matters into our own hands—the Indian courts had not lived up the promise of justice."

The *granthi* said, "My parents got really scared when the news came that the thirteen Sikhs had gotten killed. There was one person on that list who had the same name as me, and my parents thought I had been killed. They came the next day to cremate my body.

"The sad part was that the Akali government [Akai Dal was and is the main political party of the Sikhs] was elected because of Damdami Taksal's role in the Emergency, as Dr. Amarjit Singh just said. People thought it was kind of Santji's government. When people were elected they would ask for Santji's blessing and they would ask him to tell people to support them. But after this episode there was not much support for Santji. People felt he had let them down because the Akali government let them down. He didn't appear publicly for a few weeks, but he started quietly preparing himself for a fight . . . well, not exactly for a fight in the literal sense, but you could say . . . he was just thinking for some time."

"He was thinking about what to do next?" I prompted.

"Yes, he was just thinking. He was shocked. He could have expected such a thing from a Congress government but he was stunned that an Akali government, a Sikh government, should be so weak-kneed. Then he came to the conclusion that even the Akali government was no friend of *Sikhi* [Sikhdom, the Sikh way]. He decided that he would have to do something for the Sikhs, because no one else would."

"When did you first realize, yourself, that some plan of action was in the works?" I asked.

"It was never actually a 'plan of action,' so to speak. What Santji started doing was baptizing people. He felt that the main task was to make people aware of *Sikhi*. He would not talk against the Akalis, though, he just said clearly in his words and actions, we are Sikh, we should know how to live as Sikhs. But then the Akalis started verbally abusing Santji and these insults started going back and forth."

"This was how the rumor got started that Sant Bhindranwale was really a plant of the Congress government," said Amarjit. "The Akalis were scared. They had had control over the whole *gurudwara* system for sixty or seventy years, and then a man of charisma rose up and people started following him. They were not any match for him, so they started pushing this story that he had been bought by the Congress government to defame the Akalis." [3]

"Anyway," Iqbal Singh continued, "this was the background to the real rise of Sant Bhindranwale. Let me tell you about the key episode at Chando Kalan, a village in Haryana state where we were staying when some police officers came looking for Santji. They wanted to arrest him . . ."

"Why did they want to arrest him?" I asked, trying to follow the story.

"That was for the murder of Lala Jagat Narain, the owner of *Hind Samachar* [a chain of newspapers]. He had written some very nasty things about Guru Gobind Singh ji, and used to challenge Sikh traditions at every step. Santji had spoken against this man many times, so when he got murdered a conspiracy case was filed against him.

"Anyway, when the police reached the village of Chando Kalan they could not find Santji. They beat up one of my friends pretty badly. And they literally looted that whole village. They tortured the women. When they were ready to leave, they burnt our two buses. Those buses were like a library for us students. Everything we had we kept in those buses, including prayer books and all. And the same Santji, who could not tolerate one book falling at his feet while he slept, how could he tolerate the fact that Guru Granth Sahib was burnt by the Indian government for nothing? Santji said in interviews, 'If the government thought that Jarnail Singh was at fault, if they wanted to arrest me, why did they go and burn the buses? Why did they burn my Guru?' He used to cry, literally weep, when he described that situation.

"On September 20 he surrendered to the police at Mehta Sahib and was taken into Ludhiana jail. They established a court in the rest house there, and Santji was called to appear. And there was one interesting incident that took place there."

"What was it?"

"There is a tradition in India that they would give you a holy book, sometimes the Gita [Bhagavad Gita, a holy book of the Hindus], and you would say that you wouldn't tell a lie in court. When Santji was there he was asked to put his hand on Gurubani Gutka [a Sikh prayer book] instead.[4] He said to the court officers, 'What is this?' They said, 'It's Gurubani Gutka.' Then Santji said, 'In the constitution you call us Hindus [referring to the controversial Article 25]. But you are asking me to swear an oath on Gurubani Gutka. Why not make me swear on the Gita?' They said, 'Well, you might tell a lie then.' 'Look,' said Santji, 'you change the constitution then. Recognize me as a Sikh, and I'll happily say the oath on Gurubani Gutka.' The officers kept pushing him for two days, but he kept saying, 'Either change the constitution or change the book!' Finally they decided to skip the oath taking on a book completely. That's how strong Santji was."

"What finally happened in court, then? What was the verdict?"

"Santji was cleared. They never found any evidence against him."

"Who in fact killed Lala Jagat Narain?" This question slipped out before I could think about it. This was, actually, the sort of thing I did *not* want to know. Luckily (and predictably), my interlocutors were more careful than I was.

Amarjit said, "Two others were tried for that murder. But we don't know who really killed him."

Iqbal Singh added, "The point was that after the Nirankari episode this incident at Chando Kalan really alienated Santji. He became crystal clear on the point that justice could not be expected as far as the Sikhs were concerned."

Iqbal Singh continued. "After that Santji came out of jail and he never went anywhere after that. He stopped his roaming around and stayed at his headquarters at the Darbar Sahib [the Golden Temple Complex at Amritsar]. Then the real fight began.

"By 1979 I had finished my study at Damdami Taksal and I asked Santji whether I should go on to the Sikh Missionary College. He said that if I wanted to do it, I should. The Missionary College is in Amritsar, the same place where Santji was staying. He and I stayed together in a hostel, just like old times. My friends were there, too, so it was really just like a family. If I needed new clothes, for example, I wouldn't go to my own parents. I would go to Santji, and I would say, 'Santji, I need new clothes.' "

"Were your parents happy with your decision to stay with Bhindran-wale?"

"Not at first. When I first left Damdami Taksal they told me they didn't want me to go on with this business. In fact they sent me to Orissa to become a car mechanic!"

We all laughed at the thought of this *granthi*, in immaculate white turban, working on cars.

"I spent three or four months there but my heart wasn't in it. So I went to Sikh Missionary College and spent three years there. I used to teach students at Damdami Taksal, too—there were no real teachers there, it was a system in which the seniors taught the juniors, each generation bringing up the next.

"To tell you the truth, I got the feeling that the government actually wanted to eliminate every single individual associated with the Damdami Taksal. At one point I was at my college studying for an examination, when a friend of mine suggested that we go to his village for a vacation. It was a Saturday. I agreed and we went to get the forms we had to fill out stating that we wouldn't be staying in the dormitory that night. I had just left the clerk when a police party arrived in three jeeps, all carrying Sten guns. They started asking around for me and that clerk told them that I had already left. He knew I was there but he covered for me, and he showed them my application for leave from the dormitory. Then that clerk sent somebody to tell me to get out of there fast. I was shocked when I got this message, as I had never done anything wrong.

"I took the bicycle of my friend, and headed toward the gate. There was one gunman standing at one side and one gunman at the other. They seemed to be stopping everybody as they left through the gate. When I saw that I would be stopped, I suddenly got an idea. I faced toward the offices of the hostel and I shouted, 'How many cups?' as if I were asking whether they wanted tea. I pretended to be just a tea-boy. 'How many cups?' I yelled toward the offices."

He laughed, remembering this escapade. "I got through the police check this way. I outsmarted them. However, the police had seen the forms on which I had written my home address, and eventually they showed up at my parents' place. They arrested my mother and father and took them to Patiala jail. They were in there for two days, and they got beaten. When I heard about this, I decided to surrender. Though I hadn't done anything, I didn't want my parents to be punished on my account. So they were released, and I was taken into custody."

"So what was it like in jail?"

"Well, it was not too bad because my father had connections with some officials. In fact his best friend was a deputy inspector general of police, who told the others, 'You can ask him anything you like, but don't touch him.'

"There were two brothers, Jasdev Singh and Sukhdev Singh, and both were from Damdami Taksal. We three spent two days in jail together. I had been preparing myself for the entrance examination for Guru Nanak Dev University, and the exam was to take place the next day. I explained that I had to be released to take the exam. There was some argument among the officers about whether I should be allowed to take this test or not. On the evening before the test a police guard told us, 'This is your last day, all of you.' We got worried, and did not know what they would do.

"That night the three of us exchanged our *karas* [wrist bands]. Then I was released to go and take my exam in Amritsar. I took the exam, and afterward went with some of my friends to a tea stall. I picked up a paper there and was shocked to see that the two boys I had just left the night before had been killed in an 'encounter' with the police. Jasdev Singh and Sukhdev Singh were both dead."

He held up his arm, so that I could see the steel *kara* on his wrist. "This is the *kara* I got from one of them. I have never taken it off."

"Is that a usual thing to do, exchanging *karas* like that?" I asked.

"No, it was unusual. It was a sign of love between us . . ."

All three of us were quite emotional by this point in the story. The *granthi* had a tear splashed onto his glasses, and Amarjit swiped at the corners of his eyes, as he does. I restrained myself from reaching out to offer comfort. I was never sure how such displays would be taken.

"I couldn't drink the tea I had in front me," Iqbal Singh continued. "They had taken me off to Amritsar, and they took them outside of that jail and killed them."

"Were those two actually charged with any crime?"

"A bank robbery," he said. "The first bank robbery in Punjab was in Jandiala, district Amritsar, and we were all accused of being involved in that. Eight hundred thousand rupees had been taken out."

"They were not really involved in it, they were just charged," noted Amarjit.

"Right," said Iqbal Singh. "Those two were good friends of mine. They used to come to Sikh Missionary College and sleep there, and I used to visit them. In our childhood we spent seven or eight years together at Damdami Taksal. They were like my family, and I know that they were no more involved in a bank robbery than I was. When Sant Jarnail Singh Bhindranwale heard about this he just said, 'They are after the Damdami Taksal. They want to kill everybody in Damdami Taksal.' I started agreeing with this because I saw it with my own eyes."

"The bank robbery was just a street crime? It didn't have anything to do with Bhindranwale?" I asked, again, not very wisely.

"Yes," answered Amarjit. "While Santji was around there was always enough money just from donations. After 1984 [his martyrdom] there came a time when militants had to go to the banks to get money for the struggle, but as long as Santji was there there was never a need for that sort of thing."

"Yes, Santji always had enough money," said Iqbal Singh. He wouldn't have risked any of us over a few rupees to be gotten from robbing a bank. He used to say that his Singhs were more precious than rupees."

Amarjit continued on this theme. "'A Singh is more valuable than money,' he used to say. He was crystal clear on the point that nobody should lose his life because of money. This was made clear to everybody. This was just a fake case that was made."

After tea, the very sweet and milky *chai* that is ubiquitous on the subcontinent, Iqbal Singh continued his narrative.

"Then in November of 1982 a friend of mine and I decided to go to Delhi to launch a protest at the Asian games. We were picked up by police from the train, and we were carrying protest papers on our bodies, signs and all."

"What did the papers say?"

"That Sikhs want justice. That's all."

"You weren't thinking about a separate state or anything at that time?"

"No, there was no talk of Khalistan, nothing like that. But we were pulled off the train, and beaten up at a railway station in Haryana."

"Were you resisting, were you fighting back?"

"No. At that time we were not fighting back. Anyway, we were released after two days, in only our underwear. We went to a local *gurudwara*, where we were given clothes, and we came back. My point is that this was a constant struggle, something we ran into every day."

"These sorts of things were happening to a lot of people?"

"Yes, a lot of people were being harassed. But it wasn't until later, maybe 1983, that the name of Khalistan came into existence. Well, it may have been in existence before that, but finally people started talking about it, saying that we needed our own nation.

FIGHTING FOR KHALISTAN

"By the time I was enrolled at Khalsa College, doing divinity studies, I came around to the conclusion that we cannot live any longer with India. But my family was not with me on this; they said that Khalistan was all trash and nonsense and that I should stay away from it. I told them that they could have their opinion, but mine was different."

"What about your brother?" I asked, thinking about the elder brother who had encouraged Iqbal Singh to join Damdami Taksal in the first place.

"Some of my brothers were not into this Khalistan movement. But my elder brother, he is a Khalistani to the core. Because when you are really involved in religion, not just the forms but real spirituality, you can see the problem very clearly. The government was interfering in our practice of our religion, killing off the most devout practitioners of our religion.

"In 1984 came the army's attack on the Golden Temple Complex. This changed a lot of people's minds. I was with Bhindranwale in the weeks before that attack. On May 31, the Central Reserve Police attacked the Golden Temple and eight Sikhs were killed. Some CRP were killed, too, in the exchange of gunfire. On June 1 the curfew was announced and we could smell it, that there would be . . ."

"At that time, you were clear on the point that armed struggle was necessary?"

"Yes, definitely. We were resolved to it and prepared for it by that point.

"Listen," he stopped and thought carefully. "It was not for offensive purposes, it was for the defense of *Sikhi*. We needed to defend ourselves. In the courts there was no justice, in the police there was only corruption, in the government there was no friend anywhere. You cannot offend against the sixth biggest power in the world, after all! But defend you can, and you have to."

"And when you were talking among yourselves about Khalistan, were there some who said, 'OK, we need Khalistan but taking up arms is not a good idea?' "

"You have to understand that arms did not come because of Khalistan. Arms came because of self-defense. Even now, we know that we cannot win in an armed struggle against India, an armed struggle for Khalistan. What we have to do is defend ourselves as best we can, and in that defense we ask for Khalistan. Khalistan is our birthright, the right of the Sikh nation to live as Sikhs.

"And I have to tell you that Sant Jarnail Singh ji did not so much have a 'plan of action.' Rather, he was helping Khalistan emerge, letting the nation emerge, helping people become aware of themselves as Sikhs. Let me give you an example of the way Sant Jarnail Singh ji operated.

"One time Mr. Harminder Singh of Ludhiana had some business with a Hindu guy. Santji had been telling us that we should have our own businesses, have our own identity, and Harminder Singh understood this to mean that Santji was saying we should get rid of the Hindus. He wanted to split up his business with the Hindu, but he would owe that Hindu two hundred thousand rupees for his share. He had four girls, and he was not a rich man. So he came to Santji and said, 'Santji, what should I do?' Santji asked him how long it would take him to gather the two hundred thousand rupees. 'Six months,' replied Harminder Singh. Then Santji called his secretary and told him to give that Hindu guy two hundred thousand rupees. 'OK, now the Hindu is out of this,' Santji told Harminder Singh. Now you pay me back the two hundred thousand rupees in six months.'

"Well, Harminder Singh came to Santji the very next day with two hundred thousand rupees. That was the way that Sant Jarnail Singh ji was trying to create Khalistan. It was a mini-government, a parallel government which he set up for the people. Justice was being done and people were happy."

"How did Bhindranwale react when he would read what the Indian press was saying about him? That he was a terrorist, a criminal, and so on? Did he feel pained by that?" I asked.

"That was an interesting part of his personality. He never got irritated by the press people. He would say, 'I know what you are going to print, that you are working for rupees only.' He would laugh at them, but he knew they were helpless. In a way he felt sorry for them. He only used to grant interviews and so on in case he might reach other Sikhs through those."

"Were there times when you witnessed him getting angry about anything?"

"Well, he had some vengeful feelings toward Akalis particularly. He could expect anything from the others—the Indian government, journalists, foreigners—but it was really painful to him to listen to the Akalis, so-called Sikhs, talking as they were. When they accused him of being an agent of the Indian government, after all he was doing . . . Well, he understood that they were living within the system and its corruption had eaten into them, too. But the youth supported him and his ideas, as they were not corrupted."

"Did any of the Akalis ever go to Sant Bhindranwale and say, 'I was wrong to say these things, I am sorry?' " I slipped into the usage of "Sant" before Bhindranwale's name without thinking.

"A few of them did, at election time. When they needed something from him they would go, like people who go to church only when they are in trouble."

"They're called 'Sunday Christians,'" I said.

"Sunday Christians! Sunday Sikhs!" echoed the *granthi*. "They have nothing to do with real religion. A truly religious life is the most difficult life there is."

Amarjit broke in with his own comments. "Whenever Santji gave somebody some responsibility, whenever they went on some mission, he used to dismiss all the people around him and go inside and pray for hours and hours. God was never far from his mind. Then sometimes people would notice that when they got endangered in some way, suddenly help would come from nowhere to save them. Singhs became quite confident that Santji's mystic mind and his strong prayers were always with them. That is an important part of all this."

"Yes," Iqbal Singh agreed. "One of those who was martyred early in the struggle, Surinder Singh Sodhi, was a good friend of mine. We were like brothers. Wherever he would go he would have a tape of *kirtan* [Sikh hymns] with him. He used to listen to *kirtan*, nothing else. Once I asked him, 'Sodhi, why are you driving your motorcycle listening to hymns on your Walkman?' He said, 'No one knows what may happen, when death will come. I want a peaceful death. If I get killed, at least my ears will be filled with the sound of *kirtan*, not the sound of bullets.' These people were really saints and soldiers. Not only soldiers. In fact saints first, then soldiers. They never wasted a bullet on innocent people."

Amarjit added, "Santji said many times that Surinder Singh Sodhi was his right hand, his right arm. On the day that he was killed, Santji said that his right hand had been cut off. That Sodhi could handle anything—car, truck, airplaine—and if he had a rocket he could handle that, too! And let me tell you one thing about Sodhi—he was an excellent marksman. One time Bhajan Lal, the chief minister when the Asian games took place, was within his firing range. Now this was a person that Santji had warned against, saying that wherever he might hide, Sikhs would chop off his head. When Bhajan Lal came within Sodhi's range, he could have killed him. But he said, 'Santji told us to chop off his head and I couldn't do that, so I spared him.'"

Iqbal Singh then continued his narrative.

"During the actual assault on the Golden Temple Complex, Operation Blue Star, I was about four miles away at Khalsa College in Amritsar. I knew that the first tank had fired on the Akal Takht [the building in the complex where the militants were headquartered] around 2 o'clock, June 5. Before that they had been fighting with machine guns and other small arms. But on June 5 they entered with the tanks."

He started drawing a map on the back of an envelope. "Here is Harmandir Sahib. Here is the Akal Takht. Here is the sacred tank of water. You can see that the Akal Takht is right behind the Harmandir Sahib. They sent troops in from here, and here [showing two positions]. When the tanks in front were ready to fire on the Akal Takht, they had to send a message to the troops in the back to get out of the way, otherwise they might get hit.

"Santji had a wireless set inside, and somehow he intercepted that message. He knew that the area would be open to him and his group for a short time as the rear troops vacated their positions. So some of this group got away through the back. They ran into nearby houses, changed their clothes and went out as regular citizens. Only thirty-five of Santji's close followers died in the assault. The rest, two hundred or so, got out."

"And those who left at the last moment, they later played large roles in the struggle?" I asked.

"Exactly."

"And thirty-five decided they would rather stay and be martyred?"

"It was not really like that. It was just part of the overall strategy, just a plan. When the Indian army arrived on June 2, it became clear to everybody that whether we lost or won just then, eventually we would all have to fight for Khalistan. The Khalistan struggle was not just a matter of everybody dying during that first week of June. Santji said, 'OK, we are here so we will protect this Golden Temple. We will hold the army while the others get away.' It was not at all that those who left were cowards, or not also committed to die, or anything like that. Everybody was prepared to give his life for Khalistan. But as part of the whole plan some left, some stayed."

"Were many of those who left killed later?"

"Almost all of them, I think. Every one, as far as I know. Well, one or two may have surrendered later, but overall the strategy of having some leave was a good one, a successful one."

"And is it true that some of those inside tried to persuade Sant Bhindranwale to leave, but that he refused to go?" I asked.

"Yes. And I agree with his decision to die there. It is my personal feeling that though it is a loss for the Sikh community that he died, it is a proud loss. He used to always say, 'I will protect this place, I will die in this place.' If he were to leave . . . Let me put it this way. In the past century and a half at least Sikhs had no experience of the kind of leader who would not say one thing and do another. They had no experience of a Sikh leader with courage. But Santji had courage, he died there and made his point. He was an example of a real Sikh, a real saint-soldier. Why should a saint have to obey the laws of a secular government? He lived on a higher plane.

"I lived with Sant Jarnail Singh ji for seven or eight years. He was a brother, a father to me. I had no doubt that he would die when he said he would die. It was he in fact who sent those other Sikhs out."

Iqbal Singh continued. "Sant Jarnail Singh ji was both a strategist and a saint. I think it's a misconception people have, that a saintly person can't be a politician. Santji was both, and being both he knew the consequences of that kind of combination. Saint-soldiers get martyred.

"Anyway, he sent the others out to continue the fight. They fought afterwards, they died afterwards. They told people what had really happened in the Golden Temple. Eventually they went into hiding and spread out all across the world to continue the struggle. Now I believe that if any Sikh says he is not a Khalistani, he only means he is not strong enough to fight.

"After the army action against the Golden Temple, I was on a wanted list. The police came to my house and arrested my father and mother again. 'We have nothing to do with him,' they said. 'If he has done something wrong, he should be punished.' But my father had connections and he was not badly treated. When I went to see him the police gave me a paper to sign, saying that if I signed nothing more would happen to me or my family. The paper said that whatever I had done before 1984 was a mistake, that I had been brainwashed by Santji. But I said, 'No, I can't sign this. I am not sorry, I am proud of what we did. And I am thankful to Santji for the awakening he gave us.'

"A few of my friends, they did sign papers like this. That was the whole idea behind it, so that the government could show on TV that the militants were repentant. In my case, the police gave me half an hour to get away. They did not arrest me. They only wanted to publicize those cases of people who accepted this brainwashing idea. So it was a mutual thing. I ran away. My parents then told me they had no more home for me, so I said I would leave."

"That must have been difficult."

"Yes, it was. But I could see my parents' side, too. They did not want to take a risk, and they had been getting all the wrong information about Santji from here and there. That he was a womanizer, that there were drugs at his headquarters and that sort of thing. They didn't have a clear picture of what he was really doing. So even though every Sikh was against the Indian government for attacking the Golden Temple, that didn't mean that they were for Santji. These are two different things.

"Then I left home, October 1984. I drove a truck for two years, staying here and there with my friends. I remained on a wanted list because I had been a senior student at Damdami Taksal. I had been involved in some of the decisions made in the period before the 1984 assault.

So finally I bribed an official, got travel papers, and left the country."

"Did your parents eventually come around to seeing your position?" I asked.

"Yes, they did. Because after the attack on the Golden Temple Complex, Indira Gandhi was murdered, and in the riots after her assassination my sister became a victim. My parents got their eyes opened, that it was not because of Santji but because of our turbans, because we are Sikhs, that these problems exist. Then they came to understand the idea of separation.

"The concept of *Sikhi* is in fact universal. Khalistan is a need, not a destiny. It is just a matter of needing some place to enjoy religious freedom. It is a mistake to talk about Khalistan as if it were somehow preordained, an inherent part of Sikhism. Sikhs can live wherever they can live as true Sikhs. They can sit in London and wear blue jeans or listen to rock and roll if they want to—these are cultural things, not matters of faith. But if we have no place to be Sikhs, that is a problem.

"So I can actually accept the idea that somebody is not for Khalistan, if he can find another way to live as a true Sikh. But I cannot allow him to say that those who are asking for Khalistan are wrong. If he is not Khalistani, fine. But he should not get in the way of other Sikhs' demand for Khalistan. The people of Punjab are suffering, and that is why they are demanding Khalistan. Nobody should stand in their way."

I questioned, "You don't feel, then, that anybody who is not with you is against you, as somebody told me yesterday—that those who are silent are in fact complicit?"

"Dr. Cynthia," he said, "It is clear in my mind that throughout Sikh history there has been a lot of fighting and not everybody was involved in every fight. Each played his own role. The role of every Sikh is to be a true Sikh as best he can. Not everyone feels comfortable with the role of fighting. It should be the policy of fighters not to condemn anybody who is being a Sikh in another way. People are afraid. If you come to me in India and you ask me, 'Are you a Khalistani?' I will say no. Maybe you are Indian intelligence or something. But in my mind I may be sympathetic, and when the time comes I may show it.

"I am just a reader of scriptures, I am not a politician. But it seems to me that it is a problem that there is no concrete plan for Khalistan, like a constitution or something, to show people what we are really fighting for. What we are fighting *against*, that is clear, but what are we fighting *for*? This is the difference between a resistance movement and a real independence movement. We are tired of being with India, fine. But if we ask people to become Khalistani, on what grounds are we asking? We have to be clear on this."

Iqbal Singh then became deferential, nodding toward Amarjit, who had left the room to make some of the endless phone calls in which he is constantly engaged.

"I'm just a priest," he said. "You'd better ask the Panthic Committee if you want to know more about constitutions. But there are things . . . rights of women, educational system, rights of minorities, the place of the Hindus, and so on. There is the declaration of independence of Khalistan, but that's not enough." He again deferred to Amarjit. "He knows more about it," he said. "I'm just a priest."

But I didn't want to let this precious strand of conversation drop. "It's a characteristic flaw of insurgent movements that they are so busy fighting the war that they don't think about what will happen afterwards," I said. "That's why it's important to learn from history and plan ahead."

"The Indian government is the sixth biggest power in the world," Iqbal Singh responded. "Don't think they are stupid. They plan ahead, all right, and on the Sikh side we have to do the same."

Then he cut off the conversation as Amarjit re-entered the room. "I came out of India, at Dr. Amarjit Singh's hands," he said. "Now here I am, just reading scriptures."

4
BLUE STAR

"THE KHALSA is like a finely tuned instrument," it is said. "All it takes is someone to hold his finger on the right note." In recent times, that someone was Jarnail Singh Bhindranwale. The episode he provoked, the Indian army attack on the Golden Temple in June 1984, forms the raison d'être for the continuing insurgency, populated largely though not wholly by Khalsa Sikhs. In this chapter, I examine the events directly leading up to that confrontation, the battle itself, and the immediate aftermath. Whether or not the current insurgency continues or peters out, this "holocaust" of 1984 is bound to reverberate through Sikh history for a long time to come.

THE PEOPLE

Before 1984, as the conversation recorded in the previous chapter shows, those involved in militant activities were mainly individuals from the Damdami Taksal, the "moving university" of the Sikhs, and the Akhand Kirtni Jatha, a hymn-singing organization. For these people, the confrontation with the Nirankaris in 1978 forms the keystone of their commitment; that was the moment when many of them came to the conclusion that justice within an Indian framework was unattainable. For the great bulk of the Sikh population, however, this event took place somewhat on the margins of mainstream society, among highly religious people. By contrast, all Sikhs were brought up short by the 1984 debacle, which reached even those who had become avowedly secular. The attack on the Golden Temple has been compared to an attack on the Vatican or Mecca. How would Catholics, however lapsed, or Muslims, however disenchanted, feel?

The assault on the Golden Temple Complex was taken by the Sikh community not only in immediate but in deeply historical terms. It resonated with other events in the past in which enemies attacked, laid seige to, and destroyed the sanctum sanctorum. That Operation Blue Star would be perceived in these terms, that analogies would quickly be drawn with Afghan and Mughal times, was recognized by those with personal knowledge of the Sikhs; this community has always had a pervasive awareness of history and the role of the Sikhs in it. Sikhism is after all a very young religion, and the lives of the major figures in it are not shadowy legends but matters of historical record. The buildings they constructed are still around, the clothes they wore for the most part still the everyday dress of the Sikhs, as instructed by their Gurus. And though there is no recognized tradition of genealogically linking oneself to Gurus within the Khalsa, as there is in Muslim societies with regard to the Prophet and caliphs, the strong sense of siblinghood leads orthodox Sikhs to feel a strong emotive tie to members of their "family" who fought and died for Sikhism in the past.

Certainly, this deep sense of historicity helped Jarnail Singh Bhindranwale acquire the following that he had prior to his death during Operation Blue Star. Jarnail Singh was born of a rural family of modest means in Rode village in 1947. He was of Jat background, the caste group that provided the backbone of Sikh militancy from historical times to the present. (Various authors have in fact attempted to interpret Sikh violence as an aspect of Jat culture,[1] an attempt that has antagonized militants today who feel their stance is prompted by religious principle, not cultural tradition.) In any case, Bhindranwale's background was no different from that of thousands of other Sikh boys who grew up in rural areas with minimal but adequate schooling and a strong family commitment to orthodox Sikhism. As the last of seven sons, he was relatively free from family or agricultural responsibilities and from an early age spent much of his time with the Sikh scriptures.

Joginder Singh, Jarnail Singh's father, sent the boy to study at Damdami Taksal after his primary schooling, the seminary described as a "moving university" by Jarnail Singh's boyhood companion and later follower, Iqbal Singh. *Taksal* means "mint" in Punjabi, and the institution of the Damdami Taksal, believed to have been established by none other than Baba Deep Singh, can be appropriately understood as a place where spiritual individuals are shaped, like coins from a mint. As the presumed founder of Damdami Taksal, Baba Deep Singh's commitment to avenge the destruction of the Golden Temple by the Afghans stands as a continuing model for Damdami Taksal activism in defense of the faith.

Though the Taksal education is purely religious in nature and is hence dismissed by many commentators, I am not the only one to have noticed that its products can be remarkably sophisticated. Mark Tully, the BBC correspondent who closely followed the rise of Bhindranwale and the subsequent debacle at Amritsar, wrote with surprise that a young teacher there was able to engage in a complex argument involving the Bible and the Qur'an as well as the Sikh scriptures.[2] Certainly the tendency of those with secular educations to dismiss the Damdami Taksal as nurturant solely of fanaticism is both misplaced and arrogant. To be sure, its members (a more appropriate term than "graduates") did form the core of the original militancy, and in that sense it could perhaps be compared with the religious schools at Qom, which nurtured the Ayatollah Khomeini and other key figures of the Iranian revolution. But the articulate quality of Iqbal Singh, among others, belies the accusation of narrowness directed at the Taksal. Its headquarters at Chowk Mehta, about twenty-five miles from Amritsar, still serves as a fountainhead of orthodox Sikh learning.

Under the stewardship of Kartar Singh, the Damdami Taksal's alienation from the central government of India grew. Of course, during the abuses of the Emergency years (1975–1977), many Indians' alienation from the central government grew, but the Akali Dal, the major Sikh political party, was notably outspoken about its discontent with Indira Gandhi's censorship of the press, arrest of opposition leaders, and dramatic enhancement of police powers. The "Save Democracy Protest" launched by the Sikh party resulted in the detainment of some forty-five thousand activists, and *gurudwaras* across Punjab were centers of anti-Emergency sentiment. (The opposition party under the leadership of socialist Jayaprakash Narayan called the Akali Dal "the last bastion of democracy."[3]) Jarnail Singh, like Iqbal Singh, grew to maturity in an atmosphere in which political activities against the central government went hand in hand at Damdami Taksal with the chanting of scripture and theological debate. These were all of a piece, as Iqbal Singh said in the interview when he claimed that it was not "politics" but a way of life, a seamless whole, that engaged the Taksal students in the 1970s.

Kartar Singh, Bhindranwale's predecessor as head of the "moving university," was killed in a car crash in 1977, as Iqbal Singh noted.[4] Jarnail Singh was appointed head at the young age of thirty-one and immediately rose to the challenge of continuing Kartar Singh's political activism. He had been married at the age of nineteen and had two sons, but when he was recognized as "sant" Bhindranwale he relinquished most of his family responsibilities to devote full time to the Taksal. In this he followed a long tradition of *sants*, who were historically an important part

3. Sant Jarnail Singh Bhindranwale, founding figure of the Khalistan movement. This is one of the many photos and portraits of Bhindranwale that appear regularly in Khalistani posters and movement publications.

of rural Sikh life, bringing news and a quality of entertainment from village to village with their dramatic public sermons and readings of scripture. The British, it seems, recognized the political potential of the *sant* role, devoting attention to tracking these wandering holy men.[5]

By all accounts, Sant Jarnail Singh Bhindranwale was a charismatic personality. Tall and lean, with deep-set eyes, a prominent nose, and a ready grin, his blue turban tied in characteristic tiers, he was as photogenic as he was personally impressive. Though he never learned English, his command of Punjabi was superb, and soon his speeches were making the rounds of Punjabi villages on cassette tapes, radically increasing the range of his influence. He eventually became adept at radio, press, and television interviews as well.

Since Jarnail Singh Bhindranwale was largely responsible for launching the current Sikh militancy, he is now valorized by militants and demonized by their enemies, and accounts from these divergent sources seem often to be referring to two completely different people. Though the Indian press at various times compared him with Rasputin and Hitler, those who knew him personally uniformly report his general likeability and ready humor as well as his total dedication to Sikhism. Joyce Pettigrew, a Scottish anthropologist who has studied the Sikh militancy closely, witnessed the close relationship between Bhindranwale and his followers.[6] A Sikh reared in the West, clean-shaven (that is, not orthodox), told of his first acquaintance with Bhindranwale:

> The first thing I noticed about Bhindranwale was that he made everybody feel welcome. Nobody was an outsider with him, no matter what their appearance, clean-shaven or bearded. He was very human, very soft. He was firm on his views, of course, but he had a sense of humor, too. He asked me, "When are you going to become my brother [when are you going to become orthodox, grow a beard]?" I answered, "Well, I'll try." But he laughed and said, "If you just stop trying, you'll become my brother quicker. From the facial aspect, I mean!" What he meant was that if I just let nature take its course, if I didn't shave, I would look like a Sikh more quickly. This was the way he would gently remind people to live as Sikhs. He was clear in his example, but he didn't put pressure on me or anything. Everyone would feel comfortable in his presence.

Bhindranwale's appeal was such that the frequency of initiations into the Khalsa rose dramatically across Punjab, as did the level of rhetoric regarding the perceived "assault" on Sikh values from the Hindu community. Bhindranwale and his closest companions, including Amrik Singh, the son of Sant Kartar Singh and head of the All-India Sikh Students Federation, started carrying firearms with them regularly. This action was defended as within the bounds of the Sikh tradition, whose primary symbol, the double-edged sword, was itself a weapon.

One man reports:

> After I met Sant Bhindranwale, my son asked me, "How many weapons did Santji have, what kind of weapons did he have?" I said that the weapons of Sant Bhindranwale, nobody has weapons like those in all the world. The way the devotion and commitment to Sant Bhindranwale came, that was some kind of mystery, some kind of mystic inspiration.
>
> There used to be baptism ceremonies at least twice a month, later more often as Santji became more popular. Sometimes thousands of people would get baptized in a single day. Santji's impact was so powerful, people would rush forward not only to get baptized but to join him, to give up their homes and their families to stay with him. He was a great lover of humanity, sensitive to the down-trodden. And he was a very disciplined man, spending hours and hours with the scriptures even in his busy schedule. He expected the same devotion from everybody who joined him. We follow in the footsteps of Baba Deep Singh, he would say, heads in our palms. Such an inspiration he gave, will never be forgotten. Anybody who saw him was touched by him.

The 1978 clash between the followers of Jarnail Singh Bhindranwale and the Sant Nirankari sect at Amritsar was the beginning of the serious turn toward militancy for many who would become leaders in the upcoming struggle. Not only were the core of Damdami Taksal activists involved here, but they were joined by another group commited to orthodox Sikh tradition called the Akhand Kirtni Jatha. The Akhand Kirtni Jatha was founded by Bhai Randhir Singh (1878–1961), who had been active in the Ghadr and Independence movements and had been sentenced to imprisonment by the British. It focused on hymn singing (*kirtan)* as the path to preservation of orthodox Sikh tradition.

The original Nirankaris had taken a more mystical approach to Sikhism (*nirankar* means "formless") since their founding in the nineteenth century by Baba Dayal Das. The followers of that Nirankari sect coexist peacefully with mainstream Sikh tradition. But the practices of one group, the "Sant Nirankaris," were seen as directly heretical to the orthodox Sikhism expounded by Bhindranwale. Not only did they begin to revere their new founder and his successors as Gurus, but they also added their own scriptures to the Adi Granth. The movement grew quickly.

On April 13, 1978, the Sant Nirankaris were to hold a convention in

Amritsar. April 13 was celebrated as the founding day of the Khalsa, and the proposed Nirankari convention on this day, in the holy city, was particularly galling to orthodox Sikhs. Some felt, in fact, that the entire Nirankari episode was provoked on purpose by the central government to destabilize and disunify Sikhs. In any case, about two hundred members of Damdami Taksal and Akhand Kirtni Jatha formed a procession headed by Bhai Fauja Singh, a prominent member of Akhand Kirtni Jatha, to protest the Nirankari heresy. (Bhindranwale was not present, though he played an important role in launching the protest.[7]) It is not clear exactly who provoked whom in the actual encounter; some observers assert that Fauja Singh made a threatening gesture, or swiped at, Baba Gurbachan Singh, the Nirankari leader, with his sword, while others place him inside an auditorium at the time when the fight broke out on the streets. He did have a group of guards, who opened fire on the orthodox Sikhs. A fight ensued, and at the end of the melee thirteen orthodox Sikhs and two Nirankaris lay dead.

Eventually a case was registered against sixty-two Nirankaris by the Akali-led government of Punjab. It was heard in Hindu-majority Haryana, however, and all sixty-two Sant Nirankaris were acquitted. Lala Jagat Narain, chief editor and owner of the *Hind Samachar* group of newspapers, appeared as a witness in defense of the Nirankaris, and they received widespread support in the media. Orthodox Sikhs in Punjab mobilized against what seemed to be anti-Sikh sentiment in India nationally and began to talk of an outright conspiracy to defame Sikhism. A *hukmnama*, or letter of authority, was issued by the Akal Takht in which Sikhs were instructed to ostracize the Sant Nirankaris. Bhindranwale stepped up his rhetoric several notches.

In the years following the Nirankari debacle, a series of murders took place in Punjab and surrounding areas, many certainly the work of Bhindranwale's group or a newly founded parallel organization, the Babbar Khalsa, which, following its historical namesake the Babbar Akalis, vowed to avenge the deaths of Sikhs killed in defense of the faith. Baba Gurbachan Singh, the Nirankari guru, was killed in 1980, and Lala Jagat Narain, the incendiary newspaper editor, was killed in 1981. The Babbar Khalsa activists took up residence in the Golden Temple Complex as well, to which they would retreat after going on missions to "punish" or "deliver justice to" those who offended against orthodox Sikh tenets. There were episodes of heavily symbolic communal violence: cow's heads deposited in temples; cigarette packages tossed into *gurudwaras*.

Bhindranwale started urging all Sikhs to buy weapons and motorcycles rather than television sets. "When the Hindus come with their Sten guns, what are you going to do, fight them with your television aerials?" he asked. He believed that all *amritdharis*, those who had taken *amrit*, should also be *shastradharis*, weapons-bearers. Though Bhindranwale was not using the word "Khalistan" and talked in terms of greater autonomy for Punjab rather than national sovereignty per se, he used the term *qaum* to refer to the Sikh people, a word with the connotation of nationhood. (It had been used, for example, by Mohammed Ali Jinnah in the effort to achieve the Muslim state of Pakistan.) "From the teeth of the wheel to the edge of the sword"—from being ground to death on the wheel of torture to the drawing of swords—was a typical rhetorical leap made by Bhindranwale and other activists.[8] And draw swords they did, not only against the prominent figures noted previously but against more than a hundred, possibly three hundred, other people perceived as anathema to orthodox Sikhism.

Nearly every academic and media source on the rise of Bhindranwale notes his apparent ties to the Congress party, particularly through Giani Zail Singh, the president of India, up through the early 1980s. The intent was allegedly to use Bhindranwale as a pawn against the Akali Dal, Congress's chief political rival in Punjab. Several of my interlocutors claim an opposite scenario; that is, that the Akali Dal itself started rumors of Bhindranwale's links to Congress as a way of thwarting his growing popularity among its own constituency. There is evidence for both of these possibilities, and I believe Robin Jeffrey may be most accurate in his assessment when he writes that "the evidence suggests that Bhindranwale exercised a cunning independence, playing the factional antagonisms of Punjab politics with knowledge and skill. . . . In this independence lay much of Bhindranwale's appeal. It left him untainted by close association with any of the older political leaders, yet at the same time suggested that he knew how to handle them."[9] Whatever ties Bhindranwale may have had with Congress in the early days, it would be misleading to suggest that Congress "created" the Bhindranwale phenomenon. It was, in my opinion, sui generis. Help may have been received from outside, as later the Khalistani militancy would be helped by Pakistan, but the dynamic to be understood here is internal. Emphasizing the role of outside agencies, rather, is a way of minimizing the seriousness of the challenge presented by Bhindranwale himself.

By the early 1980s, the sight of armed Sikhs sitting atop buses or riding around on motorcycles became common, and though the majority of Sikhs condemned the violence of the "extremists," Bhindranwale nonetheless attracted huge crowds everywhere he went. Increasing discontent with the central government was expressed in other forums as well. The *Dharm Yudh Morcha*, or "righteous protest," launched in August 1982 by Bhindranwale and Akali leader Harchand Singh Longowal resulted in the arrest of tens of thousands of Sikhs at a time, overflowing the capacity of the Punjab criminal and judicial system. Riots were set off in September of that year when a bus-train accident resulted in the deaths of thirty-eight Akali protestors, and police fired on a largely unarmed Sikh crowd gathered in protest outside the Parliament buildings in New Delhi. When Bhindranwale was arrested in connection with the murder of Lala Jagat Narain, his supporters sprayed a crowded marketplace in Jallandhar with machine gun fire in retaliation.[10] By the time of the much-publicized Asian Games, hosted for the first time in New Delhi, Sikhs were seen as a security threat to the capital. Chief Minister Bhajan Lal of Haryana issued orders to stop Sikhs from attending the games, and even prominent military figures like retired Indian air force Chief Marshal Arjun Singh and Lieutenant General Jagjit Singh Aurora, who had accepted the surrender of Pakistan after the 1971 Bangladesh war, were stopped en route and questioned, as was former Foreign Minister of India Swaran Singh. Though the Sikh community as a whole was stunned by this treatment, little about the attempt to prevent Sikhs from attending the Asian Games appeared in the Indian press.

The interesting thing about the growing extremism of Bhindranwale and others was that it was supported by a wide range of people in significant government and, particularly, police and military posts. At one point Chief Minister of Punjab Darbara Singh constructed a list of twenty-two senior government officials affiliated in some way with the extremists, and between 1981 and 1984 Indian intelligence agents drew up a list of some four thousand police personnel with links to the nascent militancy.[11] As many as 170 army, navy, and air force officers above the rank of colonel supported the Sikh cause.[12] (Because of the Sikhs' traditional prominence in the armed services, many in the state had substantial military training, leading Robin Jeffrey to comment that "Punjab [had] the makings of a formidable people's army."[13]) Two top officers (major-generals) from the Indian army, in fact, became advisers to Bhindranwale in the period preceding Operation Blue Star: Jaswant Singh Bhullar, who later fled to the United States, and Shabeg Singh, who was killed in the 1984 assault. Shabeg Singh was of particular importance here, as he was an expert in guerilla warfare who had played a prominent role in training the Bangladeshi insurgents during the 1971 Pakistan war. He was largely responsible for preparing the defenses at the Golden Temple Complex, which, according to Lieutenant General K. S. Brar, who commanded the Indian army assault, were excellent.[14] Shabeg Singh has said that it was the humiliation meted out to him at the Asian Games that prompted him to join forces with Bhindranwale.[15]

Already, then, there is something puzzling about the "extremism" and "terrorism" of the Bhindranwale group, which, it is true, were vociferously condemned by more moderate Sikhs all over India, but which attracted support from various quarters not obviously allied to the quest for religious orthodoxy characteristic of Bhindranwale's own rhetoric. The police crackdown in Punjab ordered by Darbara Singh, which by 1983 resulted in an average of fifty Sikh youths detained and a half-dozen killed each week, prompted a wider acceptance of Bhindranwale's claim that the government was out to destroy the Sikhs. (BBC correspondent Mark Tully and his colleague Satish Jacob report that Darbara Singh himself admitted that many of the police encounters with suspected militants amounted to cold-blooded murder.[16]) Some eight hundred Sikhs were in jails as suspected terrorists, and extra battalions of police personnel appeared in Punjabi cities. The People's Union for Civil Liberties, an Indian human rights group, accused the Punjab police of behaving like a "barbarian force."[17] In response, Akali initiatives like *Rasta Roko* (Block the Roads) and *Kam Roko* (Stop Work) drew massive popular support in Punjab. Seven other states also supported Sikh demands for greater autonomy for Punjab and the decentralization of government power.[18]

Meanwhile, violence on both sides escalated in Punjab. Militants raided three armories in April in a (successful) attempt to enlarge their arsenal. Police opened fire on crowds of demonstrators and killed dozens; a bus was stopped by turbaned Sikhs, and Hindu passengers executed on the road.[19] A plane was hijacked to Lahore by Sikh militants in protest against the arrest of Bhindranwale, and bank robberies occurred as well. Punjab was declared a "disturbed area" and President's Rule was imposed in October 1983.

Government figures claimed there were some twenty-five hundred "suspected terrorists" by the spring of 1984.[20] In April organized groups of militants attacked thirty-seven railway stations in twelve districts in a concerted attempt to disrupt Punjab's transportation system. The All-India Sikh Students Federation was banned (it claimed some forty thousand members), and the Central Reserve Police Force and the Border Security Force were called into Punjab. They were fighting against both Bhindranwale's group[21] and the Babbar Khalsa, which feuded and possibly fought each other as well. In addition, there was the Dal Khalsa or "army of the pure," founded by Gajinder Singh of Chandigarh (one of the hijackers of the plane to Lahore). The militants remained, however, at least temporarily safe in their refuge in the precincts of the Golden Temple Complex. Whether Prime Minister Indira Gandhi would have the nerve to attack it or not was the question on everyone's minds as spring turned to summer in 1984.

The political party of the Sikhs, the Akali Dal, had raised crucial political issues with the central government that remained unresolved as tensions escalated in 1984. These issues included a settlement of a long-standing dispute over the apportionment of Punjab's river waters, the question of the allocation of the city of Chandigarh as the joint capital of Punjab and Haryana, and the implementation of a resolution calling for more autonomy for the state. Furthermore, there were religious demands that were highlighted by the militants at the Golden Temple Complex. Bhindranwale called for the establishment of a "holy city" status for Amritsar, which he believed was unfairly granted to Hindu cities like Hardwar and Benares;[22] renaming the train from Delhi to Amritsar as the "Golden Temple Express;" setting up a powerful transmitter to broadcast hymns from the Golden Temple; and arranging for the SGPC, the Sikh organization that governs *gurudwaras*, to have full control over all historical Sikh shrines throughout India. What happened was that at the last moment Indira Gandhi and her negotiators conceded some of the religious demands, which were from the viewpoint of the government relatively trivial, but the more serious political issues remained unresolved. Meanwhile, the level of violence and counterviolence had reached such a point that even as discussions about the issues were proceeding, preparations were being made for a military solution to the crisis.

Such are the bare facts of the events that led up to the dramatic confrontation of June 1984 at the Golden Temple Complex. This spare recitation does not convey the atmosphere of tension that had built to a crescendo not only in Punjab but in neighboring areas as well in the months preceding that face-off. I happened to be in Delhi in the fall of 1983, and saw personally what was happening to totally uninvolved and apolitical Sikhs I knew. They were stopped and searched before going into movie theaters for fear they might be carrying bombs. Hindu shopkeepers with whom they had always dealt suddenly refused to serve them. Although my Sikh friends held no brief for Bhindranwale or his methods, they felt insulted and hurt by the presumed association between their turbans and the increasing violence in Punjab. The image of the Sikh community was, indeed, changing. As one Hindu woman told me at the time, "It used to be that if we were riding on a train and saw a Sikh in our carriage, we would feel protected. Now if we see one, we feel scared." When I told this to a Sikh friend, he was quite upset. (This person was later missing after the November 1984 anti-Sikh riots in Delhi.)

The broader historical factors that contributed to the rise of a Sikh revivalist movement in the 1970s, and the political and religious context that encouraged various others to sympathize with it, are considered in the following chapter. Here, I concentrate on the epochal battle at the Golden Temple between the militants and the Indian army that has spawned what we now know as the Khalistan movement. "If the Indian army attacks the Golden Temple," Bhindranwale used to say, "the foundations of Khalistan will be laid." In June 1984, the army did just that, thus magnifying the danger of Sikh separatism a hundredfold.

CHILDHOOD MEMORIES

"My uncle Sukhdev Singh Babbar [founder of the Babbar Khalsa] took *amrit* in 1977. After a year there was the Nirankari episode, but I was just a small girl then. I remember how my father and everybody left when they heard what was going on, and when they came back home some of them had been shot and blood was coming out of their bodies. It was terrible. I still have some vivid pictures in my mind from that time. One Sikh was shot on the shoulders and I can still see the blood soaked through his shirt. I later heard how my dad and uncle and others didn't have any guns with them, that they borrowed wooden sticks from a shop-keeper and tried to fight the Nirankaris with those.

"One of the Singhs was killed there, Bhai Fauja Singh. He was a dear friend of my uncle's and after he got killed it was real hard for my uncle to sit around and do nothing. There was another Singh killed, Bhai Raghbir Singh, and his wife was a real nice person. She told us how no-body she knew was doing anything about her husband's death. So my uncle told her that he was her brother too, and that he would do some-thing about it.

"My dad's brother used to go to my uncle's room and he told us that he saw him making arrowheads, sitting there by himself. He wondered whether something was up with my uncle. Within two or three months it seemed he was never home. We later learned that they had established camps where the Singhs could get training in swords and guns.

"One day they all came over to my house and they said, 'Let's go for rehearsal.' They made a statue of Indira Gandhi and stuck it on a tree, and all the Singhs stood in line and shot arrows at her. They were making comments like, 'She's going to get killed,' 'We will get her,' and things like that. That was in 1981 or 1982, I think. I was around ten years old.

"My uncle was a really nice person, really friendly. Like one day he had a fight with some people, and after he became a Babbar and went to live at Darbar Sahib [the Golden Temple] as *jathedar* the people he had fought with came to apologize. 'It's OK,' he told them. 'That was before I had taken *amrit*. I don't hold a grudge now.' My uncle was not a violent person at all. It was the circumstances that made him do what he did.

"As a child I witnessed some Singhs getting killed myself. But we are taught that it's OK to die if you die with pride. So I didn't feel scared or anything. I was proud of them.

"Police were harassing everybody by the early 1980s. They took all my relatives to jail at one time or another, even my blind uncle. My father then decided that rather than sit around and wait to be picked up, he would join my uncle at Darbar Sahib. We would then go to visit the two of them there during our vacations.

"I still have these times in my mind. I can't describe how wonderful it was there. It was the best thing I ever saw in my life. How the Singhs were living together, how they knew so much and how dedicated they were. They would wake up early in the morning and do *nam simran*, then go to the temple and listen to *kirtan*. The whole year we waited for vacations so that we could go to see them there. On the last day of the vacation we wouldn't get any sleep, because we wanted to spend as much time there as we could.

"We used to live basically in hiding because of my father and my uncle. We stayed inside all the time and didn't go out into the open. Then neighbors would start saying, 'Who are they? Why don't those children go outside?' This sort of thing. Then we would move somewhere else.

"I knew all the Singhs who were active at that time. They treated me as a daughter or a younger sister. Whenever a Singh would get killed, we would all feel sad for a few days. But sometimes I would see them in my dreams. Sometimes I still see them in my dreams! They were people we could always count on, for anything. We could always trust the Singhs.

"In June 1984 I was at my cousin's marriage when we heard the news that the Darbar Sahib had been attacked. My brothers were there and my uncle's sons were also there, but all the ladies, my mom, my aunts and all, were all at the wedding. But we decided it would be better if we left right away. When we went to the bus some of the people at the wedding tried to stop us, saying that there was fighting going on in Amritsar and that if we went we might get killed. But we left anyway. We went straight to Amritsar.

"We were all feeling happy at that time that if we were going to die we would all die together. Early the next morning at four o'clock when the shooting started again everyone became alert. The Singhs asked the ladies to gather up all the kids, and while we did this they went on with their fighting. We saw one Singh, a very good person, get killed. But it was hard to tell exactly what was happening. There was a lot of noise, a lot of gunfire.

"On June 4 the Singhs told us to leave the building and to go to safer places nearby. But none of the women wanted to leave. They said that if the Singhs were going to die, then they wanted to die, too. At that point my uncle Sukhdev Singh came to the women and he said that we really had to leave. He explained that if the army was going to grab us and dishonor us in front of them, it would be real hard for the Singhs to stand it. That they might be made to speak like that. So to avoid that circumstance, Sukhdev Singh told us we had better leave. Eventually, we did.

"We stayed in a house nearby for two days. There was no water in that building and nothing to cook either. All the women did gather together and made *prashad* [unleavened bread, which Sikhs call by the same name as the consecrated offerings distributed in temples] for the Singhs who were fighting. One or two of the Singhs would come and get it and somehow take it in packs on their backs to where the other Singhs were fighting. They knew the Darbar Sahib inside and out.

"At night it was real dark because there was a curfew in Amritsar. But we could see the bombs going off at the Darbar Sahib. It was very colorful and noisy, and no one could sleep at all. We were wondering what was happening to the Singhs, how they were faring inside the complex.

"On June 6 most of the Singhs left the Darbar Sahib. My uncle apparently didn't want to go, but then five Singhs came before him, *panj piaras*, and said they were ordering him to leave. We need people to organize the struggle after this, they told him. If all of us die here it won't accomplish anything. So he left by a back route.

"That day we were told to come out of the house where we were staying. It was hard for us kids because we were wearing our *kirpans* underneath our clothes and holding our hands up in the air. One of my uncle's kids was only two and a half years old at the time and he got kind of permanently shocked by that experience.

"When all the people came out of the Darbar Sahib nobody was wearing shoes. Everybody was bare-footed, and people who were watching them started giving them shoes. I just remember all those people with bare feet and all the people passing shoes to them from the streets.

"We then stayed in my cousin's house for about two weeks, surviving on only flour, which we made into bread, and salt. We were worried because ten members of the family had been inside Darbar Sahib, and we couldn't hear any news about them. After the curfew was relaxed, we all piled onto a rickshaw and made for a village we knew. We stayed there some time before we went home. It was like a celebration there when the people saw us return safely.

"Then the police started coming to our home. They knew that many Babbars had escaped, and they wanted to know where they had gone. But we didn't know. We were being harassed in various ways and eventually we decided to leave that place. We hid in Amritsar for five or six years after that, but nobody knew where we had gone, not even my grandparents.

"I couldn't talk to anybody else about my situation, no girl friends or anything like that. Nobody knew I was the daughter of Mehel Singh [currently a major figure in the Babbar Khalsa force]. There was one girl, a Hindu, who became a good friend of mine, and she was always saying that she didn't like the Singhs who were fighting. She thought this way because that's what they teach the Hindus, that the Singhs are bad and scary people. I kept it a secret that my own family were among the top Singhs in the movement.

"At one point the police heard from somebody that we were in Amritsar and they started bothering another family there by the name of Mehel Singh, my father's name. But they had the wrong Mehel Singh. Then one day we suddenly found our house surrounded, with police on all the rooftops around us. Everything was searched, even my schoolbooks, page by page. But they didn't find anything to incriminate us.

"Things had become quite dicey for us, so the Singhs found a way for me to get out of India. Two days after I left, my mother was picked up by the police along with my aunt, and they were taken to the torture center in Batala. They were heavily beaten and the worst humiliation was that the police chief there made my mother drink his urine. He taunted her that it was *amrit*. Finally my mother was released from there and got admitted to a hospital. I never saw her after that, but she wrote me a letter. She said, 'Don't worry about me, girl, you be courageous and you face whatever is in store for you in that new land.'

"My uncle was killed by the police. And the police then picked up my brother from his college and tortured him and his friend. They got electric shocks, which permanently affected them. They are now hiding here and there, from place to place. They hadn't done anything, as they were quite young. It would be better if they would do something to fight back, rather than just getting tortured and killed for no reason.

"Some of my uncles arranged a marriage for me, but otherwise I am entirely alone here. Now I have a son, who was born here. I'm planning to tell him all the things I have gone through and explain what our family has done. One day I asked my husband if we should ask our son to go over there and fight when he grows up. My father-in-law was sitting there and he said, 'Wait till he grows up? That will be too late. Why not send him now so that he can learn all the things he needs to do?' But I think that if he is educated then he can fight in a more sophisticated way. He should get educated first, then think about the best way to fight.

"Maybe now that Hindu girl has seen my family's pictures in the paper and all, and maybe now she realizes that the Singhs are just ordinary people. Not some kind of devils."

THE ACTION

I don't propose to give a minute-by-minute account of Operation Blue Star here, which can be found by any interested reader in the various accounts mentioned in the notes to this chapter. Probably the most frequently cited one is *Amritsar: Mrs. Gandhi's Last Battle*, by Mark Tully and Satish Jacob. The most intricate narrative, from the military perspective, is that of Lieutenant General K. S. Brar, *Operation Blue Star: The True Story*.

Militant sympathizers reject his account out of hand, but I believe it to be an honest and straightforward appraisal. *India Commits Suicide*, by Gurdarshan Singh Dhillon,[23] is slanted in the opposite direction and is most valuable for the first-hand narratives from pilgrims caught in the crossfire at Amritsar during the confrontation. Reports on abuses carried out during the operation can also be found in the Citizens for Democracy report, *Oppression in Punjab*.[24]

The Indian army was called into Punjab "in aid of civil authorities" in mid-May, but there was no talk at that time of an impending assault on the Golden Temple Complex. The army set up a command post near the entrance to the shrine as well as laying seige to thirty-seven other *gurudwaras* throughout Punjab, Haryana, and Himachal Pradesh thought to be sheltering militants. Both Bhindranwale and Harchand Singh Longowal, the Akali leader, called for the army to withdraw, threatening massive demonstrations if it did not. Prime Minister Indira Gandhi went on national television on June 2, calling on Indians "not to shed blood, but to shed hatred," but it is now clear that as she spoke instructions had already in fact been given to top military officers to prepare for an all-out assault.[25] General A. S. Vaidya, Army chief of staff (later assassinated), Lieutenant General K. Sundarji, Lieutenant General Ranjit Singh Dayal, and Major General K. S. Brar were the major military figures involved in the planning and execution of the assault; some seventy thousand troops were eventually involved.

On Sunday, June 3, all communications between Punjab and the outside were cut off, reporters were asked to leave, and a total curfew was imposed on the streets. Everyone knew that something was up; as Iqbal Singh said in Chapter 3, "We could smell it . . ." Mark Tully describes the eerie quiet that descended on the state:

As the sun rose I saw a spectacle I had never expected—the Grand Trunk Road empty. During the five and a half hours it took us to drive to the border I did not see a single civilian vehicle, not even a bullock cart. The shops in the villages we passed through were all closed and most of the villagers were in their homes. The only trains I saw were troop trains. . . . Punjab was cut off from the rest of the world in preparation for the final assault.[26]

June 3 was the martyrdom day of Guru Arjun, and thousands of pilgrims (though possibly fewer than in previous years) were visiting the Golden Temple Complex when the curfew was imposed. It is important to note that the complex not only contains the Harmandir Sahib (the Golden Temple) and the Akal Takht (the Eternal Throne), the Sikh Reference Library, and other religious buildings, but also incorporates large hostels for the accommodation of visitors as well as offices of major Sikh organizations. The militants had moved from the hostel in which they had been staying to the Akal Takht itself, which they had heavily fortified. As pilgrims walked around the *parikrama* (pavement), took a dip in the sacred pool, and paid obeisance to the Guru Granth Sahib, they must have been aware of the military preparations that had been made. Even at that point, however, few thought that the army would actually attack the sacred precincts. There were certainly hundreds of them caught at the Golden Temple at the time of the confrontation, possibly thousands.

On June 4, the army operation began. Intermittent fire was exchanged throughout the day, not only to and from the Akal Takht but also between the army and the large towers on which the militants had prepared machine-gun emplacements and other perimeter fortifications. The houses and buildings directly surrounding the complex, many of which were occupied by militants, also came under fire during an initial clearing operation that lasted seventeen hours. During lulls, the army would announce over loudspeakers that the pilgrims should come out, but only a few ventured to do so. Nevertheless, military commanders planned to go ahead on June 5 with the major thrust of the assault, to be directed at the Akal Takht itself.

The widow of Labh Singh, a close confederate of Bhindranwale's who was later martyred as head of the Khalistan Commando Force, remembers:

> On May 25 I went with my two sons to the Golden Temple to see my husband. My father and mother were with us, as they had decided to ask for baptism on that day. We stayed until June 2, when there was a sudden burst of police fire from all directions. I was coming out of the *langar* [kitchen] with my husband, Santji, and my parents, and the Singhs immediately got started preparing defensive positions in the Akal Takht. There were announcements being made that all the pilgrims and visitors should leave, as things would likely become quite dangerous. My husband told us to get out and to take his two sons out. My mother and I said, "How are we supposed to take care of them without you? If you are staying, we want to stay, too." But he said, "I can't show my back to Santji. I'll fight with him and face martyrdom in this place. So take my sons out and let me do what I have to do." Seeing him so firm and determined on this point, we decided to leave. We came out on June 4 , 1984, amidst a lot of indiscriminate firing on all sides.
>
> There was an atmosphere of fear all around, but among Santji and his companions spirits were high when we left. During June 5 and 6, there was curfew on in Amritsar, and everything was deadly quiet in the streets. The only thing that could be heard was the sound of fierce fighting at the Golden Temple. Flames were lighting up the whole area

and you could smell the smoke from every place in the city. The final hour is drawing near, I kept thinking. In the end Santji and his companions were martyred, and my two sons were spared.

By all accounts, the defense of the Golden Temple Complex by the Sikh militants was far in excess of what the Indian army had been led to believe. Although many had thought that the entire place could be taken within a few hours, it took a pitched battle lasting several days to accomplish the goal. It also took the use of Vijayanta tanks, perhaps the most controversial aspect of the operation,[27] which inflicted heavy structural damage on the Akal Takht. Tully and Jacob note that "to say that Bhindranwale was flushed out would be, to put it mildly, an understatement. He was blasted out."[28] But the military personnel involved in Operation Blue Star are all clear on the point that they were not to harm the actual Harmandir, the Golden Temple itself, which sits in the middle of the sacred pool. Lieutenant General Sundarji said, "We entered with humility in our hearts and prayers on our lips," and despite some evidence of bullet marks on the Harmandir Sahib, this structure did survive the battle relatively intact.

The Golden Temple Complex is honeycombed by tunnels, and the militants kept the army under withering machine-gun fire from the manholes out of which they would pop up and then quickly retreat. Shabeg Singh had apparently taught them to fire at knee height on the supposition that the troops would be crawling across the *parikrama*, hence many of the injuries suffered by the army were to the lower legs. Nevertheless, this strategy did stop their advance, and the casualty levels were reaching one-third in some units. (Brar notes the extraordinarily high proportion of officers killed or wounded in Operation Blue Star, which he attributes to the desire to keep the troops under control so as to minimize damage to the sacred buildings.[29]) Finally, in order to put a stop to the massacre of the troops as well as to forestall the possibility of Sikhs converging on Amritsar as news of the assault spread, permission was requested from Delhi to make use of the tanks.

Though the numbers of rifles, machine guns, and homemade grenades were greater than had been expected, the range of types they represented were pretty much what the army had assumed would be in militant hands. The commanders in charge of Operation Blue Star were, however, shocked to discover on June 6 that the militants in the Akal Takht had two Chinese-made rocket-propelled grenade launchers with armor-piercing capabilities. Against these, the Vijayanta tanks let loose a barrage of high-explosive squash-head shells, which tore off the entire front of the Akal Takht, set off fires in many of the internal rooms (some of which housed precious historical relics), and badly damaged the signature dome. Brar says at this point that "it was amply clear to us now that the Temple of God had been turned into a full fledged battlefield."[30] He blamed, of course, Bhindranwale and his men, who certainly provided the provocation for the incident. But there was plenty of blame to go around.

As for the fighting capabilities of the militants, Brar comments: "Notwithstanding the fact that by converting the House of God into a battlefield, all the principles and precepts of the ten Sikh gurus were thrown overboard, it must be admitted that the tenacity with which the militants held their ground, the stubborn valour with which they fought the battle, and the high degree of confidence displayed by them merits praise and recognition."[31] One officer told Satish Jacob, more pithily, "Boy, what a fight they gave us. If I had three Divs like that I would fuck the hell out of Zia [the Pakistan president] any day."[32]

The bodies of Bhindranwale, Shabeg Singh, and Amrik Singh were discovered when the army finally entered the Akal Takht on June 7.[33] There were bodies of other militants in the stairways of the building, which had become scenes of major gun battles, and in its labyrinthine halls. Some had tried to swim across the sacred pool to the Harmandir Sahib and, gunned down in the water, their bodies floated on the surface, quickly bloating in the intense heat of summer. Other bodies were strewn across the *parikrama*, toppled from towers or shot on the flat pavement itself. Every eyewitness comments on the stench.

One of the major disasters of the Operation Blue Star debacle was the fire in the Sikh Reference Library at the tail end of the battle. Each side has accused the other of being at fault; the militants claim that the army set out purposely to destroy a crucial part of the Sikh heritage, while the army claims that engagement with the militants prevented it from bringing in fire-fighting equipment once the blaze began. In the middle of a ferocious battle, it is perhaps not unexpected that a fire like this should break out and that the minds of fighters on both sides might be devoted to the battle at hand rather than combatting one of what were at that point dozens of fires. In any case, the library was gutted. When the smoke cleared, everything was gone—irreplaceable copies of the Guru Granth Sahib, archives of documents from every period of Sikh history, and artifacts from the lives of the Gurus. Given the place of the written word in Sikh religious tradition, the destruction of the library had an impact that reached well beyond the world of scholarship. One man recalls:

I stood there watching the smoke, black at first then a kind of gray, curling over the rooftops around the Golden Temple Complex. When I found out later that it was the library that had burnt I kept seeing that smoke, smelling that smoke in my mind. It seemed to me that I could feel the pages burning, the precious pages of my Guru Granth Sahib. It seemed like that smoke was stinging my eyes. I cried and cried when I found out about the library. Many people had died, but I was crying most about my Guru [Granth Sahib].

As for the pilgrims, tragedies abounded. Bhan Singh, the secretary of the SGPC that had offices in the complex and an eyewitness extensively cited in the Citizens for Democracy's report on Blue Star, paints a horrifying picture:

On the 6th morning when hundreds of people were killed or wounded, everywhere there were cries of those people who were wounded and injured. . . . Many young people aged between 18 and 22 years were killed and so were some ladies. A lady carrying a child of only a few months saw her husband lying before her. The child was also killed on account of the firing. It was a very touching scene when she placed the dead body of the child alongside her husband's body. Many people were crying for drinking water but they were not provided any. Some had to take water out of the drains where dead bodies were lying and the water was red with blood. They way the injured were quenching their thirst was an awful sight which could not be tolerated.[34]

Thirst played a role in other narratives of pilgrims caught in the complex, as Operation Blue Star took place at the peak of the hot season when sustained temperatures reach over a hundred degrees Fahrenheit. A schoolteacher, Ranbir Kaur, locked herself into a room with the twelve children she was looking after. She reports,

We were all huddled together. We didn't know what was happening. The noise was terrifying. We had not been out of the room for more than twenty-four hours and we had no food or water. It was a very hot summer night. I told the children that we must be ready to die. They kept on crying.[35]

An elder of a Punjabi village wrote a letter to the president of India, Zail Singh, with another story:

The army locked up sixty pilgrims in that room [of the hostel] and shut not only the door but the window also. Electric supply was disconnected. The night between June 5th and June 6th was extremely hot. The locked-in young men felt very thirsty after some time, and loudly knocked on the door from inside to ask the army men on duty for water. They got abuses in return, but no water. The door was not opened. Feeling suffocated and extremely thirsty, the men inside began to faint and otherwise suffer untold misery. The door of the room was opened at 8 a.m. on June 6th. By this time fifty-five out of sixty had died. The remaining five were also semi-dead.[36]

Sikh visitors to the Golden Temple Complex after the army assault were seen touching their foreheads to the fresh bullet marks on the walls

4. Painting by Sobha Singh of the Golden Temple Complex, Amritsar, after Operation Blue Star. Bodies litter the sacred pool and *parikrama*; the Sikh Reference Library burns. Guru Nanak looks on in sorrow. This painting has gone through multiple reprintings and is now distributed widely in the Sikh community.

of the Harmandir Sahib and sobbing. Others pressed their bodies against the shattered trunk of the historic *elaichi beri* tree, whose branches had been blasted off in the attack. One eyewitness saw a woman lie full out on the *parikrama*, the pavement surrounding the sacred pool, spreading out her arms on the blood-stained surface and pressing her cheek against one of its crumbled tiles. Another sat in a quiet corner, sifting bits of rubble and ash through his fingers for hours at a stretch, dazedly repeating, "Waheguru, Waheguru."

In the White Paper published by the government of India after Operation Blue Star, militant and nonmilitant casualties are (apallingly) lumped under the category "civilian/terrorist," and are listed at 493.[37] Tully and Jacob note that this figure leaves 1,600 people unaccounted for,[38] based on a relatively conservative estimation of the numbers of people at the Golden Temple Complex at the time. Citizens for Democracy, a respected Indian civil liberties group headed by the distinguished jurist V. M. Tarkunde, sent an investigative team to Punjab and came out with its own response to the White Paper, *Report to the Nation: Oppression in Punjab.* Though Citizens for Democracy rejects the high claims of six or seven thousand casualties put forward by various Sikh eyewitnesses, it notes that the mounds of dead bodies on the *parikrama* in the wake of Operation Blue Star and the truckload after truckload of bodies brought out of the Golden Temple Complex, observed by many people, point to a much higher casualty figure than the one claimed by the government. Estimating that about ten thousand pilgrims were at the complex during Operation Blue Star, Citizens for Democracy notes that the actual number of alleged terrorists at the site was quite small relative to the number of innocent worshipers. "It was indeed a mass massacre mostly of innocents," their report states.[39]

Most disturbing about the reports that started coming out of Punjab in response to the government's White Paper were those that portrayed the army as committing direct atrocities against unarmed people. Brahma Chellany, an Associated Press correspondent who managed to remain in Amritsar after all the other journalists were escorted out, records the shooting in cold blood of Sikhs who had been taken prisoner, their hands tied behind their backs with their turbans. (He was later charged with sedition.)[40]

As for the number of army casualties, figures range from a low of 83 (White Paper/Brar) to a high of 700 (Nayar and Singh).[41] According to army officers with whom I spoke, many of the casualties could be put down to an abysmal failure in intelligence. The complex layout of the site, with all its tunnels and twisting corridors, was simply not in hand when the operation took place. As important, I believe, was the simple failure of the government to understand just who it was up against in that first week of June. Tully and Jacob report that

The failure to estimate Bhindranwale's will to fight is . . . easy to explain. Bhindranwale had a reputation for cowardice. He was reported to have ducked out of the march against the Nirankaris at the start of his rise to fame, and he had three times taken shelter in *gurudwaras* to avoid arrest. . . .

It is also understandable that the army underestimated the training of the terrorists. The young men who used to surround Bhindranwale when he held his morning congregations were an unimpressive lot. They used to loaf around, leaning against the parapet of the Langar [community kitchen] and chatting with each other. They looked more like thugs than skilled fighters prepared to give their lives for their leader.[42]

This impression, formed without direct knowledge of the militants and passed along by a compliant media, obviously turned out to be wrong. Tully may have thought the companions of Bhindranwale "an unimpressive lot," but they were, when push came to shove, skilled fighters prepared to give their lives. This same underestimation continues, in my opinion, today, despite the lesson of Operation Blue Star. Even as Brar commends the militants for their fighting ability and courage, he describes those who stayed with the gunny bags of cash at the Akal Takht as "looking for opportunities of getting away with huge sums of money, subsequently to enjoy their acquired riches."[43] That there were such individuals within the movement is probable. But shouldn't an army commander at least consider the possibility that those same dedicated fighters might try to escape with funding in the interests of pursuing their battle with the Indian Government at a later point? Pursue the battle they did, in fact; Blue Star turned out to be not an end but a beginning. Khushwant Singh, who despised the militants but consistently warned the Indian government of the dangers of launching an attack on the holiest of holy places, commented that

Things have never been the same again. Sikhs who had nothing to do with Bhindranwale or politics felt deeply humiliated. Bhindranwale was killed which gave him a halo of martyrdom he did not deserve. It gave a filip to the terrorist groups. Bhindranwale's ghost still stalks the Punjab countryside disturbing the sleep of the Punjabi Hindu and the conscience of the Punjabi Sikh.[44]

Khushwant Singh returned the decoration that had been awarded him by Indira Gandhi, as did several other Sikhs in high positions in the government. So did Bhagat Puran Singh, known as "the bearded Mother Theresa" for his service to lepers, orphans, and other afflicted people. Two Sikh members of parliament resigned their seats. Indian troops mutinied at various locations across India, the largest mutiny ocurring at Ramgarh (Bihar) where almost fifteen hundred soldiers tried to desert.

Lieutenant General Brar, worried about the boost given to Bhindranwale's reputation by his martyrdom during Operation Blue Star, said that "overnight, Jarnail Singh Bhindranwale became a hero, even with those who had hated his guts and despised his earlier actions." [45] One of my interlocutors praises Bhindranwale and his performance during Blue Star fulsomely:

> Sant Jarnail Singh Bhindranwale was a truthful, devout saint-soldier of the tenth Guru. He was not of a type who would care for his safety or security, but he was so much immersed in the love of Guru that he devoted his whole self to the preaching of Sikhism. In our tradition, we believe that Guru Nanak told Babar [a Mughal emperor] that he was a tyrant, right to his face. In the same way Sant Jarnail Singh Bhindranwale stood up to tell the truth, no matter who should feel offended. Our sixth Guru, Guru Hargobind, and our tenth Guru, Guru Gobind Singh, raised their voices against tyranny and had to raise their swords, too. In the same way Sant Jarnail Singh Bhindranwale raised his voice and took out his sword. Sant Jarnail Singh Bhindranwale courageously tread on the path of the best Sikh traditions and values.

Last autumn I had the chance to visit the new Holocaust Museum in Washington, D.C. The power and sorrow of that museum was enhanced for me by the fact that I was accompanied by Amarjit and Iqbal Singh of Chapter 3. I could feel the way the exhibits moved them, and I imagined wordlessly the analogies they were probably drawing with their own community's situation. In one part of the museum there is a walkway inscribed with the names of places in which Jewish communities had been destroyed during World War II. As I watched, a bent old man, apparently blind, was being led by a young boy along the walkway. He was running his fingers up and down the list of place names. Stopping at one, he leaned over and kissed the name, holding his face there against the glass, his eyes shut tight. The boy, presumably a grandson or great-grandson, looked away, embarassed by the show of emotion. But the poignancy of that old man's gesture was not lost on me, nor on the Sikhs with me. The conversation shifted from the Jews to the Sikhs.

Some Sikhs have in fact taken up the term "holocaust" (*ghallughara*) to describe the events that befell their community in 1984. As far as I can tell, not many of those who use the term are actually very familiar with the World War II holocaust, which differed in many significant ways from what happened to the Sikhs (however horrific) in 1984. But the holocaust theme has caught on; a newspaper article in one of the radical Sikh papers asked in its headline, "Are the Gas Chambers Next?" Seeing an especially troubling exhibit at the Holocaust Museum in which the shoes of concentration camp victims are piled high, disturbing in their very everydayness, Amarjit and Iqbal Singh got into a discussion about what happened to the shoes of the pilgrims visiting the Golden Temple Complex at the time of the attack, which had been deposited at the entranceway as required for worship. It was from the number of shoes recovered that some of the estimates of casualties were derived, and the two Sikhs thought that a future holocaust museum at Amritsar might effectively archive this piece of Sikh history. We started talking about the importance of preserving people's accounts of Operation Blue Star and events thereafter and the role that an outsider like myself might play in that preservation. An archivist or a chronicler of the Sikh militancy—that role suited me just fine, and I was happy that the Holocaust Museum brought out this convenient way of discussing and defining my niche. Somebody who takes down people's stories, another Sikh said later that evening, that's what we need. A gatherer of stories was, after all, something like what Geertz recommended for contemporary anthropology: that we should compile a consultable record of what humans have thought and done.[46]

The term *ghallughara* had been used to describe the massacre of Sikhs near Malerkotla and subsequent destruction of the Golden Temple by Ahmed Shah Abdali in 1762. It was in fighting against the occupation of Amritsar by Abdali's forces that Baba Deep Singh's head was severed from his body, making Bhindranwale's reported comparison of himself with Baba Deep Singh all the more potent. There were other historical resonances as well. The fact that the 1984 attack took place on the martyrdom day of Guru Arjun not only meant that thousands of pilgrims would be worshiping at the shrine at the moment of attack, but also invited a comparison between this first Sikh martyr and the modern-day martyrs defending the Golden Temple. (Why the Indian government allowed this to happen, despite warnings from many prominently placed individuals, is a matter of much speculation.) Finally, the 1984 confrontation took place just blocks away from Jallianwalla Bagh, where in 1919 General Dyer of the British colonial army slaughtered some four hundred people, many of them Sikhs, who had gathered for a rally. As the Jallianwalla Bagh massacre was a founding event in the Indian independence struggle, it was said, so Operation Blue Star would be a founding episode in the independence struggle of Khalistan. "He out-Dyered Dyer," commented one Sikh about Lieutenant General Vaidya.

Recognizing the potential political power of the martyrdom of Bhindranwale, the government of India initiated a sweeping crackdown on militants across Punjab under the code name Operation Wood Rose.

"They always thought that whoever had been with Sant Bhindranwale even for an hour, he had been magnetized, he is virtually a potential bomb, and their only idea was to finish off anybody who was even remotely associated with Bhindranwale," reported one young man who, indeed, had been "magnetized" by Bhindranwale. *Amritdhari* Sikhs were particular targets of surveillance; the Indian army newsletter suggested after Operation Blue Star that "any knowledge of the Amritdharis who are dangerous people pledged to commit murders, arson and act [sic] of terrorism should immediately be brought to the notice of the authorities. These people might appear harmless from the outside but they are basically committed to terrorism." [47] This blanket condemnation of all orthodox Sikhs as terrorists went a long way toward alienating even those who otherwise may have remained, if not committed to India, at least unwilling to applaud the use of violence against it.

The notion that Operation Blue Star was a matter of a secular, pluralist state protecting itself from a few religious fanatics is a much celebrated one, and it is true that there were Sikhs who fought on the side of the army at the Golden Temple (K. S. Brar among them). But it would be misleading to ignore the communal context that helped define the eventual impact of the operation. Local Hindus offered sweets to the troops as they left the front gate of the Golden Temple Complex, while local Sikhs did the same for the militants escaping through the alleys at the back. Though Brar says he sternly ordered his troops not to accept this kind of inflammatory hospitality, the myth of government neutrality was shattered by the thoughtless generalizations about *amritdhari* Sikhs from other sources. Later, the "communal card" was played shamelessly by Rajiv Gandhi in the elections of 1985. However well-intentioned some army and government leaders were in playing down the communal implications of Blue Star, it was received by Sikhs, and indeed by many Hindus, as an attack not on terrorism but on Sikhism. As Nayar and Singh note, "Punjab's tragedy is that there are no Punjabis anymore in Punjab—only Sikhs and Hindus." [48]

The clearly distorted account of the event released to the media does not speak well for India's vaunted freedom of press. Stories of prostitutes and drugs at the Akal Takht were printed on front pages one week, then recanted in back pages the next. A story suggesting that Bhindranwale had committed suicide was followed by one describing his body riddled with bullets from head to toe. [49] There is no doubt that an entire apparatus of fear dissemination worked to convince India that the Sikhs were to be distrusted. [50] And, by and large, it succeeded.

Compromises with press freedoms were accompanied by draconian legislation that was a target of criticism from human rights communities around the world, implemented in the interests of combating terrorism in Punjab. The Terrorism and Disruptive Activities (Prevention) Act, known by its acronym TADA, allowed for the detention of a person on mere suspicion in a "disturbed area" and was applied in twenty-two of India's twenty-five states (many of which could not have been said to face a terrorist threat by any stretch of imagination). In the ten years following 1984, some seventy thousand people were detained under TADA though only about 1 percent of them were eventually convicted of a crime. Moreover, TADA cases were held in special courts heard by executive magistrates who were appointed centrally, the cases were in camera, and could be held in locations far removed from the disturbed area itself. The identity of prosecuting witnesses was not revealed, rendering impotent the right of cross-examination. Human rights groups have complained that TADA was most emphatically applied to members of religious minorities, scheduled caste Hindus (former Untouchables), and tribals. Most significantly, the expedited system set up for TADA seems to have completely swamped the normal judicial channels. "Suddenly, there was no more crime in Punjab, only terrorism," said a former police officer. Retired Supreme Court Justice Krishna Iyer put it concisely: "Justice in Punjab has been crucified on the cross of law." [51]

There were other innovations in judicial procedure, too, that received less press than the notorious TADA but were equally problematic. Amendments to the Criminal Procedure Code allowed a person to be presumed guilty if she were found at the scene of a crime and to be held without charge for a year. If a person was present where an act of sedition occured, he was considered guilty of sedition (a capital crime) until he could prove himself innocent. The state could close down a newspaper or seize a book or any other material considered prejudicial to national integration. Under the National Security Act (NSA), an individual could be preventively detained for a year if judged to be likely to behave in a manner inimical to the interests of the country. Modifications to other laws such as the Arms Act and the Misuse of Religious Places Act enhanced the possibilities of judicial excesses in the name of counterinsurgency. Stanley Wolpert, writing in *A New History of India*, notes that "though India had signed the UN Declaration of Universal Human Rights, her legal system now clearly violated its basic provisions and left more and more of its citizens to languish behind prison bars without any stated cause for such action or real hope of freedom." [52]

The calling in of the Indian army "in aid of civil authority" and the growing militarization of law and order in Punjab worried many people, including some top figures in the Indian armed services. Lieutenant General J. S. Aurora specifically warned of the temptation such an army might feel to take over completely, which of course happened in the case of India's neighbors and thus would be ruled out only by the foolhardy.

"You know," he said, "if you use the army too often, the chances are that they may say we are managing it for them, why not manage it for ourselves? . . . There is no doubt that we are taking dangerous chances."[53] Lieutenant General Sundarji himself later accused the nation's leaders of forcing the army into political conflicts in which it didn't belong.[54]

The immediate impact of the militarization of Punjab and the cataclysmic implementation of "Black Laws" was the total alienation of the previously minimally involved targeted population. One Sikh militant I interviewed, later responsible for some major "combat actions" in the insurgency, said that "one thing very deep in my mind as I got out of prison was that I had gotten more than my share as punishment than I had actually put in service to the cause. I thought, if they bother me now, I'll become a living hell for them. Now I'll let them know what a Sikh is really like." Another interlocutor asserts bluntly, "All the Sikhs were wearing black turbans after the attack on the Golden Temple. I had one Hindu friend who taunted me, 'Hey, give me a black turban to wear, too.' I said, 'One day you'll get your black turban.' After that bitch Indira Gandhi was punished I went over to his place and presented him with a black turban."

Whatever the provocation provided by Jarnail Singh Bhindranwale and his associates, and certainly from the viewpoint of state security it was extreme, it is clear that the major effect of Operation Blue Star was not the eradication of terrorism in Punjab but the creation of a community with nothing to lose. As we all know, this situation is the most dangerous thing a civil society can face. As India faced it, the "largest democracy in the world" became, in fact, noticeably less civil.

A SOLDIER AND HIS WIFE REACT TO OPERATION BLUE STAR

The soldier: "I came from Bhatinda district in Punjab. In my family there were three brothers and one sister. We were not a very religious family. My father had unshorn hair but he was not a baptized Sikh. We were very far from religion and politics, both.

"In 1984 I was employed in the Indian army. I worked at the Bhatinda Railway Station as senior clerk . When I heard that the army had invaded the Golden Temple I felt very shocked and hurt, even though I was not a religious-minded person.

"As I was the seniormost man in the detachment, I heard on the radio what was going on during the attack. Everything was under curfew, so I couldn't really see what was happening outside. I heard on the radio that as news spread about the attack on the Golden Temple Sikh soldiers were deserting their posts and marching towards Amritsar. Then the BBC started reporting that the mutineers who had left their posts were being arrested and killed on the way. The thought came to me and the other Sikhs that the government might kill us here and now, so why not march to Amritsar to try to do something for our religion? We thought like this, but we didn't go. We just listened on the radio and talked and talked.

"After this I became a voracious reader. I tried to get as many Punjabi and other newspapers and magazines as were available. I tried to learn everything I could about my religious tradition and my community. Then I realized that Sikhs were being killed everywhere and that they were discriminated against in every sphere, and my religious emotions started becoming more intense.

"On 31 October Indira Gandhi was punished by Beant Singh and Satwant Singh for her misdeeds. Sikhs all over India were then murdered cold-bloodedly in retaliation. I was employed at the railway station, and trains used to come there with all the windows broken and dead bodies inside. Some who survived told gruesome stories. After listening to them and after seeing what was happening, I couldn't hold my emotions back. That was such a painful experience.

"The Sikh soldiers, who were coming in on trains and stopping at my station, kept asking me, 'Tell us, what should we do now?' But I advised them not to act in emotion, otherwise we would all get killed, too. 'We have to be organized and do something collectively,' I said.

"My superior officer, who was a Hindu, kept telling me, 'Why are you stopping the Sikh soldiers and not letting them go to their assigned duties?' I told him, 'The mobs are out to get them and they will be killed if I let them go.' Then I started using my authority and sanctioned these Sikh soldiers' leave applications. I told them not to go any place at all, to stay right where they were. In the two days following the punishment of Indira Gandhi, I must have stopped around two hundred young Sikh soldiers, who otherwise would probably have gotten killed traveling on trains. Some amongst them were so young and innocent, so unaware; they said, 'Why are you stopping us from the performance of our duties? We might be held negligent, so let us go to our posts.' But I told them, 'You can only be punished for negligence if you arrive alive there. You will likely get killed on the way, so life is more important than duty in this case.'

"After that episode I decided to get baptized as a Sikh. My whole family was baptized along with me. The Hindu officer in charge, however, got annoyed at this action and had me transferred to Rajasthan. I stayed there for almost a year, and through my newfound missionary zeal about forty out of the seventy Sikhs in that area started to grow their beards and gave up alcohol. Finally my Hindu OC there got annoyed as well and sent me off to the Madras regiment, where there were no Sikhs at all. After some time the OC there, also a Hindu, told me to either stop my religious activities or take retirement. 'You can't stay in the army preaching Sikhism,' he said. I had been transferred three times within two years, and it was difficult for my family, too.

"So I went back to my home in Bhatinda and started a small-scale business selling refrigerators. By 1989 I became known in my area and I became press secretary for the Akali Dal, the political party of the Sikhs, for my district. After a year I became that organization's general secretary. We tried to work for the Sikhs through democratic means, demonstrations, processions, rallies and so on, to convince the government that we have some rights as Indian citizens, too. We argued that our rights should not be violated.

"One time when our Akali Dal leader, Simranjit Singh Mann, was visiting Bhatinda to attend a rally, police surrounded us and without any warning started beating participants in the rally. Simranjit Singh Mann was beaten so badly he was taken to the hospital and stayed there for many days. I myself was wounded when I tried to protect Mann, and then I was arrested as well. The police charged us with canes, and nine people were seriously injured, one succumbing to his injuries later on.

"After that we used to try to help the villages where people had been victims of police harassment, and we used to help the families of those killed, imprisoned, or tortured with money or in other ways. Once we conducted an agitation for a sewer system for Bhatinda, which had been part of municipal planning but was eaten up by corruption. We were successful in that agitation.

"At that time, I still believed that things could be achieved through the political process. That was what I thought, so I didn't participate in the militant side of the Sikh struggle. But the price for that adherence to peaceful means was that I was taken to the police station, beaten mercilessly, and tortured there.

"When I and others protested another Indian army action against the Sikhs, Operation Black Thunder, we wore black flags on our arms and tied cloths around our mouths. I was arrested and thrown in jail for one month for that. We were not permitted to even hold peaceful rallies or conventions. Whatever date would be announced for our action, we would be arrested before that and we would not be allowed to reach that engagement. The police and the army were disrupting the peaceful process which we at that time believed in.

"Youngsters in our organization, who were being harassed day in and day out, they went into hiding and most of them ended up in the armed struggle. Since I knew them, they used to come out of hiding to visit me and I provided them shelter and food. Some of these freedom fighters revealed during interrogation that they had been to my house, and the police started harassing me continously.

"Then in February 1992 the government ordered elections in Punjab, and on the call of the freedom fighters the whole Sikh nation decided to boycott the elections. The militants, our sons and daughters, were supported by all the different factions and organizations, and we all stood in solidarity against Indian oppression.

"We were going to hold a meeting about the boycott of the elections in Bhatinda on 8 February, so on 6 February I was arrested. For three or four days I was tortured by the Criminal Investigation Agency in Bhatinda. They tortured me so badly that I started passing blood while urinating. My family didn't know where I was or what had happened to me.

"The officers accused me of helping in the boycott of the elections by getting some pamphlets published. They said, 'OK, we'll give you your Khalistan,' in a taunting tone. They accused me of harboring militants and telling them to come to me. I said that as general secretary of the Akali Dal (Mann) party for our district anybody who was a grieved party or in need of assistance could come to me. And anybody who comes to a Sikh's house must be provided food and shelter. This is simply the moral duty of every Sikh.

"It was also our tradition that Sikh Gurus had sacrificed their own sons, their own children, and Sikh martyrs went through all kinds of difficulties but still upheld their values. This Sikh history was my only strength during the time I spent under torture.

"Then the officers started telling me that I would be killed and that they had a list of all my relations, and they would all be killed, too. They wanted me to tell them all the names and hideouts of the militants with whom I had contact.

"I was stripped naked and kept that way during all these days in custody at the interrogation center. They used to hold me by my hair and beat me, and insult me by saying things about the Sikh religion. Eventually I was moved from the detention center to jail, where I was charged under TADA. I was bonded out after a month.

"When I came out of jail I went into hiding, and then eventually I decided to get out of India altogether. I thought for a while of joining the militant movement, but as I have a wife and children I thought that they would be harassed and humiliated if I did that. So I thought it might be more appropriate to continue to serve my nation in another capacity.

"As there is complete censorship on news media in India, it's hard to get the truth out. For us overseas, our duty should be to educate people about what is going on and let our people's sorrow be known to the world.

"Our only desire is to be a free people and to join the galaxy of free nations of the world. I believe in peaceful means. But I also believe that the militants have not gone in for militancy as a choice. After I came to this country one of my nephews was killed in an encounter. The other is in hiding and might be killed any day now. What can we do if our children have taken to that? I think we have no choice but to join them.

"Now this is the time for all the nations to stand up for the sake of humanity, for the sake of justice. They should not be silent and they should not allow the great Sikh nation to be killed in the hands of a brutal regime. This is the time for the world to speak up."

His wife: "I inherited religious teachings and a religious faith. My grandfather was a devout person, and he actually wrote a biography of one of our Sikh saints. My father was in the army. He served in the army for twenty-eight years and was a kind of preacher.

"When I got married I learned that my husband was not really of a religious bent at all. Due to his influence I also veered away from the religious path. It was a fire of modernism which engulfed me in those days! But when we heard that the Golden Temple had been attacked, we were really shocked. And when we saw that the Sikhs inside the Golden Temple resisted the Indian army with so much courage and bravery, my husband got convinced that some spiritual strength comes from Sikhism which can stand against any odds.

"Blue Star made a complete change of heart in my husband. He stopped trimming his beard and later proposed that we should get baptized. He started reading a lot and there was a total change in his behavior. It was like a threshold had been crossed that we didn't even know had been there.

"Though I had a yearning for religion right from my childhood, after my husband got converted we both were strengthened in our resolve and we got baptized. When he went back to his army post after that he got harassed and eventually decided to retire from the army. Then he started working for Akali Dal, the Sikh political party.

"As for me, I was a teacher of vernacular Hindi. I also used to teach my students about how they could defend their religion and what they needed to do. Some of the people opposed me and came to see my principal about the things I taught. Sometimes people would write my name on the walls, and whenever anything bad happened they would say I was behind it. And while I was teaching, I also helped my husband in his political work and became convinced that the militant struggle was the only way to obtain our rights.

"Militants don't come out of the womb of a mother. It is the system, the circumstances, that have converted them. The young boys, those who have time to read, to enjoy life, to travel, if they are in hiding all the time awaiting the hour of their deaths who can say what they will choose to do? Who chooses that kind of life? It is a compulsion. We fully sympathize with them, and we support them since we believe that they have no choice.

"The Indian government is our enemy, and it is clear that we cannot live with them. If they are calling us terrorists or something like that, it doesn't make much difference as they are our enemy and they can be expected to say anything. That only makes us more firm in our resolve that we can't live with these people and the only solution for us is an independent sovereign nation.

"After my husband came to the United States, police raided our house many times. They used to jump over the walls, come inside, and ask whether militants come to the house. One day one police official, drunk, came along with four constables. They said that my husband in the United States was active in political activities there and none of my relatives would be spared. He asked for a list of all my relatives, saying that he would keep it in his pocket. He said that if any of his bodyguards or any of his police were hurt in any way he would kill all the relatives on that list.

"I got scared on that night and thought it would not be safe to stay there. I thought they would deal with me as they deal with others, and that is that they enter the houses and rape the women. So I left my house with my children and went into hiding. Five or six days later police came and broke into my house. They took all the furniture and everything else that was left. I was glad I wasn't there or I would have been raped or humiliated in other ways. Thank God my honor was saved.

"I don't fear being killed but I don't want to be dishonored. My husband and I haven't come to this country out of fear, but out of desire that the world should know what is going on over there. There is such firm control in India that the news about Punjab is totally suppressed.

"We expect that the government of the United States and all human rights groups should help us in achieving our freedom. We are very broad-minded people, we are very nice people, we will have a nation of noble people. We will even forgive those who have done these wrongs, but at all costs we must get our freedom. We want to live in dignity and honor. That's what the whole Sikh nation wants.

"As for my sons, I'll feel proud if they get killed for a holy cause. Everybody has to die, but those who die for honor never die, for they are immortal.

"When some Sikh women were in the custody of the Mughal emperor in Lahore their small sons were put to death right in front of their eyes. They were thrown onto swords and their bodies were chopped up and made into garlands, and the Sikh women had to wear these necklaces made of the chopped bodies of their children. With folded hands they thanked God that their children had stood the test of their faith and had died bravely.

"I have only two sons, and if they get sacrificed it will be the great grace of the Guru that we will be able to give back what was the gift of God to us.

"As for Operation Blue Star, I can say that it gave us a rude awakening. It became clear just what the place of Sikhs was in India. Nobody could avoid facing up to the basic fact that we had no safe home there any-more. I therefore thank the Indian government for that."

5
WHY KHALISTAN?

WHAT LED UP TO THE POINT at which Jarnail Singh Bhindranwale and his companions went down in a hail of gunfire at the Akal Takht, spawning what became the militant movement for Khalistan? The history of the ten Gurus and the development of Sikhism during the Guru period provides the ideological base for Khalistani activism, but a series of events that took place from the death of the last Guru in 1708 until the rise of Bhindranwale in the 1970s pushed a section of the Sikh community to a position of readiness for militancy, to a point at which the rhetorical seeds of members of the Damdami Taksal and the Akhand Kirtni Jatha found fertile soil.

CAUSES PROXIMATE AND ULTIMATE

The link between religion and politics in Sikh tradition was made firm through the succession of Gurus from Guru Nanak to Guru Gobind Singh. But some of the greatest heroes of the Sikhs lived after this period, when Guru had become enshrined not in individuals but in the dual *Guru Granth/Guru Panth* formulation. The first was Banda Singh, a hermit who was converted to Sikhism by Guru Gobind Singh (Banda means "slave" [to Guru]). Banda Singh led Khalsa warriors in a raid on Sirhind, whose ruler had killed the Guru's sons, and was titled "Bahadur" (brave) by Guru Gobind Singh. After Guru Gobind Singh's death, Banda Singh Bahadur and his band took over most of southeastern Punjab, where they proclaimed a republic in the name of the Gurus. They fought with Mughal emperor Bahadur Shah and finally were starved into submission by his successor. Banda Singh Bahadur was eventually marched to

Delhi in chains, forced to kill his own infant son, and executed along with other Sikh prisoners.

Banda Singh Bahadur is particularly important in Sikh history because he was the first individual who was not a Guru but nevertheless assumed a leadership role. His fearlessness in battle and stoicism through his defeat eclipses, in Sikh minds, other aspects of his career like his multiple wives and his regal lifestyle. (It should by now be clear that courage eclipses a lot for militant Sikhs. As one leader commented when news of the Chechen rebellion broke out in 1994, "They are fighting with so much courage, they must be right.") But Banda Singh's band of warriors was certainly the first real guerilla force—led not by a Guru but by an ordinary human being—to which contemporary militants can look for inspiration.

By the late 1730s the Khalsa had regrouped under Nawab Kapur Singh, who gathered local chieftains together in a kind of coalition force called the Dal Khalsa, the Khalsa army. (The militant group started by Gajinder Singh in modern times took its name from this group.) The Dal Khalsa's fame stems from its bloody encounters with the Afghans, who were attacking the Mughals from the west at the same time as the British had begun their encroachment from the east. The so-called "lesser" holocaust (*Chota Ghallughara*) of the Sikhs occurred in 1747 when Sikhs were slaughtered at Kahnuwan by the Mughal forces from Lahore. In 1762 the Dal Khalsa faced a different enemy, the Afghan forces of Ahmed Shah Abdali, at Malerkotla, a battle in which thousands of Sikhs—possibly as many as twenty thousand—were killed in what is now called the "greater" holocaust (*Vadda Ghallughara*). After the massacre, Ahmed Shah Abdali attacked Amritsar, destroying the Golden Temple Complex. But the Sikhs rose up in response and eventually defeated the Afghans, putting the whole of Punjab under Sikh control for the first time in history.

The history of the Dal Khalsa and the Afghan wars is important for understanding what the Khalistani militancy has become today, not only because it ended up creating the only Sikh state that has ever existed, but because the organization of guerilla forces in the Dal Khalsa was a direct foreshadowing of how Khalistani militants are organized today. The Dal Khalsa was not really an "army" (*dal*) in the conventional sense; it was a loose confederation of independent administrative districts, or *misls*. At the height of the Dal Khalsa there were twelve such *misls* with their own militias, varying in size from over ten thousand to just a few hundred members. They would get together when military exigency demanded coordination of action but otherwise acted with relative autonomy. The leaders of the militias that comprised the Dal Khalsa also got together on specific religious occasions and took decisions that were sanctified by the presence of Guru Granth Sahib and then proclaimed as *gurumatta* or "wishes of the Guru." This model was obviously successful in confrontation with the Afghans and fits well the Punjabi cultural characteristics of individualism and self-reliance while drawing on the authority of religion to convey decisions to the population as a whole. It is less clear, as we shall see, that it is the most effective strategy for Khalistani Sikhs confronting India today.[1]

There is a sideline to the story of the Dal Khalsa, however, which is worth narrating, for it demonstrates the very deep awareness of history that permeates the Sikh community. The chieftains of Malerkotla, site of the *Vadda Ghallughara*, were members of the Sirhind court, and the nawab of Malerkota and his forces had participated in battles against Guru Gobind Singh at Anandpur Sahib. But when the governor of Sirhind, Wazir Khan, took Guru Gobind Singh's two younger sons into custody, the nawab of Malerkotla intervened on their behalf. Stating that they refused to bow before any other than *Akal Purukh* (God), the two young boys prompted the wrath of Wazir Khan, who proposed to execute them. But the nawab of Malerkotla, one Sher Mohammed Khan, pointed out that while the execution of a rebel like Guru Gobind Singh would be in accordance with Islamic law, there was no provision for the execution of children. They were bricked up inside a wall nonetheless, but Sikhs have never forgotten the attempt of Sher Mohammed Khan to intercede on behalf of the Guru's sons. In continuing gratitude for this episode (and in spite of the "holocaust" of the Afghan wars), Sikhs protected the Muslims of Malerkotla during the bloodshed of Partition in 1947, when Muslims were killing Sikhs and Hindus in west Punjab and Sikhs and Hindus were slaughtering Muslims in east Punjab. As a result of Sikh protection during the Partition massacres, Malerkotla remains today an idiosyncratic town with a substantial Muslim presence. It has in the recent past elected a Muslim MLA to the Punjab Assembly on the Akali ticket, and he wore an Akali-blue turban despite his Muslim name and affiliation.

The empire of Ranjit Singh, established amid the contending Rajput, Gurkha, and Maratha powers of the region, made its peace with the advancing British by signing a treaty of friendship in 1809. Although Maharaja Ranjit Singh was a Sikh, his administration incorporated not only persons of various ethnic and religious communities of the subcontinent but also stray Europeans. He made large endowments to *gurudwaras*, and under his administration the upper floors of the Akal Takht, which would later shelter Bhindranwale and his band, were added. The Harmandir Sahib was covered in its defining gold leaf. The separation of church and state in the empire meant a general atmosphere of tolerance and ecumenicism, however. Most would agree with Mahmud Ali's assessment: "He had raised the most modern native instrument of state in 19th century India."[2] This was despite being illiterate, enamored of strong drink, dazzling jewels (like the Koh-i-Noor diamond), and women.

Ranjit Singh built up a technically advanced, unified army on what was left of the Dal Khalsa guerilla forces, with a clear chain of command from the centralized authority down to the *jathas,* or brigades, after which the *jathas* of recent activism are named. He began a vigorous program of expansion from Kashmir in the north to the Khyber in the west (regions where Ranjit Singh's reign is remembered less fondly than in the Punjab heartland). But in the east were the British, and after Ranjit Singh's death his less effective successors eventually ended up ceding the empire to the expanding colonialists. (The last, Maharaja Dalip Singh, was converted to Christianity in his youth, but later re-embraced Sikhism.)

There is an extensive historical literature, of course, about how the British made their way into India, principality by principality, state by state. The long and short of the interaction between the Sikhs and the British was that a series of battles were fought (identified as the First and the Second Anglo-Sikh Wars[3]) and the end result was that Punjab was annexed to the Crown. The fighting abilities of the Sikhs were not lost on the British, however, despite their eventual loss of sovereignty. (Some of the British observers at the time fueled the mythos of Sikh soldiery, drawn on still now for pithy quotes about Sikh military prowess.[4]) When they took over, they lost no time in recruiting those top-notch fighters to their own military endeavors. Already by 1857, the time of the first major mutiny against British rule, Sikh troops from the princely states were serving with the British Indian Army, and after that Sikhs came to serve in that army out of all proportion to their numbers in the total population. This trend continued even after independence; Khushwant Singh notes that at some points Sikhs comprised a fifth of the total Indian army.[5]

After the threatening but unsuccessful mutiny, a special Viceroy's Commission was created to reform the armed services, along with a host of other reforms intended to thwart the possibility of such rebellion in future. The reform of the army benefited Sikhs in particular, who were labeled a "martial race" in the British biopolitical scheme. A "Punjabisation" of the infantry regiments resulted in the number of Sikh battalions increasing from twenty-eight to fifty-seven during the period 1862–1914 (while all other groups except the Nepalese Gurkhas, another "martial race," declined). During World War I, numbers of Sikh troops fighting for the British increased from 35,000 to 100,000. More to the point in terms of the history of Sikh identity, the British capitalized on and encouraged the observance of the five K's by Sikh soldiers. This preference for *amritdhari* Sikhs by British recruiters itself encouraged initiations into the Khalsa among a population increasingly dependent on income from service in the armed forces.

At the same time as martial Sikh identity received this military boost from the colonialist power, a reform movement called the Arya Samaj in which many Sikhs had originally been interested took a decided turn toward Hindu missionization. Arya Samaj activities focused on absorbing Sikhs into the broader Hindu community prompted the creation of a Sikh organization, the Singh Sabha or "assembly of lions," which would assert a separate Sikh identity and work toward purging Sikhism of various Hindu elements that had crept into it. (A famous pamphlet of the Singh Sabha movement was called "We Are Not Hindus.") The Singh Sabha movement represented the consolidation of a particular, relatively uniform understanding of what Sikhism was, which some scholars emphasize was imposed on what had been previously a much more fluid situation.[6] Significant also is the fact that the Singh Sabha, by the turn of the century, had become powerful not only in India but among Sikhs overseas, too. The Chief Khalsa Diwan, set up to coordinate all the branches of the Singh Sabha, was established in Amritsar, but a Khalsa Diwan movement that would link *gurudwaras* across North America was begun as well. From this early twinkling of modern Sikh identity, then, emphasized as uniform, unique, and separate from Hinduism, the *panth* was envisioned as a transnational entity, with a base in Punjab, to be sure, but with important tentacles extending across oceans.

Of particular interest is the formation, at about the same time, of the primarily Sikh Gadhr or "mutiny" movement, which had an important base in northern California. The Gadhr movement against colonialism gathered steam after what was called the Komagata Maru incident, when a Japanese ship loaded with potential Sikh immigrants was refused landing in Vancouver and sent back to India, where twenty-three of the returnees were shot as troublemakers and others formed the nucleus of an armed resistance movement. The entire Ghadr episode was critical to later developments in two ways. First, it underscored the important role played by the Sikh diaspora and the immigration policies of the countries that hosted it, with networks set up during Ghadr times still used today by Khalistani activists abroad. Second, the remnants of the Ghadr rebellion in India formed the basis of what became the Babbar Akalis, who rejected the Gandhian scheme of nonviolence as a means of achieving independence. (Today's Babbar Khalsa was named after them.)[7]

The potentially dangerous nationalism represented by the Ghadr rebellion drew British and Sikhs apart at home in India, even as Sikhs were being sacrificed in large numbers in British interests during World War I. On April 13, 1919, came the straw that broke the camel's back: several thousand people had gathered in a walled compound called Jallianwalla Bagh in Amritsar to protest the enactment of the Rowlatt Bills set up to enable the government to curb political activism by circumventing normal legal procedures. Sikhs also gathered nearby to commemorate the birthday of the Khalsa. The protestors in Jallianwalla Bagh were fired upon by Brigadier General R. E. H. Dyer of the British army. Nearly four hundred were killed and more than twelve hundred wounded in this massacre, which permanently alienated much of the Sikh population from the British.[8] (Michael O'Dwyer, governor of Punjab at the time, was assassinated more than twenty years later in London, a fact which Khalistani Sikhs frequently repeat as an illustration of their patience in exacting revenge.)

A Sikh movement was started called the Akali Dal ("eternal army") whose aim was to reform the *gurudwara* system, in particular replacing the British-nominated administrators of major shrines with Sikhs' own choices. (The fact that the Akal Takht had presented Dyer with a robe of honor after the slaughter at Jallianwalla Bagh made clear to many Sikhs the British influence on the major shrines.) In addition, officers at local *gurudwaras* had inherited their positions, and corruption was rampant. The committee the Akali Dal set up, the Shiromani Gurudwara Prabandhak Committee (Apex Temple Management Committee, SGPC), eventually did take over control of the *gurudwaras* through the Sikh Gurudwara Act of 1925, and this "religious parliament of the Sikhs" remains a powerful force in Sikh political life today.[9] In the campaign for the SGPC, nonviolent demonstrations by the Akalis had resulted in nearly four hundred dead, two thousand wounded, and thirty thousand jailed. The nonviolence of the Akali Dal in this period is cited today as a counter-example to the claim that Sikhs are somehow inherently violent or too quick on the trigger. Sikhs also participated heavily in the renowned civil disobedience movement led by Mahatma Gandhi.

At the same time, however, there were Sikhs who did choose to take up arms. The most famous among these was Bhagat Singh, who killed a British policeman who had assaulted a nationalist leader. Bhagat Singh was executed for this act of "terrorism" in 1931, and many Sikhs today feel he is unjustly neglected in most histories of the anticolonial movement.[10]

During World War II, many Sikhs continued to serve with valor in the British Indian Army. Others, however, played a crucial role in setting up the Indian National Army, which under the guidance of Germany and Japan would attempt a challenge to the Allied powers in South Asia in 1941–1942. Some Sikhs joined the Hindu-dominated but explicitly secular Congress party, while others went with the nearly wholly Sikh Akali Dal. After the war, these conflicts within the Sikh community were brought to a head in the discussions surrounding independence and partition.

The fact that the Akalis demanded a separate Sikh homeland in 1946 but never effectively negotiated for such a state is seen by Khalistanis as the great missed opportunity of history. An Akali Dal resolution of March 1946 asserted a separate Sikh state as a primary goal:

Whereas the Sikhs being attached to Punjab by intimate bonds of holy shrines, prosperity, language, traditions and history claim it as their homeland and holy-land and which the British took as a "trust" from the last Sikh ruler during his minority, and whereas the entity of the Sikhs is being threatened on account of the persistent demand for Pakistan by the Muslims on the one hand and the danger of absorption by the Hindus on the other, the Executive Committee of the Shiromani Akali Dal demands, for the preservation and protection of the religious, cultural and economic rights of the Sikhs, the creation of a Sikh State.

The Cripps Mission, organized to discuss India's future with the major concerned parties, ignored the Akali demand. In the eventual Cabinet Mission Plan, Punjab was bifurcated, approximately the western two-thirds going to Muslim majority and probably Islamic Pakistan and the eastern third going to Hindu majority but avowedly secular and plural-ist India.

Mahatma Gandhi made a kind of pledge to the Sikhs at the time, which has resurfaced in the Khalistani community today. In an essay on communal unity, he wrote,

I ask you to accept my word . . . and the resolution of the Congress that it will not betray a single individual, much less a community. . . . Our Sikh friends have no reason to fear that it would betray them, for, the moment it does so, the Congress would not only thereby seal its doom but that of the country too. Moreover, the Sikhs are a brave people. They know how to safeguard their rights by exercise of arms if it should ever come to that.[11]

It should be noted that Gandhi also made many statements that Kha-listanis today find anathema, such as that all the Sikh Gurus were Hin-dus and that Sikhism is part of the broader Hindu tradition. While he believed that Indian nationalism must override communal impulses, his concurrent message that Hinduism was the ocean into which the rivers of all other faiths flow alienated the non-Hindu minorities. Khali-stani Sikhs, while drawing on Gandhi's comment about the safeguarding of rights by exercise of arms, retain a deeply ambivalent attitude to-ward him.

In the bloodshed following the partition decision, Muslims in India fled across the border to Pakistan, while Sikhs and Hindus in Pakistan fled across the other direction to India. Estimates of people killed in Punjab during what was the largest mass migration in history range from 200,000 to 500,000, with most sources going with the higher figure. And the Sikhs left behind in Pakistan some two hundred shrines, most significantly the birthplace of the founder, Guru Nanak (Nankana Sahib).

The way in which administrative districts were drawn up in post-independence India meant that Sikhs would not form a majority in any state and indeed would probably be able to elect representatives in only a few constituencies in Punjab where they were particularly concentrated. This was a central problem with the original demand for a Sikhistan—Sikhs did not form a clear majority in any particular area. This situation is, of course, one of the great inadequacies of democratic representation based on demography, as any advocate of minority rights soon learns. In independent India the situation was exacerbated by a vibrant Hindu revivalist movement called the Bharatiya Jana Sangh (ancestral to today's successful Bharatiya Janata Party, the BJP), which attempted to claim the Indian heritage as a Hindu heritage and the Indian state as a Hindu state. It was linked to the Hindu militant organization Rashtriya Swayamsevak Sangh, the RSS, one of whose members killed Mahatma Gandhi for being too conciliatory to Muslims. The Bharatiya Jana Sangh spearheaded the campaign for Hindu domination in the Punjab region by urging Hindu Punjabis to list Hindi, not Punjabi, as their mother tongue on the first national census.

This critical first census in 1951 revealed some very interesting things about Punjab. It showed the Hindu-Sikh ratio as about 62 percent to 35 percent, even though 80 percent of all the Sikhs in India resided in Punjab. (Again, the point drawn from this was that because of numbers the Sikhs might be left without effective representation.) But it also showed an important class breakdown that would become critical to the separatist insurgency today: that most of the Punjabi Sikhs lived in villages and worked in agriculture, while most of the Punjabi Hindus lived in cities and worked in trades and professions. The antagonism between farmers and urbanites finds a voice in much Khalistani narrative, as it does also in the anti-Khalistani rhetoric that typically emphasizes the unintellectual and unsophisticated quality of the militants.

The Sikhs were not the only minority group that found itself without an obvious means of representing themselves in the new democratic arena, and in 1953 Prime Minister Nehru was forced to set up a States Reorganisation Commission to see to the redrawing of boundaries on more equitable lines. Nehru was adamant, however, that in secular India such boundaries would never be drawn based on religion, and what ended up happening was that language was used as a means of drawing boundary lines around particular communities. In the Punjab case, however, because of the listing of Hindi rather than Punjabi as the mother tongue of the majority Hindu population, the commission refused to countenance a redistricting along linguistic lines.

This was the beginning of the Punjabi Suba movement, an agitation for the redrawing of state boundaries that would take up the energies of the Akali Dal for over a decade.[12] Master Tara Singh, the leader of the *morcha* (protest) for Punjabi Suba, vowed to fast unto death for this cause but ignominiously retreated from his fast at the last moment. Various other nonviolent protests arose on behalf of Punjabi Suba, but at the same time Sikhs continued to serve in the Indian armed forces well out of proportion to their percentage in the overall population. (This period is used now as an example that Sikhs know how to be "the loyal opposition" when given a chance.) It was only after Sikh soldiers' "dazzling" performance in the 1965 war with Pakistan that concessions were made with regard to Punjabi Suba, the state of Punjab. From the viewpoint of Sikhs, their loyalty through the war had been rewarded.

The same retired colonel who called the performance of the Sikhs during the 1965 war "dazzling" told me that it is the utter disillusionment of Sikh officers in the Indian army today that carries the most serious portents for further trouble. They feel, he asserted, that their service through multiple wars since independence is at this point not only not being rewarded but is being mocked because of suspicion of their Khalistani sympathies. This suspicion itself, he said, which results in being passed over for promotions and otherwise side-stepped in the military scheme of things, is much more a source of alienation than the actual Khalistan movement ever would have been. A second retired officer, also a colonel, entirely agreed with this assessment. Particularly after having helped suppress the massive desertions and mutinies occurring among Sikh troops after Operation Blue Star, this second individual said, Sikh officers might have expected more from the government they chose to serve.

With the accession of Indira Gandhi to power in 1966, Punjab's boundaries were redrawn, with the Hindi-speaking plains in the east becoming what is now the state of Haryana, the Himalayan foothill region becoming Himachal Pradesh, and the remainder becoming Punjab. There were Hindu-Sikh riots in several cities following the announcement of Punjabi Suba. But after the redrawing, Sikhs constituted 56 percent, a bare majority, in Punjab state, with Sikh minorities in the other two new entities. The city of Chandigarh was appointed as the joint capital of Punjab and Haryana, which has been a point of contention ever since.

The dramatic fast-unto-death for Chandigarh accomplished by Darshan Pheruman in 1969 represents one of the few martyrdoms by fasting (not traditionally a Sikh tactic) in Sikh history. His fast also redeemed

5. Map of Punjab showing places mentioned in the text. (Courtesy of Steve Bicknell, University of Maine, 1996.)

Sikh honor after the failed fast of Tara Singh, and he is considered a hero today. His example was followed by Sant Fateh Singh, Master Tara Singh's replacement as Akali Dal leader, who vowed a similar death if Chandigarh was not awarded to Punjab alone. But Indira Gandhi interceded, suggesting that Chandigarh be exchanged for two Hindu-majority districts in current Punjab, Abohar and Fazilka. Fateh Singh broke his fast, but the issue remains unresolved (and still is). Neither Punjab nor Harayana wanted to give up what they had. The same was true for water control, important for both irrigation and electricity; the three rivers of Indian Punjab—Beas, Ravi and Sutlej—are scarce resources in the region, and everybody wants them. In a democratic system, pleasing the most numerous or most important constituents can sometimes subvert the cause of justice. Many Sikhs came to feel that the central government and Indira Gandhi had sold out the Sikhs of Punjab, with their agriculturalists' vital dependence on water, for other interests. Today, after both peaceful negotiations and horrific bloodshed, crucial water questions like the digging of the Sutlej-Yamuna Link Canal, which would divert Punjab's water to Haryaṇa, remain unresolved. (Two engineers working on the SYL canal were killed by Khalistani militants in 1990 to publicize the continuing importance of the water question.)

The Green Revolution was highly successful in Punjab in technical terms, but it created its own set of problems as well. Primary among these was that advances in agricultural technology made cultivators more dependent than ever before on factors beyond their immediate control, such as the price of fertilizer, the availability of diesel fuel, and the accessibility of credit. The level of education skyrocketed as Punjab's overall wealth grew, but employment opportunities for educated people remained restricted. Cheap migrant labor brought in from other states pushed Punjab's unskilled work force into unemployment as well. The conditions that developed were in a sense an explosion waiting to happen: farmers with a strong cultural tradition of self-reliance found themselves suddenly beholden to the decisions of others, and a growing number of educated people without jobs milled about the cities. When these people belong to a religious community historically perceived as having suffered discrimination at the hands of the majority community—which dominates the government now making the decisions that affect Sikhs—tension is bound to arise.

In 1973 the demand for Chandigarh, the issues surrounding water and hydroelectric power, and the questions relating to agriculture and economic opportunity in Punjab were expressed in a document drawn up by the Akali Dal called the Anandpur Sahib Resolution, referred to as the ASR. (Anandpur Sahib was the place where Guru Gobind Singh is believed to have created the Khalsa, a historical resonance to which Sikhs would be particularly sensitive.) The ASR also called for a general devolution of power from the central government to the states, and Indira Gandhi treated it as a secessionist document. Nowhere in it was a separate Sikh state mentioned, however (Harchand Singh Longowal, the Akali Dal president, said clearly at that time that "undoubtedly the Sikhs have the same nationality as other Indians"[13]), and its push toward a looser federation of states has been echoed in other parts of India as well. In the current Khalistani context, the Anandpur Sahib Resolution seems a rather moderate assertion of rights within the overall framework of India. But there was one big problem with the ASR, aside from the question of whether its demands could feasibly be met: that was the failure of the Akali Dal to poll a majority of the people in Punjab, even though it claimed to speak for all of the Sikhs. (The Sikhs were only 56 percent of the population, and many of them, especially urbanites and non-Jats, voted for Congress.[14]) How could the central government of a country committed to democracy based not on communal representation but on individual votes accede to demands like those put forth in the ASR? Most Indians agreed that it couldn't. But the manner in which the demands were dealt with inflamed the sense of indignity of many Akalis, who felt they were not being listened to, and pushed some toward further extremism. A former state finance minister residing in London, Dr. Jagjit Singh Chauhan, started a cry for Khalistan. Only a few joined him at the time, and the cry was widely seen as an absurd pipedream.

The discussion surrounding the Anandpur Sahib Resolution was abruptly halted by Indira Gandhi's imposition of a state of emergency in 1975. The calls for devolution of power were met with an assertion of centralized power that shocked the world. In Punjab, resistance to the Emergency was open and protracted. The Akali Dal, newly energized, led the nonviolent *morcha* for democratic freedoms. The Damdami Taksal, as we have seen, joined in this nonviolent protest and eventually spawned, with some members of the Akhand Kirtni Jatha, a violent one.

The framing of resistive discourse in the Sikh community around religion, brought most fully to the fore in the current militancy, is a phenomenon that must be placed in a broader historical context to make full sense of it. This contextualizing is exactly what most accounts of Sikh separatism fail to do, which results in making the insistence on religious orthodoxy among Khalistanis look inexplicable in terms other than backwardness, intolerance, and fanaticism. It appears "fundamentalist" particularly against the backdrop, first, of the state of India, which is explicitly committed to secularism, and, second, of the dominant Hindu tradition, which is explicitly committed to tolerance. Why the vehement assertions of orthodoxy in this situation? one wonders.

The problem is that neither of these backdrops to Sikh militancy—the Indian secular state and the tolerant Hindu community—is actually what it seems to be at first glance. It is becoming clearer to many observers, for example, that the philosophical tolerance of the Hindu tradition, emphasized by many Western admirers, is not in fact matched by a social or political tolerance for non-Hindu groups. Though there is an extensive literature emphasizing the recency of the kind of tribalistic Hinduism expressed in the orange-robed mobs tearing apart the Babri Masjid, in fact a kind of ethnic exclusivism has been a persistent undercurrent in Hindu tradition.[15] Ainslee Embree, in his important *Utopias in Conflict*, recognizes that this aspect of the Hindu tradition has played a central role in the communal conflicts that have wracked the subcontinent. He notes that the philosophical willingness to accept many kinds of truths as meaningful is the source of the "mistaken" notion of Hindu tolerance, which assumes a live-and-let-live generosity. In fact, a more appropriate explanation of Hindu tolerance would be that in this tradition various kinds of truths and their accompanying social practices can be "encapsulated" within a broader Hindu umbrella, as long as there is willingness to accept the premises on which the encapsulation is based.[16] So Hindus are quite ready to claim Sikhs, Buddhists, and Jains as part of their own community; indeed, there are even those who talk of "Hindu Muslims," a phrase that, for Muslims, who do *not* accept the premises of the overarching framework, is ridiculous, insulting, and sacreligious.

The result is a situation of miscommunication, in which Hindus think they are being generous in welcoming others to the fold, but those others feel they are the objects of a kind of spiritual imperialism. When the Arya Samaj started its campaign of *shuddhi* or purification in Punjab, so that Sikhs who had lapsed from the Hindu fold and become polluted through their noncaste practices could rejoin the family, it saw itself as extending a welcome to long-lost brothers and sisters. Singh Sabha activists, by contrast, saw it as a high-handed attempt to eradicate a religious and moral tradition that does not consider intercaste interaction as degrading but as uplifting. They looked at the historical example of Buddhism, which was absorbed into Hinduism in ancient times, and determined that Sikhism would not suffer the same fate.

Were India a secular state on the Western model, this aspect of Hindu tradition might not be as important as, in fact, it is. But the conception of secularism on which the Indian state is based is different from the "wall of separation" of church and state we usually mean when we use the term. The "secular" ideal of India is expressed in the motto *Sarva Dharma Sambhava*, "Let All Religions Prosper." The government has in fact not stayed out of the business of religion but attempts to be evenhanded in its treatment of various religious groups. The problem is that in numerical terms the Hindu community clearly dominates (83 percent), and top-caste Brahmins serve in high government posts utterly out of proportion to their numbers.[17] Thus a definition of even-handedness on the part of the government can oddly reinforce the idea of "encapsulation" of various minority groups as described by Embree—the terms of welcome being set by the largely forward-caste Hindu government officials. P. C. Upadyaya prefers to call Indian secularism "majoritarianism," the domination of an avowedly even-handed system by the majority community.[18] It makes the minorities queasy, and the fear that the system could slide into outright Hindu communalism is a real one. When Hindu revivalists today talk about the Hindu *rashtra*, the Hindu nation, and make being a Hindu equivalent to being an Indian, those Indians who don't want to be Hindus find themselves in the position of being potential traitors to India.

The entanglement of religion and politics is not, then, something limited to the Sikh community. To ignore the religion/politics axis in the majority community wrongly places the burden to defend or explain this nexus on the activist minority alone. When we ask why the Sikhs express religious and political grievances in joint terms, we have to ask at the same time how it is that religious and political domination are intertwined in the Indian state. Only then can we make some sense of why the political separatism of the Khalistani Sikhs has become tightly linked to the assertion of religious orthodoxy. The fact that rebellion against the Indian state is today fractured into multiple regional and sectarian movements itself points to the success of the system, which refracts discontent into myriad shattered and hence powerless pieces.

The complicity of Western academia with the ideology of foward-caste Hinduism also interferes with a realistic appraisal of what India is as a civilization and as a nation state. In anthropology this bias has been expressed in two major ways: first, in the "relativistic" understanding of caste as a consensual hierarchy rather than as a system of exploitation,[19] and, second, in the attribution of current communal conflicts to colonial intervention rather than to the long-term power dynamics of Hindu civilization. These two arenas are linked, of course, and amount to a forward-caste denial of its own role in perpetuating inequality and conflict. Interestingly, while a whole field of "subaltern studies" in India has appropriately challenged the harmony-and-tolerance conception of caste, the progressive scholars who comprise it have also been more interested in dissecting the disruption brought about by colonization than pursuing questions of archaeology and ancient history. But, as Sheldon Pollock notes,

domination did not enter India with European colonialism. Quite the contrary, gross asymmetries of power—the systematic exclusion from access to material and nonmaterial resources of large sections of the population—appear to have characterized India in particular times and places over the last three millennia and have formed the background against which ideological power, intellectual and spiritual resistance, and many forms of physical and psychological violence crystallized.[20]

One such crystallization was Sikhism itself, and another is the more tightly condensed crystal of the Khalistani insurgency. When Sant Jarnail Singh Bhindranwale, Sukhdev Singh Babbar, Amrik Singh, Shabeg

Singh, and others started their campaign against the Indian government, it was against a proximate backdrop of unresolved ASR claims and an increased sense of disillusionment with democratic process, which when it worked seemed to end up with Sikhs' not achieving the representation they thought they needed, and when it didn't work ended up with the dictatorship known as Emergency rule. But it was also against the ultimate backdrop of communal conflict on the subcontinent, which gave Sikhs a historical justification to fear for the future of their religion in a Hindu-dominated state. These leaders had the entire history of Sikhism to draw on for models for their resistance, from the lives of the Gurus to guerilla rebels like Banda Singh Bahadur, from whose movement eventually sprung an empire. The fact that the majority of the people of Punjab, and even the majority of the Sikhs, did not support them in their endeavors was not a deterrent but was if anything a potent symbol of just how far the Sikh *panth* had sunk. After they provoked the wrath of the Indian government in 1984, the *panth*, in fact, rallied round. The Khalistani militancy was born.

"A LITERARY MAN"

Harpal Singh had come to talk with me about "the Punjab problem," which I was told he viewed a little bit differently from most of the people with whom I was talking. He was interested not so much in Sikhism per se but in *Punjabiyat*, the Punjabi culture or Punjabi nation. Since Punjabi nationalism and Sikh revivalism have become intertwined in the struggle for an independent Khalistan in Indian Punjab, this other, usually submerged angle is of considerable interest. Whereas Iqbal Singh, the *granthi* of Chapter 3, feels that Punjabi nationalism has in some ways contaminated the more universalistic message of Sikh religious tradition, Harpal Singh views Punjabi culture and the freedom to express it as the heart of the Khalistan movement.

The home in which I was staying had just celebrated the birth of a baby boy, named "Manbir" after Manbir Singh Chaheru, founder of the Khalistan Commando Force. It was a place where Sikhs sympathetic to the Khalistan movement drifted in and out, not too far from the *gurudwara* that forms the epicenter of the local Sikh community. Blue balloons proclaiming "It's a boy!" hung incongruously in front of the ubiquitous painting of the destroyed Akal Takht, and crepe paper draped in front of the equally ubiquitous portrait of Guru Nanak. Bhindranwale, in the dining room, remained unadorned.

I asked Harpal Singh to tell me his story. I was especially interested in his description of himself as "a literary man." "I'm not a fighter, like these guys," he had said. "I'm a thinking person." So I looked forward to hearing how Harpal Singh had come to embrace the idea of Khalistan.

"My family had originally come from Pakistan," he began in fluent English, settling into the sofa, "but they went over to Amritsar in 1947. I lived there as well as in Uttar Pradesh and Bombay, as my father was in the military. Then he bought some land and settled down to do agriculture."

"How was it that you came to be interested in literary matters?" I inquired.

"As I was growing up I used to go to the library regularly to read newspapers, magazines, and books. I got this habit of reading from my mother, who used to read the Holy Book every morning and every evening. She would ask me to write one Shabad (verse) from the Holy Book every day.

"Anyway," he continued, "among the newspapers I used to read were *Ajit*, which was a Punjabi-language paper, and *Punjab Kesri* in Hindi. It became quite interesting to see the different ways they approached what was happening in the news. The editor of *Ajit* focused on Punjab and Punjabiyat, while the editor of *Punjab Kesri*, Lala Jagat Narain, emphasized Hindi, Hindustan, and Brahminism. I had the feeling even then that there was something wrong with *Punjab Kesri*. I mean, Punjabi is our mother language, so we must love it and we must read it. Why were we wasting all our resources to learn Hindi, to learn English, when so many people can't read and write Punjabi? Later on I learned that all across the world people want to read and write their own languages. But it wasn't so obvious to many Punjabis in those days that our language might be in trouble."

I told Harpal about my previous research on the Frisians, people in the Netherlands who have also become concerned about the erosion of the Frisian language. Yes, he said, he had heard of that. We talked a bit about Spanish-language issues in the United States, then he continued with his story.

"Anyway, in spite of these feelings about the neglect of our Punjabi language, I continued to read *Punjab Kesri*, because I wanted to see what those people were thinking. I also read some magazines oriented toward communism, because I wanted to see what that was all about as well. But I was always thinking that this communism was something Russian, not Punjabi, and maybe it did not suit us Punjabis very well."

"Did you agree with any of the things you were reading in those magazines?" I asked.

"Yes, on social issues they were very good. But then I started reading foreign periodicals like *Time* and *Newsweek*, and I started seeing how many different ways of thinking there really were in the world. I started reading novels and history books, mostly about new countries and how they got their freedom. 'Which ideas would help us Punjabis?' I thought. Is there anything here for us?"

"When you attended university," I asked, "was the medium of instruction English?" India retained this colonial habit, often to the eventual advantage of university graduates who were then well-prepared to function in the international arena. But various brands of nationalists continue to chafe at the prominence of the language of the colonialists in academia, and in Indian society generally.

"Yes," Harpal Singh answered. "I kept wondering why I could not use Punjabi in college. But I wanted to study law, and the law books are all in English. I used to fight with my professors as to why the law books could not be written in our own language. But of course, in the end I went ahead and read English. We all compromise like this, and in the end we find ourselves in a sick society.

"In 1978 a new newspaper came out in Chandigarh, the *Tribune*. There had been an English-language *Tribune* for over a hundred years, but finally somebody got the idea to put out the *Tribune* in Punjabi. I was very happy to see this and I wrote to the newspaper to congratulate them on this step. I then learned that our Punjabi-language radio station in Jallandhar was broadcast in medium waves, not in short waves like the other major stations. That meant that if somebody was living outside of Punjab, say in U.P. [Uttar Pradesh], they would not be able to hear Punjabi radio."

I told him about Frisian efforts at radio and TV broadcasting as part of the program to shore up the language.

"Eventually a TV station was set up in Amritsar. But I was sick to find out that most of the programs were broadcast in both Punjabi and Hindi. To me, my language is so very sweet, and I couldn't stand to see Punjabi mixed up with Hindi. Sometimes there would be a perfectly good word in Punjabi, but the TV station would use a Hindi word in its place. We are losing our language, I was thinking. I became preoccupied with this idea. Even when I would think to myself in Punjabi, the words seemed unbearably beautiful, because I was afraid they might disappear. But even I started using Hindi words here and there, because that Hindi influence was all around me."

I later learned that Indian Punjabis concerned with the language issue commonly perceive the Punjabi spoken by Pakistanis as more pure, since it has not been contaminated by Hindi. But Pakistani Punjabi has also, of course, been evolving, in that case due to influence from Persian and Arabic. Nevertheless, a "grass is greener on the other side" mentality persists.

Harpal Singh continued. "My friends started teasing me about my fixation on the language question. They used to call me 'Punjabi' as a nickname. 'Hey, that Punjabi guy is coming,' like that. Some of them in fact could barely speak adequate Punjabi, as they had been educated in convent schools."

Then he went on to relate how his interest in language translated into a broader interest in politics.

"In 1978 I had a job delivering papers in Muradabad U.P., and I read in the *Bharat Times* there about the confrontation between the Nirankaris and the Sikhs. I didn't know much about them until I read that they were a sect which worshiped a living person as a Guru. This pained me, as it is totally against the Sikh idea. It wasn't until I started reading materials from Sikh Missionary College that I was able to understand what was really happening with the Nirankaris."

"Had you heard of Bhindranwale at that time?" I asked.

"No. I read in the papers, that's all. I didn't have any personal involvement in any of it at that time. But I should say that I was at the same time coming to realize that there were economic issues facing our community, too. My family was in agriculture, and I saw that after such hard work we were not getting anything for our labor. The agents who take the grain from us and give it to the government have every facility—good refrigerators, new fans, nice clean clothes. But the people toiling in the fields every day have torn clothes, no refrigerators, old fans that don't work. Just tea and a piece of bread, just an old house that's too small and falling apart. This was also painful to me. I developed a great sense of sympathy for the rural people.

"After that I started taking correspondence courses from Agricultural University, Ludhiana. The books were all in English. In a course on 'Agriculture in Punjab' the textbooks were in English! I went to a big meeting there and stood before my professor, and I said that I refused to read English to learn about Punjabi agriculture. In front of all of them I tore up my books, then I went back to my seat."

"How did people react to that?" I queried.

"They were shocked, of course. The professor wrote to me that I had done a very bad thing. But I went to him and told him respectfully that he was not helping Punjab by assigning English books, not helping the farmers, the real sons of the land. The professors really couldn't understand this position because they had all gone to government schools to enter their profession. They didn't have real contact with people working on the land, although they were professors of agriculture.

"So these things—the economic part, the religious part, and the language part—started rumbling in the inner core of my soul. I had the sense that there was something deeply wrong with the way things were."

I asked, "So what did you do?"

Harpal Singh continued his narrative. "I started thinking about what should be done. I thought about communism, because many aspects of communism seemed to me to be quite good. A friend of mine was a leader in the Naxalbari movement [a Maoist agitation centered in Bengal] and we used to have long discussions about communism. He said that religion was the opium of the people, and that was a part of his philosophy that I didn't agree with. I said that what he was doing was right, but that in Punjab he would never suceed if he said that religion was an opium. We Sikhs are a product of our religion. Our first prophet Guru Nanak made us Sikhs. How could we say that what he said was wrong?"

I tried to pursue this further, as for many people seeking change in India, socialist movements remain a primary attraction, and given the Ghadr history there is a particular interest here for Sikhs.

"So you thought that although they were sincere about helping the people, the Naxalites were mistaken as far as religion was concerned. At least for Punjab, for Sikhs."

"Right, especially for Punjab. I told my friends that the Sikhs had sacrificed thousands of lives for this land. So why should they honor Lenin, why should they honor Marx here? I am not saying that Marx was wrong. He said many good things. But I say that although Marx might be good for Europe, although Lenin might be good for Russia, they are not good for Punjab. Because the blood of Sikhs has sunk into this land, and we have to remember Guru Nanak, we have to remember our religion, when we honor our land.

"If you bring a seed from Russia, you cannot get food from Punjab's land with that seed," Harpal said. "When you plant a seed in Punjab you have to remember Guru Nanak, who preached here, Guru Gobind Singh, who sacrificed his entire family here. On these matters I told the Naxalites, 'I am not with you. You cannot succeed in Punjab with this scheme.' Indeed, in the end they failed. They were sincere, they made great sacrifices, but they failed.

"I was not such a devout Sikh at that time," Harpal Singh continued. "But I knew a lot about history. I started thinking about Guru Arjun, the first martyr of Sikhism, and about Guru Tegh Bahadur, the ninth master. I started thinking about Maharaja Ranjit Singh, who had his own empire when the British arrived here. What was wrong with Punjab, I didn't know in any clear way. I am just saying that these kinds of historical thoughts were floating in my mind as I observed the problems before me.

"I traveled in Uttar Pradesh, Bihar, Bengal. The people there seemed rather lazy to me. They were doing nothing, just sleeping and lying around. I couldn't help thinking that they didn't know how to get money from their land. We Sikhs work hard and know how to make the land productive. We need more help, more electricity, more power, then what we grow we could give to the rest of India. But they say no, they will give those resources to the whole country, even though the others aren't using them properly . . ."

I interrupted this train of thought, because it was a common refrain that I found troubling.

"So the point is not that you don't want to share with the rest of India, but that you have to have the resources to make Punjab wealthy enough to share?" I asked.

But he pursued his own line of thinking. "Let me give you an example. There is a big electricity plant in Punjab, the Bhakhra Dam. It might be the biggest in Asia, I'm not sure. Anyway, the electricity from Bhakhra Dam is going to Rajasthan. To U.P., to Delhi, to other places. But not to Punjab. Why?"

"Why do you think the central government does that?" I questioned. I wanted to see just how purposeful he thought this strategy was.

"They gave us a thermal plant. The thermal plant is more expensive. The hydro projects, they are cheap. So they are getting cheap electricity for the whole country but giving us thermal plants that are costly. If a big train of coal from Bihar to Punjab gets stopped, we won't have electricity. We prefer the hyrdro electricity, but we don't get it, even though it comes from our rivers."

"Hindus as well as Sikhs would suffer from this sort of thing, wouldn't they?" I asked. "I mean, it would be the whole of Punjab that would be affected, not just one community."

"No, it turned out to be mostly directed against Sikhs, because Sikhs are in the majority in Punjab and because those Sikhs are the ones working the land. The Hindus are not so much concerned with agriculture. In my village there were a lot of Hindus doing the professional work in post offices, banks, schools. Why are the Sikhs not in banks, why are the Sikhs not in schools? Why are the Sikhs not nurses and doctors? They are all Hindus. They have cars and scooters, while we are on bicycles.

"And let me tell you that those Hindus also have no tie to the Punjabi language. They say that Hindi is their mother tongue on the census, to distinguish themselves from Punjabi Sikhs. Don't get me wrong, I had many Hindu friends. I went to their homes and all. And though at home they speak Punjabi, on the census they list Hindi as their language. They hate Punjabi because they think Punjabi is the language of the Sikhs. They think they are too good for it.

"So when you ask whether a movement is religious or linguistic, you can see that because of the alienation of the Hindus these two turned out to be linked in our case. *Punjabiyat* might include Hindus, you might think, but most of the Hindus have chosen otherwise. *Punjabiyat* has now become the concern of the Sikhs, because no one else cares to preserve it."

I tried to return to a more chronological narrative.

"So this was your general mood before the 1984 events?" I asked.

"Even before that, by the late 1970s. In 1981 or 1982, I don't exactly remember when, I was coming home from Delhi when I read in the *Punjabi Tribune* that the editor of *Punjab Kesri* had been killed. Somebody had gone and killed him. I realized suddenly that I was feeling happy as I read this news. Why was I happy? Because this man had told all the Hindus of Punjab that they were part of Hindustan, that their mother language was not Punjabi but Hindi. He bore a large responsibility for the alienation of the Punjabi Hindus from their heritage, the common heritage with us. So I thought that it was a good thing that he was gone, because people like this were a bad thing for Punjab.

"Get this straight: I want to live in peace. By all means let us live in peace. But if somebody is trying to disturb our peace by exciting people's minds, by creating conflict . . . One time there was an interview in *India Today* with Sant Jarnail Singh Bhindranwale. He said that we Sikhs know how to sacrifice our lives for peace, but at the same time we know how to cut others to pieces. We love peace, we die for peace, but if somebody interferes with our peace, we will not tolerate it. We cannot tolerate being slaves to a country that doesn't respect us, our religion, our culture, our language. Do you understand what I mean?"

"Your feelings were becoming very strong." The therapeutic echo again, the "uh-huh" to prompt continued narration, which at the same time avoids the interviewer's actually taking a stand or voicing an opinion. It works well.

"Yes, I was becoming clearer in my mind that the situation must be changed. I started thinking about freedom, about the freedom of my people. I used to see some graffiti written at the bus stands, that used to say 'Sikh homeland *zindabad*' [Long live the Sikh homeland]. It was written by that crowd around Jagjit Singh Chauhan [an early advocate of Khalistan, now in exile in London] and Gajinder Singh [who hijacked a plane to Pakistan, now in prison in Lahore]. At the time I was thinking, 'What is this Sikh homeland?' But as I saw the situation in Punjab developing, I remembered that graffiti. I started thinking about the idea of a Sikh homeland.

"Around that time, the early 1980s, people from the All India Sikh Students Federation started coming around my college. They were very intelligent, very sincere, and they told the students about the crimes of the Indian state and about the 'false encounters' [extrajudicial executions] that had already started happening in Punjab. I decided to become a member.

"Then in January or February of 1984 some guys from my village were on a train coming from Haryana which was stopped by a gang of Hindus. The Sikhs were taken off that train and beaten very badly. My friends told how they were beaten with sticks and even with iron rods. One of them had to get eighteen stitches on his head where he had been hit with an iron rod. I was upset by this, very upset. Why did they stop that train? Why did they beat these Sikhs?"

"Were those people ever prosecuted?" I asked.

"No, never. And there was a worse episode. The Hindus tore the clothes off a young lady. They tore the clothes off her father, too, and told her father to lay with his daughter. This was so painful to hear, I couldn't stand to hear this. Why were people so cruel? And why didn't the government do anything about it? This is the most hurtful thing in our culture, in our religion. We simply cannot stand this." He was becoming emotional as he spoke.

"I collected my close friends, and I told them, 'We are going to have to kill these people.'

"We sent messages to all the AISSF [All India Sikh Students Federation] members and held a big meeting in our village. We called all the village people to come together there, totalling more than a thousand people. We asked each other what we should do. And in that process my younger brother decided to go off to Amritsar, to Sant Jarnail Singh Bhindranwale. He said that he would never come back, but that he would live and die for his country, for the Sikh homeland. There was no more rule of law in India, that was all there was to it. We had to depend on ourselves."

"Did your family support your brother's decision to go?"

"Well," Harpal Singh answered, "my mother said that our history is like that, full of crises in religion and society, and that when there is a crisis somebody has to take care of it. My father disagreed a little. But my mom told him, 'Look, somebody has to do it, so why not your son?' In the end he agreed.

"I went three or four times myself to listen to Sant Jarnail Singh Bhindranwale. He explained clearly that what he and the others were doing was for our society, for our religion, for our nation. He said that staying in India would mean the genocide of the Sikhs, and I think he was right. His way of talking was also very impressive. It was very simple, very sincere. People used to come from all over Punjab to hear him speak. And big newspaper journalists from all over the world came to interview him."

"And when some of the Indian press started calling him a fanatic and an extremist . . ."

Harpal interrupted me. "That was wrong, plain wrong. You know that the press in India is not a real press. You can say it's a prostitute. The whole press is under the control of the Brahmins, chained to the Brahminical way of thinking. If they could not get the advertisements from the big Hindu companies, how could they run their papers? Believe me, I know how these papers operate because I worked on them for years; I read Hindi papers, English papers, Punjabi papers. The Hindi papers particularly are bad for every minority—Christians, Buddhists, Muslims as well as Sikhs. What they started saying was, 'Why are the Sikhs complaining? They have everything. That bad man Bhindranwale is misleading everybody.' But we knew what was wrong and we loved Bhindranwale, no matter what the Hindu press was saying about him.

"I should tell you that after that AISSF meeting the police started keeping a sharp eye on me. A police inspector came to my house and started asking me about it, and I explained that we were discussing that episode in Haryana. 'Do you like it that the Hindus did this?' I asked the police inspector. But he told me to just answer his questions.

"In May of 1984 there was an important episode in my village. My brother and my cousin came back from Amritsar, and they told me they had come to kill two Hindus who were talking loudly against the Sikhs. I told them they would not get anywhere by just killing a couple of Hindus who talked too freely, that they were not really responsible for anything. I thought that we had to see who were the truly responsible parties, not just respond emotionally to every insult. But they said no, we cannot tolerate those Hindus talking against the Sikh community, spreading so many rumors. So they killed them and ran.

"After that the police came and arrested me and two colleagues who were lawyers. But we all got out on bail after the whole village showed up at the police station and demanded that we be released."

"Did you feel upset with your brother and your cousin for killing the two Hindus and for putting you in that kind of situation?" I asked.

"No," Harpal Singh answered. "They were doing what they thought was the right thing. I disagreed, but I didn't blame them.

"Anyway, in the last two weeks in May we started collecting wheat to bring to the community kitchen at the Golden Temple. Twenty members of AISSF decided to collect about a thousand kilos of wheat in a large truck to bring to that *langar*. We went to farms and to people's houses to collect it. We were getting ready to bring it to the Golden Temple when we started hearing on the radio that the Indian army had been brought in and was surrounding the temple precincts.

"We listened to BBC and Voice of America until all the journalists were thrown out of Punjab so that nobody would know what was going on. We kept listening to Indian broadcasts but we knew everything we heard was false. My mother was just worried about her son, who was with Bhindranwale at the Akal Takht. But I was also thinking that if the military would actually go into the Golden Temple Complex, so many people would be killed. It was the martyrdom day of Guru Arjun, so thousands of pilgrims would be visiting there.

"Well, you know what happened in Operation Blue Star. But my brother got out of there and about a week later we all got arrested, my brother, me, my cousin, and some friends. I was sleeping on the roof, as it was the hot season, and suddenly I found the barrel of a gun poking my chest. The military were everywhere, on the whole ground floor of our house, in all the streets around the house, and sweeping through the whole neighborhood. It was like waking up and being in the middle of a war.

" 'Why are you arresting me?' I was asking. 'Shut up!' they said and they bound my hands behind my back. I heard some soldiers shouting at my mother in a very rude way, and I told them, 'Hold your tongues and speak nicely to my mother!' For that I got a hard slap on the mouth.

"We were taken from our village in a big military truck, with heavy security in front and in back. We were thrown into three cells in Jallandhar jail, where we were interrogated.

" 'Give us your arms! Give us weapons!' they were shouting. I said, 'I don't have any weapons. If I were involved in anything you wouldn't find me peacefully sleeping at home, would you?'

"Anyway, we were put into jail under tight security. It was a very bad experience. Punjab jails are terrible, and the people who work there are psychopaths."

I interrupted. "At that time, were you baptized? Had you taken *amrit*?"

"No, not yet," replied Harpal. "I was thinking that I wasn't ready to take that step yet. It is a very sacred thing, and one has to be spiritually ready for it. At that time I was only thinking that the time had come that Sikhs had to leave India, had to have Khalistan. Life had become impossible for us in India. Later when I heard more of the details of Operation Blue Star, when I heard from relatives in Amritsar how the army had slaughtered people outright, carrying the bodies in trucks through the streets, I became even more convinced about this. How could such a thing be forgotten, much less forgiven? Even those who were not very intellectual, who were simple people, reacted like this. They hadn't thought very much about Khalistan but they all knew that staying with India just wasn't an option any longer for us, whatever that decision might cost.

"After we got out of jail we started going around to the villages to hand out literature about Khalistan. We released the real story of what went on during Operation Blue Star, because everywhere else one heard only propaganda. My relatives had observed what was going on from outside the complex, and my brother had been inside, of course, with Bhindran-wale. He knew how many military personnel had been killed, and it was more than was being publicized. He himself had killed some. I asked him whether he was sure that was the right thing to do and he reminded me that Bhindranwale had said that to kill was bad, but to have arms and not to assert one's rights was worse. Our holiest shrine had to be defended, he said. He then went underground with his comrades, and we didn't see them after that.

"Police started coming to our place frequently, sometimes by day, sometimes by night. I myself had to report to the police every three days and was not supposed to leave my home."

"Did you have any thought, yourself, of joining one of the guerilla forces?" I asked.

"No," my interlocutor said. "I am not a man of the gun. I am a literary man. But even such a person as me can't avoid the hand of the Indian police!

"Now in the next part of this story," Harpal continued, "I have to introduce the character of my cousin. My cousin was a truck driver, and he had a route from Calcutta to Punjab. In June 1984 he happened to be passing through Ramghar cantonment, and you may know that there was a big mutiny there of Sikh soldiers, in protest of Operation Blue Star. The mutineers approached his truck with all their weapons and ordered my cousin to take them to Patna so that they could hijack a plane to Amritsar to save the Golden Temple. He complied with this request, but the Indian military followed the truck and killed all the mutineers riding on it. They spared my cousin, since he was the driver, but they put a big case on him and he went to jail in Allahabad.

"What eventually happened was that my cousin's brother-in-law, who was in the Middle East, sent a visa for him to get out of India. He couldn't use it, of course, because he was in jail. So I visited him and we decided that I should leave India using his name and his visa. My cousin told me, 'Look, I may be in jail forever. So you had better go someplace where you can work for Khalistan.' By that time he was convinced also."

"Is your cousin still in jail?"

"No," Harpal said. "He was eventually released. But I have to tell you that after two or three years my brother was killed in an encounter with the military forces."

"Do you know anything about the circumstances of his death?" I asked.

"Not much," he answered. "I read about it in the papers and my family wrote me a letter about it. At one point he had killed a minister, I forget his name, but it was a minister from the Congress party. An informer reported on him, and he was killed along with about twelve others. My family tried to collect his body for cremation, but they were unable to obtain it. So we never found out what happened to my brother's body."

"In the end, how did your family feel about your brother's activities?"

"Well, they were proud. Because when a boy or girl dies for Khalistan, dies for our religion, we say it's a martyrdom. We celebrate martyrdom and honor those who martyred for the cause. My family recited *gurubani* and hundreds of people came to the *gurudwara* to remember my brother. My whole village and my whole society honored him.

"You have to understand that even our enemies praise the way we sacrifice our lives if necessary. Someone who offers his life for the people becomes part of them, strengthens them. A sincere martyrdom is a very good thing, we think. That is why in the end we will succeed. Nobody can beat us for devotion.

"I'll tell you the most recent chapter in this story. Last year the black cats [death squads] of the police started killing the families of the generals who were fighting for Khalistan. They tried to to kill my father. They attacked him, they hit him with a car and broke both his legs. He got gangrene poisoning through that and died. Then the police took my mother and my sister into custody, and my sister was as yet unmarried. It's a very bad thing for unmarried girls in police stations. But you know what my mother said to me on the telephone after they were released? She said, 'Don't worry, son. It's not happening only with me or with your sister. This is happening with all the mothers, all the sisters of Punjab. So just forget about it.' Who knows what they went through. But so bravely they went on anyway, they didn't even want sympathy from me. This is why we cannot lose."

While we had been talking, a few other house guests had entered the room. "Those women are full of courage," one said. Another responded, "Well, that courage comes when people are fighting for a good cause. That's the price of getting your own country. If you can't pay it, you don't deserve a country."

Little Manbir, the new baby, was brought in by his father. "The newest Khalistani!" someone said, and everyone laughed.

I ventured an opinion. "Isn't there a danger," I asked, "of coming to think that *because* you suffer so much, you deserve a country? Of almost relishing that suffering because you see it as the birth pangs of a nation?" I thought of how Iqbal Singh had said that it was clear what Khalistanis were fighting *against*, but less clear what they were fighting *for*. "What do you expect that Khalistan will be like? What kind of a country are you suffering to achieve?" I asked.

"It will be a just country, where everybody will be respected," Harpal Singh said. "Everybody means everybody. Hindus, Christians, anybody else. Every person in Punjab will have his rights respected. How could we deny that, after what we've been through ourselves?"

"But that seems to be a hard lesson to learn," I responded. "Look at the Jews. They suffered so much persecution, but now one generation after the Holocaust they are forgetting some of their own experience in the way they treat the Palestinians. The last generation in India suffered under the British and now they are doing this to the Sikhs. So how will the Sikhs prevent a similar thing from happening?"

"Because we are a product of our religion. In our prayers we ask God to take care of *everybody*. Good food for everybody, a good life for everybody. Not just for Sikhs. You know about the Sikh kingdom of Ranjit Singh. He loved Hindus, Muslims, Christians. Even Frenchmen and Britishers served in his military. We have this in our history as well as in our faith, that we will protect and take care of others, even if they don't agree with us."

I could think of a lot of problems with this argument, not least of which was that Ranjit Singh was not a Sikh in anything like the same way that Khalistani militants are Sikhs (he drank Scotch and had multiple wives, for example), not to speak of the very different historical circumstances. And what about the militants themselves, who are factionalized into so many groups that claim to be in basic agreement but can't talk in a civil fashion to one another—let alone to people in radical disagreement? But before I could think about whether to voice these thoughts or not Harpal Singh had a semi-answer.

"Whatever we may do with Khalistan, it cannot be worse than what we already face in India. India is not a country that has any moral ground from which to criticize what we may or may not do with Khalistan. Like they have this new human rights commission [the Misra Commission]. It's a total fraud. Because the people who know the system of India, they know the truth behind the democracy rhetoric and the truth behind the secularism rhetoric. The truth is that minorities don't have a place in India. Buddhists, Christians, tribals are not safe. The Hindus, or rather the Brahmins, want to wipe out everybody. They demolished a big mosque [Babri Masjid at Ayodhya] and look what they are doing in Kashmir. The plain fact is that if you're not a Hindu, you don't belong in India. It's becoming clearer and clearer. And they think they can challenge us as to whether Khalistan will protect minorities? This is a joke. We will worry about how to protect the minorities in Khalistan, but when is the rest of the world going to pay attention to what is happening to the minorities in India now?"

He had a point, but it didn't resolve the question. I told the now-crowded roomful of Sikhs about a conversation I had had with Amarjit walking outside of the Holocaust Museum. We had been commenting on the pins being handed out at the museum that said "Never Again." I said as we walked that I hoped I would never be in a position to be writing a book about the Hindu resistance in Khalistan. Amarjit abruptly stopped. He looked at me very seriously as others bustled past us on the sidewalk and said, "Cynthia, if it should ever come to that, I will be writing that book with you." He was quite silent as we crossed the street and got into a waiting cab.

I had told a gathering of colleagues about this episode, and several of them had utterly discounted it as mere political rhetoric. When I retold it here, however, in a roomful of militants or militant-sympathizers, I got a different reaction.

"He was serious," Harpal Singh said. Others nodded. "Because his morality, his faith, wouldn't let him do otherwise. If we wouldn't stand up for the rights of a minority, what are we fighting for now? It would all be in vain."

Someone else commented, "That's why being a Sikh is really an endless commitment. Right now the injustice is taking one form, but our struggle doesn't just end there. If there is another injustice we will have to be ready to sacrifice then, too."

"Look," said a third. "Right now there are people with turbans who are killing Khalistanis, torturing people, dishonoring women. There are bad people who call themselves Sikhs in India and there will be bad people who call themselves Sikhs in Khalistan, too. It won't be some kind of heaven. But the real Sikhs, the real saint-soldiers, will be there, and they will have to try to do what is right."

This sounded reasonable to me. And I knew that Amarjit had been fully sincere in what he had said about writing a book about a Hindu resistance in Khalistan, should it ever come to that. Meanwhile, however, problematic moral decisions were being made every day by militants for whom "trying to do what is right" might not be as clear-cut as the abstract defense of a hypothetical Hindu minority in Khalistan. Harpal's brother was sincerely trying to do the right thing in killing two Hindus who spoke too loudly against Sikhs or, more prominently, in killing a Congress minister. Harpal himself seemed less convinced that these things were right, more open to the moral ambiguities involved in guerilla struggle. But then it's easier to consider ambiguity when you're an anthropologist or "a literary man" rather than a commando with an AK-47. Picking up a weapon seems to resolve an awful lot of ambiguity for far too many people. That's its danger, and perhaps some of its allure also.

6
DRAWING THE SWORD

FIVE MONTHS AFTER Operation Blue Star, Prime Minister Indira Gandhi was stepping into her garden at One Safdarjang Road, New Delhi, when she was shot by one of her Sikh bodyguards, Beant Singh. As she fell, another Sikh guard, Satwant Singh, pumped bullets from his Thompson automatic carbine into her body. The entire right side of her body was opened up by more than twenty bullets.

Beant Singh and Satwant Singh apparently did not try to escape but simply raised their hands in the air. They were taken to a nearby guardhouse, where after some twenty minutes officers of the Indo-Tibetan Border Police opened fire, killing Beant Singh instantly and wounding Satwant Singh. (Though it was later claimed that they had tried to escape, three present at the scene testified otherwise.) [1] The prime minister was taken to the All-India Institute of Medical Sciences amid much confusion and delay, but to no avail. Several hours later her death was announced on All-India Radio. Eventually Satwant Singh, along with an alleged co-conspirator, Kehar Singh, was hanged for the crime, but its repercussions are with us still. [2]

THE AFTERMATH OF ASSASSINATION

Sikhs both in India and overseas had been talking openly about "punishing" Indira Gandhi for her role in Operation Blue Star for some time, and there were rumors of Pakistani and even CIA involvement in such plans (though no one has been able to substantiate them). The Thakkar Commission, appointed to investigate the assassination, implicated Mrs. Gandhi's own special assistant, R. K. Dhawan. The government came up with a list of possible conspirators in an entirely separate assassination plot, including Simranjit Singh Mann, a former police officer and Akali Dal leader, Atinder Pal Singh, a leader of the All-India Sikh Students Federation, and two others. The charge of conspiracy to wage war against the government and conspiracy to murder Indira Gandhi against those four men was, however, withdrawn after Mrs. Gandhi's Congress party was defeated in the parliamentary elections of 1989.

In those elections, in fact, several militants or people with known sympathies or connections to militants were elected to parliament from various districts in Punjab. Although in custody at the time, Simranjit Singh Mann was elected from Tarn Taran, and Atinder Pal Singh was elected from Patiala. (These were not their home constituencies, and their elections here represent the work of activists who were able to elicit votes simply on grounds of political solidarity.) The widow of Beant Singh, the known assassin of Indira Gandhi, was elected as well, and so was his father.

The fact of these individuals' success in contesting the election shows the extreme alienation of a large part of the Sikh community in the years following the Gandhi assassination. The support expressed here for two family members of Beant Singh amounts to outright applauding his action in "delivering justice" to Mrs. Gandhi. (It would be as if Lee Harvey Oswald's wife and father were elected to Congress after the assassination of Kennedy, an unimaginable scenario in the U.S. context.) Beant Singh's family were of Dalit (formerly Untouchable) origin, so there was an added impact to the support they received from the Sikh community.

Though it is true that sweets were distributed in celebration of the assassination in some locations (including in remote Assam, where an entirely different conflict was simmering), it was only in retrospect that many Sikhs came to feel that perhaps the killing had been justified. For in the days following the murder, Sikhs were brutally massacred in cities across north India, apparently with the complicity of police as well as key figures in the Congress party. The jolt of Operation Blue Star was thus followed by a second shock to the sensibilities of Sikhs five months later, and it was this shock that prompted many to the position of solidarity with the militants that would later be expressed electorally.

One woman told me:

When I heard Indira Gandhi had been shot I was horrified. Of course I thought that Operation Blue Star had been a terrible thing, a wrong thing, but I still didn't think the right solution was to just kill the prime minister. I thought it would bring a bad name on the Sikhs. That isn't the way people are supposed to behave in a democracy.

My family was a well-placed one, and we had many connections in the government. As the riots started breaking out in Delhi after Mrs. Gandhi was killed, somebody sent a car for me and my kids, so that we should get to a safe place. We were hiding down in the back seat as the driver, a Hindu, took us through the streets. You would never believe that scene that was before my eyes. I couldn't comprehend that it was India, the same neighborhoods, the same places I had been through a thousand times. People were on fire, literally on fire—one man's turban had gotten kerosene poured on it, and he became a human torch. I saw another man leap off a roof, and flames kind of followed his body in a big arc, like a shooting star. And the thing that I will never forget was the way those Sikh bodies on fire were shaking, trembling like, as they burned. That driver in my car turned to his companion and said, "See, they are dancing *bhangra* [a Punjabi folk dance]." I just couldn't comprehend this comment, I felt such an anguish to hear this. Later it became clear that it wasn't just this driver, it was everybody. No one cared about the Sikhs. We had been deluding ourselves all this time, that we were instrumental in the nation, that people respected us.

My father was [a highly placed individual in the personal entourage of Mrs. Gandhi] and he was asked to turn in his gun after the assassination, just because he was a Sikh. He had served with loyalty for so many years, and this was a devastating blow to him.

I still don't say it was right for Beant Singh and Satwant Singh to kill Indira Gandhi. But after I saw that the whole country was after the Sikhs—the police, the Congress, the media—I decided I had no more patience with India. That was it.

The first reports that the world heard about the "riots" that took place in Delhi and other cities was that they were the spontaneous reaction of grief-stricken Hindus, with corresponding retaliation from Sikhs. Rajiv Gandhi, for example, seemed to excuse this "rioting" with his much-publicized comment that "When a great tree falls, the earth shakes." But independent commissions set up to investigate the approximately six thousand deaths, largely Sikh, resulting from the post-assassination carnage paint a rather different picture. It has now become clear that the anti-Sikh mobs shouting "blood for blood" and "*Hindu-Hindu bhai-bhai*" ("Hindus and Hindus are brothers," a distortion of the traditional "Hindus and Sikhs are brothers" slogan) were not spontaneous but contrived with the full assistance of police officers and Congress party officials. They brought in hired gangs to initiate the slaughter and to spark more by spreading rumors that Sikhs had poisoned the water supply of Delhi and that trains full of dead Hindus were arriving from Punjab (harking back to similar episodes during the trauma of Partition). Sikh homes and businesses were carefully earmarked for destruction, while neighboring structures survived intact. Sikhs were beaten to death, "necklaced" with tires soaked in kerosene and set afire, dismembered, and raped.

The People's Union for Civil Liberties, a human rights group headed by the respected political scientist Rajni Kothari, and the People's Union for Democratic Rights, another highly regarded human rights organization, produced a joint report on the anti-Sikh violence called *Who Are the Guilty?* It concludes that "the attacks on the members of the Sikh community in Delhi . . . far from being spontaneous expressions of 'madness' and of popular 'grief and anger' at Mrs. Gandhi's assassination . . . were the outcome of a well-organized plan marked by acts of both deliberate commission and omission by important politicians of the Congress . . . and by authorities in the administration."[3] Justice Ajit Singh Bains forthrightly called the riots "pogroms."[4] The Citizens' Commission, headed by former Chief Justice S. M. Sikri and counting a former governor, a former foreign secretary, a former commonwealth secretary, and a former union home secretary among its members, concluded that the anti-Sikh violence was "a massive, deliberate, planned onslaught on the life, property and honour of a comparatively small, but easily identifiable, minority community."[5] A third report put out by Citizens for Democracy echoed these findings, noting also that the reasoning behind the violence was to arouse Hindu passions in order to consolidate votes in the coming election.[6]

As the actual role of Congress party workers and police and other officials in the 1984 slaughter of the Sikhs is becoming clearer, the status of Indian democracy is increasingly called into question by outside observers as well. Paul Brass, writing in the prestigious *New Cambridge History of India* series, bluntly points to the "institutionalized riot systems" in which mob violence is spurred and manipulated by political leaders. He also comments darkly that "it is past time to note that Indian politics and society display many of the symptoms of a murderous pre-fascist stage which has already produced a multiplicity of localized *Kristallnachts* in numerous urban sites."[7] Though some will find the analogy with Nazi Germany here too extreme, both the explicit targeting of *amritdhari* Sikhs as traitors following Operation Blue Star and the clear earmarking of Sikh residences and businesses in the post-assassination carnage speak to an incipient genocidal campaign. Though most Indians would condemn both, if phrased in these terms, restraints on media coverage meant that much of the nation received the explanations of Sikh treachery and Hindu-Sikh "communal rioting" without much protest. The urban elite human rights communities spoke out, but India as a whole remained silent. For Sikhs, this silence was deafening.

The woman who was driven through the burning streets of Delhi told me that she was instructed to take her children out of school and get them to a safe place well before the "rioting" began. She suspected that a plan to create communal violence in the capital had been in place for some time, possibly scheduled for the upcoming birthday of Guru Nanak, which got pushed up to take advantage of the conditions created by the assassination. I have no way to assess what this woman told me, but note that three of her close family members were in high positions in the government. Her remarks are consistent with the findings of the independent commissions cited here.[8]

Khushwant Singh, journalist, member of Parliament, and firm critic of Sikh separatism, writes,

In most instances, mobs were led by members of Mrs. Gandhi's Congress party including some Members of Parliament. Policemen on duty turned away their faces and took their share of the booty. Sikh houses and shops were marked for destruction in much the same ways as those of the Jews in Tsarist Russia or Nazi Germany. . . . There were no signs of grief over the death of their Prime Minister [among the police] but plenty of envy, hate and malicious pleasure at seeing Sikhs . . . being cut to size.

I awaited my turn. I felt like a partridge in a partridge shoot waiting to be flushed out of cover and shot on the wing. . . . For the first time I understood what words like pogrom, holocaust and genocide really meant. I was no longer a member of an over-privileged community but of one which was the object of dire hate. All day long my telephone rang. "They are burning our gurdwara, can't you do anything? They have looted our shops, can't you do anything? . . . There are scores of Sikh corpses lying along the rail track, can't you do anything?" In my turn I rang up everyone I knew from the Commissioner of Police, the Lt. Governor, the Home Minister, right up to Rashtrapati Bhavan. The only help I received was in the form of advice: "Get out of your place and hide with your Hindu friends. At least you will be able to save your life."[9]

Khushwant Singh did save his life, by hiding out in the Swedish embassy. But so many other Sikhs, lacking Khushwant Singh's connections, had no embassies to flee to and no cars to bring them there.

Estimates of people rendered homeless by the post-assassination violence rose as high as 50,000, and camps to house these refugees were still in operation a year later. The government's offer of ten thousand rupees (about U.S. $1000) for surviving next-of-kin of riot victims seemed to many to be more of an insult than a serious attempt at compensation. Harji Malik, a journalist with the *Hindustan Times*, visited one of the areas worst hit by the carnage, Trilokpuri Block 32, eleven months afterward, and described the continuing aura of devastation poignantly:

This infamous block where the massacre of men and boys had been most savage, had not been touched for almost a year. No family had returned and it was easy to see why. Burned out houses, charred door frames, piles of rubble, heaps of half-burned clothes, a child's rubber chappal [sandal], charred paper obviously

6. Woman weeping during the anti-Sikh massacres at Delhi, November 1984, that followed the assassination of Indira Gandhi. The woman's family was slaughtered and their home burnt. This photograph is used in the international documentation of human rights violations in India.

used to light fires, heaps of ashes inside ruined rooms, remained mute witnesses to man's brutality. From the walls of many stricken homes painted plaques of Guru Nanak looked down on the evidence of human madness. The narrow street, both sides lined with gutted shells of homes, exuded its own horrors, its desolation a stark contrast to the overcrowded streets, bustling with life, on either side. In Block 32 the silence speaks, for pain and agony have been permanently recorded here.[10]

Rajiv Gandhi, Indira's son, became the next prime minister in a landslide election. The Congress party's campaign played shamelessly and dangerously on anti-Sikh sentiment among the majority Hindu community. One election poster pasted on walls all over India showed Mrs. Gandhi superimposed on a map of India with a gaping and bloody hole in her abdomen; another showed her crumpled body in the garden with two sinister-looking Sikhs hovering in the background. One asked bluntly, "Should you be afraid of your cab driver?" (a professional niche Sikhs dominate). Khushwant Singh, though a Congress loyalist, wholeheartedly disapproved of this tactic. He advised that the susceptibilities of the Sikhs had been deeply hurt and that restoring the dignity and self-respect of this community had to be a major project of the government. He told the home minister, "You are up against a community which feels unwanted, isolated, unhappy and sullen. You have to get round these people and get them on your side and free them of this atmosphere of hatred and bitterness that has been created." He also noted, "You might not have been told that a large number of young Sikhs today wear saffron turbans—no longer blue or white. They are wearing saffron because they have taken an oath of vengeance. What that means, I shudder to think." [11]

Despite the horror with which the progressive community in India greeted revelations surrounding government involvement in the massacres, on the popular level what have been called "Yes, but . . ." arguments prevailed. "Yes, but the Sikhs were distributing sweets" (to celebrate Indira Gandhi's death) was the most popular one. (As Dharma Kumar notes, "If all the sweets in India had been distributed that would not have justified the burning alive of one single Sikh." [12]) There was another "Yes, but . . ." that remained pervasive as well: the recognition that in the face of India's unspeakable poverty the Sikhs have been, in fact, a privileged community in economic terms.[13] Moreover, some Sikhs at least were "fundamentalists." So the civil rights sector, though rightly appalled at the post-assassination atrocities, retained a bit of ambivalence as to their relationship with the Sikhs. Bleeding-heart liberals were not sure whether they should bleed with the Sikhs, notes anthropologist Dipankar Gupta.[14] As for the masses, "the middle-class Hindu had nearly complete sympathy with the killing and lynching of Sikhs." [15] Ashis

7. Indian security personnel stationed at the Golden Temple Complex, Amritsar. This photo appears frequently in Khalistani publications as documenting the "occupation" of Punjab.

Nandy remembers the image of an elite boutique owner directing a gang of arsonists with his golf club.[16] Hating Sikhs had become respectable.

Those young Sikhs who had donned saffron turbans to the consternation of Khushwant Singh were not only deeply hurt by the actions of the Indian government, but they were at the same time greatly empowered by the actions of Beant Singh and Satwant Singh. In a sense, the anti-Sikh slaughter after the assassination was seen as justifying after the fact what the assassins had done. After all, they pulled it off. The fact that two Sikhs could murder the leader of "the largest democracy in the world" gave encouragement to every Sikh who thought that he or she had now to do something to avenge Operation Blue Star, avenge the anti-Sikh pogroms, and establish a state in which Sikhs would be not a susceptible minority but a majority whose rights could not be trampled.

Amrit Srinivasan of Delhi University appropriately recognizes the sense in which the anti-Sikh "riots" were seen as an echo of Operation Blue Star itself. Both were seen as violations of "home," one in the religious, the other in the domestic, sense.[17] This sense of geographic invasion contributed to a notion of Khalistan as a physical sanctuary, as a place where Indian soldiers, police, and mobs could not reach.

"Encounters" between Sikh militants and police and paramilitary forces in Punjab occurred with regularity after November 1984, and a variety of guerilla bands operated clandestinely in the cities, villages, and fields of the state. After a period of shock following Operation Blue Star, people seemed to be galvanized into action. Although Rajiv Gandhi reached an agreement with Akali Dal president Harchand Singh Longowal in July 1985 (the Rajiv-Longowal Accord), the mood among a significant section of the population had turned ugly. Longowal was shot by militants while speaking in a *gurudwara* in August for allegedly having betrayed the Sikh cause by compromising with the son of Indira Gandhi.[18] In April 1986 the independent state of Khalistan was declared, a formal military organization was established with a Panthic Committee at its helm, and "the movement" coalesced into a definable force. As a condition of *zulm* (oppression) descended upon Punjab, resistive zeal sprang up in every nook and cranny of the state.

BHAI DHANNA SINGH

It was a warm summer day in the community kitchen of the *gurudwara*, and women were bustling about cleaning dishes while a few stragglers finished their lunch. The sound of *kirtan* from the hall of worship upstairs was filtered blurrily into the room through an inadequate intercom, and the noise from a distant vacuum cleaner added to the cacophony. I was hot and tired after a series of problematic discussions. But Rajwinder, a Sikh with whom I was staying for a few days, wanted me to meet one more person.

We were sitting cross-legged in one corner of the large hall when a particularly gentle-looking man came and sat down with us, surrounded by a dense coterie of others. Some of them sat down with us and others remained standing, watching.

"Here is Bhai Dhanna Singh," said Rajwinder.

I looked at him questioningly. Was this the Dhanna Singh who was a member of the original Panthic Committee, which declared the independence of Khalistan in 1986?

Rajwinder understood my wordless question and nodded slightly. Unprepared, I stammered out some phrases about how pleased I was to meet him, thinking as I spoke what questions I most urgently wanted to ask Dhanna Singh. But the conversation flew along without time to consider much what to say.

"Great is God, Victory Belongs to God!" He began with the ritual greeting of the Khalsa Sikhs. Not sure where to start, I asked my usual introductory questions about family and background.

"I come from district Jallandhar, and the name of my village is Khera Maja. Here I was born and finished high school. After that for about a year I stayed home and worked in the fields. Of the four of us brothers, one is now in Canada, and the other two are still working on our family farm. As for me, after I worked in the fields for a while I decided to go for a career in electric welding. But then the episode of 1978 happened, when the Nirankaris attacked the Sikhs, and that was like a shock to my mind. Then I didn't feel like working in any field other than toward my faith. After that I was baptized into the Khalsa."

"Could you explain to me what is the process of being baptized?" I asked. It was not really the point of what I wanted to know from Dhanna Singh, but it was an easy question for an anthropologist to fall back on.

Bhai Dhanna Singh looked slightly bemused by my question, but he explained patiently.

"In the morning on which a Sikh is to be baptized he is to bathe completely, including washing of his hair. And then he has to have the five articles of faith on his body when he comes to the place where the baptism is to happen. Baptism is done in the presence of the Guru Granth Sahib, and in the presence of five beloved ones [panj piaras], who are already there. All of them are wearing the five articles of faith. There we express our desire, standing before those five beloved ones, to be baptized. Then we are asked about certain principles and commitments which a Sikh has to have to be baptized. Those commitments have to be met even if it comes to sacrificing oneself for the value of truth. Then the five beloved ones ask, 'Are you ready for that?' and when it is nodded yes, then the Sikh is baptized. In a bowl of iron, water and some sugar crystals are stirred with the double-edged sword by the five beloved ones, one by one, and as they are stirring they are reciting a hymn. Then those five hymns which are recited during the baptism ceremony become the prayer that the Sikh recites in the morning, afternoon, and night. After the *amrit* is ready the Sikh goes before the five beloved ones in a special posture, having his right knee on the ground, and one of the beloved ones takes the *amrit* and gives him five drinks, puts the *amrit* on his head five times, and sprinkles it on his eyes five times. All the time the seeker who is being baptized says 'Waheguru ji ka Khalsa, Waheguru ji ki Fateh' (Khalsa belongs to God and Victory belongs to God).

"After a Sikh is baptized he is told that from now on all Sikhs are brothers and sisters and there should not be any distinction on the basis of caste, color, or creed. You are all brothers and sisters, they say, and from now onwards you all belong to one Father, Guru Gobind Singh, and you will all believe in one Almighty God who is formless. Never worship any idols or anything else, never bow before graves or pseudo-saints. Guru Granth Sahib will be your holy Guru. A Sikh must say his prayers every morning and evening. A Sikh is supposed to earn his bread through the sweat of his brow, and give one-tenth of his earnings to the needy and poor. Those are the ideals of Guru Nanak which are reinforced during the baptism ceremony, which reminds the Sikh that his duty is to obey them throughout his life."

"What happened after you were baptized?" I prompted.

"Well, after being baptized I felt it was necessary that I should know the Guru Granth Sahib in its pure form, its grammar and everything. So I joined Damdami Taksal. That is an institution which is considered to be a very pious, holy institution where all the meaning of the *gurubani* is taught in the true, ancient way.

"At Damdami Taksal I was much impressed with Sant Jarnail Singh ji Khalsa Bhindranwale, who was the head of that place. I decided to stay with him permanently. I forgot about my home and all and became convinced that we Sikhs were being treated as second-class citizens in India. The police used to raid Damdami Taksal and caught hold of us students, all very devout Sikhs; they humiliated us badly. They held us by our hair and took off our turbans, and threw cigarette butts on us. That was the worst kind of humiliation for devout Sikhs, and it was difficult to tolerate. I became convinced that until and unless we get freedom we can't live as Sikhs with dignity and pride in this country.

"At Damdami Taksal I learned that the religious places of the Hindus, like Rishikesh, Hardwar, and Benares, were given the status of holy places. Buses were run on government basis for pilgrimage to these places. But when it came to our Golden Temple, the holiest of places for the Sikhs, curfews were applied, and Sikhs weren't even allowed to reach there sometimes. Even our preachers, very respectable people, even those who had nothing to do with any politics, they were stopped on the road, their swords taken off, and they were humiliated in the worst ways. Seeing this sort of thing was enough to convince me and the others at Damdami Taksal that this was not the country for Sikhs. This was a Hindu country.

"One day one of the prominent Sikhs, Bhai Kulwant Singh Nagoke, was arrested. He was tortured very badly and after hours and hours of that he died. His body was completely mutilated. In July of 1982 three very devout Sikhs were arrested while on their way to see Sant Jarnail Singh Bhindranwale. Two prominent lights of the Damdami Taksal, Baba Tara Singh ji and Bhai Amrik Singh ji, went to the police station to inquire why these religious people were arrested, and they also got arrested. It was feared they might get killed, as staged encounters had become common by this time. Sant Jarnail Singh Bhindranwale set up headquarters in Guru Nanak Niwas [a hostel] in the Golden Temple Complex, Amritsar."

I moved slightly closer to him to push the tape recorder's microphone to a more opportune position. As I did it, three men nearby quite suddenly leaned in closer to Dhanna Singh. I realized how attentive everyone around us was, despite the noise and clutter going on in the rest of the hall.

Bhai Dhanna Singh continued in his soft voice.

"The first step taken by Sant Jarnail Singh Bhindranwale was to call for an agitation [morcha] in which we would raise our voices in a peaceful and democratic manner. So the first unit [jatha] of Sikhs, fifty-one Sikhs, went to court arrest on July 16. That was the first of the peaceful agitations called by Sant Jarnail Singh Bhindranwale.

"Once Sant Jarnail Singh Bhindranwale started the agitation, Akali Dal, the Sikh political organization, also gave their support. The majority of the Sikhs were by that time convinced that we were being discriminated against in this country. So the call of Sant Jarnail Singh Bhindranwale was heard by Sikhs in their hearts, and they started to come forward to face any consequences and to sacrifice themselves for justice."

"At that time," I interrupted, " did you feel that you would be able to obtain justice within the Indian framework?" I still wasn't sure whether he knew that I knew who he was.

"At that time our struggle was not for an independent Khalistan. The agitation was only for implementation of the Anandpur Sahib Resolution, for greater autonomy. But even during that peaceful agitation atrocities were committed by the government and 183 Sikhs lost their lives. The families of those young people who participated were harassed, too, their lands were destroyed and warnings were issued to their fellow villagers that no one should look after their cattle. Sant Bhindranwale kept saying that we would continue to protest for the Anandpur Sahib Resolution focused on the autonomy of the state. But if the Indian army touched the Golden Temple then the foundation stone of Khalistan would be laid. That was what he said.

"Once the attack actually took place on June 3, 1984, and Sikhs saw what had happened not only to the Golden Temple but to thirty-seven other Sikh shrines, they made up their minds to go no more with Hindu India. Eventually we all got together at Amritsar to decide what to do. After we honored the families of those Sikhs killed during Operation Blue Star, we discussed what our plan of action should be.

"Since we have a historical tradition that things should be decided by five beloved ones, we thought of establishing a collective leadership under the command of five. I was one of those five. My name is Dhanna Singh Khalsa."

So it was out in the open. I wondered whether his identity was well known outside of his immediate circle, outside of this *gurudwara*. Did neighbors realize what a unique history this person had behind him?

"We five were given the responsibility by the Sarbat Khalsa, the Sikh Commonwealth, to lead the Sikh community," Dhanna Singh continued. "The first thing we did was to restore the religious celebrations within the *gurudwara* that had been disrupted during the attack. The next task before us was, what political goal should be laid before the Sikhs?

"Well, that political goal had already been declared by Sant Jarnail Singh Bhindranwale when he had said that on the day that the Indian Army would invade the Golden Temple, the foundation stone of Khalistan would be laid. So keeping that in mind, the five-member Panthic Committee declared an independent sovereign Khalistan as the only solution, on April 29, 1986."

"You have a copy of that declaration," Rajwinder added. I was intent on listening and barely noticed Rajwinder's continued presence.

"The next task before us was to help those families who were the victims of state repression. We went from village to village, identified them, and helped them in all ways. Then we started to recruit Sikhs from all places to help us in our goal. One thing about this declaration of April 29 was that it was resolved that armed struggle was the only way that the Sikhs could achieve Khalistan. Though we are not against peaceful agitation and peaceful strategies were not ruled out, on April 29 the armed struggle was given religious sanction through the Sarbat Khalsa. So we started to recruit people for that."

"At that time, were you convinced that all peaceful means had been exhausted, that armed struggle was the only recourse?" I asked. This was a formulaic phrase for Sikhs, but it seemed a tactful way of establishing just when the militancy was given official sanction.

"I was already convinced through the history of what happened from 1947 to 1978 that we were being severely discriminated against. I personally witnessed, from 1978 to 1984, how we worked peacefully in all ways to achieve justice, but what we got in return was killing of our boys, our brothers, humiliation and molestation of our sisters, and finally the onslaught against the Golden Temple and thirty-seven historical Sikh shrines. This left me convinced that all peaceful means were exhausted and that now it was justified to take to the hilt of the sword.

"Armed struggle was not our choice, it was forced on us. Even in that declaration of April 29 we appealed to all peace- and justice-loving people in the world to help us in getting liberated from the yoke of this tyrannical regime. We are the believers in Guru Nanak, we believe in working for the good of all, we believe in equality and justice. In that declaration we appealed to all other people to come and join us in our struggle.

"I helped in the armed part of the struggle, but don't want to disclose how, from April 29, 1986, to December 10, 1987. On December 10, 1987, I was taken out of a bus and arrested, probably on the word of some informant."

"At that time, were the other members of the Panthic Committee still alive and free?" I asked.

"Yes, I was the first member of the Panthic Committee to be arrested," he responded.

"I was imprisoned for one year and humiliated during that year. Very derogatory comments were made about Sikhism. Sometimes cigarette butts were thrown in the food. They used to say, 'You foolish Sikhs, you are asking for Khalistan, here is your Khalistan.' That was the kind of indignity I suffered for one year.

"After a ten-day police remand I was sent to another jail, Nabha jail. The police started asking me for the names of other people involved in the movement, their whereabouts and so on. I had been in jail for a whole year so of course I didn't know anything about it, but they were torturing me and asking me to disclose information about various people.

"After six weeks in Nabha I was moved to Sangrur prison. In Sangrur I saw how badly the other political prisoners were treated. For months and months they were not allowed to meet with their ailing mothers and sick parents, even those who came to see them, and when relatives tried to come to visit they were very badly abused by the jail authorities. My wife was allowed to visit me seven times during the whole year I had spent in jail.

"A usual police tactic is that whenever anybody is bonded out of jail a big police force is standing outside the court. Then when the prisoner is released he is immediately arrested again and charged with some other thing. But in the parliamentary elections of November 1989 nine members of parliament were elected who were either militants themselves or family members of militants. That was how much support the freedom fighters had. So this time when my bond was accepted by the magistrate, a big number of Sikhs had gathered outside the court and the police couldn't arrest me again."

"Did you feel that you had the support of most of the Sikhs at the time, even though there were some Sikhs who remained loyal to the central government?" I asked. Of course, he would say yes, but I wanted to hear what else he would say.

"They may be Sikh in their appearance," he responded, "but we never consider those people Sikhs. A Sikh is he who listens to the Guru's command, and Guru's command is to speak against injustice. Anybody who complies with an oppressive regime is never a Sikh." I had heard that kind of definition before.

"When I came out of jail I tried to contact different freedom fighters. A lot of them had already been killed in fake encounters. Then, as there was a constant danger that I might be killed, I thought of leaving India to pursue the struggle from outside."

"Is the Panthic Committee able to effectively guide the struggle, now that one is here, one is there, some have been killed and replaced, and so on?" I knew not much would be said about this, but I wanted to bring the conversation to the present.

"Our communication system is the same as in most other underground struggles. Wherever we may be, wherever other leaders may be, we are always able to make contact somehow." I later learned of Dhanna Singh's peripheralization in movement politics, and in retrospect thought I detected a hint of sadness in this last part of the conversation.

"Do you have a problem with some people getting out of control and doing things they shouldn't do?"

"The Indian government has criminalized the movement. A Sikh who is a devout Sikh, who has taken up armed struggle to uphold the value of Sikh Dharm, will never think of doing anything wrong. So most of the time, these criminal elements are encouraged by the government or are even government infiltrators. They try to come inside and destroy the movement."

"What do you think Khalistan will be like?" This was the first time in the conversation that I smiled at Dhanna Singh, and he smiled back readily.

"What I enshrine in my soul along with most of the Sikhs is a Khalistan that is an ideal state which the world has not seen before. A place where without distinction of caste, color, or creed all the citizens will have equality. Everybody will have the right to worship as they please. Citizens of Khalistan will be prosperous, and we will contribute toward the promotion of world peace. We will see that the whole world becomes a just place to live for the people of the Lord."

It may have been formulaic, but Bhai Dhanna Singh clearly felt the validity of this vision deeply. I tried to pursue the less savory side.

"Are you afraid that after Khalistan is established, it will be difficult to make that transition? Can we expect that some people, who have gone through so much trouble in their lives, might want to take revenge, that there might be bloodshed?"

"We don't have any malice or animosity toward the common Hindu or toward anybody. Of course there is no question that some Sikhs will take revenge on the Hindus or other innocent people, but the people who have committed heinous crimes on the Sikhs will be punished not on the street but according to the law of the land. They will be tried in the courts of Khalistan, and after their guilt is proved they will be punished according to the law."

"Like war criminals?"

"Yes, yes. We will be punishing them for their misdeeds, not harboring any ill will against them personally." Too much to be hoped for in a continent known for mob violence, but an admirable sentiment.

"But other Hindus will be able to worship freely in Khalistan?"

"Yes, Hindus will have the same rights. As we have proved during the reign of Maharaja Ranjit Singh, when Hindus and Muslims lived along with the Sikhs without any fear." This was again a common point, not entirely without justification, but problematic.

"Will there be academic freedom in the universities?" I brought up a topic dear to my scholar's heart.

"The Sikhs are basically broad-minded people. We will love to see Khalistan prosper academically, not only research in your field but in any scientific or humanistic field. There will be no bondage, no bar on any kind of research, and we will welcome this research.

"Guru Nanak's message is based on love, equality, and justice, and as Sikhs we won't be great if we don't live up to this love, equality, and justice. It's our moral duty. We can't be close-minded people. We will have to hear the viewpoints of others, and I hope you will continue your research and writing after Khalistan is established as well as now."

"Are the Khalistanis in solidarity with the people of Kashmir?" I queried.[19]

"It's not only Kashmir, though for the Kashmiris we have great love and awe, but you know that even the hymn of Guru Nanak says that all people are equal and deserve our love. None should be alien. So being bound by Guru's word we sympathize not only with the Kashmiris but with all the justice-loving peoples of the world. We should all help in the liberation movements of the world."

"Do you think your life is in danger now?"

"No, I don't fear any danger. All is in the hands of Almighty God, and it is the way of the Sikh that if martyrdom comes it should come in pursuit of truth. If the time comes and the Guru asks me, I will happily be martyred for the cause.

"Look, to die is not our only ambition. If our goal can be achieved in any other way we should do it. But if our cause demands martyrdom, we won't hesitate."

That was the conclusion of my conversation with Bhai Dhanna Singh. I asked him whether I could use his name outright in my book, since his membership in the original Panthic Committee would make him identifiable by any interested party. He said yes, and I promised to transcribe the interview in full, without editing his words.

STRUCTURING MILITANCY AT HOME AND ABROAD

The fact that a member of the Panthic Committee that declared the independence of Khalistan is now residing in the United States and that one of the initial instigators of the idea of Khalistan resides in London (Jagjit Singh Chauhan) shows the international character of the Sikh militant movement. Diaspora Sikhs have in fact been critical to the movement and have become more so as the success of the counterinsurgency within Punjab becomes firmly established.

This aspect of Sikh militancy creates both opportunities and difficulties for the researcher. Opportunities, because there is a community outside of India accessible to investigation and living in conditions in which free exchange is possible. Difficulties, however, because the transnational quality of Sikh militancy means that U.S., Canadian, and British citizens and residents may have been involved in very serious criminal activities abroad, and contact with them puts the researcher at least in the margins of these activities as well. There are security and intelligence questions here, not only from the viewpoint of India but from the viewpoint of the Western countries that host diaspora Sikhs as well.

A more immediate problem to be faced, however, concerns the extreme factionalization of the militant community. Up until this chapter, I have basically been discussing "the Sikh militancy" as a unitary entity, however split up functionally into various forces and organizations. Alas for the movement, this picture is false. In-fighting is in fact as characteristic of this movement as is a certain external solidarity. Rifts between groups are expressed not only in vehement verbal arguments but in physical disagreements ranging from fist fights to shooting incidents. At the worst, they accuse each other of being agents of the Indian government, a serious charge indeed in a national liberation movement. This in-fighting discourages not only temporary insiders like inquisitive anthropologists but also seasoned Khalistani Sikhs. They all lament this state of affairs but seem powerless to do anything about it.

The original Panthic Committee, of which Dhanna Singh was a member, also included Baba Gurbachan Singh Manochal, Bhai Wasson Singh Zaffarwal, Bhai Arur Singh, and Bhai Gurdev Singh Usmanwala. They were connected to the Damdami Taksal and were orthodox Sikhs. After a Sarbat Khalsa summoned by the Damdami Taksal on January 26, 1986, and conceived as a gathering of the entire community or *panth* of Sikhs, these five were chosen to lead the struggle that had in fact already begun during the months after the assassination of Indira Gandhi. Although Manochal was de facto head of the new Panthic Committee, it was conceived as a democratic committee of equals, in the *panj piaras* tradition.

On April 29, 1986, the Panthic Committee called a press conference at the Golden Temple Complex and presented the "Declaration of Independence of Khalistan." It is a rather loosely written document, but it includes basic guarantees of democracy in the proposed state of Khalistan as well as running through the litany of abuses suffered by Sikhs in the Indian state. All five members of the Panthic Committee were wanted by police at the time, so while the assembled journalists at the press conference were being served tea, the five members of the Panthic Committee changed into street clothes and made their escape.

The next day, the Golden Temple Complex was invaded for the second time by Indian army commandos, in an operation referred to as Operation Black Thunder I. Many Sikhs saw this as an attempt to justify the original Operation Blue Star, and the ruling Akali party led by Surjit Singh Barnala was split by the issue. Many party members resigned in protest and Barnala himself was declared *tankhaya* (excommunicated) by the Akal Takht for his role in allowing this second sacrilege to happen.

The Panthic Committee members remained in hiding after their initial pronouncement of Khalistan, participating in various elements of what was evolving into a full-blown guerilla operation, until they were arrested, killed, or forced to flee the country. None of the members of the original Panthic Committee are alive in India today; three were killed and the other two now live in other countries.

The Declaration of Independence of Khalistan cites the Khalistan Commando Force, under the leadership of General Hari Singh (an alias of Bhai Manbir Singh Chaheru, after a Sikh hero of the Afghan wars), as the core of the defense force of Khalistan. The Khalistan Commando Force (KCF) was one of a handful of guerilla organizations that sprang up after Operation Blue Star, a good number of its members being from the Majha region of Punjab (districts Amritsar and Gurdaspur). The Majha region, northeast of the Beas river, was historically known for its fierce and stubborn fighters. It is the site of Sikhism's holiest shrine and is located on the Grand Trunk road to Delhi. Flat and treeless like most of Punjab, the Majha zone is not an ideal setting for a guerilla insurgency. From the beginning, militants who joined the Khalistan Commando Force depended upon shelter from the people.

The fact that Sikh militant organizations have been able to sustain themselves in a territory as unsuited to insurgency as Punjab has not received the attention it deserves. Although it is clear that shelter was sometimes given at gunpoint, all the classic theorists of guerilla warfare agree that an insurgent army simply cannot survive without substantial support from the general population. (The guerilla among his people like a fish in the water, and so on.) Though the activists in the Sikh militancy are generally quite unaware either of theories about guerilla warfare or of other guerilla movements (with the exception of Kashmir, linked historically and strategically to the Punjab question), one interlocutor noted specifically the impact of Che Guevara on his thinking:

I will tell you about my friend, who was always a very polite boy who never fought with anybody or did anything wrong. He was a good student. After the Golden Temple event he went into the movement. His family got upset and they were telling him to come home, as he was the only son. But he said, "When you used to read in the paper about how brave the other boys were you used to praise them, but now when it comes to your own house you start crying. I won't come home. Consider me as dead."

The first action he got involved in was a very big action, in which eight police officers at a detective training academy were killed. The first gun he ever shot was an AK-47, in that raid. He and his comrades also pulled off an immense bank robbery, and a lot of the money was in his hands. But he didn't misuse a penny of it. He became in fact very pious and spiritual, as he became more involved in the movement.

One time he gave me a book by Che Guevara to read, and that

helped me understand what was going on with the militants. I used to wonder how they could survive, how they could succeed. But then I realized that there were other courageous people standing up for the rights of minorities and poor people in other places, too, and sometimes they managed to achieve those.

The way my brave friend finally died, it was horrible. When his body was found he had no teeth, no nails on his hands and feet, and his chest was entirely blackened. That was how he died. He was a skinny guy, only about 120 pounds although he was six feet tall. But he had a lot of conviction. He died with his convictions.

The continuing claim of Indian government sources that the militants were extremists without a popular basis was consistently belied by the ability of militants to hide underground for long periods of time. Despite claims of high numbers of militants killed, there were always more emerging from villages and towns across Punjab. But, as in the case with the estimation of the threat posed by Bhindranwale in 1984, the Indian government could not concede widespread popular support without turning what it saw as a law and order problem into a full-blown political issue. Just as the actions of the Indian armed forces during Operation Blue Star undercut the idea that the heart of the problem was a mere band of criminals, the weight of the government counterinsurgency, which fell on all and sundry in the state of Punjab, betrayed the notion that it was a few terrorists who were the problem. A substantial proportion of the population was the problem, despite rhetoric to the contrary.

Though the fortunes of a number of guerilla organizations have waxed and waned over the past fifteen years, the militant movement overall has never lacked recruits. They were and are drawn primarily from young males, aged 15–25, although women may also join, and older individuals may also play key roles. There seems to be a general pattern of incorporation into a militant organization, in which an individual moves from providing shelter to militants to carrying out subsidiary tasks like transporting weapons, to full-scale "combat" participation.

Like all the guerilla organizations, the KCF has a command structure with a "general" at the helm, "lieutenant-generals" beneath him, followed by "area commanders," and general cadres. But the extreme decentralization of the movement means that the tight hierarchy implied by these titles is often illusory. Local bands seem to frequently decide on missions quite independent of "orders" (or restraints) from above, leading both to a certain resiliency in terms of the law (one cell doesn't know what another is up to) and to a tendency for general strategies on behalf of Khalistan to turn into personal raids of vengeance on the local level.

Already in 1978 Pettigrew had noted the strength of the cultural tradition of egalitarian individualism in Punjab, with personal friendships and enmities playing a significant role in episodes of violence.[20]

Many outside writers in fact scoff at the military titles used by Sikh militants, believing they are trying to claim a dignity and power they do not have ("the self-proclaimed 'general'"; "the 'so-called lieutenant,'" and so forth). I think, rather, that we might see these titles as honors awarded to fighters viewed as especially heroic or gifted, without necessarily treating them as direct analogues of ranks in a state-based military order. A general of the Khalistan Commando Force doesn't have the controlling power of a general in the Indian Army—but he has a lot more freedom of action. And whatever outsiders may think, the title of "general" carries as much respect in the Khalistani community as Schwarzkopf or Powell carries in the United States.

One of the incidents that won the KCF notoriety in India was a dramatic rescue in which Manbir Singh Chaheru ("Hari Singh") and three others sprang Sukhdev Singh Sukha (also called Labh Singh) from Jallandhar police custody. After General Hari Singh was arrested and "disappeared," Labh Singh went on to assume the leadership of the KCF. He had been a member of the police force for twelve years before he turned to militancy. He, too, was eventually killed, and his widow and sons fled overseas, where they are now supported by the expatriate militant community.

A second major episode in which the KCF was involved was the assassination of General Vaidya, who had led the Indian armed forces in Operation Blue Star. The story of his "punishment" is a dramatic one, involving two young Sikhs, Sukhjinder Singh and Harjinder Singh (known affectionately as "Sukha" and "Jinda"), who shaved their beards, cut their hair, and infiltrated Vaidya's golf club. (Some have challenged the suitability of shaving one's beard, but one KCF colleague commented that if fighters can't give their hair in the Guru's service, how will they be able to give their heads?) After "delivering justice" to General Vaidya, Sukha and Jinda were able to escape and remained in hiding for several months. Once captured, however, they freely confessed their guilt, and requested the death sentence. When the sentence was handed down, Sukha and Jinda distributed sweets to their fellow jailmates in celebration. They were eventually hanged. The two had, however, written copious essays about their mission in the interim, and these have become staple fare in the militant community. A photo of Sukha and Jinda in jail awaiting their executions is a common household decoration.

The fact that the assassins of General Vaidya have already acquired legendary status in the Sikh militant community is demonstrated by the following story about a seven-year-old boy, who has at this young age internalized the idea of Sukha and Jinda as heroes:

> My nephew, he's only seven years old, he used to have dreams about Sukha and Jinda. He would wake up at night crying, saying that he was dreaming they were being hanged. We would say, no, it's OK, go back to sleep. Then in the morning he would tell us that the bad police were killing our people and we were killing the bad police, and then the bad police arrested Sukha and Jinda and they were hanging them up. Then I got the chance, he said, I took out my gun and I shot the rope. I shot the rope, he would say, I shot the rope and I saved them!

The Babbar Khalsa, established at the time of the Nirankari episode in 1978, remained independent of the new Panthic Commitee structure. The Babbars were in a way an outgrowth of the Akhand Kirtni Jatha, with Sukhdev Singh Babbar heading the mainline Babbar Khalsa and Talwinder Singh Parmar, a Canadian, leading an overseas wing called the Babbar Khalsa International. The Babbar Khalsa has always had a slightly different character than the other guerilla groups, being perceived as very puritan in religious terms.[21] They do not tolerate compromise on the issue of hair, for example, even in the exigencies of guerilla warfare. The spirituality that permeates the Babbars has led some experts to call them a cult rather than simply a guerilla band. Their leader, instead of being called a "general," is called a *jathedar*, a term with a more indigenous connotation. One former militant who was an expert in conducting remote-controlled bomb blasts for the Babbar Khalsa explained,

> I always yearned to be a member of the Babbar Khalsa. It was a well reputed organization and whenever anybody mentioned the word Babbar I had a throb in my heart, thinking, "Oh God, can I one day be a Babbar, too?" So I always felt proud that in fact I accomplished that goal, that I had found a way to be of service.
> Looking at my face now [clean-shaven], the way I look, nobody will believe that what I am saying is true. From my old picture and the way I used to live, nobody could believe that I could have so compromised my principles in this alien land. Can anybody imagine that this mild white-collar worker was at one time bold enough to be a Babbar? Nobody here knows me, knows what I am capable of. What a shame it is that we are reduced to living like this.

The Babbar Khalsa International was implicated in what was probably the best-known episode of the insurgency from the viewpoint of the West. That was the downing of Air India Flight 182 off the coast of Ire-

did look the other way (at the least). Human rights organizations in India did of course investigate these things, with great courage in fact, but their reports were not as accessible to the masses of uneducated Sikhs as the house-to-house, village-to-village campaigns of the militants. People had a sense of homecoming when they embraced the militancy; they were then able to reject government rhetoric as enemy rhetoric and to cease the constant attempt to reconcile what they heard with what they knew.

In an atmosphere of deceit and denial, the massacres surrounding the assault on the Golden Temple Complex and following the assassination of Indira Gandhi seemed in themselves to be assertions of truth. Suddenly, what had been gray was black and white. "The government wanted to *kill* us," one woman said, incredulously, expressing this recognition. Massacre art—in particular depictions of the torn, broken, and seeping bodies lying before the Akal Takht—was distributed and hung in Sikh homes. In their very gruesomeness, these paintings, drawings, and photos assert themselves in a room; they are impossible to ignore, and intrude in conversation, meditation, and everyday activities. Their potency derives only in part from their blood; it derives also from their unwillingness to be masked, covered, or distorted. The slaughter is there for all to see, whatever statistics are released or policies promulgated. Hanging such a painting in one's home is therefore a continuing assertion of the unsuppressible quality of truth—a truth that, in the vision of the militants, is worth dying and killing for. It is a kind of witness that will not allow one to rest.

The element of witness is crucial to understanding how militants are received in the Khalistani community and accounts for some of the style of their combat actions as well. The tradition of *wanggar* (inform and challenge) in the early phases of the Khalistani insurgency is an example: a fighter would call out his identity to his enemies and challenge them to respond, rather than simply eliminating them quietly. (We saw Ajmer Singh Lodhiwal calling out his identity in this way in the last chapter, for example.) As Pettigrew points out, this kind of swagger, resulting as it did in numerous unnecessary casualties, was later discouraged as a routine tactic. But she notes appropriately that the point of this behavior was to deny the enemy's ability to claim that one did not exist, that one was a Pakistani agent or a criminal, and to affirm loudly, clearly, and at risk to oneself, that one was a Sikh, resisting injustice *as a Sikh*. "The martyr is one whom terror does not silence," she concludes.[7]

Guru Tegh Bahadur's execution at Delhi in 1675, as traditionally recounted, exemplifies the element of undying witness in Sikh conceptions of martyrdom. Challenged by his Mughal captors to produce a miracle to prove his divine status, Guru Tegh Bahadur said that he would write a charm, and the executioner's sword would harmlessly fall on the neck around which it was hung. He placed the note around his own neck and offered it to the excutioners, who severed it with a single blow. When Guru Tegh Bahadur's captors opened the note, it said "I have given my head but not my determination."

Sikhs who have been initiated into the siblinghood of the Khalsa use their very bodies to refuse the silence of submission or complicity. The external symbols of faith, particularly the turban and the sword, make Sikhs a conspicuous presence in any crowd, even an Indian crowd in which a multitude of religious adornments and paraphernalia compete raucously for attention. As we saw in Chapter 2, Khalsa Sikhs take these external symbols quite seriously; people have died for the right to wear them (Sant Kartar Singh refusing to be shaved for surgery, for example) and are involved in legal battles in several nations over the right to carry swords in schools, the right to wear turbans in armed service, and so on. How can we account for this deep attachment to the externalities of faith, in a tradition that began when Guru Nanak questioned similar externalities in Islam and Hinduism? How can we understand the five K's in something other than the comic vein of the jokes about Sikhs endemic in the subcontinent?

The *amritdhari* Sikh, in simply being there in an inescapably obvious saffron turban, is using his or her own body as a witness to truth. In this perpetual challenge, *amritdhari* Sikhs are particularly unnerving to governments trying to control them, as stated explicitly in the Indian army's newsletter just after the 1984 events in which *amritdhari* Sikhs were declared outright to be "dangerous." The five K's, as symbols of truth in which people have invested their very lives, become then critical aspects of witness; relinquishing them under any circumstances appears to *amritdhari* Sikhs as an unforgiveable capitulation. And insults to the five K's, a common experience of Sikhs in custody (being forced to drink the urine of a police officer as *amrit*), are unerasable components of militant consciousness. "Truth is pure steel," the Guru Granth Sahib advises, and *amritdhari* Sikhs remember this stipulation through the *karas* they keep on their sword arms. They might die, but they will die *as Sikhs*, standing up fearlessly for truth as they know it. As Paulo Freire commented about the death of Tiradentes, "[they] could quarter his body, but they could not erase his witness."[8] Khalsa Sikhs would understand this sentiment implicitly. And in a climate in which the lives and deaths of Sikhs seem not to be taken seriously, the image of the Sikh militant, defiantly and seriously *present*, is an appealing one indeed. In this context it is not surprising that the image garnered so much ready support. In his very undeniability and unignorability, the *amritdhari* Sikh gave expression to a population whose realities had come to be denied and ignored. Frank

Pieke's comment about the Tienanmen protest in 1989 could be applied to the Sikh militancy also: "Violence was not a rational choice made during a life-and-death struggle but the expression of [the people's] moral outrage and frustration at not being taken seriously." [9]

The Sikh who has been initiated into the Khalsa is not only a witness, however, but also a martyr from the moment of initiation. In the sipping of *amrit* he or she has committed to play Nanak's game of love "with head in hands," utterly selflessly and therefore without fear for one's personal mortality. It is the moment of initiation, the moment of imbibing *amrit*, that is actually the significant moment in the creation of the Sikh martyr; the literal moment of bodily death is something of an afterthought, since the *amritdhari* Sikh is to have "died" to his or her individual self already. The internalization of the idea that death holds no threat accounts for the extraordinary "grace under fire" of Sikh soldiers, the reported serenity of historical heroes under torture, and the otherwise insanely bold actions of Khalistani militants in combat. "Our entire nation has taken birth from the art of keeping its head in its palms," wrote Sukha and Jinda. "The guns of evil will never frighten us." [10]

Death in battle is even welcomed, sometimes positively embraced, as a loss for the individual that paradoxically becomes a victory for the community. A ditty about a Mughal oppressor goes, "Mir Mannu is our sickle, we the fodder for him to mow; the more he reaps, the more we grow." Robin Jeffrey, commenting a bit cynically on the Sikh rhetoric of martyrdom, writes that "no Sikh . . . ever dies or is killed. Sikhs 'slaughter' their enemies, but they themselves 'attain martyrdom' or 'sacrifice their lives.' " [11] In other words, Sikhs perceive themselves as always in control of their destinies, even in the face of death, that one thing that overcomes any human attempt to control. A major task of a human being is then, in a way, to figure out how to die meaningfully. Sikhs are joyous about martyrdom because it represents the liberation of utter control over fate.

To maintain such a stance, which flies against our entire biological heritage, is not an easy thing. Anybody involved in persuading human beings to sacrifice their lives (e.g., a military commander) has to find a way to overcome the basic impulse to self-preservation, not only at the moment of recruitment but in the heat of battle also. In the Vietnam debacle, the U.S. military establishment found itself in many cases inadequate to this task, on the levels both of recruiting and combat performance. Militant Sikhs, however, have three major means by which an attitude of heroic devotion is sustained: first, the constancy of meditation and prayer in the lives of Sikhs; second, the relative insulation of the militant community from the surrounding society, particularly overseas; and, third, the perception of the present as but an echo and repetition

8. "Five Beloved Ones" in ceremonial dress at a *gurudwara* in Surrey, British Columbia. The turbans they wear are saffron, the traditional color of martyrdom. Western Canada continues to be a major center of Khalistani activism.

of the past, which pushes Sikhs to live up to the heroic models of history and to devote their individual lives to their faith in the evanescent present.

We have seen that meditation and prayer occupy a large part of the waking hours of top militants, many of whom "pray twenty hours a day." I have heard one "terrorism expert" comment that these practices put Sikhs in a hypnotic state in which they are hyper-suggestible, a variant of the "brain-washing" theory by which groups we don't approve of are regularly dismissed. Although the psychology, and perhaps the neurology, of meditative states is no doubt relevant here, it doesn't help us much in understanding how Sikhs themselves comprehend the meditation experience. It is at once a union with the transcendent and a rigorous personal discipline, both of which are important components of the head-in-hands humility, including readiness to die, that characterizes the devout Sikh. Deep identification with a spirit beyond oneself, to the point of virtually eradicating self-awareness, provides the sense of refreshment and refuge that Sikhs find in meditative prayer. The discipline of the prayer regimen, alternatively, builds the will that is necessary to overcome all the instincts of flight and preservation. Sikhs *choose* to engage in these meditative activities, knowing and aiming for the results that are obtained. In the fact of this choice lies the negligibility of theories about brainwashing. The effects may be similar, but the motivation to achieve them comes from elsewhere. Bhindranwale instructed his followers outright, "You cannot have courage without reading *gurubani*. Only the *bani*-reader can suffer torture and be capable of feats of strength."

The second factor here, the isolated quality of militant Sikh social life, is what allows free play to the peculiar psychological/philosophical stance described here. In the West, where now the most vehement assertions of militancy are being expressed, expatriate communities totally dominate certain neighborhoods, which become "Little Punjabs" with their own restaurants, Punjabi markets, prominent *gurudwaras*, and so on. In Delta, British Columbia (outside of Vancouver), street after street of houses built to accommodate joint-family living were constructed entirely by Sikh building firms, and whole grades at the local elementary school are composed of boys wearing *patkas* (a precursor to the full turban of the adult) and girls in *salwar-kameez* (Punjabi tunic and pants). In Mississauga, Ontario (a suburb of Toronto), one hears Indian film music blaring from the open windows of houses just as one does in Punjab, and the pungent smell of curry wafts out of kitchens. There are TV and radio programs that cater specifically not only to the Sikh but to the Khalistani Sikh audiences. Militant newspapers abound, both in English and Punjabi. (As Bharati Mukherjee notes in the novel *Jasmine*, "Flushing was a neighborhood in Jullundhar."[12])

Of course, there is accommodation and syncretism. There are Sikh pizza parlors in Delta, for example. In a rather grotesque cultural contortion, two young Sikh girls who were fond of American horror movies compared the indestructibility of the monster-doll Chucky with the immortality of Sikh martyrs, who can be cut to pieces but never die. And yet, despite these kinds of syntheses, I have yet to encounter a militant Sikh household in North America that maintained more than superficial contact with non-Sikh Americans or Canadians. Whether in New York, San Francisco, Washington, or Toronto, Sikhs form a largely self-contained community. Ethnographic research here feels therefore just like fieldwork in any other "exotic" locale; it doesn't seem like it's here, at home. The geographic location is North America, but the cultural location is worlds away.

"Why should they assimilate?" one person queried. "They are only here in exile. When they are needed in Punjab, they have to be ready to go." Whether this sense of being only temporarily resident can persist in the next generation is doubtful. For now, however, the insulation of the militant community, greater here than it could possibly be in Punjab, means that the norms of militant resistance become general cultural norms effortlessly. Kids are growing up venerating the heroes of the Khalistan struggle and, moreover, barely realizing that the rest of the world doesn't think of them that way. They talk about Khalistan as nearly a fait accompli. The older ones, particularly boys, fully expect to fight and die for it.

In this atmosphere, the relinquishing of self that characterizes the *gurumukh*, the Sikh with his face turned toward Guru, is therefore attained through prayer as well as passed along through the process of socialization itself. An attitude of fearlessless is simply normative in this community, and few members would dream of saying that they were not ready to die for the cause. Some of this is plain old peer pressure, but a great deal of it is deeply internalized. The Sikh militancy is therefore best seen not only as a political movement, but as an entire culture coalesced around the concept of resistance. It is not surprising that this culture has flourished in exile, not only because of the greater freedoms enjoyed outside of India but in the simple fact of marginalization itself.

Certainly the fact that young Sikh boys think of themselves as following in the footsteps of Baba Deep Singh and other heroes also gives a special sense of the weight of their actions today. They are contributing to a grander narrative than just the possible overthrow of the Indian government in the late twentieth century; they are fighting Mughals, Afghans, and British at the same time. The Babbar Khalsa fighter in Chapter 2 said that it seemed that the historical martyrs he had read and sung about were taking some of the pain of the torture he underwent with him; likewise, he participates in their glory, and they in his, when he guns down a local official. Veena Das calls this idea that every current event repeats a past one the idée fixe of the Sikhs, noting that it involves both the remembering of some aspects of history and the willful forgetting of others.[13] It is this aspect of resistance to injustice and defense of the faith that is echoed and re-echoed in cyclic accretion, that makes the sacrifice of one puny life today seem a miniscule event against the backdrop of five hundred years of heroism. The Babbar Khalsa fighter asked himself, "Would I live up to the brave deeds of those heroic people, my ancestors?" And indeed, with this in mind, he "passed the test of [his] generation courageously."

Five hundred years of fighting and martyrdom would seem a great weight to bear for a young kid from a rural Punjabi village, or indeed, a high school student in the United States or Canada. But there is a great sense of joy and warmth that permeates that Sikh militant community in the West, which seems to overcome thoughts of suffering and death. How can people with so much violence all around them be so happy and so seemingly at peace with themselves? The name of one of the expatriate Khalistani newspapers, *Chardhi Kala*, gives a hint here. *Chardhi kala* means "rising spirits," and it is a sense of boundless optimism that braces and invigorates someone who has chosen the path of Guru. The rising spirits of the Guru-oriented Sikh stem from the dual exercise of spiritual and temporal power, *miri* and *piri*, that reinforce and enhance one another in an escalating cycle. Prayer and action, action and prayer. Through one, a Sikh becomes stronger in the other. As in the case of the militants who were described as handling their weapons as if in worship or in the case of the guerilla who listened to hymns while going on combat missions, sometimes they are one and the same thing. "Rising spirits" means, really, empowerment, to which both religion and politics, as we all know, contribute. In some traditions these kinds of power are seen as parallel; in some as totally separate. In the militant interpretation of Sikhism, they are identical.

The feeling of *chardhi kala* is also one of liberation. "I was in Jodhpur jail, but I was free as a bird," one Sikh reported. I read him a passage from Thoreau, who had also written of his own (brief) prison experience:

as I stood considering the walls of solid stone, two or three feet thick, the door of wood and iron, a foot thick, and the iron gratings which strained the light, I could not help being struck with the foolishness of that institution which treated me as if I were mere flesh and blood and bones, to be locked up. . . . I saw that, if there was a wall of stone between me and my townsmen, there was a still more difficult one to climb or break through, before they could get to be as free as I was. I did not for a moment feel confined, and the walls seemd a great waste of stone and mortar. . . . They plainly did not know how to treat me, but behaved like persons who are underbred. In every threat and in every compliment there was a blunder; for they thought that my chief desire was to stand the other side of that stone wall. I could not but smile to see how industriously they locked the door on my meditations, which followed them out again without let or hinderance, and *they* were really all that was dangerous. As they could not reach me, they had resolved to punish my body; just as boys, if they cannot come at some person against whom they have a spite, will abuse his dog. I saw that the State was half-witted, that it was as timid as a lone woman with her silver spoons, and that it did not know its friends from its foes, and I lost all my remaining respect for it, and pitied it.[14]

The haughty disdain for the State that thought it could contain Thoreau by jailing him is matched by militant Sikh arrogance toward India. "They had better treat us well," one interlocutor said, "because someday they'll be begging at the steps of Khalistan for some grain for their starving masses." Unlike Thoreau, however, an apostle of individual self-reliance, Sikhs want not to exalt but to erode self, and they do this through the mechanism of prayer, scripture reading, and hymn singing.

The Guru-facing Sikh loses his individual sense of self by being, as one person put it, "drenched" in *bani*. "Why do I repeat the name of God over and over in my mind?" a young student queried. "Because if I wasn't saying 'Guru' I would be saying 'Harman' [the student's name]. I mean not consciously but that selfishness, that ego-centeredness, would be there in everything I did if I didn't replace it with Guru-centeredness. When I eat, I eat for Guru. When I sleep, I rest for Guru's work." I told the militant who felt free in Jodhpur jail the student's words and he added, "When I die, I die for Guru."

Unlike Islam, a religious tradition with an equally prominent tradition of martyrdom, Sikhs who die in battle do not look forward to an eternal life in paradise. Though some elements of heavenly aspiration and of reincarnation have crept into Sikh popular religion, on the whole this is a tradition focused on this life as the only life there is. The emphasis is on praxis here, now, in this world. G. S. Mansukhani, who wrote a popular primer on Sikhism, instructs that "Those who know the art of true living also know that of true dying. True living is dying to the self, the ego, and living up to God. True dying is the privilege of the brave." [15]

Resistance to perceived injustice is an existential stance for the militant Sikh, something one does as meaningful in itself. "I resist, therefore I am," wrote Camus, in a similar spirit.[16] One doesn't necessarily expect to get something out of it, either for oneself or even for one's movement. One engineering student who was part of the Bidar massacre in the late 1980s, for example, explained that he had been far removed from his

9. Young man killed in an "encounter" in Punjab. Some of these encounters are actually gun battles between militants and army or police personnel, but others are "fake encounters" (extrajudicial executions) in which noncombatant Sikhs are shot outright. This is one of a collection of photos of dead bodies that regularly circulate through the Khalistani community.

Sikh origins until, as a Hindu mob bore down on the *gurudwara* in which the students had taken refuge, someone handed him a *kirpan*.

"What was I supposed to do with a *kirpan*?" he recounted. "I was just an engineer. But I kind of held it out in front of me, and you know, somehow I suddenly felt like a real Sikh. In that gesture I knew what being a Sikh meant. I didn't know if we would get out of there or if I would actually kill anybody, but just the feel of that dagger made me recognize that I was a Sikh."

Although Sikh history contains ample elements of both resistance to power and complicity with power,[17] it is in postures of resistance that *amritdhari* Sikhs today feel most fully at home, most fully Sikh. "The Khalsa either rules or is in resistance," they say, harking back to Guru Gobind Singh's motto *Raj Karega Khalsa*. Since they are not ruling, there is no other stance to take than that of resistance, even if the resistance has little immediate chance of success. Militants perceive that they simply have no other option but to continue in resistance as a meaningful lifestyle in itself. Those hoping to contain the militancy are in for a long haul, for resistance is tied to the very identities, both personal and spiritual, of the militants.

VIOLENCE AND LOVE

There is a further and more enigmatic component of Sikh militant consciousness, however, centered on the notion of love. Life as a game of love, as Guru Nanak put it, is a rather different life than the one most of us experience and is certainly not what we typically envision as characteristic of guerilla fighters. But captured by photographers in poses of militancy, holding AK-47s, bandoliers across the shoulder, the martyred militants are regularly described as "gentle," "quite soft," and "full of love." Other observers of guerillas have made similar, problematic, assertions. "They died of an excess of love," wrote Yeats in reference to the Irish uprising of 1916. "Let me say, with the risk of appearing ridiculous," said Che Guevara, "that the true revolutionary is guided by strong feelings of love. It is impossible to think of an authentic revolutionary without this quality." [18]

The union of the kettle to feed the hungry and the sword to defend the weak in Sikh symbolism (the *Deg Tegh Fateh* motto) is expressive of the relationship between violence and charity in Sikh theology. It is not so very different from elements of Christian history: the Hospitaler knights of the Crusader Kingdom, for example, were an army of Christian soldiers who saw their mission in terms of helping the poor and sick as well as riding out to slaughter people in the name of Christ. The same spirit motivated both, however paradoxical it appears.

A British-reared Sikh who visited the Golden Temple Complex shortly before Operation Blue Star made this instructive comment:

> From a clean-shaven perspective [from a European perspective], things must have looked a bit dodgey at the Akal Takht. There were a lot of weapons around. But for Sikhs, we know that Sikhism actually came out of a weapon. If you look at a *gurudwara*, what does it have on top? A *khanda* [double-edged sword]. We know that this emphasis on weapons is entirely from a defensive perspective. It is not a symbol of hate for us but a symbol of love. So when I saw my relatives standing around there with guns I thought, well, they must have a good reason for it. A clean-shaven person might see it differently, of course.

Indeed, the clean-shaven saw it differently, and so did some prominent Sikhs like Khushwant Singh. He wrote in his commentary on the Punjab conflict, *My Bleeding Punjab*:

Bhindranwale promised his audiences the establishment of *Khalsa Raj*. He compared the present time with the worst days of Mughal tyranny: "If a handful of Sikhs could then triumph over the Mughals, it should not be difficult for the Sikhs to oust the government of today." He exhorted villagers to arm themselves, and be ready for action when the time came.

If this was not preaching hatred and violence, I don't know what else it was.[19]

The thing is, it *was* preaching hatred, and then again, it was not. The same words and actions carried multiple, highly divergent meanings within the orthodox community and outside of it. Outside, it was hatred. Inside, it was love, with guns.

One runs the serious risk here, talking about love and militancy, of creating a deadly pornography of violence, of making murder seem romantic, maybe even of encouraging murder, succumbing to the "anthropological temptation" to explain away violence as a form of culture.[20] This is a criticism that in one form or another has faced every scholar who has attempted to grapple with the common perception of people in militancy that what they are doing is a type of love and not of hate. Recently, *Past Imperfect* has squarely accused the postwar French intellectuals like Sartre and Camus of fomenting terrible violence with their elegant rhetorics of liberation,[21] and Yeats, in a reflective moment, asked himself also,

Did that play of mine send out
Certain men the English shot?
Did words of mine put too great strain
On that woman's reeling brain?
Could my spoken words have checked
That whereby a house lay wrecked?

Despite this serious problem (and with great trepidation about the uses to which my own words may be put), I remain convinced that the real obscenity here is not the sentences that drip from the pens of academics or poets but the blood that spurts from the arteries of people in conflict. Conflicts like the one in Punjab simply cannot be resolved by political compromises alone; they are a matter of alien ways of thinking, speaking, and acting that have to be understood before the parties involved can sit down at that bargaining table. To date, most of the actions taken by the Indian government have shown that people making decisions about Punjab don't have much grasp of who Sikh militants are, and they therefore produce policies that are ineffective. To my mind, if Sikh militants go on combat missions out of a spirit of love, we had better try to understand what they mean by that rather than denying it as impossible pornography. An ethnography of militant violence can be, I hope, *anti*pornographic, in that it can lessen the real obscenity whereby people who can't talk to one another hurl bombs instead.

The steel wristbands worn by Sikhs carry multiple meanings for individuals involved in militancy, and the "truth is pure steel" metaphor is only one of them. Another facet of the symbolism of the *kara* is the notion that the bracelet "handcuffs" the wearer to the world.

"It is a bond of love," one militant told me. "Not only to my brothers and sisters of the *panth* but to all human beings."

"We can't express our faith through renunciation," another said. "Being a Sikh is entirely tied to being in the real world. It's a link forged by steel, unbreakable."

Although the universalist sense of common ground with all people permeates Sikh rhetoric (like that of the militant who talked about fighting in Bosnia and Somalia in Chapter 2), the bond of siblinghood among initiates to the Khalsa is the most concrete expression of this "love" of the Sikhs. When "sisters" are sexually dishonored, "brothers" react with anger and shame. Men frequently remember not their own experience of torture in prison but the cries of comrades; women not their own rapes but the insults to their sisters, mothers, and daughters.

The portrait of Sukha and Jinda, hanged for the assassination of General Vaidya, that many militants have hanging on their walls shows not their martial valor but their comradely love. Squatting down, arms about each other's shoulders, they look like the young boys they in fact were, not much like fearsome assassins. They were *yar*, a Punjabi term that means "friends" but carries a much stronger and more committed connotation than the English rendition. The tight bond of solidarity among comrades-in-arms accounts for much of the courageous behavior of Sikh militants in the field and contributes to the cycles of killing and revenge killing that escalated so quickly in Punjab. The U.S. military, recognizing this phenomenon, now keeps "cohorts" of soldiers together through training and combat in the interests of creating a similar inspirational bond.

I suggest that the immediacy of the sense of siblinghood with others in the *panth* affects the behavior of Sikh militants in two other significant ways. The first relates to the torture situation, in which, as Elaine Scarry points out insightfully, the major effect is the radical narrowing of the world of the victim to the space of the pain inflicted, with a corresponding widening of the world of the torturer, which becomes hegemonic.[22]

Resistance to torture, or more accurately, ability to survive torture, depends heavily on the victim's hold on a world wider than his or her pain, and it is in this context that the "handcuffed" quality of a Sikh to the world becomes critically important. One may, out of adherence to principle and individual courage, "refuse to talk" under torture. But surviving it with spirit intact depends on the ability to physically and mentally reject the narrowing of one's world that is the ultimate aim of the torture enterprise, and the elevated attention to the cries of a cellmate or the shame of a sister one hears in narratives of Sikh militants are best understood as part of this attempt to retain a shred of a space, a world, beyond and outside of one's own searing, demanding pain. A tradition that celebrates community bonds is one, in fact, with a latent capacity to mobilize these bonds as a form of resistance, and in the Khalistani insurgency we see this mobilization effected at all levels.

When we come to the ultimate physical affront, death, the capacity of bonds of love to mold individual experience are at their strongest. A death conceived as martyrdom turns what looks like defeat into victory; the individual died, but in his or her bloody witness the truth lives on; the individual died, but the community to which he or she was linked continues. The embracing of death by Khalistani guerillas is often conceptualized as an expression both of witness and of love. Sukha and Jinda said in their farewell address that they imagined the hangman's rope as the embrace of a lover, longed for death as for the marital bed, and hoped that their dripping blood, the outcome of this union, would fertilize the fields of Khalistan. Others compared the martyr's death to a shower of fireworks, which illuminates and guides the entire community; to provide light, the martyr selflessly grasps death. Death in struggle is defined here not only as a feature of courage but as a feature above all of generosity, of selflessness, of love. Hence descriptions of martyred men and women as kind, soft, and gentle ("he was a good listener," said one person about Manbir Singh Chaheru, founder of the Khalistan Commando Force), and the immediate repudiation of leaders who, however bold, acquire the reputation of being greedy, inflated, or selfish. "We are tiny particles of dust of the numberless heroic jewels of the Sikh nation," wrote Sukha and Jinda.[23] And Bhindranwale's wish was to have his ashes scattered at the gate of the Golden Temple Complex so that they would be touched by the loving feet of pilgrims.

Sukha and Jinda also expounded poetically on their love not only for people but for the entire universe in their famous farewell letter. "We are not touched even a bit by hatred for the people of India," they wrote. "Not only to embrace our people, we are restless to embrace all of the earth and sky. We intoxicatingly remember the entire cosmos and worship the life [that] vibrates in it."[24]

Two interesting examples of syncretism among Khalistanis living in the West involve the assimilation of the Sikh tradition of martyrdom to the theme of romantic love in North American popular culture. Commenting on a Fleetwood Mac song that makes reference to "the sea of love, where everyone would love to drown," one expatriate Sikh suggested, "That's what martyrdom is— drowning in a sea of love." Another, noting a cinema advertisement for the movie *Waiting to Exhale*, said "That's what we're like. A community holding its breath." When I responded that I thought the movie was about love, he said "Yes, that's what our struggle is about, too."

One man I interviewed had just gotten out of India a month before I met him, and in the intervening time his wife and infant son had been arrested. Police apparently tied the child to a block of ice in order to make this militant's wife tell them where he was. Rather than succumbing to the temptation to try to spare her child, she asked for a glass of water and when it arrived, she smashed in on the desktop and slit her throat with the ragged edge. She died on the spot. Aside from the inherent horror of this story, with its image of a both bold and gruesome death, is the significant commentary of the husband.

"She was so full of love, she martyred," he said. He was clearly desperately saddened as well as fiercely proud as he told this story. "Resham Kaur, she was a real Sikh," somebody else in the room murmured as both the husband and I were momentarily overcome with emotion.

"What happened to the infant?" I managed to ask. But Resham Kaur's husband had gotten up to compose himself in another room.

Deaths of militants in battle are narrated somewhat differently from deaths of family members, as in the case of Resham Kaur, or in the case of noncombatants who are executed outright (as in the case of the *granthi*'s friends who exchanged their *karas*, then were shot). Despite the many occasions in which Sikh militants saved one another's lives, they typically talk about these episodes without the heightened sense of drama such stories would usually provoke in the Western military tradition. Rather, they are recounted in quite matter-of-fact tones. "X stayed behind, so that Y and I could go on with the second part of our mission." Since X, Y, and Z were already walking around in a state of total dedication, of already presumed martyrdom, the actual embrace of death by X is a matter of personal sorrow, of course, but not of radical heroism. *All* are perceived as heroic. ("It wasn't just a matter of everybody dying in that first week of June," the *granthi* said in Chapter 3. "Everybody knew they would die for the cause sooner or later. So as part of the overall plan some left, some stayed.") What seems a cold-blooded recollection of the demise of a friend—the kind of hyper-rationality that many people fear characterizes "terrorists"—is in fact a phenomenon of an entirely different order. We need to understand the philosophy behind it to comprehend in human terms what Sikh militancy is all about. The friends who let X stay behind were "in love with" him (a commonly used phrase to describe comradely bonds), but felt more strongly their common commitment to the cause than their selfish attachment to him as an individual. Their efforts on behalf of their broader love (for Guru, for Sikhi) was what was being narrated, not their narrower love for X as a friend. Life as a game of love means life unafraid of death, for oneself or for others.

Of course, as long as everyone is playing by the same rules, this works. The enemy in this case, however, has different rules. The Hindu shopkeeper who as a loyal citizen of India reports on Sikh militants is probably not ready to die for it. He has not adopted an existential stance of permanent martyrdom in which such a death could make sense. He is not part of a culture that will valorize his death, put his photo up on its walls, sing hymns on his behalf. When he is gunned down at point-blank range by Sikh militants it is then nothing other than grotesque. Here is the real problem of conflict, as obvious as it is frequently overlooked— the parties to it are playing different games.

In his research on Ilongot headhunters of the Philippines, Renato Rosaldo listened to many stories about why, after the death of a loved one, Ilongot men felt compelled to go out and take a human head. It was only after his own grief and rage following the sudden death of his wife Michelle in the field that Rosaldo comprehended what his interlocutors meant when they said this.[25] This indigenous understanding that the hunting of heads is a natural part of mourning the dead is relevant here because, whereas sometimes the people who are killed in the process are part of the same cultural group—that is, are playing by the same rules— other times the Ilongot prey upon strangers they happen to come across on the road. In the former case, we can in some way understand the killing as part of an implied contract, much like that of soliders who agree to be part of a system based on killing and then are killed in battle. In the latter case, however, we see a real conflict, for the meaning of the act of murder is differently understood by the killer and the victim. This scenario is true in many criminal cases of murder, of course, which we may resolve by labeling the murder as insane, as outside of the range of conventional normality. It's harder when a whole cultural system, Ilongot or Khalistani, has made murder in some way normative.

The very natural assumption that a military enemy thinks like oneself has been challenged by anthropologists from Ruth Benedict onward. When *The Chrysanthemum and the Sword* came out in 1946, despite its various failings, it became clear that the Japanese enemy did not conceptualize the war effort in anything like the way the Allies did; the cultural

10. The aftermath of a bomb blast in rural Punjab, provided by an anonymous source at a *gurudwara* in Toronto in 1993.

context of fighting, and certainly the cultural context of dying, was radically different. It took a suspension of Western preconceptions about violence to comprehend what was going on with kamikazes, for example. The fact is that despite the entangled rhetoric of sports and wars in the West, particularly in the United States, the two endeavors are wildly different—in war the opposing teams have not really agreed on the basic rules (Geneva Convention, war crimes trials, and so on notwithstanding). This disjunction is especially true, of course, of guerilla wars. In a war of resistance, rejection of the rules of the dominant power is in itself a part of the struggle against its hegemonic control.

One Sikh, defending the notion that even militant Khalistanis can be good guests and citizens of the Western countries in which many now live, said, "We will obey every law of every country outside of India. But in India, we will break every law." Where breaking the laws of a (perceived) unlawful power is seen as a revolutionary act, criminality itself becomes militancy. The boundary between crime and political action blurs, because every flaunting of the law is experienced as an assertion of sovereignty.

I suggest that this conscious refusal to play the game of the oppressor, the decision to start a new game of one's own, with one's own rules and not India's, is what is responsible for the failure of militant Sikhs to condemn rather obvious atrocities committed by other militants. Amnesty International, Human Rights Watch, Physicians for Human Rights, and the People's Union for Civil Liberties have all condemned out of hand the massacre of innocents that has occurred *despite Sikh militant claims of morality.* In the third narrative of the last chapter, we see a young man who has "upheld all the highest values of the Sikh religion" building bombs that probably killed, in his own estimation, untold numbers of civilians in Chakri bazaar. I think it's too easy to say that he is simply a hypocrite, and it's certainly *not* true that killing large numbers of innocent people is a value of the Sikh religion. What he has done in this action, and the reason why most others refuse to condemn it, is to flaunt the rules. Since the rules were made up by India, whose demise the militants seek, this bold rejection is in itself a revolutionary action that empowers militant Sikhs whatever the effects on the enemy (possibly negligible, in military terms) or on the outside world (highly negative, in public relations terms). The way the narrator tells the story of the bomb blasts, not only unapologetically but in fact with great pride, is an aspect of this sense of rejecting the old game and creating a new one, which other militants have to admire *even though none of them want to hurt innocent people.* Since Sher Singh at the same time exhibited extraordinary courage, this admiration comes through as nearly unconditional.

"Well, it is not a good thing, in fact it's a very bad thing, that innocent people should be killed," one person commented in a discussion about this episode. "But we love the militants so much because they have sacrificed their whole lives for us. They have so much courage and strength. Maybe mistakes are made or somebody's judgment could have been better. But they are doing all this for us."

Then, too, there is the continual justification for such events based on the extraordinary quality of the current historical moment, seen as a do-or-die cusp for the Sikh community. The need to "save the faith" excuses or covers a variety of sins. "Precisely because the nature of time is seen as extraordinary," Das writes, "it is also assumed that ordinary morality does not apply." [26] The sense that the whole weight of Sikh history has led to the current, demanding moment is one that encourages great heroism, as we have seen, but also tends to crowd out more quotidian moral hesitations. If the entire Sikh tradition is at stake, a few lives here or there seem to weigh rather less—whether these are of martyrs or of victims.

Given the hothouse quality of Sikh militant life, the failure of the *gurumukh* to extend his "love" to those who are either targeted by or fall innocent victim to militant violence is not surprising. Rather, bold actions are applauded as empowering the militant cause and therefore worthy of celebration despite the costs in terms of lives. Dramatic acts of violence, as Franz Fanon noted, have the capacity to jolt the silent masses into an awareness of their power.[27] This experience of sudden empowerment seems to overcome hesitations relating to concern for victims, on the part of both the perpetrators of the violent acts and the audiences who applaud them. Were the sense of being disempowered not so strong, acts of violent empowerment would not resonate as they do in the Khalistani Sikh community—virtually all of whose members assert the primacy of moral considerations in the separatist struggle.

A young student, Canadian-born, explained it in a different way. If he were totally sincere in his belief, a true *gurumukh*, God would simply not allow him to do something really wrong. The Batala bomber was a sincere believer, so God would not have permitted him to commit an unethical act; therefore the bombing must have been morally justified. I asked the student whether he realized what this sounded like, that a sincere believer in fact could do no wrong. He realized, of course, exactly what that sounded like to a nonbeliever (very frightening). Nevertheless, he rested his faith on it; the cornerstone of morality is belief in Guru. All else would follow from that.

RESPONDING TO TERROR

During the writing of this book the Alfred P. Murrah Federal Building in Oklahoma City was blown up, and this occasion, the most devastating act of terrorism yet on American soil, provided the context for further discussion with militant Sikhs about civilian deaths. They were uniformly horrified at what had happened in Oklahoma City. Interestingly, several noted the emphasis the American media placed on the children's deaths associated with the day-care center and the prominence of images of bloodied and limp children on magazine covers and on television newscasts.

"Why do you think there's this emphasis on children?" I asked in one session.

After some silence, someone in the room said, "Kids are too young to know what's going on. They haven't had the chance to make a choice. So it's unfair that they should be killed."

Fair enough. That's what most of us would say also, though it's doubtful whether other workers in that federal building "chose" to put their lives on the line in their jobs, not to speak of various visitors to the building who were also killed in the blast. Nevertheless, the innocence of children is, for us, a given. I then, with a concentrated attempt at tact, tried to draw a parallel with episodes in which innocents were killed by Sikh militants in Punjab.

"That would be a very dangerous analogy to make," one said. I knew that, but pushed on, carefully.

It became clear during a very difficult and halting discussion that the main reason why the two cases were perceived as incomparable by the people with whom I was talking was because the Sikhs had a serious grievance, a just cause, while the bombers in Oklahoma City really didn't. That is, the moral evaluation here was at the level of the perpetrators, not at the level of the effects (dead people). Eventually the talk turned back to the issue of kids.

"The thing is about children," one Sikh said, "they are not ready to die. We are ready to die. We could die at any minute. But a child has not thought about death. He's not prepared."

"What about people in Punjab, say, living in a neighborhood in which a bomb goes off . . . ?" I tried to ask.

"Look, they're in a war. Anybody who is in a war has to be prepared to die. Maybe people in Oklahoma are just living peacefully, and somebody blows them up, then that's terrible, horrible. Whoever did that should pay for it. But in Punjab it's a situation of war. Somebody may not 'deserve' to die, may not be personally guilty like a police officer or a military commander or something, but if you're living there you are, well, ready. It's a war. People get killed. It's too bad, but there's no point hiding from that reality." [28]

Of course, the great failure of imagination here, the tragic failure of imagination, centers on the fact that for the civilian "other" in Punjab, there is no war. There's just "terrorism," blind, utterly meaningless, and horrific.

The militants think that what they've got is a war, with both sides ready to sacrifice, but the Indian government thinks it's got a crime problem, in which deaths on one side are acceptable but deaths on the other atrocious. Since it is usually governments, not insurgents, that have money, power, and propaganda at their disposal, most of the world thinks of "the Punjab problem" in the latter terms. The reason why I say here that this is tragic is not on the merits of the Khalistani Sikh cause or the demerits of the case for viewing Sikh militancy as a version of crime but on simple strategic grounds. For a person fighting a war, losing family members to a war, sacrificing a whole life plan for a war, to be labeled a criminal and treated like one is an insult that can only be met with redoubled efforts. Sikh militants are quite ready to die, as we have all seen clearly. What they are not ready for is capitulation to somebody else's definition of who they are. Therefore every attempt to discredit the Khalistan movement by recourse to the language of crime and terrorism will, I believe, backfire tenfold. And it will encourage the most dangerous kind of back-fire, the kind in which people actively flaunt the rules, create their own definitions, establish new playing fields.

"You succeeded in driving us to a point of utter frustration," wrote Sukha and Jinda in their farewell letter to the President of India, just before their executions. "Very subtle arrangements have been made at the psychological level to destroy . . . the Khalsa Panth. . . . You have tried your hardest to humiliate us as a nation. . . . We have chosen the path of martrydom so that the ever fresh face of the Khalsa and its unique glory can come into its own once again." [29]

When India appointed Governor Chibber, who played a role in Opera-tion Blue Star, to the top appointed position in Punjab in 1994, it was rubbing salt in a wound as far as militant Sikhs were concerned. The fact that the commission created to look into the anti-Sikh atrocities in No-vember of 1984 was not more aggressive in prosecuting higher-ups in the police force and in the Congress Party rankles deeply. The appointment of S. S. Ray, who served as governor of Punjab during a period of some of the most serious human rights abuses (called "The Butcher of Pun-jab" by militant Sikhs), as ambassador to the United States was likewise virtually calculated to alienate. (Julio Ribiero, director general of police during Ray's administration, became ambassador to Romania, where he was later assaulted by Sikhs.) K. P. S. Gill, as director general of police in Punjab, was cited by human rights organizations as personally respon-sible for the widespread atrocities of torture, rape, and "encounter" kill-ings, but remained at his post for years.

It seems obvious that the only way to win back the loyalties of disaf-fected Sikhs would be, for a start, to apologize publicly for Operation Blue Star, seriously look into what happened there, and compensate the families of victims (*not* reward people involved in it with high gov-ernment posts). One could go on to a more serious investigation into the anti-Sikh pogroms and to the human rights abuses that the Indian government has simply refused to admit exist on a widespread basis, sanctioned at the highest levels. In the past two years, a start has been made on some of these fronts—Ray is gone; Gill is gone; some human rights initiatives are making their way up through the Indian courts. These are positive developments. But atrocities continue, not only in Punjab but in Kashmir and the northeast as well. And for Sikh militants, whatever is done now is simply too little, too late. Khalistan has now be-come a matter of defending one's honor.

The study of separatist Sikhs makes clear that a major factor in their alienation is simply *feeling insulted* (remember that picture of the humili-ated Sikh crouching on the floor?), *feeling that they are not taken seriously*. "The Sikh psyche knows no other medicine except that every insult must be avenged," writes Dr. Sohan Singh, founder of the Second Panthic Committee.[30] "Fearful states" that respond to political challenges with military crackdowns, then celebrate the effectiveness of those crackdowns over the bodies of slain citizens, themselves provoke the continuing obscenity of terrorism.[31] It may well be too late for India to win back the allegiance of Sikh militants who feel their honor has been irreparably compromised. But it is hard to see how government appointments and proclamations that rub salt in open wounds contribute to anything more than the escalation of public fears and hatreds. Though useful in terms of electioneering among the majority community, they are disastrous in terms of resolving conflict with a severely alienated minority.

In Brar's account of Operation Blue Star he cites a description of "the Sikh character," which as a Sikh in command of forces arrayed against Sikhs he finds a propos, as follows:

But the Sikh is always the same—the same in peace, in war, in barracks or in the field. Ever genial, good tempered and uncomplaining—a fair horseman, a stubborn infantry soldier, as steady under fire as he is eager for a charge. However, when his self-respect or honour of the womenfolk is at stake, he becomes desperate and will stop at nothing short of murder. He does not pocket an insult, bides his opportunity for revenge and becomes quite unmindful of the consequences. When aroused, he has the fury of ten elephants. It is difficult to check him. He becomes exercised, loses his mental equilibrium and does not care for the consequences of his action. You may break him, but you cannot bend him. When he is in a desperate mood, he responds only to tactful handling, sympathetic treatment, and persuasion. Any coercive measures taken against him, hardens his mood of desperation. Handled in tactful measure, he easily forgives and forgets, and is ready to side with erstwhile enemies.[32]

Although the essentializing tone of this passage is out of sync with contemporary academic writing, the author describes an ethos that Lieutenant General Brar finds quite realistic. It is, I suppose, one of the ironies of history that he himself played a central role in "breaking" the unbendable militants who had taken refuge in the Golden Temple, in taking the strongest of coercive measures that did indeed harden "the mood of desperation." He cannot have been surprised at the outcome, however confident he was that Operation Blue Star was an appropriate and necessary response from the viewpoint of state security.

Paulo Freire, the Brazilian educator, has written most persuasively about the embrace of revolutionary violence as a reclamation of human dignity. Asserting that people have an "ontological vocation" to define and defend their own humanity, he accuses the powerful of dehumanizing those whom they subordinate by imposing their own view of the world on them. Though Freire's neglect of the actual structures of domination—police barricades and so on—may strike some readers as overly abstract, it meshes perfectly, in my view, with Sikh experience. What hurts is being treated like a criminal (as "Boxer" said in the last chapter), not the roller on one's legs. It hurts as much to be told that one is another form of Hindu as to see one's river waters diverted. It is in this sense that Roy D'Andrade's comment, that the mystifications of the powerful play little role in maintaining oppression[33] (and that therefore the efforts of morally minded scholars to demystify such ideologies are futile) is inadequate. Though we shouldn't delude ourselves as to our actual power to affect events (very minor), in my perception *and in that of militant Sikhs*, "to speak a true word is to transform the world," as Freire suggests.[34] It is not only "honor" and "self-determination" that are named as goals of the Sikh community in a popular book by Sangat Singh, but also "voice."[35]

In the same way that the dramatic actions of militants attempt to break through the rules set up in a framework in which they are "criminals" in order to establish a new terrain in which they are "freedom fighters," the person who by dint of circumstance finds herself in a position to give voice to this process by the pen rather than the sword I think has a moral imperative to do so. "Limit-situations," as Freire calls them, moments of decision when one either goes ahead and breaks through the barriers of established frameworks or not, occur in Punjabi bazaars and in the halls of academia both. People who have been denied their voices in the civilized forum of public debate, or who perceive that what they say will not be heard in that forum, set off bombs in bazaars. If we abhor the setting off of bombs, those of us who have the good fortune to have other options have to make good use of them.

Nancy Scheper-Hughes insists that anthropologists are not only "spectators" accountable to science but also "witnesses" accountable to history. She writes that

Anthropologists who are privileged to witness human events close up and over time, who are privy to community secrets that are generally hidden from the view of outsiders or from historical scrutiny until much later—after the collective graves have been discovered and the body counts made—have . . . an ethical obligation to identify the ills in a spirit of solidarity.[36]

When the parties to a conflict are as uneven as they are in Punjab (or Northern Ireland), the scholar-as-witness has a special responsibility to speak what she knows of the truth. The massive propaganda put out by the Indian government and its various allies in India on the subject of Punjab has achieved nearly total sway on world opinion. Milan Kundera, in *The Book of Laughter and Forgetting*, wrote of another unequal conflict,

The first step in liquidating a people is to erase its memory. Destroy its books, its culture, its history. Then have somebody write new books, manufacture a new culture, invent a new history. Before long that nation will begin to forget what it is and what it was. . . . The struggle of man against power is the struggle of memory against forgetting.[37]

In an age of Holocaust-deniers, the responsibility of scholars to persist in writing and preserving truths should be self-evident. (Recently, an "Assembly of Turkish Americans" took out a quarter-page ad in the *New York Times* denying the Armenian genocide; there are more denials than the anti-semitic one that need to be challenged.) However one feels about the Khalistani militants, the primary duty of a scholar to investigate and write about the abuses suffered by the Sikh community, to speak truth to power, is clear.

Scheper-Hughes wants to be a *companheira* to the people with whom she works, and Julie Peteet was called *rafiqah*, comrade, by her Palestinian interlocutors.[38] But the situation in Punjab is ethically more complicated that that of the impoverished cane-workers with whom Scheper-Hughes lived in Brazil and more problematic in several ways than that of the refugee-camp Palestinians Peteet knows. It is impossible to estimate, for one thing, what proportion of the Sikh community actually supports the Khalistan movement: in the absence of a referendum, without a true free press, and with much of the population living under conditions of extreme fear, no one can come up with a believable assessment. (Wildly divergent figures are thrown around all the time, with no evidential basis as far as I can see.) In addition, the way in which religious rhetoric intertwines uneasily with the theme of national liberation in the Khalistan movement, and the tendency of militants to focus more on the quest for sovereignty as an abstract goal than on explicit consideration of what a Sikh state would be like, give potential sympathizers reason to tread carefully.

Outright solidarity with militant Sikhs is therefore not the position I choose here. I recognize their grievances and admire their courage, but I cannot make their cause my own. Although my interlocutors may not appreciate this, I believe that what I can best do here is not to embrace their movement and to write on its behalf but to serve as a translator between their cultural world and that of the outside (shared largely by secular Indians as well as the West). This bridging role is one for which I am temperamentally as well as professionally suited. It does not mean that I am "neutral." How can I be? I have put, virtually, my head in the hands of Sikh friends, and they have reciprocated that existential risk. But recognized or not, the true "act of love" here, as Freire calls it,[39] the real act of solidarity, is not becoming an apologist for Khalistan but critically and respectfully examining what these people are up to, how they are figuring out how to be human. In the long run, it is this kind of witness, sometimes harsh, that will be the most valuable service.

Scheper-Hughes notes also that "participant-observation has a way of drawing ethnographers into spaces of human life where they might really prefer not to go at all."[40] Nobody really wants to have to recognize that there can be a certain comprehensibility to bomb throwing, or, in Scheper-Hughes's case, to maternal neglect. The complexity of a world in which "magnificent" human beings end up slaughtering civilians is hard to take sometimes; it would all be so much easier if there were a simple good and evil dichotomy going on. But anthropologists' jobs are to unsettle, to pull the rug out from under conventional formulae, to ask difficult questions. A "womanly ethic," as Scheper-Hughes, following Gilligan, calls it,[41] a professional ethic of care and responsibility, means, for me, celebrating human attachments while finding the courage to speak the truth. The game of love I play is not the same one as the game played by Sikhs, but they intersect in that critical ethnographic moment when I and Thou sit side by side, heads in each other's hands, full of our different anguishes and expectations, hopeful and fearful.

9

THE PRINCESS AND THE LION

AMANDEEP KAUR

"**W**ELL, I DIDN'T HAVE any interest in politics prior to 1988. But when I went to college I saw some victims of the brutality of the state, and this shook my conscience. One girl, Harjinder Kaur Khalsa, had come from Australia to get married in Punjab, and on the way back she was arrested at the airport in Delhi and was martyred. Then there was a boy, Gurmukh Singh, who was the captain of the hockey team at my college. He was tortured so badly by police that he was admitted to the hospital and died on the fifth day there due to profuse bleeding. It occured to me then that I could try to make some changes, some social reform, and change the face of my religion on which there are many black spots at this time.

"After our college mate Gurmukh Singh died, some of us went to his house to express our sympathy to his family. We found out that he was the only son. There were four sisters and Gurmukh Singh was the eldest. When I saw those little girls crying I thought, why can't the police be held answerable for these atrocities? My mind was in a state of excitement. Why shouldn't it be me who should ask these police why this innocent boy was killed?

"But asking for answers from the police would mean two things. Either I would be killed like Gurmukh Singh in an encounter, or else they would put ammunition on me and I would languish in jail for years. So I didn't do anything.

"I was the best athlete of my college for four years, and I became captain of our team of girl's hockey. I was considered to be a brilliant sportswoman and an intelligent girl, and I came from a good family, but it was paining my heart that Sikh boys and girls who were really deserving couldn't reach the positions in life they deserved. I saw discrimination everywhere.

"Then by the grace of Waheguru I met one Singh, Gurdev Singh, who was related to me distantly. He knew that I belonged to a devout family and that I could do anything I was told to do very responsibly. One day he told me bluntly that there was some ammunition that had to be taken to some particular place. Could I do that?

"I said, 'Yes, I will do it,' and Gurdev Singh handed over all the ammunition. Why did I do this? I did it because I wanted to know the answer as to why Gurmukh Singh was martyred. I wanted to hold the police answerable for their crimes and there was no way to do it other than this way. I couldn't stand the torturing and killing of innocent boys.

"I decided not to tell my family about this decision to take action, because I feared they might obstruct my path. I had made up my mind to do it, come what may. And with my fellow friends I wasn't sure they were as serious as I was, and I thought they might make fun of me or something. I told nobody what I was going to do.

"There happened to be two police checkposts on the way to where that ammunition had to be deposited. I was wearing my track suit and I took the ammunition and hid it under my clothes. When I came to the bus stand I saw the brother of a close friend of mine, and he had a scooter. I asked him if I could borrow that scooter as I had house guests at my place and needed to go into the village. He said that would be fine, and I took his scooter and drove off.

"I was stopped at the first police checkpost. It's not a very common sight in Punjab for girls to be driving scooters, so if somebody does it people notice it and question it. A policeman said, 'Where are you going? Where are you coming from?' It turned out that they were looking for two young men, and one of them was in fact Gurdev Singh, who had assigned me this responsibility. I didn't tell them anything, just mentioned the name of my father, who was a respected man in the area. They let me go on.

"At the second police checkpost the police on duty also knew my father well and respected his name. So I was not detained there either. With God's grace I was successful in getting the ammunition to its destination where it was received by the Singhs. When I returned back home I felt satisfied that I had done my work well. I was contented and actually jubilant.

"In this moment of jubilation it occurred to me that if I could be successful in this, why couldn't I join my Sikh brothers in direct combat action? After all, Sikh girls are as brave as Sikh men, and I knew they always stood by their brothers and husbands in times of need. I knew I was capable of taking any risk, that nothing could scare or deter a Sikh woman.

"I didn't know of any women, though, who were actually involved in combat. But I requested brother Gurdev Singh to let me join him in the movement. 'I will be with you through thick and thin,' I said. 'I am capable of taking as many risks as you are.'

"Gurdev Singh said, 'You are a girl, you can't join us.'

"I realized that to be a girl is really a big sin in India. But through my repetitive and persistent requests and my bold assertions he finally said, 'OK, you can be a member of Khalistan Commando Force, but we can't take you on any combat actions.' I settled for that, but in my mind I knew what I wanted to do.

"They first had me sign up as a member of the Sikh Students Federation, on November 12, 1988. That was not a banned organization at the time. It became my routine task to take ammunition from one place to another, and I swear by God I never had a grain of fear in my mind. I always felt satisfied and contented after I had carried out my duties.

"During all this time, I didn't mention a word to my family and especially not to my mother. It is a well-known fact that women can't keep secrets. I thought that out of fear my mother might mention to somebody that her daughter has gone on this path. As far as I was concerned, I had taken a stern vow that I would not allow any police person to touch my body. I would martyr before I would let anybody come close to me. I was not scared of death in any way, but I feared that my secrets should come out.

"There was also such a climate of terror that sometimes even parents of boys or girls killed in police actions refused to identify or claim the bodies. If they did claim the bodies the police would compel them to issue a statement that their son or daughter was a terrorist. If the parents made that statement, even then they didn't escape the wrath of the police. They always humiliated and tortured them. That's why I refused to involve my family. I was not afraid for myself but I didn't want to disturb the peaceful life of my little brothers and my parents.

"I began preaching with a missionary zeal to my fellow college students. I started telling them to abide by the teachings of Guru Granth Sahib. My particular focus was those who had been led astray by the materialistic life and were not living as devout Sikhs. I preached to them peacefully for some time, but then I noticed some spoiled boys who were continually giving a hard time to the college girls. They used to tease them, standing by the roadside. I decided to teach them a lesson.

"One day, a girl complained to me that two boys stopped her on the path, chased her, and made her life miserable. I summoned those boys to me at the library, and I gave them a warning. I asked them to desist from what they were doing, plaguing the college girls. They were adamant, though, and they said they would do whatever they wanted, and I could do whatever I wanted to do about it.

"Within the college campus there was a lot of security, so I couldn't put any plan into action there. There was a local bus stand nearby, where the girl who had been teased used to catch a motor rickshaw to get home. I went there, and saw one of those boys approach that girl and start making rude comments to her. The girl looked at me in a very piteous manner, so I decided I had to take some bold action. I walked up to that boy and Waheguru gave me the strength to hold him by the collar and give him a big punch on the nose!

"That boy fell at my feet immediately. I was wearing sports shoes, and in the full presence of all those people at the bus stand I went ahead and kicked him. I beat him so badly that one of his front teeth got broken. He didn't even fight back, as I suppose he couldn't imagine in his wildest dreams that some girl could hit him and teach him a lesson. It was a usual practice that girls used to take everything silently. I say firmly now that not only boys but girls, too, were to be blamed for the sad state of affairs. They took everything too quietly.

"As for the other boy, his companion, he left the area and was never seen again.

"There was a professor of my college at that time who was a witness to that whole episode. He came up to me and, patting my back, he said, 'You are a brave girl. If you can teach these boys a lesson in front of these people, you might accomplish a lot if you had proper training.' It turned out that that professor was not only the well-wisher of the Singhs but one of them. He did everything stealthily, and no one knew of his involvement.

"As I was always looking for the right man to guide me, I said to this professor, 'Sir, I want to do something. I want to ask for some answers from the police. I want to know why they are killing so many innocent people. Please guide me on the right path.'

"That professor said, 'Well, if you want to just ask that question in an honest way, in a peaceful way, that simply means that you will be dead.'

"I said, 'If the police can martyr all these young boys who are a good match for them, I would be just a small prey before them. I am just a helpless girl.'

"Professor knew what I wanted to do, and he told me, 'On the path that you are choosing, there is no place for sentimentalism. Even if your near and dear may be killed. Women are of a more sentimental nature, and it may be hard to tread this very difficult path.'

"There was a portrait of the tenth Guru, Guru Gobind Singh, hanging on the wall of the office where we were talking. I prayed before the tenth Guru and I said earnestly, 'Oh, you rider of the blue steed, give me strength that I can fight against tyranny alongside my brother Singhs. If I can't, then tell me why you gave me so much courage and strength, if you made me a girl? Why didn't you make me a boy?'

"That professor was very much impressed by my sincerity as a I prayed before the tenth Guru, and he decided that I was fit to join the ranks of freedom fighters. He asked me to vow before the picture of Guru Gobind Singh that I would never be captured alive, that if at any time this some-how happened I would stand all the torture and agony I might suffer but I would never leak any secrets. I took this vow.

"And so a simple, naive girl from a rural spot became a terrorist in the eyes of Punjab police!

"I became really sick of the way some of these professors, who tie big turbans on their heads, behave in anti-Sikh fashion. Why don't they have the courage to stand by the teachings of Guru Granth Sahib? I challenged them on this sort of thing. What's the point of all these sacrifices if the consciousness of the people is not raised?

"One day some time later, I was on my usual routine of taking ammunition from one place to another. I was stopped by a notorious police person who had earned the nickname *Ghotna* ('Pestle') since he was fond of a particular torture in which a wooden roller crushed the legs of his victims. He caught me right outside the college complex and said he wanted to frisk me.

"It occured to me that if I showed any fear in my reaction then 'Pestle' and his companions would frisk me and the whole secret would be out. So I made up my mind to deal with this situation with boldness. I said, 'If you want to frisk me, you have to first show the warrants of my arrest.' The police said they didn't have any warrants but they would frisk me anyway. Then I asked, 'Haven't you read in your police training that if a girl is to be frisked it can only be done with a woman police present? Without a warrant and without a woman officer around, you can't frisk me.'

"Hearing this bold response, the police seemed to be shaken. I guess it occurred to them that if a young girl like me was not afraid in a situation like this she must have nothing to hide. At that time, I was twenty-one, but I looked only sixteen or seventeen, as I used to knit my hair in two plaits like children do, and I always wore track suits and not women's clothing. Anyway, they let me go and with God's grace I reached my destination.

"One of the Singhs there was disturbed when I told him about this encounter. He said that it could happen again and that I might not be so lucky the next time. It turned out that it was a Hindu shopkeeper who alerted the police to watch out for me. The Singhs told me that if I wanted to take revenge on him it would be OK.

"I thought about this carefully. I thought that I had escaped from 'Pestle' with God's grace, but I might not be safe in the future. So I decided that some action was warranted.

"When night came two boys, two other girls, and me went out to find the house of that Hindu informant. I used to tell my parents that sometimes we had to practice at the hockey field until late at night, so nobody worried about where I was. But the five of us finally got to Lala's [shopkeeper's] house. His family had gone out to attend a marriage ceremony nearby, and Lala was alone in the house. My four companions went ahead but when I joined them this Lala looked at me with his mouth wide open in surprise. 'Oh, it's you?' he asked.

" 'Why did you complain against me to the police?' I demanded. 'The police were not able to get anything out of me, but now I will tell you who I am.'

"Lala started begging for pardon and crying that I was like his daughter. 'Forgive me, forgive me,' he was saying. But I shot him down with my revolver, with my own hands. That was my first experience in direct assault.

"After that I used to go to a village where the Singh brothers got weapons training. At first we girls cooked meals for our Singh brothers, but after some time I felt more free with them and I asked them to give me training in the use of weapons. At first they refused, but eventually they said, 'OK, you are so brave, we are ready to teach you.' Gurdev Singh, that boy who had originally involved me in the carrying of ammunition, vouched for me and told about all the risks I had already taken and the difficult situations I had already been in.

"I was thinking about that shooting of Lala, too. I thought that if only every Sikh girl punished people who were responsible for informing or for other crimes, then our objective of an independent nation would come sooner. I also saw that the boys who were with us reacted to my bold action with appreciation. I thought that it must have given them a boost in confidence. If girls could be so brave, then they could be even more brave, they probably thought.

"In our religion there is equality for women. But if the woman herself is not courageous, then why should she blame the man for not giving her equality? It should be that if the man takes a step ahead, the woman should be courageous enough to take two steps ahead. With baptized Sikhs, I am confident that women don't face any real hindrances. If they believe in Guru they get the respect and dignity they deserve. And those Sikhs sitting behind and not joining in the struggle, they may get inspired by the participation of the women to come forward and fight for the liberation of Khalistan.

"One of those boys with us during the killing of the informant Lala was Manpreet Singh, who attended Guru Nanak Dev University in Amritsar. He was killed by the police two or three months later after severe torture. They threw his body in front of Lyallpur Khalsa College in Jallandhar. Since he was our comrade, we wanted to hold a continuous recitation of Guru Granth Sahib after seeking the permission of the college administrators. But the Jallandhar police didn't permit us to hold this recitation for the peace of his soul.

"We were determined to hold this function in our comrade's memory, so we started the ceremony right on the roadside. A big traffic jam developed as we recited the Guru Granth Sahib. There were long lines of traffic on both sides of the road. Finally a police official came by and agreed to let us have the recitation inside the college complex. I realized then that there were two sets of laws in this country, one for Hindus who can hold their ceremonies anyplace they like, and another for us, who can't even commemorate the death of one of our young boys. The clear message was that this country doesn't belong to us.

"During all this time my name became known in various districts. We used to hold meetings of the Sikh Students Federation in our home under the guise of celebrating the birthday of one of my relatives or friends. My parents thought that since I was in college it must have become a fashionable ritual for us to celebrate so many birthdays in this way. No one knew what the meetings were really about.

"The same notorious police officer, 'Pestle,' used to patrol that area and he stopped me again one time. I can only say that with the grace of Waheguru I had nothing on my person that time. There were two lady police officers with him, though, and I thought they they were perhaps jealous of me because my reputation had spread and they themselves had rather missed that opportunity. Those two lady constables used to be assigned to stay at the bus stands so that girls should not be harassed, but nobody ever listened to them. Rather, girls who felt afraid would call my name, and the boys who were bothering them would run away!

"My brother Singhs found out that it was again a Hindu informer who was responsible for 'Pestle' picking me up. After I was released on the word of one MLA who knew that I was the leading student of my college, I made up my mind that this kind of informing had to be stopped. This rich Hindu would have to pay the price of being an informant against me.

"We reached this Lala's home at about midnight. The whole family had gone to sleep. Again there were five of us, three girls and two boys. We huddled all the family into one room and warned them to keep quiet, and we brought that Lala into another room. We made him sit in a chair in the front veranda. Actually it was the four of them who did all this, as I was standing somewhat behind. Then my companions called me loudly and I appeared on the scene. I looked at this Lala and I said, 'Look at this lady. You want me to be arrested by the police?' He promptly said, 'Oh, I have not reported against you to the police.'

"I said, 'Well, you told the police that I was a dangerous girl, and now you are about to find out for yourself just how dangerous I really am.' My companions tied him to his chair with a rope, and I shot him down.

"The next day at home, my mother mentioned to me that freedom fighters had killed that rich Lala from Tarn Taran. I kept quiet, but in my heart I was happy that I had accomplished this mission and nobody had caught wind of it.

"On Monday I went back to college, and I got the impression that the boys and girls were looking at me in a different way. In my dreams I started getting a vision of unidentified bodies at a crossroads, and I saw my own body among them. I was haunted by all this. I thought about how it is a known fact of history that brutal governments try to destroy the youth of a nation so that nobody can challenge them. And I though about how sad it is for us girls, too. No matter what righteous path a girl might follow in full sincerity, she is always looked upon with suspicion or contempt. Today people hail that Tamil girl who killed Rajiv Gandhi, but tomorrow if I should accomplish such a thing people might scold my parents for not bringing me up properly. In the case of women you can never tell what the reaction might be. I was disturbed by these thoughts.

"Eventually, I slipped out of the country and went to the Middle East. It was my commitment to my family that made me feel restricted as to what I could do for the Sikh nation. They never knew what I was involved in, and I didn't want to bring any harm or shame to them. Other members of families of freedom fighters have been tortured and killed by police, even their distant relatives. I was constrained by this thought, and eventually I left.

"I know that whenever my Sikh nation will really need my help, however, I am capable of breaking all these shackles that bind me. If need be I will break them. I will be back there in a second with a gun in my hand, and no one will stop me."

A WOMANLY ETHIC?

Sikhism is probably the only major religion of the world that claims gender equality as one of its central precepts. The texts are unequivocal on this point, and though Sikhs recognize that they do not always live up to the desideratum of equality, it remains an ideal accepted by all. To my knowledge, there has never been any debate about whether or not women should become scripture readers, caretakers of *gurudwaras*, baptized members of the Khalsa, or freedom fighters. All career paths are, in the ideal, fully open to members of either gender. The third Guru, Guru Amar Das, had forbidden widow burning, seclusion of women, and female infanticide—practices still common in much of India. Guru Gobind Singh made woman, *kaur* or princess, and man, *singh* or lion, siblings in the Guru's family.

In fact, of course, this ideal has not exactly worked out. Equal opportunity is there, but actual equality is not. What we see in the preceding testimony is a young girl struggling with the contradictions of her society, which culturally restricts women in so many ways and yet is, in the end, responsive to insistent demands of equal treatment if an individual has the wherewithal to pursue them. Why this particular woman developed the character that would allow her to persist in her determination to take part in the militant movement is a crucial, but perhaps unanswerable, question. When I asked her about it, she responded in terms of her parents' devotion to the Guru Granth Sahib and the strength that devotion gives her to do what she feels Guru asks her to do. Petite in stature, demure under a filmy head covering, soft spoken, with pink nail polish on fingers and toes, this young woman does not appear to be capable of executing informers in cold blood. Her deference to men, apparent in her narrative, runs right alongside her obvious strength and courage. She thinks that her own demonstrations of these qualities will push men to even further acts of strength and courage. (As one of Julie Peteet's Palestinian women comments, "Men are braver when women are around."[1]) She repeats cultural stereotypes of women as sentimental and as unable to keep secrets even as her own life story belies them.

Like many Sikh women, she does not experience the cultural tradition of female deference as conflicting with the ultimate respect for women as human beings, and as human beings who fight. Western feminism, with its insistence on refusal to defer in any sphere, strikes many Sikh women as rather silly. How many of those women who won't let a man open a door for them would be capable of fighting in a guerilla war? This is the unstated challenge behind many of the discussions Sikh women have about women in the West, who seem so patronizing in their apparent equality with men. From the viewpoint of women who daily risk death, discussion of who washes the dishes seems an absurdity. Among Sikh women with whom I have spoken there is an aura of bemused tolerance, occasionally verging on outright pity, for Western women who may not have to wash dishes but who dare not gain a pound for fear of male disapproval, who face at least a 50–50 prospect of divorce, who juggle careers and children in a never-ending whirlwind of stress, and who are still struggling to achieve the right to equal opportunity in combat.

Sikh women have always had the right to participate fully in war activities, but in fact they have been more noticeably prominent in support roles than in actual combat. These include the usual sheltering of militants, cooking for militants, sewing clothes for militants, and performing other domestic tasks. The role most lauded in Sikh tradition is of the woman who, through her own stance of courage and determination, prods the men around her to militancy. Mai Bhago, a woman who refused to let forty Sikh soldiers retreat from a battle, is the historical model here, and Amandeep Kaur draws on this tradition even as she herself does more than simply spur her male comrades to action. She is inspired perhaps more by the literary heroine Sundari, who, in a popular turn-of-the-century novel by Bhai Vir Singh, fights in the jungle alongside her male comrades.

Julie Peteet's study of Palestinian women in resistance is an important

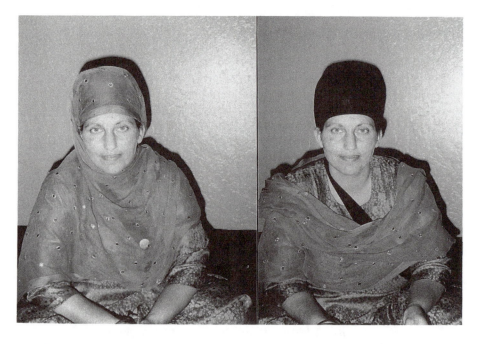

11. Photos of an *amritdhari* Sikh woman wearing the turban and *kirpan* (the strap is visible) under her traditional head covering. These photos were taken at a *gurudwara* in Fremont, California, in 1993.

ethnography of women who fight. While describing the full participation of some Palestinian women in guerilla activities, it brings out at the same time some of the paradoxes faced by these women against the backdrop of Islamic doctrine and Arab culture. The classic separation of female and male spheres as private and public, with women largely remaining in the private domestic arena, was shattered, Peteet notes, by the actual physical invasion of homes during the expulsion of the Palestinians from Palestine, and it continues to be challenged in exile locations and in refugee camps by searches of domestic spaces and raids on private locales. When women's private arena was forcibly deprivatized, classic gender roles were also effectively challenged. Women in public meant, for one thing, a challenge to the traditional understanding of sexuality, in which a state of chaos was presumed to result from the free interaction of men and women. Palestinian women who ventured into, or found themselves in, the public arena found their sexual comportment crucial to their ability to function effectively; they became "sisters" (that is, desexualized) to the men around them.[2]

The Sikh tradition of the Khalsa siblinghood forms a ready context for the same desexualization of female Khalistani militants. All women other than one's wife are to be treated as mothers, sisters and daughters, Khalsa Sikhs assert. This interpretation has two effects. One is that women with whom one works in the context of guerilla struggle are sexually off limits, making possible otherwise problematic situations in which close physical contact is mandated. A second impact of this conceptualization of all women as mothers, sisters, and daughters is the element of protection, which male Sikhs accord to their biological and to their fictive female relatives. Female sexual honor, in the Sikh as in the Palestinian community, is traditionally a responsibility of men, and, in an extension of this, protection of the female is a significant part of nationalism (an extension of the idea of family) itself.

It is clear that men have often gone to war over questions of female honor, to start with the most basic element in the complex theater of princesses and lions in Sikhism. South Asia is no exception; as Peter van der Veer points out in his book on religious nationalism on the subcontinent, protection of the female is critical to both Hindu and Muslim conceptions of national identity.[3] It certainly became clear to me early in my dialogue with Sikh militants (both male and female) that stories of insults to female sexual honor were the most likely to provoke tears. Several interviews came to a wrenching halt because of the emotionalism surrounding reports of such humiliations, and one informant said outright that Khalistan was needed as a space in which women could live without harassment.

All human rights reports emanating from Punjab point out the prevalence of rape and other sexual atrocities as methods of torture and punishment. The terroristic aspect of sexual crime as a war tool in Punjab is made clear by the many episodes in which such crimes were staged in public arenas. Several eyewitness accounts of these atrocities have already been presented here, and most Sikhs know stories about them, if they have not been direct observers. When female *sexual* honor is seen as something to be protected as a matter of *national* honor, insults to it will be used as a tool of war, as we have all seen horrifically in Bosnia. But the linking of traditional understandings of sexuality, women's status, and sexual war crimes is not one that is made by many Sikhs.

Since Sikhs believe that all men and women of the *panth* are brothers and sisters, insults of a sexual nature are taken both in a very personal way, as insults to one's family, and in a very political way, as attacks on one's nation. As the opening narrative of this chapter indicates, it is not only men but women, too, who view the protection of the sexual honor of Sikh women as central to the dignity of the community as a whole. The young girl who eventually became a member of the Khalistan Commando Force started out beating up boys who harassed Sikh college girls. One aspect of female involvement in the guerilla forces is the likelihood that they would be sexually abused if caught, a factor that several men told me they felt was a defining reason to discourage women's involvement in combat. Though they themselves are ready to suffer any tortures meted out to them, the idea of a woman being violated serves as a restraint on encouraging more women to join in combat actions. Amandeep Kaur promised that she would martyr herself before she would let any police touch her. I suspect that this vow reassured her male colleagues considerably. Sometimes men in fact use this threat of sexual abuse in a roundabout way to protect women as well, as we saw in two narratives related to the Operation Blue Star episode, in which women were asked to leave the complex so that abuse of them could not be used to force men to surrender.

Another problem with the idea of sexual honor and the family, real or fictive, as a mechanism to protect it, is that it is linked also to the reciprocal idea of sexual shame. The honor/shame dynamic plays a role among Sikhs, as it does across the Mediterranean and Southwest Asian regions. I have personally heard first-hand descriptions of sexual abuse at the hands of police from women who did not report it to their own fathers, husbands, and sons. In one case, a woman had been viciously raped no less than six times while in custody and had had chili peppers forced into her vagina and anus, and the male members of her family did not know about it. (Indeed, one said, "Luckily, my sister escaped insult when she was in jail.") As the woman told me this story, she forbade me to tell her brother or anyone else in her family, because she thought it would bring shame to the family name. Indeed, even the word "rape" is never used; euphemisms like "dishonor" or "insult" are as far as Sikhs typically go in describing what happens to women in custody. While everyone is aware of the atrocities endured by Sikh women, the honor/shame dichotomy encourages silence rather than publicity of these. Women are then doubly punished, first by the abuse itself and then by being at least implicitly held responsible for it as a source of family shame.

One interesting effect of Khalistani militancy related to the sexual honor question is in the marriage market, where now sisters and daughters of "freedom fighters" have a new avenue through which to acquire spouses. For a man, marrying a girl from a militant family who may have lost her sources of support to martyrdom or who may need protection from police harassment is yet another way of serving the nation. Though I am sure none of those involved in such militant matchmaking would view it this way, this tendency is also serving as a new route to upward mobility, replacing increasingly irrelevant notions of caste (anathema to Sikhism but recognized nonetheless). There is a strong sense that the militant brotherhood should collectively take care of Sikh women, including marrying those without male support or protection. Women whose relatives have become famous for heroic deeds for Khalistan are especially carefully provided for.

One young woman, whose husband specifically sought a bride whose relatives were militants, said, "So many girls my age had been dishonored, raped, or even killed. So it was prearranged that if the police seemed to be close to finding me I should escape. That's what I did. I came to Britain and Kulbir was waiting to marry me. I didn't have any problem."

The Sikh case differs from the Palestinian one studied by Peteet in that the significant ideal of gender equality and flexibility of sex roles in Sikh tradition is not matched by Islam. On the practical level, however, both Sikh and Palestinian women find themselves having to continue the primary responsibilities of domestic and child-care tasks, even if they become involved in another career (including militancy) as well. At a recent convention of the International Sikh Youth Federation, there were few, if any, female delegates. Though all the men were quick to express the sentiment that they would be welcomed and respected, there were also comments to the effect that, after all, they were taking care of homes and kids. The idea that men might take the initiative in freeing women from some of these activities to make a delegate role at a convention possible, which I expressed with hesitation, seemed not to be taken as a serious possibility.

Of course, this scenario is nothing new, and it has analogues in the

West and probably every other part of the world in which women have attempted to move beyond domesticity. Among the Palestinians Peteet studied, women organized groups to help each other deal with the continuing tasks revolving around home and children; rather than presenting a direct challenge to the authority and privilege of men, they acted in solidarity to make the new avenues they were pursuing (including fighting for the resistance) possible. Khalistani Sikh women have nowhere near this level of consicousness or organization, and the density of refugee camp life that makes such organization feasible has no parallel among Khalistani Sikhs.

Total stoicism in the face of danger and death characterizes both Palestinian and Sikh women, however. They become mothers to bring up children who will "pick up their fathers' guns"; like the Sikh woman who told me that if her two sons got sacrificed, she would only regret that she had only those two, "not even enough to make a necklace" (referring to the historical episode in which mothers were forced to wear garlands of the flesh of their children). The militarization of motherhood, expressed vividly in the West in the Nazi movement, also plays an important role in the "militant wombs" of the Palestinians.[4] Some Khalistani Sikhs have been public about their opposition to abortion, not on grounds of religion but on grounds of demography; who will "pick up our guns" if there are no sons and daughters to do so?

In Plutarch's *Moralia*, a Spartan mother with five sons on the battlefield asks a Helot for news of the battle. When he tells her that her five sons have been killed, she reprimands him that she had not asked about the fate of her sons, she had asked for news of the battle. Informed that victory had been won, she replies, "I accept gladly also the death of my sons." This example of maternal patriotism later formed the basis of Rousseau's conception of the female citizen, who would not participate directly in the bearing of arms but would serve the nation through unselfish bearing and rearing of future citizen-soldiers.

Sikh men who renounce wives and children to enter the militancy are celebrated in the long Indian tradition of renunciation of family to serve a larger cause. Gandhi did it; the Buddha did it; Guru Nanak did it. "Guru will take care of them," is the common expression used by Sikh men who have renounced family in this way. Guru Nanak is said to have borne the pain of separation from loved ones in order to immerse himself in the broader pain of the world, and in this he is followed by contemporary militants who now serve not their immediate family, but their broader family, the nation. As one might expect, sometimes the family members of militants reconcile themselves to this, and other times they do not.

The widow of General Labh Singh eloquently describes her transition from a worried wife to a fellow warrior:

While we were at Amritsar I sometimes used to quarrel with [my husband], that he shouldn't go into this way of life. That he should live like a common householder. But one night I had a dream, and in that dream the tenth master, rider of the blue steed, came before me. He made me bow before him over and over to repent by rubbing my nose in the ground. He warned me that I shouldn't criticize his Singh, and he would bless me with another son. In my dream he gave me something and he told me to tie it to my cot and then I would never feel scared. He said, "You are also my Singhni, and it doesn't look good that my Singhni should try to stop my Singh." So after that I would pray to Guru to give him strength. I didn't try to argue with him anymore. I prayed that whatever mission he went on he should succeed.

The dramatic martyrdom of Resham Kaur, who slit her throat with a glass so that she might not reveal her husband's whereabouts under threat of her infant's torture, is another prime example of wifely support. A female martyr, Gurnam Kaur, is venerated in the most flowery terms:

Gurnam Kaur was a great heroine of the Khalistan struggle. Her husband Mokkam Singh of the Babbar Khalsa had absconded, and Gurnam Kaur was arrested by the police. She herself had also been of great service in the movement, providing food to the fighters and carrying weapons from place to place. She was really a brave lady, and our hearts went out to her when we learned that she was in custody.

Anyway, after torturing Gurnam Kaur continuously for forty-five days, the police finally killed her. She had two children, whose whereabouts remain unknown. And her body was never released, so nobody knows exactly what was done to her.

Many of the actions of the Babbar Khalsa over the years would not have been possible without Gurnam Kaur. She talked very little, and most of her time was spent in prayer. But when she was needed for some action, she was always ready.

As long as the stars are in the sky, the heroic deeds of Gurnam Kaur will not be forgotten by the Sikh nation. When Khalistan is liberated, those people who are responsible for perpetrating such heinous crimes against women will be punished. We look forward to that.

The young woman who described joining the KCF in the opening narrative of this chapter obviously feared that her family members would not take this kind of Rousseauian posture, so she kept her activities entirely secret from them. Despite the common rhetoric of sacrifice, it is clear that the support of family members cannot simply be assumed. The stories that are told concern wives who heroically martyr themselves and mothers who rejoice in the victorious battles in which their sons have died, but realities are often more complex. One militant's sister, from whom we shall hear shortly, wanted to get him away from a life of drinking and hunting and urged baptism at the hands of Bhindranwale. But she later found herself caught in a bind of accepting responsibility for his wife and children, despite her painful conclusion that some of the things he ended up doing were wrong.

There are a range of ways in which Sikh women relate to militancy, then, from shooting informers to committing suicide for husbands to desperately trying to take care of sons in a situation in which nurturance is impossible, a dilemma I heard about from several anguished mothers. Whenever discussion of gender came up, however (and my presence, as a presumed Western feminist, prompted it fairly often), both men and women supported the notion that members of either gender were equally likely to take on a warrior role. The idea that women are somehow more naturally peaceful, which plays a role in some contemporary feminist thinking, struck nearly every Sikh I talked to as absurd.

The notion of males as "just warriors" and women as "beautiful souls" in our culture is described by Jean Bethke Elshtain in *Women and War*, where she notes that the Western linkages between men and war and between women and peace continue to frame most discourse about gender and violence today.[5] This stereotypical construction clearly does a disservice both to pacifist males and to militant females, but the strength of the woman-as-nurturer motif in the Western cultural heritage makes it very difficult for many Westerners to accept the claims of women warriors that what they do comes quite naturally to them. Even the classical myth of the Amazons, at the foundation of Western culture, pictures them with breasts cut off, that is, as less than fully female. Joan of Arc, our other major woman warrior, pretended to be a man. It is not surprising, then, given this heritage, that when women get involved in violence they are accused by some feminists of the "beautiful soul" persuasion of simply falling under the sway of violence-inclined men.[6]

Though there is substantial evidence of a relationship between sex hormones and aggressive behavior, and though virtually all wars in world history have been fought predominantly by men, neither fact in itself can appropriately be used to substantiate the claim that men are more warlike than women. The first argument, that of the link between biology and individual aggression, has in my mind been definitively dealt with by Marshall Sahlins's classic counter to sociobiology, to the effect that if you laid all the motivations of individual soldiers end to end, you still wouldn't be able to understand why there was a battle.[7] Wars are fought not between individuals but between social groups, and we have to understand how those groups are constituted and how relations among them are defined to explain why people end up facing one another with arrows drawn. The second argument, that men have historically predominated in all situations of war, is tied to the fact that men have historically predominated in all situations outside of the home generally. Feminists who hope to change the fact that men dominate politics, science, and the arts cannot assume that challenges to male domination in the military will not ensue also.

The one situation in which women have in fact commonly fought alongside men has been guerilla warfare. Where "people," "army," and "state," the Clausewitzian trinity, are not separable—where people are fighting on their own behalf on their own home turf—women have picked up weapons with the best of them and in some struggles have attained high positions (the Sandinistas come readily to mind here[8]). Whether this is a good thing or not is another question. I only note that evidence for female peaceability rests on shaky empirical grounds and cannot simply be assumed no matter what ideological benefits might accrue from this presumption. Particularly where people that one knows personally are involved, as in guerilla insurgencies, women appear to participate quite heavily.

I suspect, however, that women and men in struggle may well experience their involvement in different terms, less polarized than the Just Warrior/Beautiful Soul dichotomy, but as complex human beings with demonstrably different ways of understanding the world. Carol Gilligan, in her pathbreaking work *In a Different Voice*, describes best the different ways in which men and women understand issues of morality, for example. Drawing on evidence from child development, she notes that women tend to base their actions on relationships more than on abstract principles, to ground their perceptions and judgments in a field of other human beings. She further asserts that a "womanly ethic" of engagement must not be read as a female lack of self-esteem or limited ego development but should be respected as a viable, and perhaps desperately needed, ethic for the modern world.[9] This notion of engagement has been adopted by feminist anthropologists, and we will return to it in the next chapter. But I think that the idea of a womanly ethic of engagement can be usefully used to understand the important *feminine* contribution made by women to the Sikh militancy. Amandeep Kaur, the young woman whose narrative opens this chapter, appears classically feminine with her filmy veil, pink nail polish, and soft, deferent voice. Yet she was capable of killing informers in cold blood, a fact that points to the limitations of superficial impressions of masculine and feminine, especially in cultures different from one's own. I take her story also to mean that she acted in a combat capacity *as a woman*, that her actions were not seen by herself or by others as in any way negating her essential femininity. Furthermore, her narration is "engaged" in the manner described by Carol Gilligan; she talks not of abstract ideals like Khalistan but in terms of individuals she knew who were hurt or killed, people who informed on her personally, considerations for her family. My point is not that there is an inherent or dramatic rift between the way this woman perceived things and the way that male militants do. I only point out that it was as a woman, not as a masculinized Sikh or a generic Sikh, that Amandeep Kaur killed.

Noting the empirical fact that women are often at the forefront of guerilla insurgencies and accepting the evidence for differential understandings of moral action on the part of men and women, I suggest that a research program focusing on how women fight is critically needed. I have only the barest hints here of what "a womanly ethic" of engagement means in the face of insurgency and counterinsurgency in Punjab. No doubt it means something different here than among women Palestinians or female Sandinistas. But to gloss over the possibility of a gendered experience of violence, or to consider that women fight only as Sikhs or as Viet Cong but not *as women*, is to miss, I suspect, an important part of the human story.

The colloquial understanding of a "masculine" quality to the Sikhs as a community, elaborated more formally by several academics,[10] is not one with which any of the Sikh women with whom I have spoken agrees. Indeed, Nikky Guninder Kaur Singh, a prominent female Sikh academic, has written an important volume detailing the centrality of the feminine principle in Sikh philosophy. She notes that the Divine Presence in Sikh philosophy is conceived explicitly as neither male nor female, though various translators and interpreters have distorted this point by referring to the divine as "He." (Culture, that is, has eclipsed philosophy.) The *bani*, the sacred words, are grammatically feminine, and the metaphor of the bride longing for her groom as symbolic of humanity's longing for the divine, common in Sikh tradition, identifies woman with human, attributing the most important kind of agency, the impulse to spirituality, to her. Woman is the vessel from which all else flows: "Of woman are all born, without woman none could exist."[11]

While it is obvious that the celebrated virtues of courage, bold action, and strong speech are consonant with masculinity as understood in the West, among Sikhs these qualities are treated as neither masculine nor feminine, but simply as Sikh, values. Women may be bound to the kitchen and may have babies in their arms, but they are still fully expected to behave as soldiers, if necessary. The frail woman fainting at the sight of blood or hysterical in the face of danger is not a stereotype that has any parallel among Sikhs. The fictional Sundari, paradigmatic of the Sikh conception of woman, is utterly without fear yet gently nurturant, boldly pragmatic yet deeply spiritual. The ideal is of a full human being—however problematic to achieve in real life.

Sikh women, then, enjoy a real sense of personhood and a definite respect within their families and communities and, ideally, may pursue lives as full as that of Sundari. At the same time they face some important cultural constraints. A long tradition of deference to men continues, even among those women, like Amandeep Kaur, who have assumed combat roles. Most important, though unrecognized by most Sikhs, being held responsible for the sexual honor of family and nation is a severe burden to bear. Every Sikh woman who is raped in custody and every custodial rape that goes unreported are part of the price exacted by the honor/shame tradition. Here I am speaking for myself, however, not for my Sikh interlocutors, who do not link sexual abuse with sexual politics. For them, it is the image of Sundari, who is capable of everything, that remains the desideratum. And most, in fact, see that goal as not out of reach.

A MOTHER, A DAUGHTER, AND A SON

Mother: "My son used to be so fond of hunting, and I used to tell him that he should give it up and become a devout Sikh. He was not as disciplined as some boys might be. One day his sister told him that he should get baptized, and that he should get it from Sant Bhindranwale. He took this advice deeply to his heart and he got baptized.

"After that Ranjit went to stay with Santji. He told me, 'Look, mom, now I won't come to see you but you come here to see me now and then.' Every seven or eight days we used to visit there. Santji used to say, 'Are you here to get Ranjit?' 'No,' we would say, 'We just came to have a glimpse of you and of Guru Granth Sahib. Ranjit is yours now. We are not here to ask that he should go home.'

"Ranjit looked his loveliest over there. When I saw that I was convinced that he was on the right path. We told Santji, 'Santji, we are very happy that our son is now on the right path.' Eventually he became a trusted bodyguard of Sant Bhindranwale. He was with him at the Golden Temple in June 1984 and escaped along with General Labh Singh and the others. We thought he was martyred but found out after six months that he was alive. He continued working for the cause.

"Ranjit never talked about anything to me. He never talked about his missions or expeditions in any detail, as men usually think that women are chicken-hearted. He had big spots on his chest so we wondered what had happened to him, but he would not comment on it. He always reiterated, though, 'Mother, we are here working for the nation and you should be glad that we are on the right path. Whenever you feel like seeing me, you just come over here.'

"At that time there was never a grain of fear in my mind with regard to Ranjit. Now, some scary things come to my mind when I think of those times. But in the past, in those days, there was never a grain of fear. Actually when my son used to hold a Sten gun, just standing there, he looked very smart. I was very proud.

"After some time Ranjit had to go underground. He used to go from one place to another. Wherever Ranjit was then I used to follow, spend two or three days with him, and then he would say, 'OK, mother, let us be separated again for some time so that they will not bother you.' Then later I would come again to where he was and see him once more.

"We lived like this for about two years. The same story was repeated again and again. We went from one place to another. 'Mother, come see me,' was the message my son would send. One time we had a car, and we went to several historical places together. One time we stayed at a *gurudwara* for some time. In this manner the time passed.

"I hadn't seen him for a month when I learned that he had been killed in an encounter. I don't know any more about it. There were different versions of what happened. One fact is known, and that is that he had no weapons at the time that he was arrested. He fought with his fists and the jaw of one of the constables was dislocated as my son gave a strong resistance. It was not easy for them to arrest him.

"Sometimes I didn't like what Ranjit was doing. But he used to remind me, 'Mother, you were the one who first told me to get baptized. Be firm now on this path.' These were the words of strength he gave me."

Sister: "I was also one who wanted my brother to be baptized, but later on I changed my mind about his activities. He told me he had taken an oath when he was in the Golden Temple, and he couldn't break it. Over there there were a lot of guns, and those Singhs were trying to kill people. But they used to say they were serving their nation.

"In our village the situation for teenagers was not so good. You know how teenagers like to drink and hunt, and I didn't like it when Ranjit did that. He drank sometimes at midnight, and he used to bring meat and tell me to cook it. I hated that. I said, 'Ranjit, I would like it if you would go to Sant Bhindranwale and take *amrit.*' He said, 'OK, sister, you go there and see what is going on.' I went there and had a look, and when I came back I told him that there were some bad people over there. But he said, 'I want to go there.'

"I knew what would happen in the future. I knew, but I couldn't do anything. I just prayed to God. Give good health and long life to Ranjit, I said, because he is in service of the nation. One time I went to bring him over here but he didn't want to come. He used to say, 'Canada is your battlefield, but this is my battlefield.' He reminded me that I should take *amrit*, too. He said he would stay in Punjab and that Guru would take care of his wife and daughter. But he told me to look after them, too. I accepted that responsibility, but at the time I was so upset. I told my parents, 'How can I take this responsibility?' But I couldn't refuse my brother. 'OK,' I said, 'I will take that responsibility.' But I kept praying that he should have a long life. I prayed and prayed for his health and safety."

Mother: "At one point I felt that I was having some physical problems, I wasn't feeling well. I felt that Ranjit needed a wife and he said, 'OK, mother, if it is your will, I will do it.' I was visiting a historical shrine in memory of the fifth master when a girl's parents caught a glimpse of Ranjit and proposed that their daughter should marry him. It was just his handsome looks or maybe some kind of divine bond between them, but anyway that decision to marry was very spontaneous.

"After their marriage, Ranjit's wife might have felt at heart that it was not the life she had looked for in her dreams. A husband, good home, prosperity. But she was very firm in her resolve to be with Ranjit. I suggested to her that if he goes out and doesn't show up for many nights that she should go to her parent's house where at least the police wouldn't bother her. But she said, 'Whatever is my fate is already written. I can't leave Ranjit in any way. Wherever he will be, I will be with him. That is what destiny wants me to do.' She never compromised this in any way although the police used to bother her often. Eventually her whole family was arrested and her brother was beaten up, on account of their link to Ranjit.

"This girl is now missing. They took all the belongings from the house and took Ranjit's wife and one-year-old daughter with them. She was also pregnant with another when she was taken into custody. Hearsay is that she gave birth to a son during that time. The daughter would now be three years old and the son would be two.

"We don't know what happened to her now, as she has disappeared. Before her disappearance we spoke on the phone and she never mentioned her agony or her pain. She always said, 'Don't worry, take care of your health. We will see each other again soon.' But she also said there was no guarantee as to how long she would live. No one knows what happened to her now."

Sister: "I took responsibility for Ranjit's wife and children but now no one knows their whereabouts. This is what happens when people decide they want to make their own country."

10

CULTURE, RESISTANCE, AND DIALOGUE

THE IDEA OF ETHNOGRAPHY as a kind of conversation is now common in anthropology, as common as the idea of ethnography as a kind of natural science once was. Some people misinterpret the presence of ethnographers in their texts as a form of narcissism and condemn what they see as the "navel-gazing" quality of current ethnographic narrative. Those critics will not be happy with this effort. But I see the reflexivity of contemporary ethnography as an honesty about the limitations of our vision that has too long been suppressed in the interests of creating a false aura of authority about our work. Relinquishing that authority is not easy, and it is particularly not easy to share authority with one's interlocutors without denying one's own ultimate responsibility for a text.

Dialogical ethnography with a community in struggle is even more fraught with difficulties—moral, methodological, and literary—than usual. Extraordinary circumstances create extraordinary demands for anthropology. Who knows whether I did it right, in a way that is enlightening rather than mystifying, in a way that will help rather than hurt, or, at least, in a way that will do minimum harm to those on whose welcome this work was predicated? With other scholars—and perhaps particularly with other women scholars [1]—I believe we have to reflect carefully on these matters, too long neglected in the name of academic freedom and scientific hegemony.

While I cogitated on these questions toward the end of 1994 as transcriptions of interviews with Sikh militants were proceeding apace, a debate broke out among the Sikh community with regard to a new book on Sikhism by Harjot Oberoi, holder of a chair in Sikh and Punjabi Studies at the University of British Columbia in Vancouver. I watched this interaction with great interest, and I found myself weighing my own relationships with Sikhs against those of Oberoi and discussing both with them. The dialogue between myself and the Sikhs intersected with the dialogue between myself and other scholars at this critical point, expressed in the publication of an academic volume that excited vehement argument in the community under study. I therefore go into this juncture in some detail as a means of bringing together the complex point at which author, subjects, and academic audience are joined in somewhat dissonant conversation. Since it is into this nexus that the present book will be inserted, it seems necessary to flesh out this context in order to convey to the reader the fuller meaning of this book, whose political and academic context makes it more than the words typed on these pages and the meanings construed from them by individual readers.

WEAPONS AT THE DOOR

One of my first encounters with militant Sikhs, at San Pedro prison, is described in the first chapter of this book. At the main gates of the prison I, Amarjit, and the other Sikh were asked to remove all metal objects from our persons, including the swords of the two Sikhs. They were loath to part with their swords, and Amarjit indeed had tears in his eyes as the guard explained to us that even the tiny one-inch version of the *kirpan*, often used in emergencies such as this one, was not allowed. In the end, we had to put all our things (my jewelry, their swords) by a pole at the gate; the guard did not want to even claim responsibility for their safekeeping while we visited the prison. Thus denuded, we went in to interview Sikh prisoners.

I came to see this initial encounter as a metaphor for much of what passes for dialogue in contemporary ethnography, which I have attempted to move beyond in this volume. In his address to the American Anthropological Association in 1987, Edward Said pointed to the salon-like quality of many current conceptions of anthropology's interlocution with its subjects, possibly stemming from the roots of these conceptions in literary criticism. "The interlocutor is someone who has perhaps been found clamoring on the doorstep, where from outside a discipline or field he or she has made so unseemly a disturbance as to be let in, guns or stones checked in with the porter, for further discussion," he writes.[2] The gentle civility implied by this image of the exchange of ideas across divides of culture and power is as artificial and misleading as the nondialogic scientism of another anthropology, now criticized vehemently. In the messy, sometimes bloody real world the swords on the hips of contemporary interlocutors won't be taken off for anthropologists (who lack the bureaucratic power of the U.S. prison system). "[The] scrubbed, disinfected interlocutor," Said continues, "is a laboratory creation with sup-pressed, and therefore falsified, connections to the urgent situation of crisis and conflict that brought him or her to attention in the first place."[3] We can't learn much of importance from de-sworded Sikhs (a contradiction in terms for the orthodox); we therefore have to find a way to talk to them with weapons on. This weapons-at-the-door image, con-cretized for me at San Pedro prison, was in my mind as I pursued a dia-logue with Sikhs in struggle.

Harjot Oberoi has written a book on Sikh identity that has prompted nothing short of an uproar among the orthodox. Originally published in India, *The Construction of Religious Boundaries* had already established it-self as an important resource for scholars and a bone of serious conten-tion for Sikhs by the time of its North American publication in 1994.[4] The North American Sikh community quickly generated an entire vol-ume of critical response called *The Invasion of Religious Boundaries.*[5] Be-cause Oberoi became controversial, I, as a fellow-traveler, a member of the same academic tribe, found myself newly challenged by my interlo-cutors as well. Why should we bother with you, when you might write something like *The Construction of Religious Boundaries?* Facing these ques-tions, it became critical to me to find out what it was about Oberoi's work that prompted such vehemence.

The theme of Oberoi's volume, indicated by the subtitle *Culture, Iden-tity, and Diversity in the Sikh Tradition,* is the historical pluralism of the Sikh tradition and the amorphous boundaries between Sikhs and non-Sikhs up until the early 1900s, at which point his study ends. The diffuse identities subsumed under the general heading "Sikh" have been, as Ob-eroi notes, an area of silence in much religious scholarship, since these various identities do not mesh with the contemporary formulation of or-thodox Sikhism as described in this volume. (What you read in Chapter 2 is a hagiographic, not a strictly academic, reading of Sikh history.) By contrast, Oberoi follows W. H. McLeod in tracing the gradual evolution of contemporary Sikh identity,[6] calling into question contemporary Sikh claims to the separateness of Sikh tradition and the historical persistence of an identifiable Sikh community. In its challenge to "received" notions of Sikh identity, Oberoi's book is recognizable as an example of the cur-rent deconstructive genre in academia, unpacking invented traditions and imagined communities to reveal a much more fluid picture of social life. With similar efforts in other religious and ethnic forums, however, Oberoi's work brings forth insistent political questions that I believe can-not be neglected. Our interlocutors, in any case, won't let us neglect them.

Oberoi begins his study with what has become a commonplace ques-tioning of the usefulness of religious categories in reference to India, starting with the diffuse quality of the Hindu tradition and the recency of the label "Hindu" and moving on to propose a parallel vagueness in the category "Sikh." Although it is clear that the idea of uniform textual communities is utterly inapplicable to the Indian situation, as Oberoi and others note, the level of conflict among religious groups both historically and presently suggests some measure of indigenous categorical identification. (From Wittgenstein, we know that not all members of a category must share a fixed set of features for the category to be cognitively viable, a fact apparently lost on academicians who, failing to find a set of shared attributes, announce the nonexistence of community.[7]) For Oberoi, however, the disestablishment of classically conceived religious categories provides the backdrop to his chronological examination of Sikh identity from the inception of the tradition in the fifteenth century through the Singh Sabha reforms of the nineteenth. It is only then, according to Oberoi, that we can speak of "the Sikhs" as something like a demarcated community. This notion is not really new, but Oberoi fleshes out this thesis better than anyone else has done, and the book won a prestigious award from the American Academy of Religion as a result.

The central role of the ten Gurus in Sikhism is downplayed by Oberoi, fascinated as he is more by boundary phenomena, by the fuzzy edges of the Sikh arena, than by its center. He treats the biographical accounts of Guru Nanak, for example, as "wonder stories," emphasizing the constructed quality of notions about this founding figure of Sikhism as well as the syncretic quality of the Sikh holy book, the Adi Granth. Here we have an obviously important disjunction between Oberoi's view and that of orthodox Sikhism; where he sees the catholicity of stories about the first Guru and the diversity of contributions to the Adi Granth as indicators of the lack of a separate or definable identity on the part of the Sikhs, they treat these as measures of the spiritual universalism of their tradition. The radically different morality espoused by Guru Nanak and his successors (e.g., the rejection of caste) is deemphasized by Oberoi, who follows mainstream Hindu thought in considering the Sikhs themselves as one branch of a broader Hindu (Indian) social and spiritual world, with caste affiliation as a crucial component of that world. He writes of Hinduism as a large inn, with the Sikhs as one wing, and describes the moral code later articulated by the Khalsa or orthodox Sikhs (*rahit*) as of the same status as the *dharmas* of various other caste groups in Indian society.

The question of just how "heterodox" traditions fit into, alongside of, or against the overarching Hindu framework in India goes beyond the case of the Sikhs alone, of course, as noted in Chapter 5 of this book. Buddhists and Jains, classed with Sikhs as part of the Hindu community for some purposes (e.g., in the controversial Article 25 of the Indian constitution), are also focal points of issues of category definition on the subcontinent. In fact, Oberoi's comment at the end of his book, "[The Gurus'] only intention in initiating Sikh tradition was to remove the social and moral evils which had seeped into the fabric of Hindu society," is a near paraphrase of former president Radhakrishnan's formulation of the-Buddha-as-Hindu-reformer, now as axiomatic to Hindus as it is abhorred by Buddhists.[8] The congruence between Oberoi's vision and that of Brahminic Hinduism is inescapable for non-Hindu readers though unremarked by the author. This subtext of the book is not immediately apparent to the nonspecialist audience, which may not be aware of the extent to which mainstream Western scholarship on India follows traditionally Brahminic conceptions of the Indian social order. But these congruities, being linked literally to life or death questions in India today, leap out persistently for the politically situated Sikh reader.

Continuing this tradition, Oberoi sets up a dichotomy between what he calls "Sanatan" Sikhs and Khalsa or orthodox Sikhs, proposing that the pluralistic eclecticism of the wider Sikh community (including continuing attention to caste, celebration of Hindu festivals, veneration of *pirs*, and so on) was simply a way of life in rural Punjab seen as *sanatan* or "from time immemorial." Oberoi draws on Foucault to discuss the ways in which the "Sanatan episteme" was gradually overshadowed by the "Khalsa episteme" that rejected the poetic, ludic, magical qualities of Sanatan Sikhism in favor of a more linearly defined and ethically puritan scriptural orthodoxy. Culminating in the Singh Sabha reforms that formed the foundation of contemporary Sikhism, the Khalsa episteme focuses, Oberoi says, on "the three G's" of Guru, Granth, and Gurudwara, and can most effectively be seen as the movement of an indigenous elite to appropriate the wider tradition in its own interests. That this appropriation led to the current situation of polarization between the Khalsa-dominated Sikh tradition and the Hindu community it perceives as both alien and repressive is the political message left hanging in the air, as the book concludes well before the current Sikh-Hindu tensions.

Although *The Construction of Religious Boundaries* is an objectivist rendering of Sikh history without an explicit political message, the way Sikh history is construed here effectively subverts any understanding of Sikh militancy in terms other than fanaticism. The fact of conflict, which has spawned the resistive posture of the Khalsa Sikh, is entirely absent from his book. There is barely a mention in the book of Afghan wars, Mughal domination, the persecution of Sikhs and Hindus both, and the eventual Hindu nationalism that molded the anticolonial movement and the current state of India. Without the context of this endemic conflict, the formation of the militant ethos that largely defines the Khalsa episteme is left opaque. We first hear of Sikh martyrs, for example, in the discussion of the distribution of tales about them by Singh Sabha activists in the nineteenth century, so that one is left with more of an impression of the propagandistic telling of the stories of martyrs than with the fact of historical martyrdom itself. (It is clear that history gets rewritten, accounts arc cmbellished, put to particular uses, and so on, but to leave out the actual fact of persecution and execution of Sikhs is itself a rewriting with important repercussions.) Likewise, the missionary aspects of Arya Samaj activities, which played a significant role in prompting calls for orthodoxy among the Sikhs, is ignored, giving a lopsided picture of why Sikh sentiment coalesced around a relatively uniform understanding of Sikh identity. The consolidation of the Sikh community expressed through and since the Singh Sabha movement is both a matter of "fundamentalism" and of resistance, and the way in which these axes intersect is of critical interest. Without attention to intergroup conflict, one perceives the solidification of collective identity solely as the result of the first part of this equation. Community boundaries are thereby effectively depoliticized and, for secular Western readers, undermined.[9]

For those interested in demonstrating the separateness of the Sikh "nation" and in justifying the struggle to achieve a Sikh homeland today, Oberoi's book is highly problematic. And indeed the response provoked by *The Construction of Religious Boundaries* in the orthodox Sikh community has been dramatic. Not only are Sikh critics of Oberoi upset by this "aggressive work of mischievous propaganda," as one contributor to the new volume of criticism calls it, but they are taking action to try to unseat Oberoi from the academic chair he holds at U.B.C., which is partially funded by contributions from the Sikh community. They have held meetings at various locations in North America and Punjab to discuss the situation, as well as bringing the Akal Takht into the fray. Oberoi himself has addressed criticisms from the orthodox circle but eventually found it unamenable to dialogue. Indeed, the angry calls launched by the most strident amount to attempts at censorship and verge on the personally threatening.

This is not the first time a dispute has occured between orthodox Sikhs and scholars of the Western tradition. Just before the controversy over *The Construction of Religious Boundaries*, there was a great debate about a Ph.D. dissertation at the University of Toronto by Pashaura Singh, a student of Hew McLeod's, who was eventually given a penance to perform by the Akal Takht, including cleaning the shoes of Sikh pilgrims.[10] "McLeodism" has in fact become an epithet of choice among orthodox Sikh academics who reject what they see as the disrespect for Sikh belief from the Western scholarly community (some of whose members are in fact of Sikh origin but are lumped together with outsiders as complicit with the Western academic paradigm). Ernest Trumpp, a Western scholar of Sikhism of the nineteenth century, is said to have smoked cigarettes, anathema to Sikhism, while studying the holy book; whether true or not, this image is stamped in orthodox Sikh minds as characteristic of the Western attitude toward religion, one devoid of respect for the sensitivities of the faithful.[11]

The conversation about Harjot Oberoi, his new book, and his chair in Sikh Studies, is going on as I write this, so the outcome is not yet clear. While the debate clearly brings out the dangerously intolerant quality of orthodox Sikhs whose ire has been roused, it can also provide an important window into two aspects of current scholarship that I would like to problematize here. First is the trend toward the deconstruction of group identities, which Oberoi celebrates in this volume, a phenomenon as repellent to people conceiving themselves as members of the challenged groups as it is attractive to postmodern academics. Second is the unwillingness of many academics to engage in dialogue with people who refuse to play the conversation game our way, whose behavior is, as Said says, "unseemly," who decline to converse if it means taking off their swords. Because many of those involved in the assertion of political identities today in fact "have swords on," so to speak (i.e., are in the middle of struggle), these two are intertwined. By not talking to Sikh "fundamentalists," many scholars of religion fail to grasp the sensitivity to talk of ambiguous identities that prompts negative reactions to works of scholarship like *The Construction of Religious Boundaries*. With appropriate care, I believe that the impasse between Harjot Oberoi—a rigorous and innovative scholar—and the orthodox Sikhs—devout and embattled believers—could have been avoided.

IDENTITIES IMPOSED AND DENIED

A common theme in current Indological scholarship is the impact of British colonialism on communal identities, typically conceived as quite fluid before the "divide and rule" strategies of the imperial power solidified them into the more definable units we witness today. Though this formulation neglects the very real conflicts between religious communities that took place long before the British arrived on the scene with their categorization schemes, it is clear that the colonial differentiation of groups on the subcontinent into "martial races," "criminal tribes," and so on had an important impact on the development of contemporary communal divisions, particularly with regard to groups like the Sikhs, who benefited from British patronage insofar as they retained the symbols of their separateness. We know that the same sort of thing happened in other colonial areas. Tribal divisions in Africa were artificially reified, and anthropologists are now accused of complicity in this with their over-determined formulations of *the* Nuer, *the* Tiv, *the* this and that character-istic of traditional ethnography. Now that the age of colonization is over (the explicit kind, at least), anthropology is trying to disengage itself from this heritage by, among other things, rejecting the "essentialism" of classic conceptualizations of cultures as definable entities. We are cur-rently interested in flux, ambiguity; the polyphony or cacophony of mul-tiple voices that speak or shout across, between and within traditional boundaries. Oberoi's perspective on Sikhs as goddess worshipers, vener-ators of Muslim *pirs*, and caste-based social actors is of this genre and will therefore certainly be applauded by those up to date on postmodern ethnography.

So why does this vision anger many Sikhs? Why does Richard Handler's vision of Québecois culture, so challenging theoretically and so impor-tant substantively,[12] anger many Québecois? (One could name countless similar examples.) The answer often given is that these perspectives undercut the ideological formulations of indigenous elites, whose own power base depends on the acceptance of invented traditions and imag-ined communities as wholly real. Thus Oberoi talks about resistance *to* orthodox elites in Sikhism, making the orthodoxy-as-resistance narrative of Sikh history appear to be propaganda. The subversion of this narra-tive, as in *The Construction of Religious Boundaries*, can then be seen as actually liberatory. But, predicated as it is on a consideration of Sikhism utterly independent of the domination/subordination dynamic vis-à-vis other communities, this model is a charade. Orthodox "elites" suc-ceeded in redefining Sikhism because people saw them as taking the lead in resistance to first Muslims, then Hindus, just as Québecois nationalist "elites" succeed (insofar as they do) because of Québec's historical rela-tionship of subordination to anglophone Canada. If one looks just at Sikh or Québecois tradition, this success is enigmatic. It's the broader political context that makes it understandable in terms other than the acquiescence of the masses to fanaticism.

Richard Handler (who has been most forthright in explicitly grap-pling with these issues) says bluntly that ethnography should be "destruc-tive" of group myths; that one should be careful *not* to echo the ideologies of the people one studies, even to reject calling them what they want to be called, for example, *the* Québecois, as an act of complicity in myth-making.[13] This metaphor is echoed, ironically, in the title of the Mann, Sodhi, and Gill volume responding to Oberoi, which was origi-nally titled "The Destruction of Religious Boundaries." (The title was changed when the editors realized it might be taken to imply that Sikh identity could indeed be destroyed!) These critics, in any case, probably do not imagine that there are academics who might take pride in "destruction" as indicative of acute ethnographic acumen. The two valuations of destructive/destruction here show the semantic gulf that divides the worlds of academia and politics. Is there any way to talk with people who reject "destruction" without giving up the usefully skeptical attitude of contemporary ethnography, to stand up for the human rights of suppressed groups without going along with the myths they have (however understandably) created? Can we talk about making culture without making enemies? [14]

The problem here is that the artificial reification of groups that scholars like Handler and Oberoi appropriately react against is both a theoretical and a political matter. When the people whose group identities we deconstruct are using those identities as leverage points against domination by others, experiencing a collective identity "with swords on," so to speak, academic discussion of the historical constructedness of categories not only seems absurdly abstract but can be taken as the outright sabotage of assertions of group rights. Hence the tension between Harjot Oberoi and separatist Sikhs; what he writes as an avowedly nonpolitical, ethnohistorical tract is taken by the sworded as "mischievous propaganda." There is undeniably paranoia here, but there is also something we can learn from.

Part of the current popularity of the deconstruction of group identities in anthropology resulted from a belated recognition of the discipline's partnership with the colonial enterprise, which used imposed identities to control and ultimately exclude others. The ignored fact in most discussions of the reification of group identities by the powerful, however, is that such reification is only one way in which power can be maintained. Aware as we now are of the impact of European colonial domination on the world and on our discipline, and evident as it has become that the superordinate definition of groups was a key part of this domination, we now emphasize it to the neglect of strategies of domination on the part of liberal democracies and postcolonial states today that involve not the imposition, but the denial, of group identities. It is no longer acceptable in the international forum to label people as belonging to alien groups and then to ghettoize them or "cleanse" them (witness the global condemnation of apartheid South Africa or Serbian expansion). These are easy targets for liberal sentiment—as white South Africans and Serbs assert their power in the way of colonial or totalitarian states, they are reminiscent of fascism; in their labeling of people as "other" they hint of concentration camps and gas chambers. But the more insidious kind of domination, far more common in the world today, is the kind that exalts the individual and claims the equality of individuals before the state, while in fact replicating a status quo in which a majority community holds continuing power over minority communities. In a one-person-one-vote situation, minorities will generally lose, and, recognizing this, assert themselves *as a group*. This kind of resistive identity is different from the subservient identities imposed by imperial powers or from the hegemonic identities claimed by expansionist communities like the Nazis, a fact that eludes many theorists of group identity today, who see in every assertion of collectivity a potential pogrom (e.g. Arthur Schlesinger's popular tract warning against the excesses of multiculturalism, *The Disuniting of America*[15]).

In postcolonial India this trend is particularly dangerous, as it mirrors traditional forms of hegemony that refused to acknowledge difference (of Buddhists, of Jains, of Sikhs, viewed simply as another form of Hindu). The domination of a Brahminic/Hindu center throughout Indian history is replicated today in the Hindu resurgence which claims that being Hindu means simply being Indian, a stance which sounds like an aspect of tolerance but is taken by non-Hindus as exclusionary, since it equates assertions of the separateness of their religious traditions with treason. That the secular intelligentsia of India has largely gone along with the formulation that it is the intransigence of the minority communities and not the appropriation of Indian identity by the majority community that is the problem here reflects the same liberalism that sees black nationalism, not white racism, as the problem in the United States.

The congruence of postmodern ethnography with the kind of power that asserts itself not by imposing but by denying group identities, and the subtle convergence of Western intellectual tradition with the rhetoric of the liberal state (including India), is obvious to those outside our paradigms or resisting our states. As Talal Asad points out, "It is a notorious tactic of political power to deny a distinct unity to populations it seeks to govern, to treat them as contingent and indeterminate. . . . It is precisely the viewpoint of interventionist power that insists on the permeability of social groups, and unboundedness of cultural unities, and the instability of individual selves." [16] This was not true of the colonial state, but it is an appropriate insight into the functioning of the liberal state. In a United States that upholds a melting pot rhetoric while continuing to keep its African-origin ingredients subordinate and condemning black nationalists as chauvinists, the confluence of an academic milieu bent on "destroying" group identity with the perpetuation of a status-quo based on denial of group identities is clear. The denial of a Kurdish identity in Turkey (where they used to be called just "mountain Turks"), the denial of a Pukhtoonistan in Pakistan (where it is still called just "the northwest frontier"), and the denial of a Sikh religion in India (where it is called just "a wing in a large Hindu inn") are equally prominent examples of the kind of power that claims egalitarian individualism but supports continued status differences among groups.

As Edward Said notes, the implicit "consent" of intellectuals to the colonial project played a key role in its success.[17] In anthropology this took the form of the celebration of imposed group identities through classic ethnography, which we rightly criticize today. But now the terms of power have changed. In the postcolonial state, the "destruction" of group identities is not a progressive but a regressive act, and it is the exploration of *denied* group identities that is the most politically challenging avenue of contemporary research. This kind of exploration does not sit comfortably in the current academic literature on ethnic and religous identities, particularly when the identities in question seem to be leading in the direction of national sovereignty (Sikhs, Québecois). One line of argument suggests that nationalism is itself a Western idea only secondarily imitated by others, and Handler intimates the same in arguing that the idea of "having" a nation of one's own is an aspect of possessive individualism. Ernest Gellner and Eric Hobsbawm, more famously, view nationalism as an essentially outmoded philosophy in an increasingly interconnected world.[18] These ways of thinking sound progressive in the circles of Western intelligentsia, but carry a very different message for people who have developed nationalist aspirations today as a means of acquiring the recognition they are denied in the liberal states in which they find themselves. Said observes that there is a marked "discomfort with non-Western societies acquiring national independence, which is believed to be 'foreign' to their ethos. Hence the repeated insistence on the *Western* provenance of nationalist philosophies that are therefore ill-suited to, and likely to be abused by, Arabs, Zulus, Indonesians, Irish, or Jamaicans."[19]

Carol Breckenridge and Peter van der Veer, in an important book on the "predicament" faced by postcolonial academics, note that "By deconstructing the categories, we certainly do not dissolve the political realities. . . . The deconstruction of secularism, nationalism, and communalism cannot be separated from an arena in which the nature of the postcolonial state is the subject of violent confrontations."[20]

The fact that orthodox Sikhs now feel wholly alienated from Harjot Oberoi is symptomatic, then, of the different trajectories being followed by Western academia, especially contemporary ethnography, and minority communities around the world. The rebirth of ethnicity, the revival of religion, and the wildfire spread of separatist movements, are all phenomena which, as they draw our attention in theoretical terms, pull us away from our so-called "interlocutors," in political terms. But what shall we do about this widening gap? Is it possible to shout conversations across it?

NO WHALES ANYMORE

Salman Rushdie, in a 1984 essay, drew on Orwell's metaphor of life inside a whale, insulated from worldly reality, to note that today's artists live "outside the whale," in a world that is in fact whaleless, where there are no corners in which we can escape the hubbub and turmoil.[21] Given Rushdie's later situation of permanent hiding, this comment is particularly poignant. It also belies the major argument of the thousands of liberal supporters of Rushdie who rely on the idea that a work of art is basically to be seen as independent of context, that one has to be free to write whatever one wants regardless of consequences. This celebration of the text-in-itself, with the studied neglect of authorial intention and even greater neglect of audience reception, is in line both with the current mood of literary criticism and the ideology of the liberal state. The rally around Salman Rushdie gave at the same time a new vigor and unity to the intellectual community and a fresh chance for denunciations on the part of politicians of the West's current nemesis, the world of Islam.

Now, obviously no right-minded person would support the idea of a death penalty for Salman Rushdie; indeed, we should all condemn it vociferously. No one denies the limitations on personal liberties in various Muslim societies, which reach their apogee in a *fatwa* extended halfway around the world to reach a naturalized citizen of Britain. But, as Talal Asad points out, along with our solidarity with Salman Rushdie in this sense, we can profit from examining the "aggressively enthusiastic" support of this beleagured writer for what it can tell us about the state of Western intellectual culture.[22] There is a great deal of censorship in the world today; much imprisonment; many executions. Why has this case in particular inspired so passionately the imagination of the intellectual community?

One angle on the Rushdie controversy might be provided by looking further into the "new cold war" between religion and secularism, as Juergensmeyer puts it, particularly between the Western secular state and Islamic nationalism. This is certainly an important part of the dynamic here—also related to the received Western view of orthodox Sikhs as religious fanatics. But for the purposes of the current essay I would like to emphasize the sense in which Westernized writers like Salman Rushdie (one could name a host of others) have become important symbols for our supposed dialogue with the non-West. As Tim Brennan notes, such writers are immediately celebrated by Western literati as providing an "inside view" of various Third World societies, though they in fact write for a clearly Western target audience and live lives far removed from their distant origins.[23] Rushdie used to be heralded as a kind of spokesperson for Islamic South Asia, for immigrant communities, and so on, until that same supposed constituency started burning his book. It turned out that he was more of a spokesperson for what the intellectual world *thought* Islam was like or the immigrant experience was like; in embracing him, it could pride itself on its cultural open-mindedness while not really taking the risk of confronting truly alien ways of thinking. Since it's easier to converse with Salman Rushdie than the Aytollah Khomeini and his ilk, by all means let's make it possible for Rushdie to continue to function. (*Shame*, praised as particularly insightful with regard to postcolonial Pakistan, is so Western that it is unreadable by all except the most elite Pakistanis.) Concepts like "fundamentalism" and "terrorism," which form the cornerstones of most discussions of Khalistani Sikhs, are to my mind words we use to comfort ourselves about our own civility, while excusing our inability to actually grapple with radical others. They are accusatory and dismissive, and therefore not useful in the endeavor to understand.

In his discussion of anthropology's interlocutors, Said describes the difference between the *evolué* taken into confidence by the French colonial regime and the person who "refuses to talk, deciding that only a radically antagonistic, perhaps violent riposte is the only interlocution that is possible with colonial power." [24] Despite our disicpline's admirable new insistence on dialogue, it remains easier for us to exchange ideas with those who will come into our parlor than with those who, refusing to leave their weapons at the door, challenge us, condemn us, even sentence us, with rude ignorance of the rules of the "academic freedom" game. When we see a volume like the response to Oberoi just put out by Jasbir Singh Mann, Surinder Singh Sodhi, and Gurbaksh Singh Gill, much of it strikes us as way beyond the norms of accepted academic exchange. There are ad hominem remarks, tirades against the whole of Western social science, defenses of scriptural dogma, and so on. Harjot Oberoi, seeing that orthodox Sikhs seem to be unwilling to enter the conversation on his/our terms, now refrains from responding to this explosion, which is easily brushed aside as evidence of narrow-minded zealotry.

I suggest that anthropology, of all disciplines, shall have to come to terms with the radically alien quality of some of its most important interlocutors, those who reject interlocution on the terms we prefer. Religious "fundamentalists" like the orthodox Sikhs, many of whom now carry not only swords but AK-47s, making them "terrorists" as well, are a case in point. Is it futile to think of productive dialogue with people who intransigently refuse to hear divergent interpretations of their community's history, who respond to investigation into the textual sources of Sikh belief with cries of blasphemy, who are ready with accusations of government conspiracies at the slightest sign of an anti-Khalistan bias?

Most Western scholars of religion are, sadly, coming to the conclusion that this is the case.

My experience with orthodox Sikhs indicates that such radical interlocution is, in fact, quite possible. It means, however, accepting a compromise framework in which a dialogue between equals becomes possible, and this compromise will antagonize those most fixed on the notion of inviolable academic sovereignty. Such sovereignty, held up as a wall of separation between the politicized real world and the supposedly nonpoliticized *république des lettres*, is an effect of the professionalization of intellectuals that has taken place over the past half-century in the Western metropolis.[25] The Gramscian concept of the "organic" intellectual, the public intellectual whose voice is engaged in the affairs of the world rather than distant from it, takes a back seat today to the image of the academic specialist, the "expert" whose credibility rests on his or her mastery of an increasingly narrow body of knowledge and on a critical distance from political debate. As an antidote to this kind of withdrawal from public discourse, Said suggests an "amateur" (i.e. nonprofessional, engaged) approach to intellectual life.[26] With Noam Chomsky, Gore Vidal, and a handful of others, Said insists on the critical permeability of the membrane that holds academic dialogue apart from that of the rest of the world. I suggest that insofar as this membrane is *not* permeable, accepting exchanges of views in both directions, academia becomes, simply, impotent.

Postmodern interpretations of the intellectual, which conceive of the intellectual not as "legislator" of absolute truths but as "interpreter" between communities,[27] can help anthropologists construct viable frameworks for dialogue that enable conversation with radical "others" without denying the continuing importance of academic freedom. As interpreters, we want to establish a terrain on which we can be mutually intelligible[28] as a logical precondition to responsible assertions of truth-as-we-see-it. For orthodox Sikhs, the framing of a conversational terrain must take into account respect for the sacred scriptures and the historical Gurus, as well as some recognition of the current political dilemmas facing the Sikh community. Our (professional academic) terrain is obviously contoured by ideas about the integrity of research and the importance of the free exchange of ideas. Are these unbridgeable? I don't think so. One can recognize and acknowledge publicly what the sacred scriptures and historical Gurus mean to orthodox Sikhs, while at the same time offering textual or historical critique. One can state that Sikh identity is at the moment closely tied up with politics that hinge partly on the separateness or lack of it of the Sikh community, and go on to present one's own ideas about group boundaries. One can work for human rights in Punjab, and criticize at the same time the definite atrocities committed by Khalistanis; respect the militant resistance yet suggest that leaders have further thinking to do on the nature of an eventual Khalistan. Orthodox Sikhs, upholding a religious tradition in which "truth is pure steel," as they say, are in my opinion ready to recognize other interpretations of truth, if perceived as sincerely offered (i.e. respectfully and in good faith).

The reason why orthodox Sikhs are upset with Oberoi is, in fact, only superficially related to his ideas about Sanatan Sikhs and other aspects of Sikh history. What they are upset about is his unwillingness to establish a common terrain, to treat practicing Sikhs as colleagues in the endeavor of understanding their religious tradition. (This is not the same thing as inviting them to join into the liberal academic terrain.) Oberoi writes about Sikh history from inside a whale, seemingly without concern for those whose deepest religious sensibilities are at stake and whose political fates may hang on the question of identities and boundaries. I don't think it is bowing down to censorship to suggest that one could effectively deconstruct Sikh identity while acknowledging the current human rights abuses being perpetrated against the Sikhs *as a community* (however "constructed" that community may seem to academicians), or that one could discuss scriptural disputes while recognizing and stating the viewpoints of those who hold one version as sacred.

One telling aspect of my own interactions with orthodox Sikhs is the way in which these interactions are received by colleagues, some of whom seem to feel that willingness to engage in dialogue on compromise terms—respect for the Guru Granth Sahib as axiomatic, for example—implies a total suspension of critical judgment on my part. (One even questioned the appropriateness of touching one's head to the floor before the Guru Granth Sahib at a *gurudwara,* a part of the worship service every participant performs out of respect; that Sikhs would take this gesture as indicating the willingness of a visitor submit to their authority is absurd.) When orthodox Sikh interlocutors are also involved in an armed insurgency, the hackles go up even further ("You'll lose your credibility as a neutral observer if you talk to them" sort of thing). This is plain silly, and undermines our discipline's claim, or hope, to be able to engage in serious cross-cultural dialogue. I talk to orthodox Sikhs, to separatist Sikhs, and disagree with much of what they tell me. But it's their religion, and their war, that I am trying to understand, on their terms as well as others'. And in fact, being engaged in conversation with them enables a degree of criticism that has the potential to be effective (heard) rather than simply reacted against. The fact is that however much many of us disagree with "fundamentalism" per se, fundamentalists will not be deterred by our condemnation from on high. We retain a level of personal integrity at the cost of actually ameliorating the worst aspects of religious orthodoxy, and stay self-righteously neutral in the middle of an armed conflict at the cost of its perpetuation. Blindly condemning "terrorism" provokes nothing more, as far as I can see, than further terror.

The "worldliness" of the texts we write[29] implicates us in the problems of this whaleless world. It is failure to recognize the context of his writing that is, in the end, the central problem with Harjot Oberoi's book. He has written an account of Sikh history that is fascinating, informative, and theoretically challenging, and he did so in a climate in which this act alone required some amount of courage. I focus on his work here not to deprecate what is in fact a substantial achievement, but to point to the shadowy region behind and around it, full of prayer and drawn swords, which gives it its ultimate meaning. Had this netherworld been brought explicitly into the text, the work would not have suffered, I suggest, and we of the academic world would be closer to, not further from, productive collaboration with the people we study.

In the middle of the discussion with Sikhs about Oberoi's book and what it meant for them and for me, Joyce Pettigrew's volume on the Punjab conflict came out.[30] The Sikhs had a copy of it before I did, demonstrating once again that we are seriously deluding ourselves if we think we write solely or even primarily for other scholars. When culture has become politicized, every work about culture has a political impact and is read and responded to in political terms. This is simply a fact of life in doing anthropology in the highly politicized late twentieth century. Like it or not, our work has unignorable real-world consequences.

Amarjit attended the American Anthropological Association meetings with me in 1993, as I noted in Chapter 1. In our forum, he kept his *kirpan* tucked tactfully under a suit jacket, though his bright saffron turban made him, to put it mildly, conspicuous. Since I was giving a paper on Sikh separatism, we talked about whether his presence at the meetings might be taken as some attempt at surveillance or censorship, whether my talk would carry less credibility because of it. Looking back on this incident, its absurdity—or tragedy—seems evident. While it is perfectly acceptable to have a turbaned, sworded Sikh as an "informant," to accept one as a colleague at a professional meeting is a step that not all are ready to take. The potential loss of authority represented by the attendence of such a person at the sanctum sanctorum of our discipline is scary. Though Johannes Fabian pointed out the clearly non-reciprocal quality of anthropology's dialogue with its subjects, the continuing sense that we are not coeval with them,[31] it is still easier for most of us to visualize an anthropologist in a *gurudwara* than a Sikh at the AAA. (We now see representatives of various indigenous groups at the AAA, but I suggest these are relatively safe, because relatively powerless, entrants to our discussions.) Yet if we are to avoid the kind of impasse we now see between Oberoi and the orthodox Sikh community, we shall have to come to grips with the notion of interlocution with not only radically different but occasionally radically opposed others. There is no more "field" to go to, separate from ourselves and unable or unwilling to talk back. The field is at the AAA, sword and all.

The alienation of the academic study of religion from religious people, to the point where willingness to truly converse with "fundamentalists" is taken as a symptom of irretrievable loss of integrity, and the alienation of the academic study of group identity from people in groups, to the point where an anthropologist has to caution others not to use the names preferred by group members themselves, represent serious failures in communication between the ivory tower and the world. Mascia-Lees and others point to a similar problem in their classic article on the disjunction between postmodernism and feminism; just as women are asserting themselves as subjects, they note, academia wants to do away with subjectivity.[32] Academia seems to have declared the end of modernism, the end of "grand narratives" of emancipation,[33] before everyone has had the chance to reap their benefits. We deconstruct boundaries at the very historical moment that those boundaries are being mobilized for political resistance: we challenge the sanctity of religious texts as those texts are giving fresh inspiration to increasing numbers of believers. It is not surprising that people disparage academics in light of this scenario; that some give up on talking with us altogether.

Feminist scholars have already shown that there is much to gain by redefining the contours of academic inquiry, with explicit attention to the "outside the whale" consequences of scholarship in a world in which our priorities seem at the moment to be at odds with those of people we study. I suggest here that taking the risk of talking with radically different others, on jointly defined terms, in other people's parlors and in our own, will enhance our understanding of the resistive identities that form such a key part of the late twentieth-century global order. Not only will failure to engage in such dialogue impoverish academia, but it can lead to a dangerous downward spiral into Manichean intransigence on the part of those excluded from the debate. Academia will then itself share the blame for the intolerance of the fundamentalists and the chauvinism of the separatists.

KHALISTAN-IN-AMERICA

We came here so we could organize a stronger political movement and a more sophisticated militancy. Everywhere in India Sikhs are being killed. So instead of just getting wiped out we want to gather here so we can prepare ourselves for future struggle. We want to convey our message to the democratic people here. Man to man, we want to say that we need our own country. We are not related socially, morally or religiously to Hindu people. We are different. We had a country before the British came, but through various devious means we ended up losing it. We have a good culture, a strong culture, and we are good people. We need help to establish a Sikh nation. Man to man we want to say, help us.

Yes, I was in Perth and I don't remember the name of the pub, but anyway one guy came up to me and grabbed me by my coat. He said, "Are you a follower of Ayatollah Khomeini? What the hell are you doing over here?" At that time the Ayatollah Khomeini thing was really hot. I was just dazed. I said, "Whoa, man, what are you saying?" Then I had to explain the whole thing, that this is not the same turban that Khomeini tied, nor the same beard, that I was from a totally different religion. So little do people know about our faith.

I was in my cab and I picked up a fare one evening, two drunken businessmen. They started laughing and falling over each other and one said, "Take us to the World Trade Center!" They thought this was really funny. I stopped the cab and hauled them out by their collars. I stood them there on the sidewalk and gave them an education about Sikhism. They were really shocked. Finally I told them to never taunt a Sikh that way again and I drove off.

We are ordinary people. We are not terrorists. But if you see the list from the Indian Embassy we will be listed as terrorists, because we are fighting for our rights. If you say that right is right and wrong is wrong, you are a terrorist. Here you have free speech. But if we stand in front of the Indian Embassy and raise our voices, we are put on record as being terrorists. It's quite embarassing. But anyway, at least we are not killed here. We have shelter in this country and we can work for our living in this country. We are respected in this country. How thankful we are!

To tell you the truth, I would die if somebody gave me a gun and told me to shoot a person. I am just not capable of it. But you see, when you have to run a country, you can't run a country just by guns. It wouldn't last very long if you tried. Khalistan will need people from a wide spectrum, with different capabilities. There will be room for everybody. Even room for you!

Anthropologists have been making a virtue of necessity ever since Malinowski, who managed to write one of the classic ethnographies in the canon while interned in the Trobriand Islands during World War I. I started out studying North American Sikhs because, quite simply, things had become difficult for me in India. My Muslim last name, sadly, became an issue on my last visit to Bihar, and I knew that with Sikhs, unlike with Hindus, this facet of my identity would help rather than hurt. (I will surely be accused of working for Pakistan by some more devious or paranoid Indian critics, which is, to my mind, an idea beneath comment.) Investigating militancy in Punjab itself, besides being dangerous, is difficult because people are simply not free to express themselves in the way they can overseas, and are far more suspicious about inquisitive outsiders. (Joyce Pettigrew, who did do fieldwork in Punjab, nevertheless had to ask a Sikh in London to acquire taped interviews on her behalf for her book.) So what with one thing and another, I ended up pursuing expatriates, and though I originally considered it a second-best option, I ended up valuing it as an especially fruitful window into Khalistani nationalism.

Sikhs overseas have always been heavily involved in affairs in the homeland, playing a particularly critical political role in the Ghadr rebellion and in the current separatist insurgency. Today, they are helped in their continuing involvement by technology; Khalistani leaders never go anywhere without being connected by multiple fax and phone lines to each other, not to speak of the KhalsaNet computer network that links Sikhs around the world. Such connection, unlike the telegraph and mail system of Ghadr times, is instantaneous. Sikhs in California often hear the latest news before Sikhs in Delhi do.

I used the word "Khalistani" at various points in this book, but I sometimes asked myself whether "Khalistani" was an adjective that made sense in the absence of an actual country called Khalistan. Once I voiced this concern to a group of Sikhs with whom I was talking. My interlocutors were way ahead of me. "Of course we are Khalistani," they said. "We are all part of the Khalistan nation wherever we are." In effect, they were saying that Khalistan is a state of mind. In this they were following the spirit of Benedict Anderson, whose concept of the "imagined community" helped launch the new, denaturalized understanding of collectivity just discussed.[34] He linked his conception to territory in a way that Khalistani Sikhs cannot, however—at least not yet. Wherever Khalistani Sikhs are, Khalistan is.

Recent works of scholarship have emphasized the de-linking of ethnicity and territory in the postmodern world, celebrating "transnationalisms" that cut across cartographic and political boundaries. This is reshaping traditional understandings of "immigration," "emigration," "country of origin," "host country," and so on, as *transmigrants* are reconceived not as people who leave one nation behind to adopt a new national identity, but as people whose nationhood and identity criss-cross classically imagined frontiers.[35] So Portuguese are Portuguese everywhere, not only in the southwestern tip of Europe; Chinese are Chinese wherever they may be.

While it would seem that such a deterritorialization of identity presents a challenge to the paradigm of the nation-state which links people to territory in a definitve way, in fact the picture is more complicated. Zionism is only the most notable example of a diasporan collectivity that inscribed its identity onto a piece of territory, making the maintenance of that territory as a permanent homeland critical to diasporan identity despite the failure of most diasporan Jews to actually "return" to it. Akhil Gupta highlights this "re-inscription" of identities onto geographical spaces as a critical feature of ethnicity in the current era,[36] and this makes sense of the seemingly paradoxical trends of deterritorialization, on the one hand, and increasing nationalism, on the other. If we apply this idea to the area under study here, it seems clear that the power of the Khalistan idea is enhanced, not diminished, by the dispersion of Sikhs outside of Punjab and India. And this is expressed in monetary, political, and moral support for Khalistan from diasporan Sikhs despite the fact that many or most would not move to Khalistan if it were indeed created.

The idea that Khalistan is where Sikhs are is really a way of inscribing nationhood onto what was classically conceived as the *panth*—implied also by Bhindranwale's use of *qaum* to talk about *panth* in the days before "Khalistan" became the rallying cry of the discontented. Despite the linkage of the territory of Punjab with Khalistani nationalism in contemporary militant rhetoric and despite the fact that historically there is no doubt that Punjab was the center and heartbeat of the *panth*, the world of Sikhism was traditionally in no way constrained by the geography of the land of five rivers. In Guru Nanak's legendary travels he in effect circumambulated the world, metaphorically incorporating the entire universe within the realm of Sikhism. Two of the five *takhts* or "thrones" of Sikhism are outside of Punjab (one in Bihar and one in Maharashtra), reflecting the fact that the lives of the ten Gurus were in no way restricted to the northwestern corner of the subcontinent. The Adi Granth is explicitly ecumenical. And all of this has led to the perfectly appropriate appeal of the Sikh faith to people outside Punjab; for example, in the small but steadfast community of American converts to Sikhism.[37]

But the universalist message of Sikhism is, in the Khalistan movement, tied up with a specifically Punjabi nationalism in a way troubling, for example, to Iqbal Singh of Chapter 3, who expressed his unease by asserting that "Khalistan is a need, not a destiny," and that Sikhs simply

12. A demonstration in Washington, D.C., organized by the Council of Khalistan. The Sikh emblem of the double swords is visible on the flag. (Courtesy of the Council of Khalistan and the *World Sikh News*.)

needed someplace where they could live as "true Sikhs" whether that be London or Amritsar. Harpal Singh of Chapter 5, however, feels the opposite, exalting *Punjabiyat* as a critical component of the Khalistan idea. In the tension between these two viewpoints lies a problematic ambiguity in the notion of "self-determination" for a Sikh homeland of Khalistan. Are we talking about some kind of theocratic state here, in which Sikh=Punjabi=Khalistani? (In which case, we will be concerned about the fate of minorities, democratic freedoms, and so on—points typically raised by those fearing exactly this future.) Or are we talking about what is really a mere practical expedient, whereby a community whose rights have been trampled seeks to set up an alternative framework within which those rights could be guaranteed? In Pakistan, the question of whether the founders intended an *Islamic* state, that is, following a particular theopolitical line, or a *Muslim* state, that is, a place where Muslims could live freely, remains unresolved, as its parallel does in Israel.

The gradual linkage of the idea of the Sikh community to the idea of a Sikh nation inscribed on the territory of Punjab developed primarily since Independence, even though it now claims much earlier roots.[38] (The kingdom of Maharaja Ranjit Singh is, as we have seen, frequently drawn on in the discussion of Khalistan because it was the only time when something like a Sikh state was in existence. The theme of communal harmony and tolerance under the enlightened rule of Ranjit Singh is as celebrated by Khalistanis as other aspects of Ranjit Singh's rule are suppressed.) Without denying the historical evidence of a definable Sikh *community*, the point is that the notion of Sikh *nationhood*, linked to Punjabi *territory*, is not a traditional one. The claim to Khalistan as a nation-state and reliance on the principle of self-determination to achieve it are part of the discourse of modernity.

The rise of the state as a political form in ancient times was accompanied by the rise of warfare as we know it, and the rise of the modern nation-state in the West since 1648 (the Treaty of Westphalia) likewise gave rise to the particular understanding of warfare expressed by Clausewitz in *On War*. The same Sikhs who defend the idea of self-determination in the form of one people=one nation=one state, and who try to imagine Khalistan/*qaum*/*panth* in these terms also understand the legitimation of organized violence (war) provided by statehood, in the Clausewitzian (what could generally be called "modern") framework. In commenting that they are George Washingtons or Menachem Begins of sorts, Sikh militants rely on the idea that the establishment of a future state will legitimate what they are doing now, turn acts of terrorism into acts of war. This has always been a problematic part of the Clausewitzian legacy—what to make of guerilla (nonstate) warfare.

It pushes guerillas in the direction of separatism, aimed at the formation of independent states, rather than toward regional autonomies, national reforms, or other compromise solutions, for it is primarily in the achievement of independence that the violence of the guerillas will be vindicated.

Sukha and Jinda, who "delivered justice" to General Vaidya, consciously placed the activities of Khalistanis squarely amongst those of other revolutionaries in their farewell missive:

When nations wake up, even history begins to shiver. During such . . . moments a Banda Bahadur bids farewell to his peace[ful] dwelling and destroys a state of suppression like Sirhind, a Che Guevara turns down a ministership of Cuba, loads a gun on his breast and entrenches against the enemies in the forests of Bolivia, a Nelson Mandela rejects the ideology of apartheid and prefers to spend his life in a dark prison cell.[39]

Fighting a war of independence plays well abroad today, since self-determination is one thing everybody understands, whatever they may know or not know about Sikhism or Punjab. (Sikhs are not linked to Khomeini; Sikhs didn't blow up the World Trade Center.) The rhetoric of peoplehood, nationhood, and statehood has come to dominate discussion among expatriate Sikhs, totally eclipsing talk of particulars like grain prices or water distribution. The flurry of movements of self-determination across the globe, comprising what Bernard Nietschmann calls "the third world war,"[40] is a logical outcome of the ideal of the nation-state, now extended to previously unrepresented or submerged groups. And the explosion of violent conflicts over it is traceable to the Clausewitzian scheme that legitimates political violence only by linking it to state authority.

In a deterritorialized world, people are increasingly getting involved in self-determination movements and their violent concomitants in regions far from the ones in which they reside. Certainly in the Khalistani Sikh case, the diasporan Sikh community has been not only part of but at the forefront of the Khalistani insurgency. This fact has inspired a considerable body of scholarship. Arthur Helweg cites the alienation of migrant Sikhs from host societies abroad, their limited opportunities there, and the organizational vigor of expatriate *gurudwaras* to explain why Khalistani activism becomes a likely path to honor and achievement.[41] Mark Juergensmeyer, alternatively, emphasizes the migrants' marginalization vis-à-vis the home (Punjabi) community as the source of their desire to push forward a new framework in which they would be not peripheral but central.[42] Other studies focus on not the migrants' own situation but the situation of the host countries in which they reside, exemplified most clearly by the Ghadr movement in which nationalist aspirations among expatriate Sikhs were sparked by Canadian and American exclusionary policies and critically tied to the failure of British Indian authorities to protect Indians abroad.[43] This last perspective resonates well with many Sikhs outside of India today, who perceive the Indian embassy and consular apparatus not only as unwilling or unable to protect them but as in itself persecutorial.[44]

Verne Dusenberry's insights into the politics of diasporan Sikh identity are particularly interesting, however, as they tie in usefully to the bigger picture before us of a virtual florescence of self-determination movements worldwide, of which the Khalistan case is but one. Dusenberry relates the shift in Canada from allegiance to NACOI (the National Association of Canadians of Origins in India) to loyalty to local *gurudwaras* and the term "Canadian Sikhs" rather than "East Indians." This shift, importantly, happened in Canada *before* the major developments in Punjab itself that would make definition as a Sikh rather than as an Indian politically acceptable—before Operation Blue Star, before the post-assassination pogroms, before the Declaration of Khalistan, and so on. Dusenberry traces it to Canada's multiculturalism policy put in place in 1971, noting that "the local logic of multiculturalism in these pluralist polities requires a distinctive source 'culture' derived form a recognized homeland or country of origin."[45]

The point is not that separatist movements overseas are created by multiculturalism policies in Canada: that would be absurd. The roots of Sikh separatism are clearly in Punjab. But what Dusenberry's work does show is how a North American sociopolitical trajectory intersected with a different one in India to produce the interesting situation in which the Canadian Sikh community has become a key center of the Khalistan movement. The resurgence of cultural identities and the rise of separatist nationalisms, West and East, are intertwined parts of the same global phenomenon.

The demography of South Asian emigration patterns plays a role in diaspora Sikh nationalism as well. In several countries the proportion of Sikh immigrants relative to all Indian immigrants is much higher than the proportion of Sikhs at home in India. In Britain as many of half of all Indian immigrations may be of Sikh origin,[46] and Sikhs have dominated the South Asian immigration scene in Canada at several points in history (e.g., Ghadr times in British Columbia). What this means is that in the ordinary perception of an overseas Sikh, the Sikh community is a major piece of the South Asian mosaic. When he or she sees the relatively lesser attention paid to Sikhs in India, where they are only 2 percent of the population, it appears as if the Sikh community's voice is being purposely ignored.

This dynamic is exemplified by the controversy over All-India Radio broadcasts in the late 1970s. As an avowedly secular state, India compels its state-run radio to schedule proportionately equal amounts of religious programming aimed at the various religious communities. But this formula, problematic even in India, was disastrous overseas, where Sikhs were never satisfied with the small amount of Sikh religious programming allotted (aimed at the 2 percent Indian minority, not the up to 50 percent diaspora contingent). Southall was full of turbans, but there was little *kirtan* to be heard on Indian short-wave radio. A demand for a Sikh radio transmitter, to be set up at the Golden Temple Complex, ensued, but was rejected as a "communal" demand not in keeping with the Indian policy of equal treatment of all faiths. Finally, Jagjit Singh Chauhan, the apostle of Khalistan based in London, went to Amritsar and illegally set one up. What was seen as inflammatory communalism in India played as an appropriate redress of grievance in Britain.[47]

As noted in the previous discussion, there has been something of a backlash among erstwhile liberals against the multiculturalist paradigm, and this has gone hand in hand with a similar critique of the idea of self-determination. Daniel Patrick Moynihan, in *Pandaemonium*, suggests that the principle of one people/one state, initiated in the very particular historical circumstances of World War I and brought to a peak in the era of decolonization, has in the deterritorialized world of the late twentieth century resulted in total chaos.[48] Any reader of newspapers today would be hard pressed to disagree with this, and a spate of books portraying movements of self-determination as dangerously undermining the international order are widely read and cited. These are typically conceived as tribalistic revivals of long-simmering ethnic hatreds, suddenly let loose due to political changes, economic upheavals, and so on. Though anthropology has relinquished this primordial image of ethnic conflict in favor of a more complex understanding of how changing group identities tie into dynamics of domination and resistance, on the popular level the "tribal" (non-Western, uncivilized, retrogressive) quality of such conflicts is increasingly emphasized.[49]

Letting loose a tirade of condemnation against such tribalesque movements (which goes hand-in-hand with the unspoken claim that we in "civil society" have outgrown them) can only provoke further expressions of just the sentiments of national identity and pride we scorn. Obviously, what we have to do is work toward changing the conditions that prompt the dismay, despair, and anger that turn into movements of revitalized nationhood or religious mobilization. It is true that there are leaders in these sorts of movements who seek to build a following in order to consolidate their own holds on power, a common theme in much of the current literature on ethnic conflict.[50] But there are also large numbers of willing followers who, rather than being duped by manipulative demogogues, are seeking a way to assert themselves collectively in forums in which they perceive their voices will not be heard as individuals.

Although we might well consider what psychological and sociological factors prompted the initial resurgence of Sikh orthodoxy amongst Bhindranwale and his cohort in the late 1970s and early 1980s, this part of the movement only ever attracted a minority of Sikhs. Focusing on "fundamentalism," as expressed in the Bhindranwale period, will miss the driving point of the movement for Khalistan today, which is that it is essentially a movement of political resistance. This is, to my mind, an inescapable fact for anybody who immerses herself in the Khalistani community. The celebration of religious orthodoxy is a symptom of discontent and a vehicle for military mobilization—but not a cause in itself, not for the great majority of people involved in fighting for separate statehood. Sikhs are fighting against the desecration of their holy sites and against the humiliation of their bodies. Indeed, this "against" feeling is a problem for some, like our friend Iqbal Singh who asks just what it is that Khalistanis are fighting *for*. But it is the element of resistance that in any case comes strongly to the fore in my encounter with Khalistani Sikhs.

The comparative study of religious fundamentalism, while a fruitful area of research across several disciplines, faces the key issue of whether the various kinds of religious revivalisms now emerging around the world are in fact comparable. Are we talking about apples and oranges when we try to juxtapose Sikh with Christian with Jewish with Islamic forms of religious revival? A problem with looking at disparate movements along a common axis of religious orthodoxy is that by its nature this enterprise wrenches them from their political contexts, turning what is better understood as a *symptom* (of political distress) or a *method* (of mobilization) into an object in itself.[51] The study of terrorism parallels the study of fundamentalism nicely, privileging commonality of symptom and method (violence, in this case) over great diversity in political context. Both the FMLN and the Salvadoran government used to set off bombs, but if we focus on the bombing to the neglect of the politics we'll not understand either. Beyond the glaring surface of mutilated bodies and burning buildings lay an immense diversity of meanings. Likewise, Palestinian and Israeli expressions of fundamentalism share surface features, but this common ground masks radically divergent political contexts. Nehru himself had made a similar distinction when he noted that "Honest communalism is fear; false communalism is political reaction."[52]

When we think of Khalistanis as religious zealots and as terrorists (and it is clear that most of the academic and popular literature portrays them that way), we wonder whether, in Dipankar Gupta's fortuitous phrase, our bleeding hearts should bleed with them.[53] Violent fundamentalists disrupting what most of the world thinks of as a democratic and tolerant state would seem a source of pandaemonium we wouldn't want to encourage. Yet it is clear that every act of state suppression targeting this community has spurred, not dampened, its ardor. People want self-determination when the state in which they live doesn't protect their rights, and despite the religious rhetoric of many of the militants, the majority of the people who support them do so for precisely this pragmatic reason. If we want to prevent the chaos of unlimited conflicts surrounding self-determination, as I believe, with Moynihan, we must, the answer is to work clearly and unhesitatingly for the protection of human rights—and particularly minority rights—within existing states. If those rights can't be protected, then self-determination claims, however havoc-provoking, have a moral justification that is hard to deny.

India since independence has enjoyed an inexplicable immunity from international censure, as Barbara Crossette notes in her clear-eyed portrait, *India: Facing the Twenty-First Century*. The images of Gandhian pacifism and Eastern mysticism cover up a multitude of abuses, not only vis-à-vis the outside but within India as well, where a huge media apparatus functions to keep people largely in the dark about the level of popular disaffection and the erosions of democracy that are both on the increase. She notes that more Indians fall victim to their own army and police each year than were killed during the entire seventeen-year dictatorship of Pinochet in Chile. Despite this apalling level of state violence, there have been no mass protests in India and there is no significant international outcry. The "mantra" of democracy, as Crossette dubs it, overwhelms all dissenting voices.[54]

It would be too easy to say that if there had been no Operation Blue Star, no anti-Sikh massacres, no extrajudicial executions, no custodial rapes, that there would be no Khalistan movement. The example of Québec is right here to haunt us in that regard. But a great deal of the moral justification for insurgency, for many people both inside and outside the movement, wouldn't be there without this horrific crackdown. And it is clear that the repression of Sikhs makes every aspect of Khalistani activism more vehement and the potential for a kind of reactive fascism more dangerous. This is particularly the case when the *panth*, the *qaum*, the nation, is spread across several continents, and has access to education, communications, and weapons on a global scale.

But what can an anthropologist do in this situation? Where do our responsibilities lie when the people we study decide to fight a nationalist war?

11
LOOKING INTO DRAGONS

HADN'T ENTERED into this project with any idea that I was doing "applied" anthropology—that is, anthropology with a practical outcome. Although in a vague way the reason I was interested in violent conflict was because I wanted to contribute to ending it, the reason I was interested in the question of justice because I wanted to contribute to achieving it, I, like most scholars, assumed that the way I would do these things was simply by writing about them. I criticized the inflated notions of "culture wars" that pervade humanities corridors in academia these days, but planned on doing something similar myself—to try to be an activist without really risking anything. However, events intervened. I was pulled out of the ivory tower, into the real world in which conclusions are demanded, in which ambiguities and subtleties are blurred over, and in which the opinions of scholars (who become "experts") can have life and death consequences.

THE WORK OF RECOGNITION *

After I had been working among the North American Sikh community for about a year I found myself called on to contribute information to people involved in the refugee determination process in the United States and Canada. While I had been careful not to find out about the exact immigration status of my interlocutors, for fear of discovering some to be illegals, I realized that in addition to immigrants coming to North America through regular channels there were also many Sikhs who were

*Parts of this section were taken from a paper I wrote for *Human Organization*. I thank *Human Organization* for permission to use this material.

determined to be refugees under the Geneva Convention. Officials in the United States and Canada recognized that human rights abuses in Punjab warranted the application of refugee law to fleeing Sikhs, but there were special complications that arose because of India's refusal to allow international human rights groups in for on-the-spot reporting. So "experts" like myself were called on to provide the information on which refugee determination decisions would be made.

I should note here that, according to the Documentation and Research Center of the Immigration and Refuge Board of Canada in Ottawa, the great majority of academics appealed to for this sort of information refuse to get involved. They fear, according to a Research Officer there, "repercussions." Indeed, there can be repercussions of various sorts when scholars venture outside the ivy-covered walls. But for me there was never a question here; how could an anthropologist refuse to give information that could literally save the lives of her informants, whatever repercussions there might be? With Scheper-Hughes, I find Charles McCabe's caricature of anthropologists as "fearless spectators" of the human condition a biting one.[1] (And many anthropologists now agree, as witness the human rights theme of the 1994 American Anthropological Association meetings and the creation of a permanent human rights committee in that organization.) When interlocutors' bodies are marred by burn scars, blackened nails, and twisted leg muscles, when their minds are distorted by memories of electric shock and their dreams haunted by images of sisters' rapes, what role is there for a spectator? Discussions of cultural relativism and human rights, important in themselves, fade in the face of this kind of obvious atrocity. I didn't want to be, couldn't be, a mere voyeur of human suffering, however elegantly such a stance may be defended in the halls of academe. When I was called upon to testify, I did.

Becoming involved in this "applied" side of anthropology brought me face to face, however, with the primary ethical issue underlying my entire interaction with militant Sikhs: How was I to feel about the violence in which they were engaged? In academics we can debate this sort of thing ad nauseum, with few "repercussions." But in the real world, where fates are decided in courts of law, one has to simply come to grips with the thing, here and now, whatever the complexities surrounding it.

In coming to learn more about the legal system surrounding refugee determination, I realized that taking up arms against persecution is the great moral blind spot of international law. We all sympathize with victims, with bloated-bellied Rwandans huddled in tent camps; these inspire donations, prayer, and legal protection. People who don't flee but stay and fight are much more problematic for lawyers, scholars, and all human beings worried about both justice and peace. Do we want to help, condemn, or ignore that militant with his (or her) AK-47? The law is ambivalent on that score.

The current refugee system was set up as a response to the upheavals of World War II, with a United Nations High Commissioner for Refugees (UNHCR) established as the primary protector of refugees. The Geneva Convention of 1951, amended and extended in 1967, defines a refugee as a person who, "owing to a well-founded fear of being persecuted for reasons of race, religion, nationality, membership of a particular social group or political opinion, is outside of the country of his nationality and is unable or, owing to such fear, is unwilling to avail himself of the protection of that country."[2] Once an individual has adequately demonstrated "well-founded fear of being persecuted" on one of the five "convention" grounds, the important principle of *non-refoulement* or non-return applies. It states that "No contracting state shall expel or return a refugee in any manner whatsoever to the frontiers of territories where his life or freedom would be threatened on account of his race, religion, nationality, membership of a particular social group or political opinion."[3] This principle is echoed in the 1984 *Convention Against Torture,* which brings the right of non-return into play simply where there are substantial grounds for believing that the individual would be subject to torture if returned to the home country.[4]

On both these grounds Sikhs fleeing Punjab have been able to claim Convention refugee status and to thereby attain the right of non-return to India. (This is true not only in North America but in many other countries as well.) In any given case, the officials deciding whether a person is a legitimate refugee is basically faced with the question of just how "well-founded" his or her fear of persecution really is. If the fear is deemed to be well-founded, the person is defined as being in need of protection from the international legal system.

This is, however, the easy part, at least in moral terms. But it is possible for somebody to be deemed to be *in need* of protection (that is, having a well-founded fear of persecution) but not to be *deserving* of protection for various reasons (called "exclusions"). According to the Geneva Convention, a person cannot be considered deserving of protection if "he has committed a crime against peace, a war crime, or a crime against humanity" or if "he has committed a serious non-political crime outside the country of refuge prior to his admission to that country as a refugee."[5] This principle is repeated in the section on non-return, which asserts that the benefit of *non-refoulement* may not be claimed by somebody who has committed a serious crime or is regarded as a danger to the security of the country of asylum.[6]

This caveat introduces a big problem—how to define what constitutes a crime against peace, a war crime, a crime against humanity, a "non-political" versus a "political" crime, or a danger to security. Commentators on refugee law have come up with various means of thinking about these categories. For Sikh militants who may be claiming to be refugees based on a well-founded fear of persecution, the key distinction is between "political" and "non-political" crimes. Killing a police officer—political or non-political? Setting off a bomb in a crowded neighborhood—can it be "political?" What about assassinating a prime minister?

In strictly legal terms, committing acts of violence in the context of an organized movement to overthrow a government, if the acts of violence are commensurate with the goals and do not target innocent people, can be considered "political" and therefore do not exclude an asylum applicant. In practice, however, anybody who is actively involved in violence is likely to be looked upon with disfavor in the refugee determination process. People I have spoken with who work at various levels in the refugee system recognize the basic paradox here: while we abhor persecution, we do not condone resistance to it if that resistance takes a violent form. The problem is, we also recognize that violent resistance is in fact sometimes an effective antidote. In conditions of *zulm* (oppression), pacific resistance has definite limitations.[7]

The *Universal Declaration of Human Rights*, adopted as a keystone text by the United Nations in 1948, sets the stage for the rights/violence dilemma in its opening passages. "It is essential," the document states, if man is not to be compelled to have recourse . . . to rebellion against tyranny and oppression, that human rights should be protected by the rule of law."[8] The clear implication here is that where human rights are in fact not protected by law, people may be "compelled" to rebel. But when they do so, they are then not entitled to the refugee protections laid out in other conventions. This critical ambiguity creates the legal gap into which many Sikh militants fall.

Upendra Baxi, a leading Indian human rights theorist, confronts the issue of rights and violence squarely when he writes that

human rights discourse, premised on the view that violence is antithetical to any model of rights, rarely concedes the historical truth that violence can create rights. . . . To do so [would] inevitably raise most discomforting theoretical issues: can violence by one man against another, one class against another, ever be justified? If it can, should there be a right to violence, a right to revolution regarded as a human right? . . . In some kind of cognitive amniocentesis, the entire problematic is aborted [in the liberal human rights tradition].[9]

Though the right to self-determination is enshrined in two 1966 covenants (the *International Covenant on Economic, Social and Cultural Rights* and the *International Covenant on Civil and Political Rights*), it has primarily been Third and Fourth World activists who have chosen to interpret the concept of rights in terms of groups rather than in terms of individuals.[10] Sikh militants, celebrating this tradition, are therefore utterly unapologetic about the need for violence in the creation of Khalistan. But the fact is that despite some recognition granted the notion of self-determination and the use of violence to achieve it in international law, the definition of insurgent acts as "criminal" by the states in which guerillas operate makes it very difficult for them to ask for our protection from persecution by that state (seen by that state, of course, as prosecution, not persecution). When the states of origin are our allies or are regarded as "democracies," the situation becomes even more problematic.

The gap in the international legal system, which understands why people may be "compelled" to rebel but cannot effectively extend its protection to them when they do, exactly parallels the ethical problem I face as an anthropological witness. I can try to help victims of human rights abuses by testifying on their behalf, working to make a place in our advantaged societies for those whose lives elsewhere have become intolerable (as well as protecting the integrity of the refugee system by helping weed out false claims). But my advocacy can't legitimately extend to those who fight rather than flee, without dangerously compromising my professional stance as an anthropologist by skirting the edges of international law and perhaps compromising other anthropologists who rely on the good will of the state of India to conduct their research. I think again of Rupinder Singh Sodhi, the lawyer who could create an opportunity for Sikh assassins to die with dignity but could not help them evade the scaffold. That's about what being an engaged witness amounts to.

Sikhs who pick up guns in defense of their community and on behalf of a hypothetical homeland know full well (implicitly if not explicitly) that in doing so they are placing themselves beyond the protection of international law, beyond the compassion of most of the people of the world, and beyond the understanding of most academic scholarship. In this sense the decision to fight is a very lonely one. It is one which only history will decide as heroic, or misguided. Being a witness to that moment of decision is an oddly moving experience, as is writing about the Sikhs whose historical stature as heroes or fools has yet to be determined.

Being a scholar of Sikh militancy is a lonely occupation, too; other academics shy away from such intimacy with people with guns, but the people with guns themselves remain irrevocably distant. I try to explain them but can't defend them. A witness but not a fellow-traveler, I don't even know their real names. I am *among* them rather than *with* them, as Jean Genet described his own relationship to the Palestinians.[11]

During the initial episode at San Pedro, I described how I reached out to touch an old man's arm as he recounted his tale of torture and humiliation. Later I told Amarjit that I had felt like embracing him, but knew that culturally this is something that is just not done. At a later time, I talked with a room full of young Sikh students, and their affection and appreciation for me was obvious. "If we were Americans we would give you a hug," one said, "but we just don't do that." In fact warm handshakes is about as much as my relationship with the Sikhs can tolerate. There's a lot of mutual regard in my work with them, but there will be no embracing. I'm not a *companheira* or a *rafiqah,* though I'm certainly not their enemy.

Nancy Scheper-Hughes, commenting on the criticism of traditional anthropology's "hostile gaze" toward its subjects, defines a more human attitude, short of love but more than simple respect:

Given the perilous times in which we and our subjects live, I am inclined toward compromise, the practice of a "good-enough" ethnography. While the anthropologist is always a necessarily flawed and biased instrument of cultural translation, like every other craftsperson we can do the best we can with the limited resources we have at hand: our ability to listen and to observe carefully and with empathy and compassion. I still believe that we are best doing what we do best as ethnographers, as natural historians of people. . . . Seeing, listening, touching, recording can be, if done with care and sensitivity, acts of solidarity. Above all, they are the work of recognition. Not to look, not to touch, not to record can be the hostile act, an act of indifference and of turning away.[12]

"The work of recognition" is, I believe, the best way to define what it is that humanistically inclined ethnographers do in the research setting, in the writing of monographs, and in the courtroom. Not to praise or condemn our interlocutors, but to discover with them the challenges they face, as Freire puts it.[13] How to be a person, how to be a Sikh, in a situation of conflict—this is the challenge that faces my interlocutors, who have generously allowed me the privilege of not only eavesdropping on but being part of their ongoing conversation about it. And they have allowed it without insisting that I become one of them.

Upendra Baxi notes that human rights activists, who are not militants but work within the law, "have often to hunt with the hound and run with the hare, an exercise in which they trip, get caught, and are frequently bloodied." [14] The same can be said for anthropologists in today's world in which cultural issues become political issues, and those political issues escalate to military issues, far too often. One takes risks in studying "culture" in such circumstances. This is the substance of *our* challenge and *our* conversation, in which ethnographic interlocutors can also effectively participate, if we allow them to.

Although the problems inherent in research into violent conflict are staggering, it seems to me that the only way we can avoid the stumbling

Baxi talks about, the only way we can avoid the professional and indeed physical risks involved in such work, is to deliberately look the other way as our interlocutors kill and are killed in increasingly depressing numbers. One of the unpleasant truths of the world is that intercultural conflict is on the rise, and we who venture out into that world more than members of any other discipline must be aware of that reality and take it on board as a disciplinary challenge. "If we wanted home truths, we should have stayed at home," writes Geertz.[15] We didn't stay home, and Sikh militants didn't either. We're now sitting in parlors together, one side sworded, the other not, wondering how to talk, whether to embrace, how to face our respective challenges ethically and effectively.

Out of this sitting-together, a book emerged. Some of the Sikhs, reading this manuscript, alternately smiled and frowned, were worried, were glad, were tearful. They disagreed with some of the things that I have written here, and many of those who kindly cooperated with this venture will disagree also. I can only hope that, at the least, I did not misrepresent what they told me. Minimum harm, "good enough" ethnography—sounds far less grand than the kind of anthropology I was taught as a student, years ago. Talking about "an experimental moment in the human sciences"[16] sounds far nobler than the simple doubts and questions that plague my generation of anthropologists, for whom the older paradigms seem empty but new replacements perhaps emptier still. Anyway, we soldier on, trusting that our impulse to reach out to alien others and then write about that experience is, somehow, of use.

THE FACES OF VIOLENCE

Another professional meeting, three years later. This time I had no turbaned Sikhs with me but, rather, was sitting at a bar table being congratulated on the acceptance of this manuscript for publication. Amid the chatter of my colleagues, I noticed that one woman at the table was oddly silent. I introduced myself to her, and we started talking. But as we did so, her eyes welled up with tears, and she finally politely told me that she had had to walk out of a paper I had presented about Sikh militancy, and could not or would not be reading my book. During the rather intense encounter that followed, it came out that this anthropologist had been on one of the planes that had been hijacked by Sikh militants. She was clearly still in great pain over this episode, and in fact said that her life would never be the same again. She didn't want to talk about the Sikhs, and couldn't countenance my study of them.

This is the kind of pain, the pain of the victim, that is too easily elided in a study primarily of perpetrators. To the charge of one-sidedness here, I plead guilty (noting that this is a not the same thing as a charge of partisanship). I have been writing here of how Khalistani Sikhs suffer pain and how Khalistani Sikhs commit acts of violence, but not of how their enemies suffer pain and commit acts of violence. This one-sidedness is a practical limitation in researching venues of ongoing conflict in which, as June Nash put it, no neutrals are allowed.[17] Trying to make contact with or interview the agents of violence against the Sikhs—police, military officers, and so on—can easily appear as betrayal or sabotage to militant interlocutors. As Sluka advises, based on his fieldwork in Belfast, "It is not enough to not be a threat to your research participants; act in such a way as to *be seen* not to be a threat." [18] Even pursuing the innocent victims of Khalistani violence can be problematic in an arena like this one in which infiltrators are everwhere, spies, real or chimerical, abound, and everything is shades of gray.

One should never minimize the inherent danger in this kind of research or grow complacent about the potential for things to go wrong. At least three anthropologists have been killed in the course of conducting fieldwork on violence: Ruth First in South Africa, Arnold Ap in Indonesia, and Myrna Mack in Guatemala. While insisting on complete freedom of expression from Sikh militant interlocutors, I refuse to even *appear* to go behind their backs to talk with their enemies or victims. I urge the reader to seek out these other kinds of accounts of the Khalistani insurgency; they are numerous, indeed, hegemonic. I used most of them in an effort at balance in the current account, and references to them can be found in the bibliography.

What this book has to offer, in my mind, is a glimpse into a world that few readers will have had any contact with—the world of violent religious nationalists. The limitations on my work, reflected in this book, are many, and some critics will say that scholarship cannot or should not take place under these kinds of conditions. I disagree, and feel that this criticism is a product of the unrealistic notion that a scholarly account must be definitive. Scholarship in fact works best in coalition, and my bit of the puzzle here is the culture of Sikh militancy. There are victims of this militancy, hundreds and thousands of people who have been affected, insulted, violated, and destroyed by the "saint-soldiers" I describe here. Their suffering must never be minimized. But their pain, real and intolerable as it is, does not change the fact that the Khalistani militancy continues, and needs desperately to be understood *whether one supports or condemns it*. To use the anguish of victims as a blanket of silence over the Sikh militancy is to sentence us all to continuing spirals of violence, as the state charges "Terrorism!" and the militants respond with escalating proofs of revolutionary ardor.

I hope that this volume has shown that dialogue with militants is not impossible. As more anthropologists do this sort of work, research strategies are emerging. I agree with Sluka that total openness and honesty is the best way for an ethnographer to deal with militant interlocutors. I never hid my opinions from the Khalistanis with whom I worked, never hesitated to disagree with them, and never pretended to be a believer, in the religious sense. When invited, I spoke publicly in Sikh gatherings. I am convinced that this willingness to expose myself was an important part of the militants' ultimate respect for me. They felt they could trust me not because I was "on their side," but because they knew me to be a trustworthy and honest person in general terms. I stayed in their homes when invited; this intimacy may look problematic but is a central part of creating a framework of friendship in which, then, viewpoints could be shared openly. I was never censored by my Sikh interlocutors, and never treated with anything other than respect.

There is no doubt that it is difficult to engage in this kind of very personal encounter with individuals who do things to which one has strong moral objections. Robert Friedman tried to write about this ambivalence with regard to Zionist settlers on the West Bank, and Vincent Crapanzano did the same in his ethnography of South African whites, *Waiting*.[19] Drinking tea with a man who has set off bombs in crowded neighborhoods is an emotionally draining experience, not because one is utterly disgusted with such a person and has to sit sipping tea hypocritically, but precisely because concurrent with one's disgust one feels also the pain that led up to the moment of bomb-making, and the lonely hardness that comes from the commitment to move on, to continue living and indeed loving after having done a thing like that. Sympathy and revulsion become partners here.

In this kind of confrontation, which is not only about "culture" but about lives and deaths, many of the borders around ourselves that we construct as ethnographers simply fall apart. Our own *human* reactions to what we are hearing break through all methodological artifice and impact in turn our interlocutors, who likewise cease being "informants" and share, however fleetingly, a moment of empathy beyond categorization or judgment. Tony Robben describes the intensity of this sort of encounter movingly, experienced during his study of Argentina's "dirty war":

An Argentine anthropologist, who knew one of my interviewees, a former guerrillero, recounted to me one day his rendition of my meetings with him. He had told her that during a stirring moment of our conversation in which he was reflecting on the terrible waste of lives in the political struggle of the 1970s, he saw tears in my eyes. This intensified the awareness of his own tragedy and made him break down as well. At these moments of a complete collapse of the critical dis-

13. A Sikh boy posing as a soldier. This poignant photo was given to me by a proud relative of the child in southern California.

tance between two interlocutors, we lose all dimensions of the scientific enterprise. Overwhelmed by emotion we do not have the need for any explanation because we feel that all questions have already been answered. What else is there to ask? What else is there to tell? What more do we need to know? What more is there to know? [20]

Nevertheless, Robben does go on to take a step back, to reflect critically on the conversation that had moved him to tears. Emotional moments, however unforgettable, do not eradicate our capacity for independent and reasoned judgment. Khalistani militants all know that whatever they have told me I may have to testify to; this stipulation was part of the ground rules of our encounter, and continues to be an ethical imperative for me no matter how many tears we have shared. Militants, too, have imperatives that go beyond shared tears, so they understand this principle very well.

No matter how vociferously we anthropologists of militancy assert our commitment to maintaining an ultimate intellectual distance from our research participants, we all suffer the accusation of partisanship from their enemies. This response is to be expected. Less understandable is the common skeptical reaction from the general public and indeed the world of scholarship, which often goes beyond the charge of one-sidedness. We are accused of creating a pornography of violence, of providing an "aesthetic alibi" to terrorists, even of *being* terrorists. [21] Having transgressed the taboo of never talking to "terrorists," of never putting a face on the acts of violence we find so easily revolting on the evening news, we find ourselves contaminated and in some ways stigmatized by what we study. This phenomenon has a few parallels in other arenas: that people who study homosexuality must be themselves homosexual, for example. In this book, I have suggested that the alienation of violence from the general realm of human experience—the willed refusal to put faces on terrorists—is in itself partly responsible for escalating insurgent violence. Paradoxically, it is because we do care about victims—on both sides—that we feel compelled to take the personal and professional risks of studying violence.

Until it becomes fully normal for scholars to study violence by talking with and being with people who engage in it, the dark myth of evil and irrational terrorists will continue to overwhelm more pragmatic attempts to lucidly grapple with the problem of conflict. Hysterical calls to condemn terrorism from a distance, to find better ways of technologically defeating terrorists as we find ourselves less and less capable of politically defeating them, are of a piece with the failure of imagination that considers freedom fighters as nothing more than serial murderers. In the current world situation, in which even nuclear weapons are not out of the range of possibility for insurgent groups, nothing, I suggest, could be more dangerous.

Nordstrom and Robben, in their pathbreaking work on the ethnography of violence, write that:

For too many people everywhere in the world, violence is an all too human reality. This includes the victims of violence but also the perpetrators who themselves are caught in spiraling conflicts that their actions have set in motion but that they can no longer control. To understand their plight and to try to begin to forge solutions, we must confront violence head on, place it squarely in the center of the lives and cultures of the people who suffer it, precisely where they themselves find it. Violence may not be functional, and it is certainly not tolerable, but it is not outside the realm of human society, or that which defines it as human.[22]

The masculinist discourse on "terrorism" that has become hegemonic in policy arenas today condescendingly rejects attempts to put a human face on violence as hopelessly naive. If we think we can enter into productive dialogue with assassins, we must be "soft" on crime. But there is a greater naïveté, and a greater danger, I suggest, in continuing to insist that physically exterminating terrorists is the way to eradicate terrorism. A lethal game of one-upmanship ensues, which feeds the appetite for power on both sides and injures many innocent bystanders in the process. People build excellent careers in the counterterrorism forum, money is poured into the coffers of counterterrorism think tanks, yet more fresh new terrorists spring up every day.

Ashis Nandy, a prominent voice on the Indian intellectual scene, instructively narrates the process through which the standard rhetoric of terrorism replaced the complex experience of a Sikh hijacking in 1984 in his recent book, *The Savage Freud*. He quotes an article describing the conclusion of the hijacking in the *Sunday Observer*, penned by one of the victims who had at first "assumed the tone of a war correspondent" but was forced by events to take greater account of the *human* ambiguities of the situation. Where are the "evil terrorists" and the "terrified victims" of public imagination in the following eyewitness account?

Suddenly the passengers and hijackers were in each others' arms, crying like children as the tension of the past twenty hours visibly melted away. It was a crazy scene I shall not forget. Passengers who were hijacked, humiliated and beaten up by these nine desperadoes were actually jostling with each other to get the hijackers' autographs on the back of their air tickets. Conversely all the aggression and mental resolve of the Sikh extremists seemed to be cracking up. The fearsome Sikh with an axe ran round hugging passengers while Pinkha Singh made it a point to shake hands individually with everyone in the cabin and the fifteen-year-old boy hijacker just sat down on the floor and cried his heart out.[23]

Despite this description, which was echoed in the accounts of other passengers, the key protagonists were quickly reduced to cardboard figures by the mainstream press and by "policy analysts." Within a day of the tragicomic denouement narrated above, they were already busy "building up the hijacking as the act of a group of well-trained, well-armed, merciless commandos let loose on Indian soil by enemy countries and traitors." [24] Nandy bluntly characterizes the establishment arena of counterterrorism in India as utterly out of touch with reality:

the Indian press, the airlines bureaucracy, the foreign office, the security machinery and defence experts . . . appeared to be living in an unreal, mythical world. . . . When these outsiders talked of the hijackers, foreign involvement and security lapses in reified terms, they seemed to be totally out of touch with the real world of air piracy as it had been experienced by real persons uninitiated in sophisticated academic theories of terrorism. [25]

"Lives perturbed by violence," as Nordstrom and Robben describe them, [26] are full of contradictions and ambiguities. Laughter and "rising spirits" do sometimes coexist with suffering; hijackers do cry; bomb builders can be not beyond but within our range of understanding. Violence is "natural" only to the pathological few; most people come to it within a culturally constructed *conceptual* (not instinctual, not emotional, not customary or blind) [27] framework. As a part of culture, it is amenable to ethnographic analysis.

Nandy knows how unpopular his thinking about the Sikh hijackings is likely to be, and wryly advises any graduate student interested in furthering his or her career not to follow him in it. But without denying the obviously important security aspects of combatting terrorism, he argues for the possibility that there may be other ways of dealing with one's enemies, ways that take account of rather than overlook the multiplex quality of human personalities and human interaction. "Some will call this absurd, maudlin moralism," Nandy recognizes. "[But] to others it is the heart of politics." [28]

Whether or not it is the heart of politics, I do believe that recognition of this complexity in the lived experience of violence is the heart of ethnography. We don't deal in cardboard constructions, but in all the "thickness" of human life. We try to understand witchcraft, not to participate in witch hunts. The mythic proportions that the battle against terrorism has assumed today calls for a similar anthropological subversion.

The business of ethnography is looking into dragons, not domesticating or abominating them, according to Clifford Geertz. [29] Writing about violence that is part of the human experience but finds its context in highly specific historical circumstances and is interpreted in an idiosyncratic religious idiom means trying to walk that fine line between taming and exoticizing that faces all ethnographers. Although this arena is fraught with ethical, methodological, and legal dilemmas that rarely confront more traditional ethnography, this work does not therefore lie outside the general range of the ethnographic enterprise, any more than the fact of suffering and the commission of violence on the part of nationalist militants places them outside the general range of humankind. The simplistic trope of the Sikh-as-terrorist has done enough damage both to India itself and to the academic study of India; it is time that it be replaced by a "thicker" conception of what it means to be a Sikh who suffers, and fights. Ethnographic methods, which focus on people rather than stereotypes, can contribute here.

I still have nightmares about violence. Now that the book is nearly done and the research part of the project over, however, they sometimes take place in Punjab, with turbaned Sikhs and not vaguely defined Cambodians as the major protagonists. Each is as fear provoking, as shattering, as the last; each results in night sweats and pounding heartbeat. One doesn't "get used to" the idea of violence, as I never "got used to" hearing narratives of tortures, of assassinations, of bomb building, no matter how apparently repetitive the stories were. Of course, when I wake up from my dreams, I can go back to the nonviolent world of books and papers, students and teachers; I can forget about nightmares. But in the back of my mind I am always aware that many of the people I have come to know are waking up from nightmares to live nightmares, in the unrelenting and unforgiving world of violent conflict. I am privileged to be a part of their world, and more privileged to be able to leave it. That critical difference between anthropologist and interlocutor, an escape hatch, a way out, won't be eradicated by any amount of "experimental moments" or shared tears. For me, it's an experience; for them, a life.

"I don't really like this ending," Balraj said. "It sounds awfully negative. Like you're just talking now about what we must fear and forgetting about what we can hope."

"What can we hope?" I asked.

"That God will bless us with the courage and wisdom to do what we have to do. So far He has filled us with his love every day, and that gives us hope that we will succeed."

"You mean, succeed in getting Khalistan?"

"Not really. I mean succeed in being the best human beings we can be. We might be suffering, we might be fighting, and so on. But we are being Sikhs in the best way we can, and you should end on this note. We are happy because we have God's love, and we are filled with hope."

"OK," I said. "I will end on that note."

NOTES

CHAPTER 1: OF NIGHTMARES AND CONTACTS

1. "Culture or civilization, taken in its widest ethnographic sense, is that complex whole which includes knowledge, belief, art, morals, law, custom, and any other capabilities and habits acquired by man as a member of society." (Edward Burnett Tylor, *Primitive Culture: Researches into the Development of Mythology, Philosophy, Religion, Language, Art and Custom* [London: Murray, 1871].) For Kant's exposition, see his *Anthropology from a Pragmatic Point of View*, trans. Mary Gregor (The Hague: Martinus Nijhoff, 1974).

2. Inderjit Singh Jaijee of the Movement Against State Repression, an indigenous human rights group, estimates total casualties at over 100,000. This is the figure typically cited by Khalistanis.

3. There are actually multiple committees claiming to lead the separatist movement; more about this is explained in Chapter 6.

4. Kushwant Singh, *My Bleeding Punjab* (New Delhi: UBS Publishers, 1992), p. 164. Kushwant Singh is a Sikh who thoroughly condemns the militants.

5. Elaine Scarry, *The Body in Pain: The Making and Unmaking of the World* (New York: Oxford University Press, 1985).

6. Key among these, in chronological order, are *Punjab in Crisis: Human Rights in India* (New York: Asia Watch, 1991); *Human Rights Violations in Punjab: Use and Abuse of the Law* (London: Amnesty International, 1991); *India: Torture, Rape and Deaths in Custody* (London: Amnesty International, 1992); *An Unnatural Fate: Disappearances and Impunity in Punjab and Kashmir* (London: Amnesty International, 1993); *Dead Silence: The Legacy of Abuses in Punjab* (New York: Human Rights Watch/Physicans for Human Rights, 1994); *India: The Terrorism and Disruptive Activities (Prevention) Act: The Lack of "Scrupulous Care"* (London: Amnesty International, 1994); *Punjab Police: Beyond the Bounds of Law* (London: Amnesty International, 1995). Indian human rights groups such as the People's Union for Civil Liberties, Citizens for Democracy, and Punjab (later International) Human Rights Organization, and the Movement Against State Repression have also produced reports on specific episodes of abuse; these reports are cited throughout this book.

7. Jeffrey A. Sluka, "Participant Observation in Violent Social Contexts," *Human Organization* 49, 2 (1992): 114–205; "Reflections on Managing Danger in

Fieldwork: Dangerous Anthropology in Belfast," in *Fieldwork Under Fire: Contemporary Studies of Violence and Survival*, ed. Carolyn Nordstrom and Antonius Robben (Berkeley: University of California Press, 1995), pp. 276–294. Others who have written especially effectively on issues that arise when one studies not only victims but also perpetrators are Joseba Zulaika (*Basque Violence: Metaphor and Sacrament* [Reno: University of Nevada Press, 1988]) and David Lan (*Guns and Rain: Guerillas and Spirit Mediums in Zimbabwe* [Berkeley: University of California Press, 1984]).

8. Carolyn Nordstrom and Antonius Robben, "Anthropology and the Ethnography of Violence," in *Fieldwork Under Fire*, ed. Nordstrom and Robben, pp. 1–24.

9. See Robert Dentan, "Bad Day at Bukit Pekan," *American Anthropologist* 97, 2 (1995): 225–231.

10. J. Corbin, "The Anthropology of Violence," *International Journal of Environmental Studies* 10 (1977): 107–111.

11. Carl von Clausewitz, *On War*, ed. M. Howard and P. Parets (Princeton, N.J.: Princeton University Press, 1966).

12. Noam Chomsky, *The Culture of Terrorism* (Boston: South End Press, 1988).

13. Martin van Creveld, *The Transformation of War* (New York: The Free Press, 1991).

14. John Keegan, *The Face of Battle: Agincourt, Waterloo and the Somme* (New York: Viking, 1976).

15. For example, Carolyn Nordstrom and JoAnn Martin's *Paths to Domination, Resistance and Terror* (Berkeley: University of California Press, 1992); Kay Warren's *The Violence Within: Cultural and Political Opposition in Divided Nations* (Boulder, Colo.: Westview Press, 1993); Nordstrom and Robben's *Fieldwork Under Fire*.

16. See Kevin Avruch, ed., *Cross-Cultural Perspectives on Conflict Resolution* (New York: Greenwood Press, 1991); Alvin Wolfe and Honggang Yang, eds., *Anthropological Contributions to Conflict Resolution* (Athens: University of Georgia Press, 1996).

17. Mark Juergensmyer, *The New Cold War: Religious Nationalism Confronts the Secular State* (Berkeley: University of California Press, 1993).

18. After Singh, *My Bleeding Punjab*, p. 53.

19. Sluka, "Managing Danger in Fieldwork," p. 290.

20. Comments offered at the World Sikh Organization convention, Toronto, June 1994.

21. Martin Buber, *Between Man and Man* (New York: Macmillan, 1965).

CHAPTER 2: THE FRAGRANCE OF JASMINE

1. The classic academic view here is that of Khushwant Singh, expressed in his two-volume *History of the Sikhs* (Princeton, N.J.: Princeton University Press, 1963–1966). Many scholars follow Singh in seeing Sikhism as a merger of the two faiths. W. H. McLeod, in a competing view, places the origins of Sikhism firmly within the Hindu tradition, broadly defined, as expressed in *The Sikhs: History, Religion and Society* (New York: Oxford University Press, 1989) and other works.

2. George Foster, *A Journey from Bengal to England Through Northern India, Kashmir, Afghanistan and Persia into Russia, 1783–84* (London: R. Faulder, 1798); Joyce Pettigrew, *Robber Noblemen: A Study of the Political System of Sikh Jats* (Delhi: Ambika, 1978). See also Mark Juergensmeyer, *Religion as Social Vision: The Movement*

Against Untouchability in Twentieth Century Punjab (Berkeley: University of California Press, 1982).

3. On the rise of a separate Sikh identity see W. H. McLeod, *The Evolution of the Sikh Community* (Oxford: Clarendon Press, 1976) and *Who Is a Sikh? The Problem of Sikh Identity* (Oxford: Clarendon Press, 1989); also Richard G. Fox, *Lions of the Punjab: Culture in the Making* (Berkeley: University of California Press, 1985); Rajiv Kapur, *Sikh Separatism: The Politics of Faith* (London: Allen and Unwin, 1986); and Harjot Oberoi, *The Construction of Religious Boundaries* (Chicago: University of Chicago Press, 1994).

4. T. N. Madan, "The Double-Edged Sword: Fundamentalism and the Sikh Religious Tradition," in *Fundamentalisms Observed*, ed. Martin W. Marty and R. Scott Appleby, pp. 594–625 (Chicago: University of Chicago Press, 1991).

5. Robin Jeffrey, "Grappling with History: Sikh Politicians and the Past," *Pacific Affairs* 60 (1987): 65.

6. Jeffrey, "Grappling with History," p. 71.

7. A British colonial observer, Malcolm Darling, commented that the Sikhs "do spendidly, whether with sword or with plough, as long as conditions are adverse" (*The Punjab Peasant in Prosperity and Debt* [New Delhi: Manohar, 1977], p. 47).

CHAPTER 3: A SAINT-SOLDIER

1. Mark Juergensmeyer, *The New Cold War: Religious Nationalism Confronts the Secular State* (Berkeley: University of California Press, 1993), p. 6. For a strong critique of Juergensmeyer, see Henry Munson's "Intolerable Tolerance: Western Academics and Islamic Fundamentalism," *Contention* 5.3 (1996): 99–117.

2. There are various, highly divergent accounts of this episode. It is reviewed further in Chapter 4.

3. The idea that Bhindranwale had close ties to the Congress party is repeated in virtually every major source on the Punjab conflict. He is typically portrayed as a kind of Frankenstein's monster who was created by Congress to thwart the political power of the Akali Dal but got out of control. These informants paint a different picture.

4. The Guru Granth Sahib's sacredness prevents its being used in this way in a court of law, so Gurubani Gutka is typically used instead.

CHAPTER 4: BLUE STAR

1. Notably, W. H. McLeod, *Early Sikh Tradition* (Oxford: Clarendon Press, 1980).

2. Mark Tully and Satish Jacob, *Amritsar: Mrs. Gandhi's Last Battle* (Calcutta: Rupa and Company), p. 54.

3. Cited in Ram Narayan Kumar and Georg Sieberer, *The Sikh Struggle: Origin, Evolution and Present Phase* (Delhi: Chanakya Publishing, 1991), p. 250.

4. A book echoing his claim that the accident was contrived is Chand Joshi's *Bhindranwale: Myth and Reality* (New Delhi: Vikas, 1984), p. 4. This claim is otherwise unsubstantiated, to my knowledge.

5. R. E. Parry, *The Sikhs of the Punjab* (London: Drake, 1931), p. 102.

6. Joyce Pettigrew, *The Sikhs of the Punjab: Unheard Voices of State and Guerilla Violence* (London: Zed Books, 1995), p. 35.

7. Many sources, including some prominent academic ones (e.g., T. N. Madan, "The Double-Edged Sword: Fundamentalism and the Sikh Religion, in *Fundamentalisms Observed*, ed. Martin E. Marty and R. Scott Appleby [Chicago: University of Chicago Press, 1991], pp. 594–625), repeat the claim that Bhindranwale headed the anti-Nirankari procession. I have yet to find an eyewitness who places him there.

8. Cited by Veena Das, "Time, Self, and Community: Features of Sikh Militant Discourse," *Contributions to Indian Sociology* 26, 2 (1992): 248.

9. Robin Jeffrey, *What's Happening to India? Punjab, Ethnic Conflict, Mrs. Gandhi's Death and the Test for Federalism* (New York: Holmes and Meier, 1986), pp. 141–142.

10. This was one of several episodes that militants claim were the responsibility of the so-called "Third Agency," a super-secret division of RAW (Research and Analysis Wing) or Indian intelligence. The "Third Agency" is said by militants to have been working to defame Bhindranwale and other leaders. (For a description of the militant view of these events see Gurdarshan Singh Dhillon, *India Commits Suicide* [Chandigarh: Singh and Singh, 1992].)

11. Ian Mulgrew, *Unholy Terror: The Sikhs and International Terrorism* (Toronto: Key Porter Books, 1988), p. 71.

12. Tully and Jacob, *Amritsar: Mrs. Gandhi's Last Battle*, p. 88.

13. Jeffrey, *What's Happening to India?*, p. 149.

14. K. S. Brar, *Operation Blue Star: The True Story* (New Delhi: UBS Publishers, 1993). Brar also reports the association of many in the Punjab police with the militancy but describes this as an "infiltration" of the police by the militants (p. 36). He describes the retired military officers who supported Bhindranwale as people with "their own axes to grind" against the Indian military (p. 27). Shabeg Singh, it is true, had been dismissed from service on corruption charges, which were, however, later reversed. He was reportedly greatly pained over these charges, which he consistently denied.

15. Kumar and Sieberer, *The Sikh Struggle*, p. 260.

16. Tully and Jacob, *Amritsar: Mrs. Gandhi's Last Battle*, p. 105.

17. Kuldip Nayar and Khushwant Singh, *The Tragedy of Punjab: Operation Blue Star and After* (New Delhi: Vision Books, 1985), p. 55. Kuldip Nayar was a member of the People's Union for Civil Liberties.

18. Mulgrew, *Unholy Terror*, pp. 71–72.

19. Both Bhindranwale and the Babbar Khalsa chief condemned this massacre, and it is not clear who carried it out.

20. Mulgrew, *Unholy Terror*, p. 74.

21. A name frequently mentioned in connection with Bhindranwale is the Dashmesh Regiment, which was said to have claimed responsibility for many of the assassinations and raids of the early 1980s. There are enough ambiguities surrounding the Dashmesh Regiment (including accusations that the name was used by a "Third Agency" to implicate Bhindranwale's group in atrocities) to warrant restraint in using this name.

22. As an officially secular state, India does not have such a thing as "holy city" status. What the Sikhs were upset about were things like the running of pilgrimages to Hindu sacred sites by the government-run tourist organization, the use of government monies to restore Hindu temples classed as national treasures, regulations regarding the selling of alcohol and meat in the vicinity of temples,

and so on. This "holy city status" rhetoric had the effect of inflaming Sikhs but leading others to question the militant Sikhs' understanding of how secular India worked.

23. Gurdarshan Singh Dhillon, *India Commits Suicide* (Chandigarh: Singh and Singh, 1992).

24. Citizens for Democracy, *Report to the Nation: Oppression in Punjab* (Bombay: Citizens for Democracy, 1985).

25. The claim is frequently made that the army had been practicing storming the Golden Temple Complex at a full-scale model in the foothills of the Himalayas for weeks. Lieutenant General Brar denies this outright but says it is possible that a special paramilitary force had been preparing such an attack (*Operation Blue Star*, p. 39).

26. Tully and Jacob, *Amritsar: Mrs. Gandhi's Last Battle*, p. 154.

27. The most controversial *charge* was that chemical weapons were used. It appears that the weapon in question was CS gas, more powerful than ordinary tear gas but not deserving of the epithet "chemical weapon" in ordinary usage. It can apparently have severe effects on children, however.

28. Tully and Jacob, *Amritsar: Mrs. Gandhi's Last Battle*, p. 159.

29. Brar, *Operation Blue Star*, p. 97.

30. Ibid., p. 101.

31. Ibid., pp. 126–127.

32. Tully and Jacob, *Amritsar: Mrs. Gandhi's Last Battle*, p. 187.

33. There were rumors to the effect that Bhindranwale had in fact not died in the assault but had escaped and fled to Pakistan, a story fed by the quick cremation of the militants' bodies by the army. There is no evidence for this scenario, though now and then rumors to this effect resurface.

34. Cited in Citizens for Democracy, *Oppression in Punjab*, pp. 69–70.

35. Cited in Tully and Jacob, *Amritsar: Mrs. Gandhi's Last Battle*, p. 171. The journalists report that Ranbir Kaur, her husband, and the twelve children were taken to interrogation camps, after which nine of the children were missing. Ranbir Kaur was not released until the end of August (p. 172).

36. Cited in Tully and Jacob, *Amritsar: Mrs. Gandhi's Last Battle*, p. 172.

37. Government of India, *White Paper on the Punjab Agitation* (New Delhi, 1984).

38. Tully and Jacob, *Amritsar: Mrs. Gandhi's Last Battle*, p. 184.

39. Citizens for Democracy, *Oppression in Punjab*, p. 76.

40. Citizens for Democracy, *Oppression in Punjab*, p. 6; M. Ghazdi, "The Charge is Sedition," in *Punjab: The Fatal Miscalcuation*, ed. Patwant Singh and Harji Malik (Delhi: Crescent, 1985), pp. 196–207. In 1988 another journalist, Dhiren Bhagat, was killed under suspicious circumstances after he published an article accusing Indian intelligence of smuggling weapons from Afghanistan into the country, perhaps to plant on Sikh separatists in the interests of justifying counterinsurgency (Barbara Crossette, *India: Facing the Twenty-First Century* [Bloomington: Indiana University Press, 1993], p. 103).

41. K. S. Brar, *Operation Blue Star*, p. 124; Nayar and Singh, *The Tragedy in Punjab*, p. 102.

42. Tully and Jacob, *Amritsar: Mrs. Gandhi's Last Battle*, pp. 186–187.

43. Brar, *Operation Blue Star*, p. 122.

44. Khushwant Singh, *My Bleeding Punjab* (New Delhi: UBS Publishers, 1992), p. 71.

45. Brar, *Operation Blue Star*, p. 127

46. Clifford Geertz, *The Interpretation of Cultures* (New York: Basic Books, 1973).

47. Army Gazette, Baat Cheet Special No. 153, cited in *Oppression in Punjab*, p. 29.

48. Nayar and Singh, *The Tragedy of Punjab*, p. 7.

49. Both cases reported by Ajit Singh Bains, *Seige of the Sikhs: Violation of Human Rights in Punjab* (Toronto: New Magazine Publishing, 1988), p. 116.

50. Patwant Singh, "The Distorting Mirror," in *Punjab: The Fatal Miscalculation*, ed. Patwant Singh and Harji Malik (Delhi: Crescent, 1985), pp. 9–32.

51. Quoted in Bains, *Seige of the Sikhs*, p. 27. See also the Amnesty International report, *India: The Terrorism and Disruptive Activities (Prevention) Act: The Lack of "Scrupulous Care"* (London, 1994). In May 1995 TADA was allowed to lapse, but those imprisoned during the period of TADA's tenure are still being held.

52. Stanley Wolpert, *A New History of India*, 4th edition (New York: Oxford University Press, 1993), p. 425. For a response from the human rights community, see the report issued by the People's Union for Civil Liberties, *Black Laws* (New Delhi: PUCL, 1984).

53. Singh and Malik, *Punjab: The Fatal Miscalculation*, p. 137.

54. Crossette, *India: Facing the Twenty-First Century*, p. 98.

CHAPTER 5: WHY KHALISTAN?

1. Joyce Pettigrew says that leaders of contemporary factions "are the modern equivalent of the *misl* chiefs" (*Robber Noblemen: A Study of the Political System of the Sikh Jats* [New Delhi: Ambika Publications, 1978], p. 202). She continues this theme with regard to the current militancy in *The Sikhs of the Punjab: Unheard Voices of State and Guerilla Violence* (London: Zed Books, 1995), where she describes the organizational disarray that came to characterize phases of the Khalistani militancy.

2. S. Mahmud Ali, *The Fearful State: Power, People and Internal War in South Asia* (London: Zed Books, 1993), p. 82.

3. Richard G. Fox, in *Lions of the Punjab: Culture in the Making* (Berkeley: University of California Press, 1985), calls the twentieth-century developments in Sikh activism and militancy "the Third Sikh War," harking back to this history.

4. For example, General E. J. Thackwell, on Sikh behavior during the Second Sikh War: "Seikhs caught hold of the bayonets of their assailants with their left hands and closing with their adversaries, dealt furious sword blows with the right. . . . [This will] suffice to demonstrate the rare species of courage possessed by these men" (E. J. Thackwell, *Narrative of the Second Sikh War, 1848–1849* [London, 1851], p. 213).

5. Khushwant Singh, *History of the Sikhs*, vol. 2 (Princeton, N.J.: Princeton University Press, 1966), p. 160. For details on the Indian military, see Stephen P. Cohen's classic treatment, *The Indian Army: Its Contribution to the Development of a Nation* (Berkeley: University of California Press, 1971).

6. Fox, *Lions of the Punjab;* Harjot Oberoi, *The Construction of Religious Boundaries: Culture, Identity and Diversity in Sikh Tradition* (Chicago: University of Chicago Press, 1994).

7. A definitive source on the Ghadr movement is Haresh K. Puri's *Ghadar Movement: Ideology, Organization and Strategy* (Amritsar: Guru Nanak Dev University Press, 1993).

8. Ram Narayan Kumar and Georg Sieberer assert that the majority of those killed were in fact not Sikhs. (*The Sikh Struggle: Origins, Evolution and Present Phase* [Delhi: Chanakya, 1991], pp. 102–103.)

9. See Haresh K. Puri, "Akali Politics: Emerging Compulsions," in *Political Dynamics of Punjab*, ed. Paul Wallace and Surendra Chopra (Amritsar: Guru Nanak Dev University Press, 1981), p. 35.

10. There is some dispute about just how "Sikh" Bhagat Singh was. Some claim he was a secular, even atheist, individual; others that he became a baptized Sikh at the end of his life. Sikhs today honor portraits of Bhagat Singh in the full five symbols of the Khalsa Sikh.

11. M. K. Gandhi, *Communal Unity* (Ahmedabad: Navjivan, 1948), pp. 165–167.

12. On Punjabi Suba, see Paul Brass's excellent treatment, *Language, Religion and Politics in North India* (London: Cambridge University Press, 1974).

13. Tully and Jacob, *Amritsar: Mrs. Gandhi's Last Battle*, p. 50.

14. The situation here was more complex that it sounds, however, as the Akali Dal always worked in coalition with other parties, so it is hard to say outright, based on polls, how representative it was of the Sikh population as a whole.

15. For fuller discussion, see my "Rethinking Indian Communalism: Culture and Counter-Culture" *Asian Survey* 7, 3 (1993): 722–737; "Ayodhya and the Hindu Resurgence" *Religion* 24 (1994): 73–80.

16. Ainslie Embree, *Utopias in Conflict: Religion and Nationalism in Modern India* (Berkeley: University of California Press, 1990).

17. There are problems with Indian census figures, most notably that the "Hindu" category includes Scheduled Castes (former untouchables) and many tribals, who may not actually identify themselves as Hindu. Gerald Larson adopts a usefully long-term view of the dynamic of Brahminic hegemony in India, tracking the "neo-Hindu" state of today back through ancient times (*India's Agony Over Religion* [Albany: State University of New York Press, 1984]).

18. Prakash Chandra Upadyaya, "The Politics of Indian Secularism," *Modern Asian Studies* 26, 4 (1992); see also *Contesting the Nation: Religion, Community, and the Politics of Democracy in India*, ed. David C. Ludden (Philadelphia: University of Pennsylvania Press, 1996).

19. Expressed most famously by Louis Dumont in *Homo Hierarchicus: The Caste System and Its Implications*, trans. Mark Sainsbury, Louis Dumont, and Basia Gulati (Chicago: University of Chicago Press, 1980). For a recent critcism see Peter van der Veer, "The Foreign Hand: Orientalist Discourse in Sociology and Communalism," in *Orientalism and the Postcolonial Predicament*, ed. Carol Breckenridge and Peter van der Veer (Philadelphia: University of Pennsylvania Press, 1992), pp. 23–44.

20. Sheldon Pollock, "Deep Orientalism? Notes on Sanskrit and Power Beyond the Raj," in *Orientalism and the Postcolonial Predicament*, ed. Carol Breckenridge and Peter van der Veer (Philadelphia: University of Pennsylvania Press, 1993), p. 115. On the complicity of academia with the Brahminic perspective, also see Richard Burghart, "Ethnographers and Their Local Counterparts in India," in *Localizing Strategies*, ed. R. Fardon (Washington, D.C.: Smithsonian Institution Press, 1990), pp. 260–278.

CHAPTER 6: DRAWING THE SWORD

1. Pranay Gupta, *Vengeance: India after the Assassination of Indira Gandhi* (New York: Norton, 1985), pp. 48–50.

2. The case of Kehar Singh became a complex one, with lawyers arguing the unconstitutionality of the death sentence in his case up until the last moment.

Balbir Singh, a fourth alleged conspirator, had his death sentence set aside. See Ram Narayan Kumar and Georg Sieberer, *The Sikh Struggle: Origin, Evolution and Present Phase* (Delhi: Chanakya Publications, 1991), pp. 294–296.

3. People's Union for Civil Liberties/People's Union for Democratic Rights, *Who Are the Guilty?* (New Delhi, PUCL/PUDR, 1985), pp. 2–4.

4. Ajit Singh Bains, *Seige of the Sikhs: Violations of Human Rights in Punjab* (Toronto: The New Magazine Publishing Company, 1988), pp. 11–12.

5. Citizens' Commission, *Delhi: 31 October to 4 November 1984* (New Delhi, Citizens' Commission, 1985), p. 12.

6. Citizens for Democracy, *The Truth About Delhi Violence* (New Delhi, Citizens for Democracy, 1985).

7. Paul Brass, *The Politics of India Since Independence*, 2d edition, in *The New Cambridge History of India*, vol. 4, no. 1 (New York: Cambridge University Press, 1994), pp. 353–354. It is perhaps also pertinent to note the investigations into other "riots" of the 1980s (Gujrat, Ahmedabad, Meerut) also pointed to explicit manipulation (Ali Ashgar Engineer, "Communal Fire Engulfs Ahmedabad Once Again," *Economic and Political Weekly*, July 6, 1985; "Gian Prakash Committee Reports on Meerut Riots," *Economic and Political Weekly*, January 2–9, 1988; Ashish Banerjee, "Comparative Curfew: Changing Dimensions of Communal Politics in India," in *Mirrors of Violence*, ed. Veena Das [London: Oxford University Press, 1990], pp. 37–68).

8. Robin Jeffrey cites two others who make similar claims (*What's Happening to India?*, p. 17). Sangat Singh, who had a long career in India's defense and intelligence communities, suggests bluntly that a war with Pakistan was planned for the first week of November, to be accompanied by large-scale slaughter of the Sikhs (*The Sikhs in History* [New York: Sangat Singh, 1995], p. 361).

9. Khushwant Singh, *My Bleeding Punjab* (New Delhi: UBS Publishers, 1992), pp. 93–94.

10. Harji Malik, "The Politics of Alienation," in *Punjab: The Fatal Miscalculation*, ed. Patwant Singh and Harji Malik (Delhi: Crescent, 1985), p. 55.

11. Singh, *My Bleeding Punjab*, p. 107.

12. Dharma Kumar, "A Voice from 'The Rest of India,'" in *Punjab: The Fatal Miscalculation*, ed. Patwant Singh and Harji Malik (Delhi: Crescent, 1985), p. 163.

13. A very strong image of the Sikhs as a privileged rather than an exploited minority is provided by Yogendra Malik in "Democracy, the Akali Party and the Sikhs in Indian Politics," in *Religious and Ethnic Minority Politics in South Asia*, ed. Dhirendra Vajpeyi and Yogendra Malik (Riverdale, Md.: The Riverdale Company, 1989), pp. 19–50.

14. Dipanker Gupta, "The Communalising of Punjab 1980–1985," *Economic and Political Weekly*, July 13, 1985.

15. Banerjee, "Comparative Curfew," p. 50.

16. Ashis Nandy, "The Politics of Secularism," in *Mirrors of Violence*, ed. Veena Das (London: Oxford University Press, 1990) p. 89.

17. Amrit Srinavasan, "The Survivor in the Study of Violence," in *Mirrors of Violence*, ed. Veena Das (London: Oxford University Press, 1990), pp. 304–320.

18. Paul Wallace believes the Rajiv-Longowal Accords to have been a window of opportunity for resolution of the conflict, which was tragically lost as the central government hesitated with implementing them ("Political Violence and Terrorism in India: The Crisis of Identity," in *Terrorism in Context*, ed. Martha Crenshaw [University Park: The Pennsylvania State University Press, 1995], pp. 352–409).

19. Khalistani and Kashmiri expatriates often work together on human rights issues. There has always been a suspicion that they cooperate militarily as well, but I never inquired about this, and was never told anything about it.

20. Joyce Pettigrew, *Robber Noblemen: A Study of the Political System of the Sikh Jats* (New Delhi: Ambika Publications, 1978).

21. Stories later came out in the Indian press that Sukhdev Babbar had in fact been leading a double life, with a fancy house and a wife in Patiala to complement his austere Babbar Khalsa activism. Most militants reject this as propaganda, though one leader I consulted about it said he could not "confirm or deny" the report. It should be noted that public reports on the activities of militant Sikhs are often wildly unreliable; for example, the Punjab police reported that Sukhdev Babbar was responsible for one thousand murders, while the state government of Punjab reported that he was responsible for ten.

22. Zuhair Kashmeri and Brian McAndrew, *Soft Target: How the Indian Intelligence Service Penetrated Canada* (Toronto: James Lorimer and Company, 1989).

23. For a detailed account, see Ian Mulgrew, *Unholy Terror: The Sikhs and International Terrorism* (Toronto: Key Porter Books, 1988).

24. They have been accused of gun running as well, but this is an area I stayed out of conscientiously. There is certainly no dearth of weapons available in South Asia itself, particularly since the Afghan war, so I wonder how central overseas weapons procurement really is. The charge of drug smuggling as a means of acquiring money to support the militancy is also a common one, but as far as I know there is no evidence of it. Since militants readily admit to crimes like robbing banks, killing police officers, and setting off bombs in urban areas (in India), I take seriously their denial of involvement in air disasters or drug smuggling. One can never be sure, of course.

25. See the report issued by the Punjab Human Rights Organization, *Punjab Bulldozed: Operation Black Thunder II* (Ludhiana: Punjab Human Rights Organization, 1988), which includes an interview with a member of one of these squads. I have spoken with someone close to Barnala who said under condition of anonymity that Barnala was put under great pressure to agree to "awful things."

26. For example, Sampat Singh, home minister of Haryana, who accused two ministers at the national level of patronizing terrorist groups in Punjab (Kumar and Sieberer, *The Sikh Struggle*, p. 279).

27. For a detailed eyewitness account, see Mark Tully, *The Defeat of a Congressman and Other Parables of Modern India* (New York: Alfred A. Knopf, 1992), ch. 5. Tully accepts the identity of the "militants" who surrendered during Operation Black Thunder II at face value.

28. U.S. Department of State, *Patterns of Global Terrorism 1994* (Washington, D.C.: Office of the Coordinator for Counterterrorism, 1995).

29. Pettigrew, *The Sikhs of the Punjab.*

30. It should be additionally noted that the Sikh Students Federation also comprises two unarmed wings, one led by Manjit Singh and the other by Rajinder Singh Mehta and Amarjit Singh Chawla. These focus on demonstrations and other nonviolent political activities. Because many activists fleeing to the West as asylum seekers come from these groups, it is important to recognize that involvement in them does not mean involvement in violent militancy.

31. Simranjit Singh Mann works solely in the above-ground political sphere, and has no direct links to any militant groups. A consistent voice on issues of Punjab's autonomy, however, he has the respect and support of most of them.

32. Pettigrew, *The Sikhs of the Punjab.*

33. There is substantial disagreement over the extent to which government infiltrators themselves may be responsible for continuing violence. Some at least believe several of the organizations described here to be virtual pawns of the Indian government. I suspect this accusation is used more frequently as a means for one individual or group to edge out another in the internal power politics of the movement, though infiltration can never be ruled out.

34. See Gurharpal Singh, "The Punjab Elections 1992: Breakthrough or Breakdown?" *Asian Survey* 32, 11 (1992): 988–999.

CHAPTER 8: PLAYING THE GAME OF LOVE

1. W. R. Connor, "Why Were We Surprised?" *American Scholar* (Spring 1991): 175–185.

2. Hannah Arendt, *Eichmann in Jerusalem: A Report on the Banality of Evil* (New York: Viking, 1965).

3. Michael Taussig, *The Nervous System* (New York: Routledge, 1992).

4. Amos Elon, "One Foot on the Moon," *New York Review of Books*, April 6, 1995.

5. Linda Green, "Living in a State of Fear," in *Fieldwork Under Fire: Contemporary Studies of Violence and Survival*, ed. Carolyn Nordstrom and Antonius Robben (Berkeley: University of California Press, 1995), p. 108; see J. Zur, "The Psychological Impact of Impunity," *Anthropology Today* 10, 3 (1994): 14–16.

6. Amitav Ghosh, "The Ghosts of Mrs. Gandhi," *New Yorker*, July 17, 1995, p. 38.

7. Joyce Pettigrew, "Martyrdom and Guerilla Organization in Punjab," *Journal of Comparative and Commonwealth Politics* 30, 3 (1992): 387–406.

8. Paulo Freire, *Pedagogy of the Oppressed*, trans. Myra Bergman Ramos (New York: Continuum, 1993), p. 158.

9. Frank Pieke, "Witnessing the 1989 Chinese People's Movement," in *Fieldwork Under Fire*, ed. Nordstrom and Robben, p. 73.

10. Excerpted from the farewell letter of Sukhjinder Singh and Harjinder Singh to President Vankatraman, reprinted as "When Nations Wake Up, History Begins to Shiver," *World Sikh News*, October 13, 1995.

11. Robin Jeffrey, *What's Happening to India? Ethnic Conflict, Punjab, Mrs. Gandhi's Death and the Test for Federalism* (New York: Holmes and Meier, 1986), p. 91.

12. Bharati Mukherjee, *Jasmine* (New York: Grove Weidenfeld, 1989), p. 148.

13. Veena Das, "Time, Self and Community: Features of Sikh Militant Discourse," *Contributions to Indian Sociology* 26, 2 (1992): 253.

14. Henry David Thoreau, *Civil Disobedience and Other Essays* (New York: Dover Publications, 1993), p. 12.

15. G. S. Mansukhani, *Introduction to Sikhism* (New Delhi: Hemkunt Press, 1977), p. 51.

16. Albert Camus, *Resistance, Rebellion and Death*, trans. Justin O'Brien. (New York: Alfred A. Knopf, 1961).

17. See Joyce Pettigrew, "Betrayal and Nation-Building Among the Sikhs," *Journal of Comparative and Commonwealth Politics* 30, 3 (1992): 387–406.

18. Ernesto Che Guevara, *Venceremos: The Speeches and Writings of Che Guevara*, ed. John Gerassi (New York: Simon and Schuster, 1969), p. 398.

19. Singh, *My Bleeding Punjab*, (New Delhi: UBS Publishers, 1992), p. 52.

20. Adam Gopnik, "Violence as Style," *New Yorker*, May 8, 1995, pp. 6–8.

21. Tony Judt, *Past Imperfect: French Intellectuals 1945–1956* (Berkeley: University of California Press, 1992).

22. Elaine Scarry, *The Body in Pain: The Making and Unmaking of the World* (New York: Oxford University Press, 1985).

23. Singh and Singh, "When Nations Wake Up, History Begins to Shiver."

24. Ibid.

25. Renato Rosaldo, *Ilongot Headhunting, 1883–1974: A Study in Society and History* (Stanford: Stanford University Press, 1980).

26. Das, "Time, Self, and Community," p. 256.

27. Franz Fanon, *The Wretched of the Earth*, trans. Constance Farrington (New York: Grove Press, 1968).

28. One highly placed interlocutor who read this part of the manuscript suggested here that more noncombatants than combatants are killed in most wars, and that the stringent moral standards that outsiders would like to apply to the Khalistanis should be equally applied to the Indian government, which made Punjab's citizenry the field of battle. Another militant who heard this remark acknowledged its legitimacy, but added that as saint-soldiers the Khalistanis had to take the moral high ground despite all provocation—"saints first, soldiers second."

29. Singh and Singh, "When Nations Wake Up, History Begins to Shiver."

30. Sohan Singh, *India and Khalistan* (Sohan Singh, 1991).

31. The phrase is from S. Mahmud Ali, *The Fearful State: Power, People and Internal War in South Asia* (London: Zed Books, 1993).

32. Lepil Griffin, *Maharaja Ranjit Singh and the Sikhs*, cited in Brar, *Operation Blue Star*, pp. 9–10.

33. Roy D'Andrade, "Moral Models in Anthropology," *Current Anthropology* 36, 3 (1995): 408.

34. Freire, *Pedagogy of the Oppressed*, p. 68.

35. Sangat Singh, *The Sikhs in History* (New York: Sangat Singh, 1995), p. xiv.

36. Nancy Scheper-Hughes, "The Primacy of the Ethical: Propositions for a Militant Anthropology," *Current Anthropology* 36, 3 (1995): 418–419.

37. Milan Kundera, cited in Arthur Schlesinger, *The Disuniting of America*, (New York: Norton, 1992), p. 52.

38. Scheper-Hughes, "The Primacy of the Ethical"; Julie M. Peteet, *Gender in Crisis: Women in the Palestinian Resistance Movement* (New York: Columbia University Press, 1991), p. 17.

39. Freire, *Pedagogy of the Oppressed*, p. 32

40. Scheper-Hughes, "The Primacy of the Ethical," p. 419.

41. Ibid.

CHAPTER 9: THE PRINCESS AND THE LION

1. Julie M. Peteet, *Gender in Crisis: Women and the Palestinian Resistance Movement* (New York: Columbia University Press, 1991), p. 92.

2. Peteet, *Gender in Crisis*, p. 91; pp. 152–157.

3. Peter van der Veer, *Religious Nationalism: Hindus and Muslims in India* (Berkeley: University of California Press, 1994); on women and nationalism in global context, see *Identity, Politics, and Women: Cultural Reassertions and Feminisms in International Perspective*, ed. Valantine M. Moghadam (Boulder, Colo.: Westview, 1994).

4. Claudia Koonz, *Mothers in the Fatherland: Women, the Family, and Nazi Politics* (New York: St. Martin's Press, 1987); Peteet, *Gender in Crisis*, p. 185.

5. Jean Bethke Elshtain, *Women and War* (New York, Basic Books, 1987).

6. For example, Robin Morgan, *The Demon Lover: Sexuality and Terrorism* (New York: Norton, 1989).

7. Marshall Sahlins, *The Uses and Abuses of Biology* (Ann Arbor: University of Michigan Press, 1976).

8. Margaret Randall, *Sandino's Daughters: Testimonies of Nicaraguan Women in Struggle* (Vancouver: New Star Books, 1981); *Sandino's Daughters Revisited: Feminism in Nicaragua* (New Brunswick, N.J.: Rutgers University Press, 1994).

9. Carol Gilligan, *In a Different Voice* (Cambridge, Mass.: Harvard University Press, 1982).

10. For example, Veena Das, "Time, Self and Community: Features of Sikh Militant Discourse," *Contributions to Indian Sociology* 26, 2 (1992): 245–259.

11. Nikky Guninder Kaur Singh, *The Feminine Principle in the Sikh Vision of the Transcendent* (London: Cambridge University Press, 1993).

CHAPTER 10: CULTURE, RESISTANCE, AND DIALOGUE

1. Suzanne R. Kirschner, " 'Then What Have I to Do with Thee?' On Identity, Fieldwork, and Ethnographic Knowledge," *Cultural Anthropology* 2, 2 (1987): 204–211.

2. Edward Said, "Representing the Colonized: Anthropology's Interlocutors," *Critical Inquiry* 15 (1989): 210.

3. Ibid.

4. Harjot Oberoi, *The Construction of Religious Boundaries: Culture, Identity and Diversity in the Sikh Tradition* (Chicago: University of Chicago Press, 1994).

5. Jasbir Singh Mann, Surinder Singh Sodhi, and Gurbaksh Singh Gill, eds., *The Invasion of Religious Boundaries* (Vancouver: Canadian Sikh Study and Teaching Society, 1995).

6. W. H. McLeod, *The Evolution of the Sikh Community* (Oxford: Clarendon Press, 1976); *Who Is a Sikh? The Problem of Sikh Identity* (Oxford: Clarendon Press, 1989).

7. C. K. Mahmood and S. L. Armstrong, "Do Ethnic Groups Exist? A Cognitive Perspective on the Concept of Cultures," *Ethnology* 31, 1 (1992): 1–14.

8. Oberoi, *The Construction of Religious Boundaries*, p. 39; S. Radhakrishnan, Foreward to *2500 Years of Buddhism* (Delhi: Ministry of Information, 1956). The parallel quote (p. 25 of that volume) is: "The Buddha's main object was to bring about a reformation in religious practices and a return to the basic principles . . . the Buddha was accepted as an avatara who reclaimed Hindus from sanguinary rites and erroneous practices and purified their religion of the numberous abuses which had crept into it."

9. For Oberoi's perspective on current "fundamentalism," see his "Sikh Fundamentalism: Translating History into Theory," in *Fundamentalisms and the State*, ed. Martin E. Marty and R. Scott Appleby (Chicago: University of Chicago Press, 1993), pp. 256–285.

10. See Bachittar Singh Giani, *Planned Attack on Aad Sri Guru Granth Sahib: Academics or Blasphemy* (Chandigarh: Institute of Sikh Studies, 1994).

11. Trilochan Singh, *Ernest Trumpp and W.H. McLeod as Scholars of Sikh History, Religion, and Culture* (Chandigarh: Institute of Sikh Studies, 1994).

12. Richard Handler, *Nationalism and the Politics of Culture in Quebec* (Madison: University of Wisconsin Press, 1988). I would like to thank Richard Handler for continuing critical exchange on this and other topics.

13. Richard Handler, "On Dialogue and Destructive Analysis: Problems in Narrating Nationalism and Ethnicity," *Journal of Anthropological Research* 41, 2 (1985): 171–182.

14. From Jean Jackson, "Is There a Way to Talk About Making Culture Without Making Enemies?" *Dialectical Anthropology* 14 (1989): 127–143.

15. Arthur Schlesinger, *The Disuniting of America* (New York: Norton, 1992).

16. Talal Asad, "Ethnography, Literature and Politics," *Cultural Anthropology* 5, 1 (1990): 239–269.

17. Edward Said, *Culture and Imperialism* (New York: Alfred A. Knopf, 1993).

18. Ernest Gellner, *Nations and Nationalism* (Ithaca, N.Y.: Cornell University Press, 1983); Eric Hobsbawm, *Nations and Nationalism Since 1780: Programme, Myth, Reality* (Cambridge: Cambridge University Press, 1990).

19. Said, *Culture and Imperialism*, p. 216.

20. Carol Breckenridge and Peter van der Veer, eds., *Orientalism and the Postcolonial Predicament* (Philadelphia: University of Pennsylvania Press, 1993), p. 17.

21. Salman Rushdie, "Outside the Whale," *Granta* (1984).

22. Talal Asad, "Multiculturalism and British Identity in the Wake of the Rushdie Affair," *Politics and Society* 18, 4 (1990): 455–480.

23. Tim Brennan, "The National Longing for Form," in *Nations and Narration*, ed. Homi Bhabha (London: Routledge, 1990), pp. 44–70.

24. Said, "Representing the Colonized," p. 210.

25. See Russell Jacoby, *The Last Intellectuals: American Culture in the Age of Academe* (New York: Basic Books, 1987); Bruce Robbins, *Secular Vocations: Intellectuals, Professionalism, Culture* (London: Verso, 1993).

26. Edward Said, *Representations of the Intellectual* (New York: Pantheon, 1994).

27. Zygmunt Bauman, *Legislators and Interpretors: On Modernity, Post-Modernity, and Intellectuals* (Ithaca, N.Y.: Cornell University Press, 1987).

28. After Maurice Merleau-Ponty, "The Philosopher and Sociology," in *Phenomenology and Sociology*, ed. Thomas Luckman (Hammondsworth: Penguin, 1978).

29. From Said, *Culture and Imperialism*.

30. Joyce Pettigrew, *The Sikhs of the Punjab: Unheard Voices of State and Guerilla Violence* (London: Zed Books, 1995).

31. Johannes Fabian, *Time and the Other: How Anthropology Makes Its Object* (New York: Columbia University Press, 1983).

32. F. E. Mascia-Lees, P. Sharpe, and C. Ballerino Cohen, "The Postmodernist Turn in Anthropology: Cautions from a Feminist Perspective," *Signs* 15, 1 (1989): 7–34.

33. After Jean-François Lyotard, *The Post-Modern Condition: A Report on Knowledge*, trans. Geoff Bennington and Brian Massumi (Minneapolis: University of Minnesota Press, 1984).

34. Benedict Anderson, *Imagined Communities: Reflections on the Origin and Spread of Nationalism* (London: Verso, 1991).

35. Arjun Appadurai, "Global Ethnospaces: Notes and Queries for a Transnational Anthropology," in *Recapturing Anthropology*, ed. R. Fox (Santa Fe, N.M.: School of American Research Press, 1991); Akhil Gupta and James Fergerson, "Beyond Culture: Space, Identity and the Politics of Difference," *Cultural Anthropology* 7, 1 (1992): 6–23; Nina Glick Schiller, Linda Basch, and Cristina

Szanton Blanc, "From Immigrant to Transmigrant: Theorizing Transnational Migration," *Anthropological Quarterly* 68, 1 (1995): 48–63.

36. Akhil Gupta, "The Song of the Nonaligned World: Transnational Identities and the Reinscription of Space in Late Capitalism," *Cultural Anthropology* 7, 1 (1992): 63–77.

37. Many of these converts are uncomfortable with the "Punjabi" quality of current political rhetoric. See Verne A. Dusenberry, "Punjabi Sikhs and Gora Sikhs: Conflicting Assertions of Sikh Identity in North America," in *Sikh History and Religion in the Twentieth Century*, ed. Joseph T. O'Connell et al. (Toronto: University of Toronto Press, 1988), pp. 334–355.

38. See Harjot Oberoi, "From Punjab to Khalistan: Territoritality and Metacommentary," *Pacific Affairs* 60 (1987): 26–41.

39. Sukhjinder Singh and Harjinder Singh, "When Nations Wake Up, History Begins to Shiver," *World Sikh News*, October 13, 1995.

40. Bernard Nietschmann, "The Third World War," *Cultural Survival Quarterly* 11, 3 (1987): 1–16.

41. Arthur Helweg, "Sikh Politics in India: The Emigrant Factor," in *The Sikh Diaspora: Migration and Experience Beyond Punjab*, ed. Gerald Barrier and Verne Dusenberry (Delhi: Chanakya Publications, 1989).

42. Mark Juergensmeyer, "The Ghadr Syndrome: Immigrant Sikhs and Nationalist Pride," in *Sikh Studies: Immigration and the Experience Beyond Punjab*, ed. Mark Juergensmeyer and Gerald Barrier (Delhi: Chanakya, 1989), pp. 173–190.

43. Peter van der Veer, introduction to *Nation and Migration: The Politics of Space in the South Asian Diaspora* (Philadelphia: University of Pennsylvania Press, 1995).

44. What they mean by this is the alleged keeping of lists of "troublemakers," withholding of visas and other necessary documents, surveillance and infiltration of Sikh organizations and *gurudwaras*, and propagating anti-Sikh propaganda. This perception is echoed by Barbara Crossette in *India: Facing the Twenty-First Century* (Bloomington: Indiana University Press, 1993), p. 104.

45. Verne Dusenberry, "A Sikh Diaspora? Contested Identities and Constructed Realities," in *Nation and Migration*, ed. van der Veer, p. 33.

46. Cited by Robin Jeffrey, *What's Happening to India? Punjab, Ethnic Conflict, Mrs. Gandhi's Death and the Test for Federalism* (New York: Holmes and Meier, 1986), p. 74.

47. See Jeffrey, *What's Happening to India?* pp. 73–78.

48. Daniel Patrick Moynihan, *Pandaemonium: Ethnicity in International Politics* (New York: Oxford University Press, 1993).

49. A popular recent example: Michael Ignatieff, *Blood and Belonging: Journeys into the New Nationalism* (New York: Farrar, Strauss and Giroux, 1994).

50. For example, Paul Brass, *Ethnicity and Nationalism: Theory and Comparison* (New Delhi: Sage, 1991).

51. For an opposing view on this question, see Henry Munson, "Not All Crustaceans Are Crabs: Reflections on the Comparative Study of Fundamentalism and Politics," *Contention* 4 (1995): 151–166.

52. Jawaharlal Nehru, *Selected Works*, vol. 6 (Delhi: Orient Longman, 1974), p. 164.

53. Dipankar Gupta, "The Communalising of Punjab, 1980–85," *Economic and Political Weekly*, July 13, 1985.

54. Crossette, *India: Facing the Twenty-First Century*, p. 32.

CHAPTER 11: LOOKING INTO DRAGONS

1. Nancy Scheper-Hughes, "The Primacy of the Ethical: Toward a Militant Anthropology," *Current Anthropology* 36, 3 (1995): 410.

2. *Convention Relating to the Status of Refugees*, Ch. 1, Article 1, Section A[2].

3. *Convention Relating to the Status of Refugees*, Ch. 5, Article 33, Section 1.

4. *Convention Against Torture and Other Cruel, Inhuman or Degrading Treatment or Punishment*, Part 1, Article 3, Section 1.

5. *Convention Relating to the Status of Refugees*, Ch. 1, Article 1, Sections F[a] and F[b].

6. *Convention Relating to the Status of Refugees*, Ch. 5, Article 33, Section 2.

7. For the fullest discussion of this issue, see Heather Wilson, *International Law and the Use of Force in National Liberation Movements* (Oxford: Clarendon Press, 1988).

8. *United Nations Declaration of Human Rights*, preamble.

9. Upendra Baxi, "From Human Rights to the Right to be Human: Some Heresies," in *Rethinking Human Rights: Challenges for Theory and Action*, ed. S. Kothari and M. Sethi (New Delhi: Lokayan, 1988), pp. 164–165.

10. See Michael McDonald, "Should Communities Have Rights? Reflections on Liberal Individualism," in *Human Rights in Cross-Cultural Perspectives*, ed. A. A. An-Na'im (Philadelphia: University of Pennsylvania Press, 1992), pp. 133–161.

11. Jean Genet, *Prisoner of Love*, trans. Barbara Bray (London: Picador, 1989).

12. Scheper-Hughes, "The Primacy of the Ethical," p. 418.

13. Paulo Freire, *Pedagogy of the Oppressed*, trans. Myra Bergman Ramos (New York: Continuum, 1993).

14. Baxi, "From Human Rights to the Right to be Human," p. 111.

15. Clifford Geertz, "The Uses of Diversity," in *Assessing Cultural Anthropology*, ed. Robert Borofsky (Houston: McGraw-Hill, 1994), pp. 454–466.

16. George Marcus and Michael Fischer, *Anthropology as Cultural Critique: An Experimental Moment in the Human Sciences* (Chicago: University of Chicago Press, 1986).

17. June Nash, "Ethnology in a Revolutionary Setting," in *Ethics and Anthropology: Dilemmas of Fieldwork*, ed. Michael Rynkiewich and James Spradley (New York: Wiley and Sons, 1976), pp. 148–166.

18. Jeffrey A. Sluka, "Reflections on Managing Danger in Fieldwork: Dangerous Anthropology in Belfast," in *Fieldwork Under Fire: Contemporary Studies of Violence and Survival*, ed. Carolyn Nordstrom and Antonius Robben (Berkeley: University of California Press, 1995, p. 284.

19. Robert Friedman, *Zealots for Zion: Inside Israel's West Bank Settlement Movement* (New York: Random House, 1992); Vincent Crapanzano, *Waiting: The Whites of South Africa* (New York: Random House, 1985).

20. Antonius C. G. M. Robben, "The Politics of Truth and Emotion Among Victims and Perpetrators of Violence," in *Fieldwork Under Fire*, ed. Nordstrom and Martin, p. 94.

21. Joseba Zulaika, "The Anthropologist as Terrorist," in *Fieldwork Under Fire*, ed. Nordstrom and Robben, pp. 206, 223.

22. Carolyn Nordstrom and Antonius Robben, "Anthropology and the Ethnography of Violence," in *Fieldwork Under Fire*, ed. Nordstrom and Robben, p. 3.

23. Quoted in Ashis Nandy, *The Savage Freud and Other Essays on Possible and Retrievable Selves* (Princeton, N.J.: Princeton University Press, 1995), p. 6.

24. Nandy, *The Savage Freud*, p. 7.

25. Ibid., p. 22.

26. Nordstrom and Robben, "Anthropology and the Ethnography of Violence," p. 10.

27. After J. Corbin, "The Anthropology of Violence," p. 10, *International Journal of Environmental Studies* 10 (1977): 107–111.

28. Nandy, *The Savage Freud*, p. 25.

29. Clifford Geertz, "Anti Anti-Relativism," *American Anthropologist* 86 (1984): 263–278.

GLOSSARY

akal Eternal, as in Akal Tahkt, "eternal throne," Akali Dal, "eternal army," Akal Purukh, "eternal being" (God), Sat Sri Akal, "truth is eternal" (a Sikh greeting).

akhand Continuous, as in Akhand Kirtni Jatha, the organization dedicated to continuous hymn-singing; Akhand Path, the continuous reading of scriptures.

amrit Nectar, as the sanctified sweet water imbibed during initiation into the Khalsa; forms the etymological root of Amritsar.

amritdhari One who has taken *amrit*, i.e., has been initiated into the Khalsa.

bhai Brother, used as a title of scripture readers.

bhakti Spiritual power.

bhangra A Punjabi folk dance.

bhog Properly, Bhog Akhand Path, the uninterrupted reading of Guru Granth Sahib.

chardhi kala Rising spirits, a mood of optimism and energy.

dal Army or party, as in Akali Dal or Dal Khalsa.

deg Large kettle in which food is served ("Deg Tegh Fateh," Kettle-Sword-Victory).

dharm Moral law or righteousness, as in Dharm Yudh, "righteous war."

ek oankar One God.

fateh Victory.

ghallughara Holocaust.

granthi Scripture reader.

gurubani The Guru's songs, i.e., scriptures.

gurudwara   Sikh place of worship (lit., "gateway to the Guru").

gurumatta   The Guru's wishes; a decision taken in the presence of Guru Granth Sahib by five beloved ones.

gurmuhki   Punjabi script (lit., "Guru's letters").

gursikh   A true Sikh.

gurumukh   A Guru-facing person, i.e., highly devout.

hukmnama   A decree issued by the Akal Takht; letter of Sikh Gurus addressed to the congregation.

janamsakhis   Biographical accounts of the life of Guru Nanak.

jat   A caste group central to the development of Sikhism, primarily agriculturalists.

jatha   Brigade or task group.

jathedar   The caretaker or administrator of one of the five "thrones"; a head of a group, also used as a title in the Babbar Khalsa.

jhujaru   Fighter, militant.

kachera   Breeches worn by Khalsa Sikhs (one of the five K's).

kanga   Comb carried by Khalsa Sikhs (one of the five K's).

kara   Wristband (one of the five K's).

kaur   Princess; name of all Khalsa Sikh women.

kesh   Hair (one of the five K's).

khalsa   Pure; the Khalsa, the siblinghood of devotees.

khanda   Double-edged sword.

kirpan   Sword or dagger (one of the five K's).

kirtan   Hymns.

langar   Community kitchen, attached to every *gurudwara*.

lathi   Stick used by police.

miri   Temporal power, as in *miri-piri*, the joining of temporal and spiritual power.

misl   Administrative unit with its own militia.

morcha   Protest or agitation.

nam simran   Repetition of the divine name, a form of meditative prayer.

nirankar   Formless (i.e., to express the formlessness of God).

panj piaras   Five beloved ones; the first five men initiated into the Khalsa and any group of five *amritdharis* who come together to take a decision.

panth   The whole Sikh community.

parikrama   Circumambulation; especially, the tiled pavement at the Golden Temple Complex, around which one walks to circumambulate the shrine.

patka   Underturban.

piri   Spiritual power, as in *miri-piri,* the joining of temporal and spiritual power.

prashad   Consecrated food distributed at *gurudwaras.*

Punjabiyat   Punjabi culture, Punjabi nation.

pyjama-kurta   Male indigenous dress in Punjab.

qaum   Nation.

rahit   Code of behavior.

raj   Rule, as in "Raj Karega Khalsa," the Khalsa Shall Rule.

rashtra   Nation, as in "Hindu Rashtra."

salwar kameez   Female indigenous dress in Punjab.

sanatan   From time immemorial.

sant   Saint or holy person.

sant-sipahi   Saint-soldier.

saskar   Cremation.

shaheed   Martyr.

shakti   Temporal power.

shastradhari   Bearer of weapons.

shuddhi   Purification.

sikhi   Sikhdom, the Sikh way.

singh   Lion; name of all male Khalsa Sikhs.

takht   Throne, as in Akal Takht.

taksal   Place where coins are minted; used in name of seminaries, e.g., Damdami Taksal.

tankhaya   Declaration by the Akal Takht that someone is guilty of a religious offense (can lead to excommunication or performance of penances).

tegh   Sword; "Deg Tegh Fateh," Kettle-Sword-Victory.

waheguru   Great Guru, God.

wanggar   Challenge.

yar   Friend.

zaffarnama   "Letter of Victory" sent by Guru Gobind Singh to Emperor Aurangzeb.

zindabad   A cheer, as in "Khalistan Zindabad," Long Live Khalistan.

zulm   Oppression.

BIBLIOGRAPHY

Ali, S. Mahmud. 1993. *The Fearful State: Power, People and Internal War in South Asia.* London: Zed Books.

Amnesty International. 1991. *Human Rights Violations in Punjab: Use and Abuse of the Law.* London: Amnesty International.

———. 1992. *India: Torture, Rape and Deaths in Custody.* London: Amnesty International.

———. 1993. *An Unnatural Fate: Disappearances and Impunity in Punjab and Kashmir.* London: Amnesty International.

———. 1994. *India: The Terrorism and Disruptive Activities (Prevention) Act: The Lack of "Scrupulous Care."* London: Amnesty International.

———. 1995. *Punjab Police: Beyond the Bounds of Law.* London: Amnesty International.

Anderson, Benedict. 1991. *Imagined Communities: Reflections on the Origin and Spread of Nationalism.* London: Verso.

Appadurai, Arjun. 1991. "Global Ethnospaces: Notes and Queries for a Transnational Anthropology." In *Recapturing Anthropology,* ed. R. Fox. Santa Fe, N. Mex.: School of American Research Press.

Ardrey, Robert. 1966. *The Territorial Imperative.* New York: Atheneum.

Arendt, Hannah. 1965. *Eichmann in Jerusalem: A Report on the Banality of Evil.* New York: Viking.

Asad, Talal. 1990. "Ethnography, Literature and Politics." *Cultural Anthropology* 5(1): 239–269.

———. 1990. "Multiculturalism and British Identity in the Wake of the Rushdie Affair." *Politics and Society* 18(4): 455–480.

Asia Watch. 1991. *Punjab in Crisis: Human Rights in India.* New York: Human Rights Watch.

Avruch, Kevin, ed. 1991. *Cross-Cultural Perspectives on Conflict Resolution.* New York: Greenwood Press.

Bains, Ajit Singh. 1988. *Seige of the Sikhs: Violation of Human Rights in Punjab.* Toronto: The Magazine Publishing Company.

Banerjee, Ashish. 1990. "'Comparative Curfew': Changing Dimensions of Communal Politics in India." In *Mirrors of Violence: Communities, Riots and Survivors in South Asia,* ed. Veena Das, pp. 37–68. New York: Oxford University Press.

Bauman, Zygmunt. 1987. *Legislators and Interpreters: On Modernity, Post-Modernity, and Intellectuals.* Ithaca, N.Y.: Cornell University Press.

Baxi, Upendra. 1988. "From Human Rights to the Right to be Human: Some Heresies." In *Rethinking Human Rights: Challenges for Theory and Action,* ed. S. Kothari and H. Sethi, pp. 151–166. New Delhi: Lokayan.

Benedict, Ruth. 1946. *The Chrysanthemum and the Sword: Patterns of Japanese Culture.* Boston: Houghton and Mifflin.

Brar, K. S. 1993. *Operation Blue Star: The True Story.* New Delhi: UBS Publishing.

Brass, Paul. 1974. *Language, Religion and Politics in North India.* London: Cambridge University Press.

———. 1991. *Ethnicity and Nationalism: Theory and Comparison.* New Delhi: Sage.

———. 1994. *The Politics of India Since Independence. The New Cambridge History of India,* vol. 4.1. New York: Cambridge University Press.

Breckenridge, Carol, and Peter van der Veer, eds. 1993. *Orientalism and the Postcolonial Predicament.* Philadelphia: University of Pennsylvania Press.

Brennan, Tim. 1990. "The National Longing for Form." In *Nations and Migration,* ed. Homi Bhabha, pp. 44–70. London: Routledge.

Buber, Martin. 1965. *Between Man and Man.* New York: Macmillan.

Burghart, Richard. 1990. "Ethnographers and Their Local Counterparts in India." In *Localizing Strategies,* ed. R. Farding, pp. 260–278. Washington: Smithsonian Institution Press.

Camus, Albert. 1961. *Resistance, Rebellion and Death.* Trans. Justin O'Brien. New York: Alfred A. Knopf.

Chomsky, Noam. 1988. *The Culture of Terrorism.* Boston: South End Press.

Citizens' Commission. 1985. *Delhi: 31 October to 4 November 1984.* New Delhi: Citizens' Commission.

Citizens for Democracy. 1985. *Report to the Nation: Oppression in Punjab.* Bombay: Citizens for Democracy.

———. 1985. *The Truth About Delhi Violence.* New Delhi: Citizens for Democracy.

Clausewitz, Carl von. 1966. *On War.* Ed. M. Howard and P. Parets. Princeton, N.J.: Princeton University Press.

Cohen, Stephen P. 1971. *The Indian Army: Its Contributions to the Development of a Nation.* Boulder, Colo.: Westview Press.

Connor, W. R. 1991. "Why Were We Surprised?" *American Scholar* (Spring): 175–185.

Corbin, J. 1977. "The Anthropology of Violence." *International Journal of Environmental Studies* 10: 107–111.

Crapanzano, Vincent. 1980. *Tuhami: Portrait of a Moroccan.* Chicago: University of Chicago Press.

———. 1985. *Waiting: The Whites of South Africa.* New York: Random House.

Creveld, Martin van. 1991. *The Transformation of War.* New York: The Free Press.

Crossette, Barbara. 1993. *India: Facing the Twenty-First Century.* Bloomington: Indiana University Press.

D'Andrade, Roy. 1995. "Moral Models in Anthropology." *Current Anthropology* 36(3): 399–408.

Darling, Malcolm. 1977. *The Punjab Peasant in Prosperity and Debt.* New Delhi: Manohar.

Das, Veena. 1992. "Time, Self, and Community: Features of Sikh Militant Discourse." *Contributions to Indian Sociology* 26(2): 245–259.

Dentan, Robert. 1995. "Bad Day at Bukit Pekan." *American Anthropologist* 97(2): 225–231.

Dhillon, Gurdarshan Singh. 1992. *India Commits Suicide.* Chandigarh: Singh and Singh.

Dumont, Louis. 1980. *Homo Hierarchicus: The Caste System and Its Implications.* Trans. Mark Sainsbury, Louis Dumont, and Basia Gulati. Chicago: University of Chicago Press.

Dusenberry, Verne. 1988. "Punjabi Sikhs and Gora Sikhs: Conflicting Assertions of Sikh Identity in North America." In *Sikh History and Religion in the Twentieth Century,* ed. Joseph O'Connell, et al., pp. 334–355. Toronto: University of Toronto Press.

———. 1995. "A Sikh Diaspora? Contested Identities and Constructed Realities." In *Nation and Migration: The Politics of Space in the South Asian Diaspora,* ed. Peter van der Veer, pp. 17–42. Philadelphia: University of Pennsylvania Press.

Elon, Amos. 1995. "One Foot on the Moon." *New York Review of Books,* April 6.

Elshtain, Jean Bethke. 1987. *Women and War.* New York: Basic Books.

Embree, Ainslie. 1990. *Utopias in Conflict: Religion and Nationalism in Modern India.* Berkeley: University of California Press.

Engineer, Ali Ashgar. 1985. "Communal Fire Engulfs Ahmedabad Once Again." *Economic and Political Weekly,* July 6.

———. 1988. "Gian Prakash Committee Reports on Meerut Riots." *Economic and Political Weekly,* January 2–9.

Fabian, Johannes. 1983. *Time and the Other: How Anthropology Makes Its Object.* New York: Columbia University Press.

Fanon, Franz. 1968. *The Wretched of the Earth.* Trans. Constance Farrington. New York: Grove Press.

Foster, George. 1798. *A Journey from Bengal to England Through Northern India, Kashmir, Afghanistan and Persia into Russia, 1783–84.* 2 vols. London: A. R. Faulder.

Fox, Richard G. 1985. *Lions of the Punjab: Culture in the Making.* Berkeley: University of California Press.

Freire, Paulo. 1993. *Pedagogy of the Oppressed.* Trans. Myra Bergman Ramos. New York: Continuum.

Friedman, Robert. 1992. *Zealots for Zion: Inside Israel's West Bank Settlement Movement.* New York: Random House.

Gandhi, M. K. 1948. *Communal Unity.* Ahmedabad: Navjivan.

Geertz, Clifford. 1973. *The Interpretation of Cultures.* New York: Basic Books.

———. 1984. "Anti Anti-Relativism." *American Anthropologist* 86: 263–278.

———. 1994. "The Uses of Diversity." In *Assessing Cultural Anthropology,* ed. Robert Borofsky, pp. 454–466. Houston: McGraw-Hill.

Gellner, Ernest. 1983. *Nations and Nationalism.* Ithaca, N.Y.: Cornell University Press.

Genet, Jean. 1989. *Prisoner of Love.* Trans. Barbara Bray. London: Picador.

Ghazdi, M. 1985. "The Charge Is Sedition." In *Punjab: The Fatal Miscalculation,* ed. Patwant Singh and Harji Malik, pp. 196–207. Delhi: Crescent.

Ghosh, Amitav. 1995. "The Ghosts of Mrs. Gandhi." *New Yorker,* July 17.

Giani, Bachittar Singh. 1994. *Planned Attack on Aad Sri Guru Granth Sahib: Academics or Blasphemy.* Chandigarh: Institute of Sikh Studies.

Gilligan, Carol. 1982. *In a Different Voice.* Cambridge, Mass.: Harvard University Press.

Gopnik, Adam. 1995. "Violence as Style." *New Yorker,* May 8.

Government of India. 1984. *White Paper on the Punjab Agitation.* New Delhi: Government of India.

Green, Linda. 1995. "Living in a State of Fear." In *Fieldwork Under Fire: Contempo-*

rary Studies of Violence and Survival, ed. Carolyn Nordstrom and Antonius Robben, pp. 105–127. Berkeley: University of California Press.

Guevara, Ernesto Che. 1969. *Venceremos: The Speeches and Writings of Che Guevara.* Ed. John Gerassi. New York: Simon and Schuster.

Gupta, Akhil. 1992. "The Song of the Nonaligned World: Transnational Identities and the Reinscription of Space in Late Capitalism." *Cultural Anthropology* 7(1): 63–77.

Gupta, Akhil, and Fergerson, James. 1992. "Beyond Culture: Space, Identity and the Politics of Difference." *Cultural Anthropology* 7(1): 6–23.

Gupta, Dipankar. 1985. "The Communalising of Punjab 1980–85." *Economic and Political Weekly*, July 13.

Gupta, Pranay. 1985. *Vengeance: India After the Assassination of Indira Gandhi.* New York: Norton.

Handler, Richard. 1985. "On Dialogue and Destructive Analysis: Problems in Narrating Nationalism and Ethnicity." *Journal of Anthropological Research* 41(2): 171–182.

———. 1988. *Nationalism and the Politics of Culture in Quebec.* Madison: University of Wisconsin Press.

Helweg, Arthur. 1989. "Sikh Politics in India: The Emigrant Factor." In *The Sikh Diaspora: Migration and the Experience Beyond Punjab*, ed. Gerald Barrier and Verne Dusenberry, pp. 429–436. Delhi: Chanakya Publications.

Hobsbawm, Eric. 1990. *Nations and Nationalism Since 1780: Programme, Myth, Reality.* Cambridge: Cambridge University Press.

Human Rights Watch/Physicians for Human Rights. 1994. *Dead Silence: The Legacy of Abuses in Punjab.* New York: Human Rights Watch.

Ignatieff, Michael. 1994. *Blood and Belonging: Journeys into the New Nationalism.* New York: Farrar, Strauss and Giroux.

Jackson, Jean. 1989. "Is There a Way to Talk About Making Culture Without Making Enemies?" *Dialectical Anthropology* 14: 127–143.

Jacoby, Russell. 1987. *The Last Intellectuals: American Culture in the Age of Academe.* New York: Basic Books.

Jeffrey, Robin. 1986. *What's Happening to India? Punjab, Ethnic Conflict, Mrs. Gandhi's Death and the Test for Federalism.* New York: Holmes and Meier.

———. 1987. "Grappling With History: Sikh Politicians and the Past." *Pacific Affairs* 60: 59–72.

Joshi, Chand. 1984. *Bhindranwale: Myth and Reality.* New Delhi: Vikas Publishing.

Judt, Tony. 1992. *Past Imperfect: French Intellectuals, 1945–1956.* Berkeley: University of California Press.

Juergensmeyer, Mark. 1982. *Religion as Social Vision: The Movement Against Untouchability in Twentieth Century Punjab.* Berkeley: University of California Press.

———. 1989. "The Ghadr Syndrome: Immigrant Sikhs and National Pride." In *Sikh Studies: Immigration and the Experience Beyond Punjab*, ed. Mark Juergensmeyer and Gerald Barrier, pp. 173–190. Delhi: Chanakya.

———. 1993. *The New Cold War: Religious Nationalism Confronts the Secular State.* Berkeley: University of California Press.

Kant, Immanuel. 1974. *Anthropology from a Pragmatic Point of View.* Trans. Mary Gregor. The Hague: Martinus Nijhoff.

Kapur, Rajiv. 1986. *Sikh Separatism: The Politics of Faith.* London: Allen and Unwin.

Kashmeri, Zuhair, and Brian McAndrew. 1989. *Soft Target: How the Indian Intelligence Service Penetrated Canada.* Toronto: James Lorimer and Company.

Keegan, John. 1976. *The Face of Battle: Agincourt, Waterloo and the Somme.* New York: Viking.

Kirschner, Suzanne R. 1987. " 'Then What Have I to Do with Thee': On Identity, Fieldwork, and Ethnographic Knowledge." *Cultural Anthropology* 2(2): 204– 211.

Koonz, Claudia. 1987. *Mothers in the Fatherland: Women, the Family, and Nazi Politics.* New York: St. Martin's Press.

Kumar, Dharma. 1985. "A Voice From 'The Rest of India.' " In *Punjab: The Fatal Miscalculation*, ed. Patwant Singh and Harji Malik, pp. 162–165. Delhi: Crescent.

Kumar, Ram Narayan, and Georg Sieberer. 1991. *The Sikh Struggle: Origin, Evolution and Present Phase.* Delhi: Chanakya Publishing.

Lan, David. 1984. *Guns and Rain: Guerillas and Spirit Mediums in Zimbabwe.* Berkeley: University of California Press.

Larson, Gerald. 1984. *India's Agony Over Religion.* Albany: State University of New York Press.

Lorenz, Konrad. 1967. *On Agression.* Toronto: Bantam Books.

Ludden, David C., ed. 1996. *Contesting the Nation: Religion, Community, and the Politics of Democracy in India.* Philadelphia: University of Pennsylvania Press.

Lyotard, Jean François. 1984. *The Post-Modern Condition: A Report on Knowledge.* Trans. Geoff Bennington and Brian Massumi. Minneapolis: University of Minnesota Press.

Madan, T. N. 1991. "The Double-Edged Sword: Fundamentalism and the Sikh Religious Tradition." In *Fundamentalisms Observed,* ed. Martin E. Marty and R. Scott Appleby, pp. 594–625. Chicago: University of Chicago Press.

Mahmood, Cynthia Keppley. 1993. "Rethinking Indian Communalism: Culture and Counter-Culture." *Asian Survey* 7(3): 722–737.

———. 1994. "Ayodhya and the Hindu Resurgence." *Religion* 24: 73–80.

———. 1997. "Asylum, Violence and the Limits of Advocacy." *Human Organization* 55(4): 493–498.

———. 1997. "Playing the Game of Love: Passion and Martyrdom Among Khalistani Sikhs." In *Martyrdom and National Liberation Movements,* ed. Joyce Pettigrew. Amsterdam: Free University Press.

Mahmood, C. K., and S. L. Armstrong. 1992. "Do Ethnic Groups Exist? A Cognitive Perspective on the Concept of Cultures." *Ethnology* 31(1): 1–14.

Malik, Harji. 1985. "The Politics of Alienation." In *Punjab: The Fatal Miscalculation,* ed. Patwant Singh and Harji Malik. Delhi: Crescent.

Malik, Yogendra. 1989. "Democracy, the Akali Party, and the Sikhs in Indian Politics." In *Religious and Ethnic Minority Politics in South Asia,* ed. Dhirendra Vajpeyi and Yogendra Malik, pp. 19–50. Riverdale, Md.: The Riverdale Company.

Mann, Jasbir Singh, Surinder Singh Sodhi, and Gurbaksh Singh Gill, eds. 1995. *The Invasion of Religious Boundaries.* Vancouver: Canadian Sikh Study and Teaching Society.

Mansukhani, G. S. 1977. *Introduction to Sikhism.* New Delhi: Hemkunt Press.

Marcus, George, and Michael Fischer. 1986. *Anthropology as Cultural Critique: An Experimental Moment in the Human Sciences.* Chicago: University of Chicago Press.

Mascia-Lees, F. E., P. Sharpe, and C. Ballerino Cohen. 1989. "The Postmodernist Turn in Anthropology: Cautions from a Feminist Perspective." *Signs* 15(1): 7–34.

McDonald, Michael. 1992. "Should Communities Have Rights? Reflections on Liberal Individualism." In *Human Rights in Cross-Cultural Perspectives,* ed. A. A. An-Na'im, pp. 133–161. Philadelphia: University of Pennsylvania Press.

McLeod, W. H. 1976. *The Evolution of the Sikh Community*. Oxford: Clarendon Press.

————. 1980. *Early Sikh Tradition*. Oxford: Clarendon Press.

————. 1989. *The Sikhs: History, Religion and Society*. New York: Oxford University Press.

————. 1989. *Who Is a Sikh? The Problem of Sikh Identity*. Oxford: Clarendon Press.

Merleau-Ponty, Maurice. 1978. "The Philosopher and Sociology." In *Phenomenology and Sociology*, ed. Thomas Luckman. Hammondsworth: Penguin.

Moghadam, Valentine M., ed. 1994. *Identity, Politics, and Women: Cultural Reassertions and Feminisms in International Perspectives*. Boulder, Colo.: Westview Press.

Morgan, Robin. 1989. *The Demon Lover: Sexuality and Terrorism*. New York: Norton.

Moynihan, Daniel Patrick. 1993. *Pandaemonium: Ethnicity in International Politics*. New York: Oxford University Press.

Mukherjee, Bharati. 1989. *Jasmine*. New York: Grove Weidenfeld.

Mulgrew, Ian. 1988. *Unholy Terror: The Sikhs and International Terrorism*. Toronto: Key Porter Books.

Munson, Henry. 1995. "Not All Crustaceans Are Crabs: Reflections on the Comparative Study of Fundamentalism and Politics." *Contention* 4: 151–166.

————. 1996 "Intolerable Tolerance: Western Academia and Islamic Fundamentalism." *Contention* 5(3): 99–117.

Nandy, Ashis. 1990. "The Politics of Secularism." In *Mirrors of Violence: Communities, Riots and Survivors in South Asia*, ed. Veena Das, pp. 69–93. New York: Oxford University Press.

————. 1995. *The Savage Freud and Other Essays on Possible and Retrievable Selves*. Princeton Studies in Culture/Power/History. Princeton, N.J.: Princeton University Press.

Nash, June. 1976. "Ethnology in a Revolutionary Setting." In *Ethics and Anthropology: Dilemmas of Fieldwork*, ed. Michael Rynkiewich and James Spradley, pp. 148–166. New York: Wiley and Sons.

Nayar, Kuldip, and Khushwant Singh. 1985. *The Tragedy of Punjab: Operation Blue Star and After*. New Delhi: Vision Books.

Nietschmann, Bernard. 1987. "The Third World War." *Cultural Survival* 11(3): 1–16.

Nordstrom, Carolyn, and JoAnn Martin, eds. 1992. *Paths to Domination, Resistance and Terror*. Berkeley: University of California Press.

Nordstrom, Carolyn, and Antonius Robben, eds. 1995. *Fieldwork Under Fire: Contemporary Studies of Violence and Survival*. Berkeley: University of California Press.

Oberoi, Harjot. 1987. "From Punjab to Khalistan: Territoriality and Metacommentary." *Pacific Affairs* 60: 26–41.

————. 1993. "Sikh Fundamentalism: Translating History Into Theory." In *Fundamentalisms and the State*, ed. Martin E. Marty and R. Scott Appleby, pp. 256–285. Chicago: University of Chicago Press.

————. 1994. *The Construction of Religious Boundaries: Culture, Identity, and Diversity in Sikh Tradition*. Chicago: University of Chicago Press.

Parry, R. E. 1931. *The Sikhs of the Punjab*. London: Drake.

People's Union for Civil Liberties. 1984. *Black Laws*. New Delhi: People's Union for Civil Liberties.

People's Union for Civil Liberties/ People's Union for Democratic Rights. 1985. *Who Are the Guilty?* New Delhi: PUCL/PUDR.

Peteet, Julie Marie. 1991. *Gender in Crisis: Women in the Palestinian Resistance Movement*. New York: Columbia University Press.

Pettigrew, Joyce. 1978. *Robber Noblemen: A Study of the Political System of the Sikh Jats*. New Delhi: Ambika Publications.

———. 1992. "Betrayal and Nation-Building Among the Sikhs." *Journal of Comparative and Commonwealth Politics* 30(3): 387–406.

———. 1992. "Martyrdom and Guerilla Organization in Punjab." *Journal of Commonwealth and Comparative Politics* 39(3): 387–406.

———. 1995. *The Sikhs of the Punjab: Unheard Voices of State and Guerilla Violence*. London: Zed Books.

Pieke, Frank. 1995. "Witnessing the 1989 Chinese People's Movement." In *Fieldwork Under Fire: Contemporary Studies of Violence and Survival*, ed. Carolyn Nordstrom and Antonius Robben, pp. 62–80. Berkeley: University of California Press.

Pollock, Sheldon. 1993. "Deep Orientalism? Notes on Sanskrit and Power Beyond the Raj." In *Orientalism and the Postcolonial Predicament*, ed. Carol Breckenridge and Peter van der Veer, pp. 76–133. Philadelphia: University of Pennsylvania Press.

Punjab Human Rights Organization. 1988. *Punjab Bulldozed: Operation Black Thunder II*. Ludhiana: Punjab Human Rights Organization.

Puri, Haresh K. 1989. "Akali Politics: Emerging Compulsions." In *Political Dynamics of Punjab*, ed. Paul Wallace and Surendra Chopra. Amritsar: Guru Nanak Dev University Press.

Radhakrishnan, S. 1956. *2500 Years of Buddhism*. Delhi: Ministry of Information.

Randall, Margaret. 1981. *Sandino's Daughters: Testimonies of Nicaraguan Women in Struggle*. Vancouver: New Star Books.

———. 1994. *Sandino's Daughters Revisited: Feminism in Nicaragua*. New Brunswick, N.J.: Rutgers University Press.

Robben, Antonius C. G. M. 1995. "The Politics of Truth and Emotion Among Victims and Perpetrators of Violence." In *Fieldwork Under Fire: Contemporary Studies of Violence and Survival*, ed. Carolyn Nordstrom and Antonius Robben, pp. 81–103. Berkeley: University of California Press.

Robbins, Bruce. 1993. *Secular Vocations: Intellectuals, Professionalism, Culture*. London: Verso.

Rosaldo, Renato. 1980. *Ilongot Headhunting, 1883–1974: A Study in Society and History*. Stanford, Calif.: Stanford University Press.

Rushdie, Salman. 1984. "Outside the Whale." *Granta*.

Sahlins, Marshall. 1976. *The Uses and Abuses of Biology*. Ann Arbor: University of Michigan Press.

Said, Edward. 1989. "Representing the Colonized: Anthropology's Interlocutors." *Critical Inquiry* 15: 205–225.

———. 1993. *Culture and Imperialism*. New York: Alfred A. Knopf.

———. 1994. *Representations of the Intellectual*. New York: Pantheon.

Scarry, Elaine. 1985. *The Body in Pain: The Making and Unmaking of the World*. New York: Oxford University Press.

Scheper-Hughes, Nancy. 1992. *Death Without Weeping: The Violence of Everyday Life in Brazil*. Berkeley: University of California Press.

———. 1995. "The Primacy of the Ethical: Propositions for a Militant Anthropology." *Current Anthropology* 36(3): 409–420.

Schiller, Nina Glick, Linda Basch, and Cristina Salzman Blanc. 1995. "From Immigrant to Transmigrant: Theorizing Transnational Migration." *Anthropological Quarterly* 68(1): 48–63.

Schlesinger, Arthur. 1992. *The Disuniting of America*. New York: Norton.

Shostak, Marjorie. 1981. *Nisa: The Life and Words of a !Kung Woman*. Cambridge, Mass.: Harvard University Press.

Singh, Gurharpal. 1992. "The Punjab Elections 1992: Breakthrough or Breakdown?" *Asian Survey* 32(11): 988–999.

Singh, Khushwant. 1963–1966. *History of the Sikhs*, vols. 1 and 2. Princeton, N.J.: Princeton University Press.

———. 1992. *My Bleeding Punjab*. New Delhi: UBS Publishers.

Singh, Nikky Guninder Kaur. 1993. *The Feminine Principle in the Sikh Vision of the Transcendent*. London: Cambridge University Press.

Singh, Patwant. 1985. "The Distorting Mirror." In *Punjab: The Fatal Miscalculation*, ed. Patwant Singh and Harji Malik, pp. 9–32. Delhi: Crescent.

Singh, Sangat. 1995. *The Sikhs in History*. New York: Sangat Singh.

Singh, Santokh. 1991. *India Since Independence, 1947–1991: Persecution of Religious Minorities*. Princeton, Ontario: World Sikh Organization.

Singh, Sohan. 1991. *India and Khalistan*. N.p.

Singh, Sukhjinder, and Harjinder Singh. 1995. "When Nations Wake Up, History Begins to Shiver." *World Sikh News*, October 13.

Singh, Trilochan. 1994. *Ernest Trumpp and W. H. McLeod as Scholars of Sikh History, Religion, and Culture*. Chandigarh: Institute of Sikh Studies.

Sluka, Jeffrey A. 1992. "Participant Observation in Violent Social Contexts." *Human Organization* 49(2): 114–205.

———. 1995. "Reflections on Managing Danger in Fieldwork: Dangerous Anthropology in Belfast." In *Fieldwork Under Fire: Contemporary Studies of Violence and Survival*, ed. Carolyn Nordstrom and Antonius Robben, pp. 276–294. Berkeley: University of California Press.

Srinivasan, Amrit. 1990. "The Survivor in the Study of Violence." In *Mirrors of Violence: Communities, Riots and Survivors in South Asia*, ed. Veena Das, pp. 304–320. New York: Oxford University Press.

Taussig, Michael. 1992. *The Nervous System*. New York: Routledge.

Thackwell, E. J. 1851. *Narrative of the Second Sikh War*. London.

Thoreau, Henry David. 1993. *Civil Disobedience and Other Essays*. New York: Dover Publications.

Tiger, Lionel. 1969. *Men in Groups*. New York: Random House.

Tully, Mark. 1992. *The Defeat of a Congress-man and Other Parables of Modern India*. New York: Alfred Knopf.

Tully, Mark, and Satish Jacob. 1991. *Amritsar: Mrs. Gandhi's Last Battle*. Calcutta: Rupa and Company.

Tylor, Edward Burnett. 1871. *Primitive Culture: Researches into the Development of Mythology, Philosophy, Religion, Language, Art and Custom*. London: Murray.

United States Department of State. 1995. *Patterns of Global Terrorism 1994*. Washington, D.C.: Office of Counterterrorism.

Upadyaya, Prakash Chandra. 1992. "The Politics of Indian Secularism." *Modern Asian Studies* 26(4): 815–853.

Veer, Peter van der. 1993. "The Foreign Hand: Orientalist Discourse in Sociology and Communalism." In *Orientalism and the Postcolonial Predicament*, ed. Carol Breckenridge and Peter van der Veer, pp. 23–44. Philadelphia: University of Pennsylvania Press.

———. 1994. *Religious Nationalism: Hindus and Muslims in India.* Berkeley: University of California Press.

———. 1995. Introduction to *Nation and Migration: The Politics of Space in the South Asian Diaspora,* ed. Peter van der Veer. Philadelphia: University of Pennsylvania Press.

Wallace, Paul. 1995. "Political Violence and Terrorism in India: The Crisis of Identity." In *Terrorism in Context,* ed. Martha Crenshaw, pp. 352–409. University Park: The Pennsylvania State University Press.

Warren, Kay, ed. 1993. *The Violence Within: Cultural and Political Opposition in Divided Nations.* Boulder, Colo.: Westview Press.

Wilson, Heather A. 1988. *International Law and the Use of Force in National Liberation Movements.* Oxford: Clarendon Press.

Wolfe, Alvin, and Honggang Yang, eds. 1996. *Anthropological Contributions to Conflict Resolution.* Athens: University of Georgia Press.

Wolpert, Stanley. 1993. *A New History of India.* 4th ed. New York: Oxford University Press.

Zulaika, Joseba. 1988. *Basque Violence: Metaphor and Sacrament.* Reno: University of Nevada Press.

———. 1995. "The Anthropologist as Terrorist." In *Fieldwork Under Fire: Contemporary Studies of Violence and Survival,* ed. Carolyn Nordstrom and Antonius Robben, pp. 206–223. Berkeley: University of California Press.

INDEX

Beant Singh (chief minister), 163
Benedict, Ruth, 203–204
Bhagat, Dhiren, 281 n.40
Bhagat Singh, 112, 283 n.10
Bhago, Mai, 222
Bhan Singh, 92
Bharatiya Jana Singh, 114; Bharatiya Janata
Party (BJP), 114
Bhindranwale, Jarnail Singh, 30, 40, 46–47,
51–70, 74–78, 88–89, 91, 95–98, 127–
128, 131, 145–147, 154, 158, 164, 178,
187, 199, 201, 228, 231, 280 nn. 7, 10, 14,
21, 281 n.33
Bhindranwale Tiger Force of Khalistan
(BTFK), 159; BTFK Sangha, 159
Bholla, Sukhwinder Singh, 175
Bhullar, Jaswant Singh, 81, 161
Bidar massacre, 196–197
Black Thunder, Operation. See Golden
Temple Complex
Blue Star, Operation. See Golden Temple
Complex
bombs, 46, 156, 163, 181–183, 204–207,
210, 285 n.24
Bourgois, Philippe, 18
Brahma, Avtar Singh, 47, 165, 172
Brahminism and Brahmins, 28, 58, 119,
129, 239, 244, 283 nn. 17, 20
Brar, K. S., 81, 87–88, 90–91, 94, 98, 187,
209, 280 n.14, 281 n.25
Brass, Paul, 138
British colonization of India, 108, 110–
113, 123, 133, 241–242
British Sikhs, 151, 159–160, 258–259
Buber, Martin, 25
Buddhism, 5, 28–29, 34, 119, 129, 133,
226, 238, 244, 288 n.8
Budhsinghwala, Gurjant Singh, 166, 172

Camus, Albert, 196, 199
Canadian Sikhs, 45, 111, 151, 156–157,
159, 161–162, 192–193, 240, 258
caste: in Sikhism, 27, 238; Untouchability, 99, 136, 163, 172, 283 n.17; anthropology of, 120, 283 nn. 19, 20. See also
Brahminism
casualties: in Jallianwala Bagh massacre, 97,
283 n.8; during Partition, 114; in Operation Blue Star, 94; in anti-Sikh "riots,"
139; total number in current conflict, 2–
3, 154, 277 n.2

censorship, 2, 4, 98–99, 103, 129, 281 n.40.
See also Press, in India
Chaheru, Manbir Singh. See Hari Singh
Chandigarh issue, 82, 115–117
Chando Kalan, episode at, 61–62
chardhi kala (spirit), 195–198; Chardhi Kala
(newspaper), 158, 195
charity, 27, 145, 198. See also Kettle
Chauhan, Jagjit Singh, 118, 127, 151, 160,
259
Chawla, Amarjit Singh, 285 n.30
Chellany, Brahma, 94
Chibber, Governor, 208
Chief Khalsa Diwan, 11
children, sacrifice of, 48, 103, 105–106,
108–109; as victims, 92, 165, 202, 206–
207, 233, 281 n.35; in militancy, 182,
271
Chomsky, Noam, 17, 248
Christians, 56, 110, 129, 132–133, 179–180
CIA (U.S.), rumors about, 135
Citizens Commission, 138
Citizens for Democracy, 87, 92, 94, 138,
277 n.6
Clausewitz, Wilhelm von, 17, 229, 256–257
communalism, 8, 79, 82, 98, 100–102,
126, 129, 138, 150, 164, 179–182, 259,
283 n.15
communism. See Naxalites
Congress party, 61, 136, 163; ties to Bhindranwale, 61, 80, 279 n.2; role in anti-
Sikh "riots," 136–139, 208; in history,
112–113, 118
consequences of scholarship, 3, 14, 199–
200, 246–251, 263
constitution of India, 62, 238–239
Corbin, J., 16, 274
Council of Khalistan (London), 160
Council of Khalistan (Washington), 161–
162, 255
counterinsurgency legislation, 98–100. See
also Terrorism and Disruptive Activities
(Prevention) Act
courage. See Fearlessness
Creveld, Martin van, 17–18
crime, militancy as a form of, 204, 207–
208, 210
Crossette, Barbara, 261, 290 n.44

Dal Khalsa, 82, 108
Dalip Singh, Maharaja, 110

Guru Granth Sahib (*continued*)
89, 91–92, 107, 144–145, 190, 215, 219,
231, 238–239, 241, 254, 279 n.4; verses
from, 27–33, 35–36, 43. *See also* Prayer

hair. *See* K's, the five
Handler, Richard, 242–243, 245
Hargobind (Guru), 40–42, 96
Hari Singh (Manbir Singh Chaheru), 121,
153, 155, 165
Harjinder Singh ("Jinda"), 155–156, 191,
200–201, 257
Harmandir Sahib. *See* Golden Temple
Complex
hijackings, 82, 131, 268, 273–274
Hindi. *See* Language issue
Hindus: history of, 34; and Guru Nanak,
26–27, 33–34; and Guru Arjun, 35;
Sikhs as, 62, 113, 119, 238, 247, 278 n.1;
tolerance of, 118–119; current revival
among, 114, 118–120, 239, 244, 283
n.15; Muslims as, 199; in Khalistan, 72,
133. *See also* Brahminism; Sikh identity;
Communalism
Holocaust: comparison to WWII, 96, 97,
133–134, 138–139, 211; "Lesser Holocaust," 108; "Greater Holocaust," 108
holy city status, 83, 145–146, 280–281 n.22
human rights. *See* Names of specific human rights groups (e.g. Amnesty International); Torture; Sexual abuse;
Counterinsurgency
Human Rights Watch, 205, 277 n.6
humiliation: episodes of, 10–11, 81, 87,
105, 145–146, 148, 173, 181; analysis of,
141, 187–191, 207–210
humility, 20, 33, 193, 201
hydroelectric power, 117, 126

Independence movement of India, 78, 194
Indian National Army, 112
individualism in Punjabi culture, 109, 117
infiltration of militant movement, 149,
158–160, 165, 176–177, 280 nn. 10, 21,
285 n.26, 286 n.33
informers, punishing of, 170–171, 174,
217–220
innocents, killings by militants, 23, 68, 81–
82, 129, 150, 164, 167, 171, 174, 179–
182, 205–207, 269, 287 n.28
intellectuals. *See* Consequences of
scholarship

interlocutors: contacts with, 4–5, 10, 12,
21–22; protection of, ix–x, 12–13; immi-
gration status of, ix, 262–263; in anthro-
pology, 236, 245, 247–249, 266–275
International Human Rights Organization
(IHRO), 162, 277 n.6
International Sikh Youth Federation (ISYF),
157–158, 222
Islam. *See* Muslims
Iyer, Krishna, 99

Jacob, Satish, 82, 87, 90–91, 94–95
Jaijee, Inderjit Singh, 277 n.6
Jainism, 28–29, 119, 238, 244
Jallandhar rescue episode, 155, 168
Jallianwala Bagh massacre, 97, 112
janamsakhis, 31–32, 238
Jasdev Singh, 64–65
jasmine, image of, 49
Jat Sikhs, 74, 118
Jeffrey, Robin, 32, 80–81, 191
Jews. *See* Zionism; Holocaust
Joginder Singh, 74
Juergensmeyer, Mark, xi, 20, 50, 246, 257,
279 n.1

Kant, Immanuel, 2, 19, 25
Kapur Singh, Nawab, 108
Kartar Singh, 45, 52–56, 59, 75, 279 n.4
Kashmir, 110, 133, 151, 153, 163, 208,
285 n.19
kaur, symbolism of use as surname, 44, 221
Kaur, Gurnam, 227
Kaur, Kamaljit, 162
Kaur, Mata Sahib, 43
Kaur, Ranbir, 92, 281 n.35
Keegan, John, 18
Kehar Singh, 135, 283–284 n.2
kettle, as symbol of Sikhism, 42, 198
Khalistan: historical agitation for, 113, 117;
conceptions of, 20, 54, 65–67, 71–72,
120, 132, 143, 150, 211, 253, 255–256;
Declaration of Independence of, 46, 72,
143–144, 147, 152–153; as quest, 21, 48,
196–198, 211, 275; numbers supporting,
ix, 2, 211
Khalistan Affairs Center, 162
Khalistan Commando Force (KCF), 89,
121, 153–156, 165, 167–168, 173–174,
215, 224, 227; KCF Zaffarwal, 159; KCF
Panjwar, 161

Khalistan Liberation Force (KLF), 42, 47, 159–160, 165, 172
Khalra, Jaswant Singh, 162
Khalsa: establishment and conception of, 42–47, 58, 107, 117, 190, 197, 200, 222, 238–239; initiation into, 78, 84, 101, 104, 111, 130, 144–145, 191, 231; involvement in militancy, 46, 73, 98, 138. See also *Amrit*
Khalsa, Daljit Singh ("Bittu"), 161
Khalsa, Harjinder Kaur, 213
Khan, Sher Mohammed, 109
Khushwant Singh, 7, 95, 98, 110, 139, 141, 143, 199, 277 n.4, 278 n.1
Komagata Maru incident, 11
Kothari, Rajni, 138
K's, the five: role of, 44–45, 57, 110, 144, 190; *kara*, 14, 190, 200, 202; *kesh*, 10, 58, 77, 100–101, 103–104, 145, 155–156, 172–173; *kirpan*, 5, 25, 41, 45, 59, 146, 162, 196–197, 222, 236–237. See also Turban; Sword
Kundera, Milan, 210–211

Labh Singh (Sukhdev Singh Sukha), 89, 155, 165, 170, 227, 231
Lahoria, Daya Singh, 162
Lal, Bhajan, 68, 81
langar, 27, 129
language issue, 114–115, 122–124, 126–127
liberalism, 243–245
Lodhiwal, Ajmer Singh, 171–173, 189
Longowal, Harchand Singh, 80, 88, 117, 143

Madan, T. N., 29, 280 n.7
Majha region, 153
Malerkotla, 97, 108–109
Malik, Harji, 139
Mand, Dhyan Singh, 45
Mani Singh, Bhai, 36
Manjit Singh, 285 n.30
Mann, Simranjit Singh, 45, 102, 136, 162, 185 n.31
Manochal, Gurbachan Singh, 152, 159
Manpreet Singh, 219
Mansukhani, G. S., 196
marriage, 27, 87, 104–105, 169, 172, 202, 225, 233
martyrdom: Sikh conceptions of, 34, 36, 48, 132, 151, 189–198, 201–203, 240; narratives regarding, 84–85, 89, 131–132, 151, 177–178, 227; of Guru Arjun, 35–36, 125; of Bhai Mani Singh, 36; of Guru Tegh Bahadur, 42, 189–190; of Baba Deep Singh, 40; of Bhindranwale, 40, 69, 95–97
McLeod, W. H., 237, 240, 278 n.1
Mehel Singh, 84–86, 159
Mehta, Rajinder Singh, 285 n.30
methods of research: participant-observation, 2–4, 14, 23; interview style, 12–13, 54, 127; objectivity, x, 1, 25; reflexivity, 24–25, 235; translation, 12; use of audiotapes, x; use of photos, x; danger in fieldwork, 4, 12–13, 23–24, 269, 277–278 n.7; role of anthropologist, 13–14, 97, 211–212, 266–275. See also Interlocutors; Consequences of scholarship
military personnel in Khalistan movement, 81, 115, 280 n.14
Mir, Mian, 35
miri-piri, concept of, 41, 195
misls, 108–109, 282 n.1
Misra Commission, 133
Mokkam Singh, 227
Movement Against State Repression, 277 nn. 2, 6
Moynihan, Daniel Patrick, 259
Mughals: persecution under, 34, 105, 191, 194, 199, 239; Babar, 96; Jehangir, 35; Aurangzeb, 34, 42; Bahadur, 107
Muni, Sushil, 158
murders, 80, 82, 117, 129, 131, 153, 165, 168, 172, 175, 218, 220, 285 n.24. See also Assassinations; Innocents
Muslims of India: relationship of Sikhs to, 27–28, 31, 35, 74, 133–136; as Hindus, 119. See also Babri Masjid; Kashmir; Pakistan
Mustana Singh, 182–183

Nagoke, Kulwant Singh, 146
Nanak (Guru), 14, 26–34, 41, 44, 48, 96, 125, 139, 150, 198, 226, 238, 254; birthplace of, 26, 114
Nandy, Ashis, 143, 273–274
Narain, Lala Jagat, 61–62, 79, 122
Narayan, Jayaprakash, 75
Nash, June, 269
Naxalites, 125, 171
Nayar, Kuldip, 98, 280 n.17

Nehru, Jawaharlal, 114, 260
Nikky Guninder Kaur Singh, 230–231
Nimma, Nirmaljit Singh ("Chotu"), 38, 175–178
Nirankaris, 58–60, 73–79, 84, 124, 144, 156, 280 n.7
noncombatants. *See* Innocents
nonviolence, 54, 102, 112, 115–118, 146–148, 265, 285 n.30; *Dharm Yudh Morcha*, 80
Nordstrom, Carolyn, xi, 4, 273–274

Oberoi, Harjot, 235–243, 245, 247, 249–251, 288 n.9
O'Dwyer, Michael, 112
Oklahoma City bombing, 206–207

Pakistan: Sikh history in, 26; wars of India with, 81, 115; support for insurgency by, 80, 135, 159; Islam in, 256. *See also* Partition
Palestinians, 3, 211, 222–223, 225, 230, 266
panj piaras. See Five Beloved Ones
Panjwar, Paramjit Singh, 161
panth: as repository of Guru, 48, 107; as nation, 32, 48, 80, 121, 152, 156, 200, 254, 256, 261
Panthic Committee: First, 46, 143–144, 147–148, 151–152, 156, 162; Second, 159–161, 209; Zaffarwal, 159–161
Parmar, Talwinder Singh, 157
Partition, 109, 113–114, 122, 139
Pashaura Singh, 240
People's Union for Civil Liberties (PUCL), 82, 138, 205, 277 n.6, 282 n.52
Peteet, Julie, 211, 221–223, 225
Pettigrew, Joyce, xi, 77, 155, 160, 163, 185, 189, 250, 253, 280 n.17, 282 n.1
Pheruman, Darshan, 115
Physicians for Human Rights, 205, 277 n.6
prayer: in Sikh tradition, 29, 55, 62, 122, 145; examples of, 32–33, 35, 47–48; among militants, 30, 47, 85, 165, 167, 170, 174, 191, 193, 227
President's Rule, 82
press in India, 67, 88, 94, 98–99, 101, 122, 128–129, 152; *Ajit*, 122; *Bharat Times*, 124; *Hind Samachar*, 61; *Hindustan Times*, 139; *India Today*, 121; *Punjab Kesri*, 122, 127; *Sunday Observer*, 273; *Tribune*, 123, 127. *See also* Censorship; Narain, Lala Jagat

Punjab Human Rights Organization. *See* International Human Rights Organization
Punjabi. *See* Language issue
Punjabi Suba movement, 115
Punjabiyat, 121, 126–127, 256

qaum, 80, 254, 256, 261
Quebec, 242–243, 245

Radhakrishnan, S., 239
radio: Sikh religious programming on, 83, 259; Punjabi language on, 123; news coverage on, 100–101, 129, 188; Bhindranwale on, 77; overseas, 193
Raghbir Singh, 84
Rajinder Pal Singh, 165
Ram, Gobind, 46
Ranbir Singh, 60
Randhir Singh, 78
Ranjit Singh ("Kuky"), 162
Ranjit Singh, Maharaja, 109–110, 125, 133, 150, 256
rape. *See* Sexual abuse
Rashtriya Swayamsevak Sangh (RSS), 114
Ray, S. S., 208
refugees, 262–266
renunciation, 29, 75, 78, 128, 145, 177, 226
resistance, Khalistan movement as, 19–20, 71, 118, 132, 197–198, 260
Ribiero, Julio, 208
"riots" following Gandhi assassination, 101, 136–143, 188–189, 208, 284 nn. 7, 8
river waters issue, 82, 117
Robben, Antonius, xi, 14, 270–274
Rosaldo, Renato, 3, 203
Rousseau, Jean Jacques, 226
Rushdie, Salman, 246–247

saffron, symbolism and use of, 6, 25, 118, 141, 190, 191. *See also* Turban
Sahbi, Dilbar Singh, 183
Said, Edward, 236–237, 241, 245, 247
saint-soldier, concept of, 41, 68–70, 96, 134, 287 n.28
Sampat Singh, 285 n.26
Sanatan Sikhs, 239
Sandhu, Sukhminder Singh ("Sukhy"), 162
Sangat Singh, 210, 284 n.8
Sangha, Sukhwinder Singh, 159
sant, concept of, 30, 76–77

Sarbat Khalsa, 147, 152
Satinder Pal Singh, 160–161
Satwant Singh, 101, 135, 137, 143
Sawaranjit Singh, 168
Scarry, Elaine, 9, 200
Scheper-Hughes, Nancy, 3, 210–212, 263, 267
Second Panthic Committee. *See* Panthic Committee
secularism in India, 98, 118–120, 133, 244
security personnel, 142: Central Reserve Police Force (CRPF), 11, 66, 170, 175, 182–183; Border Security Force (BSF), 82; Indo-Tibetan Border Police (ITBP), 135; Criminal Investigation Agency (CIA), 39, 103
Sekhon, Pritam Singh, 161
self-determination, 162, 245, 252, 255–261
sexual abuse, 10, 39, 85, 105, 128, 132, 165, 200, 223–225
Shabeg Singh, 81, 90–91, 120, 280 n.14
shelter of militants, 102, 153, 165, 167, 171, 173, 176, 178
Shiromani Gurudwara Prabandhak Committee (SGPC), 83, 112
shuddhi, 119
Sikh Gurudwara Act, 112
Sikh identity, separateness of, 26, 28, 34–35, 62, 111, 237–245, 248–249, 252, 279 n.3
Sikh Missionary College, 63, 124
Sikh Students Federation (SSF), 37–38, 77–78, 82, 127–129, 157–158, 160, 215, 219, 285 n.30
Sikh Youth of America (SYA), 157–158
Sikhi, concept of, 61, 66, 71, 203
Sikri, S. M., 138
sincerity, 7, 10, 125, 127–128, 249
singh, symbolism of use as surname, 43, 221
Singh (surname). *Individuals with surname Singh are indexed by first name*
Singh Sabha, 111, 119, 238, 240
Sirhind, 107, 109, 257
Sluka, Jeffrey A., xi, 10–12, 24, 269
Sobha Singh, 44, 93
Sodhi, Rupinder Singh, 24, 266
Sodhi, Surinder Singh (author), 242, 247
Sodhi, Surinder Singh (militant), 68
Sohan Singh, 159–161, 209; Sohan Singh Panthic Committee (*see* Panthic Committee)

state, as a political order, 16–18, 256
States Reorganization Commission, 114
subjects. *See* Interlocutors
suicide, 163, 169, 215, 224
Sukha, Sukhdev Singh. *See* Labh Singh
Sukhdev Singh (Damdami Taksal), 64–65
Sukhdev Singh (Babbar Khalsa), 183
Sukhjinder Singh ("Sukha"), 155–156, 191, 200–201, 257
Sultanwind, Kanwaljit Singh, 38
Sundarji, K., 88, 90, 100
Sutlej-Yamuna Link Canal (SYL Canal), 117
Swaran Singh, 81
sword: as symbol of Sikhism, 41–42, 78, 148, 198, 241, 243; in baptism, 43, 145, 255. *See also* K's, the five

Tara Singh, Baba, 146
Tara Singh, Master, 115
Tarkunde, V. M., 94
Taussig, Michael, 186
Tegh Bahadur (Guru), 42, 189–190
Telham, Kuldip Singh, 37
"terrorism," 3, 17, 21, 49, 81–82, 99, 105, 112, 154, 215, 247, 250, 252, 260, 269, 272–275
Terrorism and Disruptive Activities (Prevention) Act (TADA), 99, 103, 282 n.51
Thakkar Commission, 135
Thakur Singh, 53
Thoreau, Henry David, 195–196
tobacco, prohibition and significance of, 46, 79, 145, 148
torture: human rights reports on, 10, 277 n.6; Sikh interpretation of, 35–37, 195, 200; analysis of, 9–10, 200–201; narratives about, 8–10, 38–40, 103, 154, 172–173, 202, 213, 217. *See also* Sexual abuse
tribals, 4–5, 99, 133, 136, 283 n.17
Trumpp, Ernest, 240–241
Tully, Mark, 75, 82, 87–88, 90, 94–95, 285 n.27
turban, significance of, 10, 41, 83, 94, 100, 145, 161, 173, 190, 191, 217, 222. *See also* Saffron
Tylor, Edward Burnett, 2, 277 n.1

Udasis, 29
United Nations, 99, 162, 264–265
Upadyaya, P. C., 119

Usmanwala, Gurdev Singh, 152
U.S. Congress, 162
U.S. Sikhs, 111, 151, 157, 161–162, 193, 222, 255, 257–258, 271
U.S. State Department, 160

Vaidya, A. S., 88, 97, 155, 200, 257
Veer, Peter van der, xi, 223, 245
vengeance, 150, 154, 161, 170, 208, 227
violence: Sikh understanding of, 48, 66, 104–105, 148, 185–212; anthropological study of, 15–16, 19, 277–278 nn. 7, 15, 16; military conceptions of, 16–18; banality of, 186; "pornography of," 18, 199–200, 272; as psychopathology, 18, 186, 193; as instinct, 18; as crime, 204, 207–208; in international law, 263–266
Vir Singh, Bhai, 222

Wadawa Singh, 159
weapons, in hands of militants, 90, 281, 285 n.24

Westphalia, treaty of, 17
White Paper on the Punjab Agitation, 94
Wood Rose, Operation, 97–98
Wolpert, Stanley, 99
women, status of, 44, 213–234. *See also* Sexual abuse
World Sikh News, 162
World Sikh Organization (WSO), 161
World War I, Sikhs in, 111
World War II, Sikhs in, 112

Yeats, William Butler, 198–199

Zaffarwal, Wasson Singh, 152, 159; Zaffarwal Panthic Committee (*see* Panthic Committee)
Zail Singh, 80, 92
Zionism, 32, 254